TUDOR ROSES

It is a truth universally acknowledged that a single woman in possession of a good kingdom, must be in want of a husband...

TUDOR ROSES

From Margaret Beaufort to Elizabeth I

Amy Licence

AMBERLEY

For Rufus and Robin

First published 2022

Amberley Publishing
The Hill, Stroud
Gloucestershire, GL5 4EP

www.amberley-books.com

British Library Cataloguing in Publication Data.
A catalogue record for this book is available from the British Library.

ISBN 978 1 4456 5683 0 (hardback)
ISBN 978 1 4456 5684 7 (ebook)

1 2 3 4 5 6 7 8 9 10

Typesetting by SJmagic DESIGN SERVICES, India.
Printed in the UK.

Contents

PART ONE

Founding Mothers
1437–1485

1

Elizabeth Woodville and Margaret Beaufort

1437–1460

This story begins with the births of two girls in late medieval England. Elizabeth Woodville and Margaret Beaufort, the future mothers of the first Tudor monarchs, arrived a few years apart, Elizabeth in late 1437, and Margaret in 1443. The England they knew could not, by any stretch of the imagination, be described as a woman's world, but certain women were making their mark, and making history.

By 1450, England's population had been in steady decline for about a century, decimated by plague and famine to around 2,000,000,[1] or less than half of what it had been in the 1340s. This decrease may have allowed greater opportunities for women in working roles, increasing their wealth, and possibly in terms of choosing a husband, but they were still always subject to their menfolk. The majority of women's lives in the mid-fifteenth century were domestic. As wives, daughters, sisters and mothers they worked in the fields and home, the marketplace and workshop to further the material aspects of life and the raising of children. Few were educated or literate, some were able to own wealth and property if they were a widow or heiress, while others escaped the temporal world by entering the cloister. The average female life expectancy was significantly reduced by the dangers of childbirth and post-partum complications, as well as the acceptance of regular misogynistic violence under the guise of discipline. Male perceptions of women's abilities and characters were drawn from Biblical stereotypes and reinforced in church, the law courts and popular culture. Contemporary manuals of behaviour stressed obedience, humility and modesty as chief among desired feminine qualities. Those qualities were to be increasingly challenged and redefined over the coming century and a half. Women would help create the next dynasty, and eventually take control of it entirely.

London was by far the largest city in England, with just over 23,000 inhabitants. More than one in ten of the national population lived there. York and Bristol were next, at around 7,000 each, and Coventry fourth with almost 5,000. The country was growing prosperous on the wool trade: 1447 would mark the first peak year, with around 60,000 cloths being exported, providing one of the most significant national forms of employment, from shepherds to weavers and dyers. London's imposing Guildhall was completed in 1440 and, six years later, the foundation stone of King's College Chapel, Cambridge, was laid. In spite of urban migration in the wake of the plague, the majority of the English population still lived in the countryside, in self-sufficient villages, centres of milling, brewing, farming and other small industries. Amid these, like gems studding the map, sat new, ornate, Perpendicular churches built from merchants' wealth, flanked by swathes of woodland and fields of sheep. All around the coastline and along rivers to inland ports, a steady stream of vessels unloaded luxury goods from overseas – wine, oil, spices, dried fruits, sugar, dye, silver, flax and other luxuries – before their hulls were refilled with homespun cloth and wool. It was a country dominated by religious routine, by church services, rituals, calendars, Saints' days and the ringing of bells. After the crown, wealthy monasteries were the biggest landowners, but were also established centres of theological debate, medical knowledge, with libraries full of illuminated manuscripts. The young King and his court were peripatetic, often glimpsed travelling between various royal residences, but for most, power rested in the hands of a small number of magnates to whom all owed allegiance. Their rivalries and private squabbles dictated local politics in a way which would spiral out of control during Elizabeth and Margaret's lifetimes.

There was no English queen at the time of their births. Henry VI occupied the throne alone, young, unmarried and easily led by his advisors. The year 1437 had already marked the deaths of two queens dowager, Henry's mother, Catherine of Valois and his step-grandmother, Joan of Navarre. It was the end of an era for female influence at the English court, making it necessary to look to Europe to find examples of contemporary queenship. In France, Henry's future aunt-in-law, Marie of Anjou, had already reigned for fifteen years, presiding over the council of state and bearing Charles VII fourteen children. Isabella of Portugal, Henry's cousin through their mutual descent from John of Gaunt, had borne three children following her marriage to Philip the Good, Duke of Burgundy, and besides being regent, had acted as negotiator in trade relations with England. Isabella's portrait, painted in the 1440s by Rogier van der Weyden, depicts her looking sage in a large butterfly hennin, draped in lace. Henry's future mother-in-law, Isabella, Duchess of Lorraine, a mother of ten, ruled jointly with her husband René of Anjou, then acted as regent during the six years of his imprisonment during the 1430s. Continental queens modelled the contemporary ideal by being competent heads of state as well as fruitful wives. It was from this exemplary pool that Henry would select his own wife, Margaret of Anjou, in 1445.

Elizabeth and Margaret arrived at a time when fine art was flourishing. The influence of the early European Renaissance was beginning to creep north, bringing its ideals of female beauty and piety. These years witnessed the death of Jan van Eyck, who painted the woman in the green dress, known to the world as the wife of the merchant Arnolfini, and the birth of Sandro Botticelli, most famous for his timeless icon of beauty in the *Birth of Venus*. They saw Piero della Francesca commissioned to paint the *Madonna della Misericordia*, Filippo Lippi working on his *Coronation of the Virgin*, and Pisanello's luminous *Portrait of a Princess of the House of Este*. More than this, the 1440s witnessed the work of the first recorded female artists, Catherine of Bologna, a writer, painter and visionary Abbess, later named as the patron saint of artists; Agnes van den Bossche, designer and decorator of flags, admitted to the Painters' Guild of Bruges; and Eleanor de Poitiers, author of *Les Honneurs de la Cour*, an account of her experience of ceremony at the Burgundian court. Elizabeth and Margaret, both of whom would be depicted in contemporary works of art, belonged to a world divided from Europe by water, across which these influences would only slowly trickle.

*

It was into this world that Elizabeth Woodville and Margaret Beaufort arrived. This in itself was a victory against circumstances and odds.

Birth was notoriously dangerous, fraught with the possibility of infection, injury and death, for both mother and child. Contemporary understanding of the female body and its workings was limited, based on the Galenic model, and defined women as imperfect forms of masculinity, prey to evil humours, temptation and requiring firm male guidance. Doctors, physicians and surgeons were all male, as were the authors of most medical texts, with female practitioners being relegated to unofficial and superstitious roles. The medical profession would not be regulated until the founding of the Royal College of Surgeons in 1518, but the first midwifery oath would not be sworn until 1562. Maternal fatalities and injuries were frequent, due to a lack of basic understanding about hygiene issues such as hand washing and clean linen, and a range of potential complications contributed to what has been estimated as a maternal death rate of between one and four per cent.[2] And yet, giving birth was a cultural ideal, the necessary aim of every married woman. Jacquetta Woodville, Countess Rivers, was formerly Henry VI's aunt by marriage, and had reached her early twenties when she delivered her first child and Margaret Beaufort, Duchess of Somerset, was a decade older when she bore her eighth. Both were fortunate to survive.

Elizabeth Woodville's birthplace is likely to have been her family's main residence in the village of Grafton, eight miles south of Northampton. The Woodville home sat close to ancient woodlands, on land which had recently been devoted to worship. Previously held by the French Abbey of Grestain, it also sheltered a twelfth-century hermitage and the church of St Mary, but by the early fifteenth century the property had been transferred to the de la Pole family, headed by the Duke of Suffolk. The Woodvilles' presence there represented the currents of contemporary social mobility; a rise in rank for Elizabeth's father, but a decrease in station for her mother. By the time of Elizabeth's birth, Richard Woodville was in his early thirties and had already taken steps to advance up the social ladder. Born in 1405, he had been a knight in France in the household of John, Duke of Bedford, uncle of Henry VI, then a captain in 1429 and a lieutenant in 1435. Upon the Duke's death that year, Richard transferred into the household of William de la Pole, first Duke of Suffolk, a connection which would bring him to Grafton, probably as Suffolk's tenant.

In his early thirties, Richard Woodville contracted a secret marriage that would forever change his fortunes. His chosen spouse was his former employer's wife, Jacquetta, Duchess of Bedford, a woman far above Richard in terms of status and technically out of his league. As a daughter of the house of Luxembourg, she had been raised in Brienne, a county in the north-west of France, by her father Pierre, Count of St Pol. Her marriage to Bedford was orchestrated when she was seventeen by her uncle, Louis of Luxembourg, Archbishop of Rouen, who collaborated with the ruling Lancastrian regime in northern France. As Jacquetta was aunt-in-law to the unmarried King Henry VI, she was also first lady in the land in terms of precedence. Any child she might have borne Bedford would have been heir to the throne. Thus, even though she was widowed after only two years, she remained a very important figure politically, an intimate member of the royal family, whose future marital path could have national implications and was carefully monitored by parliament. When Bedford died in 1435, Jacquetta had been granted her widow's dower payments on the premise that she would not remarry without the permission of Henry VI. And yet, she did. At some point in the next eighteen months, she became the secret wife of Richard Woodville, the man entrusted with the task of bringing her home.

Predictably, the secret marriage did not remain so for long. Jacquetta was still only twenty-one when her actions became public knowledge, to the chagrin of her nephew, the young King. It may have been an advancing pregnancy that forced her to throw herself upon Henry's mercy and admit that she 'toke but late ago to Husband youre trewe liegeman of your Roailme of England, Richard Woodville, knight, not having thereto youre Roiall licencse and assent', for which offence she had 'suffred right grate stretness as well in their persones as in their goddes'.[3] On 23 March 1437, the couple were issued with the not inconsiderable fine of £1,000,[4] which they raised through the sale of some of Jacquetta's properties to the King's half-uncle, Cardinal Beaufort. But the marriage was a fait accompli, and a child was probably on the way. Although undesirable unions could be broken in extreme cases, there was no legitimate reason to do so in this case.

The pair were restored to royal favour seven months later, being granted a pardon that October for the act of 'intermarrying without the king's consent'.[5] The young King may have been disposed to forgive the widow's secret love match, because it reminded him of the similar union made by his own mother to her handsome Welsh squire, Owen Tudor. Catherine of Valois had also been widowed young and disobeyed parliamentary instructions forbidding her not to remarry without their permission. She bore Tudor at least two children, perhaps as many as six, a considerable feat to conceal behind the walls of Windsor Castle, although no contemporary accounts exist suggesting she was directly censured for it. Not exactly common knowledge, it is probable that the liaison was known only to the royal family's inner circle, which included a young Jacquetta, visiting England with her first husband in the mid-1430s, providing her with the precedent of tolerance towards the love affairs of a former queen. She may have even hoped that Catherine would intercede on her behalf, but Henry VI's mother died early in 1437, just two months before the Woodville match was exposed. Such illicit marriages, driven by passion in spite of the consequences, could become cankers on the Tudor dynastic tree.

The Woodvilles' eldest child, Elizabeth, probably arrived in autumn 1437. Historian David Baldwin has suggested an arrival date of October,[6] to coincide with the pardon that was issued on the 24th of that month, a theory supporting the notion that Jacquetta's confession made in March was prompted by the realisation that she was pregnant. It is also likely that Jacquetta's choice of name indicates her birthday, given the lack of Elizabeths in the Luxembourg and Woodville families. Traditionally, the celebration of St Elizabeth's day in the Catholic calendar falls on 23 September, and custom often saw children named after their patron birth saint, as a way of inviting their spiritual guidance through life. St Elizabeth also had particular connections with childbirth, having conceived in improbable circumstances, so the choice of name might represent the gratitude of a first-time mother who had prayed for a safe delivery.

Like the majority of girls of her class, the milestones of Elizabeth's early years passed by unrecorded. As a small child, she may have accompanied her parents when they sailed to France in July 1441, and again in November 1444, but it is far more likely that she and her siblings remained at Grafton, pursuing their studies in the Northamptonshire countryside. Suggestions that Elizabeth was placed in the household of Henry's new queen, Margaret of Anjou, are not illogical, given her mother's social standing, but they are unlikely. Firstly, Elizabeth was too young and secondly, the theory derives from confusion between Elizabeth's later married name and that of Isabelle, the wife of Sir Ralph Grey, who definitely was part of the queen's entourage. With the name 'Isabelle' being the French version of 'Elizabeth,' and the two used interchangeably in contemporary records relating to Margaret's arrival in England, such confusion is understandable. The first definite landmark in Elizabeth's life, following that of her birth, is 1452 or 1453, when her marriage took place. This also helps to backdate her birthdate, as she would have been required to have attained the minimum age of fourteen in order to agree to the match.

Elizabeth's first husband, Sir John Grey, came from a Leicestershire family based at Groby Old Hall, fifty miles north of Grafton. Very little is known about the man with whom she lived, and perhaps loved, and lost, before she became queen. John was not a particularly illustrious match for the daughter of a woman formerly married to the King's uncle, but his status was in line with that of Elizabeth's father. The geographical proximity of their homes, and the families' connection through Bedford's household, in which Grey's uncle had also served, suggest the two young people may have known each other whilst growing up. At the least, it was arranged to reinforce existing ties of family loyalty and service dating back to the household of the Duke of Bedford. What Elizabeth thought of her husband is unknown. Personal happiness in marriage was considered less important than the fulfilment of dynastic duty but, given that Jacquetta had been married first to satisfy her family and secondly to satisfy herself, she may have been inclined to take her daughter's feelings into account.

The newly-weds may not have lived together initially. A woman might give her legal consent to be married at the age of fourteen, but full consummation was often delayed until she reached the age of sixteen. When they did, it may have been in the house of John's parents at Groby, or in their property at Astley in Warwickshire, twenty miles to the south-west. At the latest, the union had been consummated by the end of 1454 or early in 1455, the year when their first child, Thomas, was born. A second son, Richard, arrived around 1457. As Elizabeth prepared for her second labour at the age of twenty, another young mother was delivering a son whose future would become irrevocably entwined with that of the Woodvilles.

*

Margaret Beaufort was six years younger than Elizabeth Woodville. If Elizabeth was the product of a controversial marriage, Margaret was even more so. The Beaufort family were the descendants of John of Gaunt, Duke of Lancaster, third surviving son of Edward III, and his adulterous liaison with Katherine Swynford. Although their offspring had been legitimised by papal dispensation and parliament in the 1390s, they were barred from inheriting the throne by Henry IV, and the taint of illegitimacy lingered down the generations.

Margaret's father, John, Duke of Somerset, had an initially promising career fighting with his cousin Henry V in France, but after he was captured after the Battle of Baugé in 1421 he spent the following seventeen years in captivity. He resumed his military activity after his release, although his final years in France proved a string of disasters, complicated by ill-health, financial mismanagement and military mistakes. Somerset's marriage to Margaret Beauchamp of Bletsoe had been a fairly unambitious one on his part. She was an heiress from a gentry family, the twenty-nine-year-old widow of a knight, who brought with her seven children. The ceremony can be dated to after August 1441, but the couple were destined to enjoy little time together as Somerset was busy planning his next campaign. In 1443 Margaret prepared to give birth at her residence of Bletsoe Castle, in Bedfordshire, and her daughter arrived at the end of May, just months before Somerset's career fell apart.

In January 1444, Somerset returned from France with little to show for his campaign, save for broken promises and mounting debts. Rejected by the King and court, he retreated to the west country where he died that May, days before his daughter's first birthday. Only just into his forties, and recently active, this unexpected death was interpreted by some chroniclers as suicide. There is no doubt that such failure would have been shameful to a man already broken by his defeats, but no concrete evidence survives to support the rumour that he took his own life. The times were against it. While medieval concepts of 'self-murder' and eternal damnation did not entirely prevent suicides from taking place, contemporary literature presents a persuasive case for making a 'good' death, a resignation to one's fate that would pave the way to forgiveness in the afterlife. Other chroniclers stated, more simply, that the Duke had died of illness. The taint of her father's failure may have hung over the young Margaret, but it was offset by the huge inheritance he left her as his only surviving legitimate child.

Margaret was left fatherless after her first birthday, but her position was not as friendless as it might seem. A wealthy heiress, with royal blood, she was a significant figure in her own right despite her infancy, and although she was allowed to remain in the custody of her mother, King Henry granted her wardship to William de la Pole, Duke of Suffolk. Margaret's new guardian was the same Duke of Suffolk from whom Richard Woodville had bought Grafton, an ambitious man in his fifties who stepped into the role of the King's closest advisor after Somerset's death. Keen to secure Margaret's inheritance for his own use, Suffolk planned her marriage to his eldest son, John de la Pole, who was just a year older than his bride. Such arrangements were not binding in canon law, merely constituting a promise to wed in the future, dependent upon the agreement of the two children once they had come of age. Yet Suffolk ran out of time. In January 1450, the Duke's enemies closed in. He was accused of conducting treasonous negotiations with the French, of passing over details of Council meetings and even supporting a foreign invasion. Hurriedly, in the next few days, he orchestrated a formal ceremony of marriage between the six-year-old Margaret and seven-year-old John. It came too late. Impeached by parliament and accused of treason, Suffolk was banished from England for five years, but his ship was intercepted in the Channel, he was murdered on board, and his body was cast into the sea.

Margaret's brief union was annulled and her wardship granted to the King's half-brothers, Edmund and Jasper Tudor, the products of that secret union between Henry VI's mother, Catherine of Valois, and her servant Owen Tudor in the late 1420s. The family originated from Penmynydd on the isle of Anglesey, North Wales, and had fought on the side of their cousin, Owen Glendower, against English rule, for which they lost their fortune and status. Owen Tudor's efforts to regain the confiscated family lands brought him to the court of Henry VI, where he caught the eye of the lonely ex-Queen. In 1453, Edmund and Jasper were formally recognised as half-brothers of the King and granted the titles of Earl of Richmond and Earl of Pembroke. Margaret and her mother were invited to court on this occasion, and Henry VI provided 100 marks for the purchase of new clothes for the girl, raiments intended to impress on the occasion of her betrothal.

Just as Suffolk had, the Tudor brothers were keen to utilise the advantages of status and wealth Margaret brought, but they had no young son of her age to which they might ally her in marriage. Both Tudors were fully grown men, unmarried in their twenties, and they now considered her future in terms of their own marital aspirations.

In later life, Margaret would relate these events to her confessor, Bishop John Fisher, as being activated by her choice rather than political necessity, and not unduly influenced by her guardians. She claimed that the decision to leave Suffolk's heir and wed Edmund Tudor was hers to make after she offered prayers to St Nicholas, who confirmed to her that her future lay with the Tudors. Her strong sense of personal destiny was not untypical of aristocratic women of the period who had been raised to make dynastic marriages, especially those with royal blood, but her young age underlines the intensity of her focus. Her retelling of her personal narrative was also an important tool in the justification of her son's rule thirty years later. Just how much real choice she was able to exercise as a child, as the ward of her future husband, is less clear. She may have been as ambitious as he. Her subsequent career certainly suggests so.

*

It took two acts, by two women, to embed the Tudor dynasty into English royalty. Both were marriages, one for love and one for advancement. Catherine of Valois was responsible for the first, by falling in love with Owen Tudor, becoming his secret wife and bearing his children. Whatever the circumstances and legalities of her union with Tudor, Catherine's birth and marriage meant that her sons by him were also the grandsons of Charles VI, King of France, and the half-brothers of Henry VI of England. Their royal blood could not be denied. Thus, the name of Tudor was connected for the first time in 1437 to the ruling dynasties of England and France, forever changing their prospects. Love made the first Tudors royal.

The second act was Margaret Beaufort's marriage to Edmund Tudor, by which the family were united to the descendants of John of Gaunt. As the chief name in the land, only comparable to that of the Duke of York, it was the formerly illegitimate Beaufort bloodline that gave the Tudors greater legitimacy and wealth in the 1450s. The union of Margaret and Edmund was, no doubt, one of political expediency, but it cemented Henry VI's validation of his half-brothers as holding a central place in the hierarchy. In three decades, this branch of the Tudor line had gone from obscurity and poverty to royal blood. This was the direct result of a choice made by Catherine of Valois and the agreement of Margaret Beaufort.

The year of Margaret's betrothal, 1453, was to prove a significant one. The old world was falling and a new one was being forged. That spring, the Byzantine Empire that had survived for a thousand years after the fall of the western Roman Empire came to an end after the siege and fall of Constantinople. Secluded in her Italian convent, Catherine of Bologna had received visitations from Christ, the Virgin Mary, Thomas Becket and others, predicting this eventuality, as she rewrote her *Le Sette Armi Spirituali*, or Seven Weapons for Spiritual Warfare. A partial lunar eclipse, observed towards the end of the siege, seemed to confirm the intervention of divine mercy, although this did not lessen the rape, murder and enslavement experienced by women in the sacked city.

Also in 1453, Florentine hermit and manuscript illustrator, Maria Ormani degli Abizzi, painted, signed and dated her self-portrait in a breviary. Framed in a scroll, the portrait's Latin inscription described her as the 'handmaid of God, daughter of Orman and the writer of this book'. Such individuality and identification were rare among male scribes and illustrators, but the conscious self-fashioning of Maria's work is indicative of an increasing sense of women recognising themselves as authors of their own destiny, which chimes with Margaret Beaufort's narrative. Just three years later, Antonia di Paolo di Dono, daughter of the artist Uccello, would become the first listed in civic documents as a 'pittoressa', a female painter.

That July, the English and French armies clashed at the Battle of Castillon, resulting in a defeat for the forces of Henry VI, and the loss of the final territory in England's once-great Angevin empire. One glimmer of hope for England was that Henry VI's queen, Margaret of Anjou, had finally conceived after eight years of marriage. That August, though, when the queen was seven months pregnant, Henry fell into a catatonic state and was unable to move, communicate or feed himself. The reasons for this are unclear, perhaps deriving from a condition inherited from his grandfather, Charles VI, also known as 'the mad', which had manifested in violence and paranoia. Initially, the royal Council attempted to cover up this problem but during his long period of infirmity that followed, Henry was clearly unable to rule. When Margaret of Anjou delivered a healthy boy, named Edward, after the patron saint who shared his October birthday, Henry was presented with the child but could not understand who it was. The Council rejected Margaret's bold request to act as regent and appointed a Protector until such time that Henry recovered, or Prince Edward came of age. That Protector was Henry's nearest adult male relative, the former Lieutenant of France and great-grandson of Edward III, Richard, Duke of York.

On 1 November 1455, at Bletsoe, the twenty-four-year-old Edmund was married to the twelve-year-old Margaret. The pair departed for Wales, moving between the Bishop's Palace in Lamphey, seat of the Bishops of St David's, Pembroke Castle in Pembrokeshire, given to Jasper by the King in 1452, and perhaps also at Caldicot Castle in Monmouthshire, which had passed into royal ownership from Mary de Bohun, mother of Henry V. Edmund's task was to defend Lancastrian-held territories against the encroachment of Richard, Duke of York. Margaret's task was to be his wife. The 1393 'Ménagier de Paris' guidebook of behaviour was aimed at young wives, containing the usual advice on obedience, thrift, medicine, socialising, cookery and pleasing a husband; but Margaret's age and isolation makes her case atypical.

No evidence survives to help us understand how the twelve-year-old Margaret experienced marriage and her new life. Her character is best known to us through her later actions and writings, which convey her as strong, pious and focused, as well as erudite, intelligent and astute. Her confessor, John Fisher, wrote that Margaret was 'of singular easiness to be spoken unto, and full courteous answer she would make to all that came unto her. Of marvellous gentleness she was unto all folks, but specially unto her own, whom she loved and trusted right tenderly.' She never forgot any kindness or service done to her, 'which is no little part of very nobleness', and she was 'always ready to forgive and forget an injury'.[7] It must be remembered that these are tributes to the mother of a king. Margaret's character at the age of twelve, still evolving, must have been sorely tried, if not permanently scarred, by the events that were to follow.

Six months after the wedding, in April 1456, Margaret fell pregnant. She was only twelve, a few weeks short of her thirteenth birthday. To the twenty-first century, this seems brutally, criminally, young, but laws and moralities change, necessitating the analysis of this circumstance within the context of her times. In the fifteenth century, fourteen was considered the age of consent for girls, when they had reached their majority and were able to enter a full marriage. In reality, though, marriages conducted at this time were usually just formal promises.

Occasionally, youthful couples were permitted to sleep together just once, following the church vows, making the match legally binding, but then it was common practice for the couple to separate for a few years, to complete their education and development. There were sound gynaecological reasons for this too, for the safety of mother and child, as well as the girl's future ability to bear children. Even then, it was unusual for marriages to be consummated while the bride was so young, especially given Margaret's well-documented small stature and girlish fragility. Aristocratic brides might exist at the age of twelve, but very few became pregnant.

Yet the Tudor-Beaufort marriage was not typical. Other factors were at play in 1456. Edmund Tudor was keen to fully validate the marriage to ensure his ownership of his new wife's estates, an event which would only be guaranteed once he had fathered an heir. This 'Courtesy of England' or Courtesy Tenure, was a legal concept granting a lifetime's access for a husband or widower to a woman's estates regardless of the survival of that woman or her child. The terms of the tenure specified that a marriage ceremony had to have taken place, the estates must have been in the wife's possession and that the union must have resulted in live issue. Edmund did not have the benefit of hindsight when it came to his impending death. He did not know he needed to hurry up and father a son, or that he lacked time. His decision to try and impregnate Margaret at such a young age was prompted more by impatience and financial motives. In this, he was behaving as an aristocrat of his times, for whom marriages were economic arrangements rather than affectionate unions.

Recently, some historians have commented upon Margaret's marriage in ways that border upon censure or openly condemn Edmund Tudor's actions. Clearly, marriage and sexual consummation with a girl of twelve is understood in the modern world to be deeply damaging, emotionally and physically, and would breach a number of moral, ethical and legal codes. In the twenty-first century, in the Western world, such an act would be considered a clear case of paedophilia and rape, incurring criminal charges. Margaret's marriage was not conducted in this context. Her later actions imply an understanding that her early pregnancy had been traumatic and damaging, but she would not have accepted modern accusations of rape levelled at her husband. The pair were man and wife in the eyes of the church and, as such, Margaret had no legal recourse to resist her husband's advances.

It was considered part of her duties, and although the medieval church did debate circumstances where this could be injurious to a woman's health or endanger her life, it had reached no universal conclusions. As her husband's property, the concept of marital rape had no legal basis during Margaret's lifetime, nor did it, in fact, for the intervening five centuries, only becoming law in 1993. No court would have convicted Edmund Tudor of rape in 1456, thus it is anachronistic to apply the terminology of modern sensibilities to his case, no matter how morally wrong it appears today. Margaret's early pregnancy is a valuable reminder of how human experience remains constant, but moral and legal sensibilities change over time.

In August 1456, Edmund was captured by William Herbert, acting on behalf of Richard, Duke of York, and imprisoned in Carmarthen Castle. After three months in confinement, possibly suffering neglect after his enemies moved north, Edmund contracted the plague and died. Margaret was left a widow at thirteen, entering the third trimester of her pregnancy and terrified that she, and her unborn child, would suffer the same fate as her husband.[8] Margaret turned to her brother-in-law, Jasper, for help, who offered her protection in his remote stronghold of Pembroke Castle. On this bleak promontory at the tip of the little town, Margaret passed the final weeks of her confinement. According to tradition, it was in a tower to the west of the gatehouse, in the outer ward, that she bore her son on 28 January 1457. The tiny rooms inside are dark but solid, with a great fireplace and thick walls, both secure and warm, which may explain the choice for her to lie-in there, instead of the larger keep. Recent excavations on the grass inside the walls suggest the presence of a now-demolished building of considerable size, which may indicate an alternative location. The labour was long and difficult[9] and may have led to lasting physical damage, which explains why Margaret never conceived another child despite making two more marriages. In later life, she would be keen to protect her granddaughter and namesake, Princess Margaret Tudor, from a similar fate by delaying the consummation of her marriage to James IV of Scotland.

Widowed and a mother, Margaret was still a valuable commodity on the marriage market. Events after her delivery moved very swiftly, barely allowing her time to recover after her month of lying-in and churching. By March 1457, she had recovered sufficiently to travel a hundred miles west, with Jasper, to Greenfield Manor, also known as

Ebboth, near Newport in Gwent. There, discussions were undertaken to betroth her to her second cousin, Henry Stafford, son of the powerful Duke of Buckingham. Margaret's proven fertility and the survival of a male child may have counted in her favour, but her presence at the negotiations was unusual, suggesting that she was given a voice in shaping her future. It has been suggested that with Jasper's help she took steps to avoid an alternative marriage of her mother's choosing, but there is little evidence to support this. Certainly, she did not return to her mother's care but put herself in the hands of the family of her son's father. A papal dispensation was issued on 6 April and the marriage took place on 3 January 1458, possibly at Maxstoke Castle in Warwickshire, the Duke's favourite residence with octagonal towers overlooking the moat. Margaret was fourteen, her new husband thirty-two, and her young son almost a year old.

Women as Witnesses
1460–1463

In 1460, Francesco del Cossa, a young stonemason's son from Ferrara, completed his depiction of Polyhymnia, the muse of sacred poetry, hymn, eloquence and agriculture. Although she typified abstract early Renaissance ideals, Ferrara portrayed his subject as a working figure in simple clothes, a sturdy, strong woman shouldering an axe, leaning on a shovel, with a bunch of grapes hanging from her hand. Del Cossa's juxtaposition of earthy fertility and poetry in part captures the dichotomy of expectations faced by Elizabeth, Margaret and their peers. As women of rank, they were bound to represent a standard of behaviour, maintain a purity of conduct and reputation, inspire with their demure piety, whilst conceiving and delivering children, risking all the dangers that entailed.

Another image from the same year, Rogier van der Weyden's *Portrait of a Lady,* captured a more recognisable face of medieval womanhood, in simple black and white planes. The woman's clothing is severe and modest, quasi-religious, but revealing touches of bodily humanity. The sheer lace pinned over her breast and throat covers but does not conceal her skin. Equally, it reveals her hairline and the pins holding her hat in place, skims her eyebrows and the tops of her ears. The eyes are downcast demurely but are as sensuous as the full lips and the fingers that lace together with their gold bands visible. The face combines modesty and knowledge, the dangerous path which both Elizabeth and Margaret would be required to walk in the coming years.

Enclosed in the quiet of their country estates, Margaret and Elizabeth may not have sensed the coming crisis. By 1460, rumours of national insecurity probably reached them, but the business of life continued.

Their concerns were still primarily domestic, overseeing payments and arrangements, balancing the books, meals and linen, patronage and piety, raising children. The ways in which women engaged with national and dynastic events differed vastly from the experience of men. Far more frequently, they were facilitators, observers, organisers and providers, rather than the active warheads that society expected their husbands to be. Yet Margaret and Elizabeth were not necessarily so far removed from the centre of life as might be assumed from their locations. For once, the royal drama was being played out elsewhere than the usual arena of the capital. Following their conflict with the Yorks, the Lancastrian royal family had established an alternative court at Coventry, a hundred miles north of London in the West Midlands, with around 5,000 residents. Parliament was held there in 1459. Queen Margaret considered Coventry to be her 'secret harbour' and was welcomed there amid much pageantry.

The Greys and Staffords were close enough to Coventry to be involved in the new court. John and Elizabeth were based at Groby, only twenty-five miles to the north-east, or perhaps at the other family property at Astley, a mere nine miles north of the new royal capital. On at least one occasion Elizabeth's father visited the city with her, as the Coventry Leet Book records that he paid two shillings for a 'glasse of rose water'.[1] In the early years of their marriage, Henry and Margaret Stafford lived at Bourne Castle in Lincolnshire and, although it lay seventy miles east from Coventry, the north-south divide made that less significant than the one hundred and twenty miles between Bourne and Westminster. Bletsoe Castle was situated fifty miles east but even closer was Stafford's Maxstoke Castle, ten miles away. Grafton was thirty-eight miles south-east, a two-day ride. Both women were geographically located within the Lancastrian stronghold, but soon their Yorkist enemies were to bring the war to them.

Conflict broke out again in the summer of 1460. For Margaret and Elizabeth, it must have been deeply unsettling to hear the Yorkist army was marching north, coming closer and closer to home. Perhaps Elizabeth, her children and Jacquetta fled before the Yorkists passed just ten miles north of Grafton on their way to Northampton. Margaret was safer at Bourne, forty-eight miles away, but the paths of armies and the fall-out of battlefields could be notoriously unpredictable. Edward, Earl of March, son of the Duke of York, met Henry's men on 10 June in the grounds of Delapré Abbey, on the bank of the River

Nene. Living comparatively near the site, Sir John Grey, the Woodville men and Henry Stafford would have been among those who attended Henry as the rebels closed in. With the resident nuns looking on in terror, the battle raged in the driving rain until the King was captured. Before their victory was declared, the Yorkists claimed the life of Margaret's father-in-law, Humphrey, Duke of Buckingham, who died attempting to protect the King from capture. As a result of his father's death, Henry Stafford came home as the head of the family, although he was not to receive the title, which passed to his deceased brother's little son. Elizabeth's prayers were answered, as Sir John returned to her and his two little boys.

*

Recasting these events from the female perspective is not easy. Women's sphere of influence was largely informal: they did not come together on the battlefield or in the council chamber as men did. They did not undergo the intense, terrifying trial of hand-to-hand combat, so definitive in the shaping of this era. Instead, they waited separately, or in small family groupings, spread across the country, watching at windows, kneeling before altars, attending children, writing letters. On a more active front, they might temporarily undertake 'male' activities, such as overseeing local courts and resolving disputes, keeping their estates running smoothly and gathering harvests. The domestic spaces which framed women's responses were defined by their relationship to the men involved, and the patriarchal code of conduct which required their passivity and patience. The nature of their activities means they frequently went unrecorded.

One notable example was the patient strength of Cecily, Duchess of York, paternal grandmother of the first Tudor queen. The Duchess is reputed to have stood proud in the marketplace at Ludlow while the Lancastrian army looted the town in 1459. Such an anecdote sounds apocryphal, but two contemporary sources place Cecily there, with *Hearne's Fragment* describing how she 'had her wardrobe rifled and her furniture spoiled'[2] and the Abbot of Whethamsted stating the 'noble duches of York unmanly and cruelly was entreted and spoyled'.[3] This comment must be read in terms of gender and status. Those despoiling the Duchess's possessions were acting outside a gendered code, disgracing their masculinity by disrespecting a woman of rank, even one on the opposing side. Conflict had clearly defined boundaries for the sexes; men fought, women waited, prayed and tended their wounds. The failure to respect those roles, especially the violation of women, was a state of barbarism akin to the fall of civilisations, as at the sack of Constantinople seven years earlier. Most of the time, when it came to aristocratic women, these rules were entrenched in English culture.

On many occasions, women must have found the unfolding political situation to be equally terrifying and frustrating. What united them in such times was an emotional landscape rather than that of a battlefield. Secluded in their homes, they represented, in microcosm, the ideals of motherhood and dynasty that their men fought to protect on a national scale. Late medieval society was defined by procreation and inheritance, so women's contributions had a significance beyond that of their individual identities. For women themselves, though, cast as witnesses, reliant upon delayed, imperfect information, there was one way to commute their passivity into something useful. That was through prayer. Prayer was considered an active, powerful way of asking God to influence the outcome of unpredictable events. The more devout a woman could become, the more prayers she offered, the more prostrate she could make herself before the altar, the more 'control' she could feel, in the belief that everything was in God's hands. Men should be pious too, but during marches, meetings and battles, their attention was elsewhere. Women could be spiritual warriors in the new parish churches erected by their families to the glory of God. Thus, the correlation between pious activity and military, or political, success, could become a painful commentary upon the extent of one's personal favour in the eyes of the Lord.

Women did not always submit passively, especially when they perceived an injustice had been done. Many chose an active faith, reinterpreting themselves as instruments of God's will, determined to overcome the trials he had sent them and triumph as Christian warriors, a theme visible through the line of Tudor queens to come.

*

In 1460, the Lancastrian Queen, Margaret of Anjou, responded to the unfolding political drama as a mother. When the Duke of York returned from exile in Ireland, he made the extraordinary assertion that he was the rightful king, and forced Henry VI to sign the Act of Accord, recognising the inheritance of York and his sons. The Act entirely bypassed the claim of Henry's own son, the seven-year-old Prince Edward of Westminster, a situation that Margaret was not prepared to tolerate. She had been raised in that European tradition of strong women who fought for their rights, acted as regent in their husbands' absences, led campaigns, raised funds, championed their children's inheritances and remained determined until the bitter end. Her own mother, Isabella, Duchess of Lorraine, and grandmother, Yolande of Aragon, had done no less.

The Lancastrian wives, Elizabeth and Margaret, both mothers of sons whose inheritance they would fight to ensure, would have sympathised with the Queen's predicament. If they had much knowledge of her character, and Margaret had certainly met her in 1453, they would have known that the Anjou bride would not sit by and allow her son's rights to be signed away. It would have come as no surprise then, in the opening days of 1461, when news arrived at the Grey and Stafford homes that York had been ambushed and killed by the Queen's troops at Wakefield. Such a victory for the Lancastrians may have given John, Henry and their wives cause for relief, but they had reckoned without York's son, Edward, Earl of March, the victor of Northampton.

Edward, then an eighteen-year-old, standing over six-foot-three, was determined to avenge his father's death. By the terms of the Act of Accord, to threaten the life of York or his sons was treason, and March now used this to his advantage to assert his position as the Duke's heir. Word spread that he was gathering an army on the Welsh borders, prompting Margaret's former brother-in-law Jasper Tudor and father-in-law Owen Tudor to raise troops in their homelands of Pembrokeshire and Carmarthenshire, as well as hiring mercenaries from Brittany and Ireland. Neither Henry Stafford nor John Grey fought among the Lancastrian troops on this occasion, temporarily placed out of danger by virtue of geographical distance. The two sides met at Mortimer's Cross in Herefordshire where, on the morning of 3 February, support for the Tudors crumbled and Edward's men pursued their enemies as far as the city of Hereford, seventeen miles away. The defeat took on greater significance for Margaret when she learned that her former father-in-law, Owen Tudor, her son's grandfather, had been captured and beheaded by Edward's men outside the cathedral.

Grey and Stafford may already have armed and departed by the time news of the defeat at Mortimer's Cross reached them. If not, they were soon galvanised to act for the Lancastrian cause. By mid-February,

Sir John Grey had joined the Queen's army, with Margaret's cousin, Henry Beaufort. Bent on revenge, they intended to claim London before the victorious Edward could arrive from the west. However, Edward's ally, the Earl of Warwick, had possession of King Henry and stood between them and the capital, preparing to clash for a second time at St Albans. The unfortunate town, only recently recovered from the bloodshed and destruction in its streets six years earlier, braced itself for another onslaught.

The Queen's forces attacked the town from the north-east in the early hours of 17 February 1461, with Sir John Grey among them. After a long day of fighting, the Yorkist forces were overcome and withdrew, allowing Queen Margaret to enter the town and regain control of her husband. Estimates suggest that the Lancastrians lost around 2,000 men out of their entire army of 15,000, one of whom was Elizabeth's husband John. No one knows the exact circumstances of how and when he met his death, nor where his body was laid to rest. He passed out of history without record, leaving Elizabeth a widow with two small sons. At the time, this loss would have been a personal tragedy for his family, but the opportunity afforded by his death would change the future course of three dynasties. Hindsight reveals that it was as the result of the death of John Grey that the houses of Lancaster, York and Tudor took a different turn. Without his death, there would have been no Henry VIII or Elizabeth I. Of course, his widow knew nothing of this in 1461. She went into mourning, wondering what would become of herself and her children.

After St Albans, Queen Margaret failed to capitalise on her victory. Had she marched successfully upon London, there was every chance she would have prevented the arrival of her enemies. As it was, though, London feared her unruly soldiers, tales of their apparently lawless behaviour had already reached the city in lurid detail. Disposed to support the Yorkists, the city planned to close its gates against its long-absent Queen. A deputation of Lancastrian noblewomen was sent north to plead with Margaret, who heeded their concerns and turned north. Shortly afterwards, Edward entered the capital and declared himself king on 4 March, announcing that the Lancastrians had broken the peace established by the Act of Accord and offered amnesty to any who came over to his side.

In comparison with the pious, pacific Henry, the active, martial Edward IV conformed more readily to the contemporary concept of kinship. He offered an alternative to the years of illness, confusion, debt and influential favourites that had dogged the last decade of Lancastrian rule. Supporters flocked to his side as he joined with Warwick to pursue the Queen and her allies. Henry Stafford was among the tens of thousands of Lancastrians who marched under the leadership of Margaret's cousin, Henry Beaufort, and Sir Andrew Trollope, towards a field located between the villages of Towton and Saxton. They set up their lines on a snowy Palm Sunday, 29 March 1461. Faced with such terrible conditions, staring into the driving weather, even the experienced Stafford would have realised this was going to be one of the most gruelling fights of his life. Again, the women could do little but wait and pray.

In the days following the battle, eyewitnesses estimated that as many as 28,000 men had died at Towton or its immediate aftermath. Certainly, it was one of the bloodiest encounters ever fought on English soil, as attested by the graves excavated in 1996 by a team from the University of Bradford. After hours of fighting in the constant snow, with the wind behind the Yorkists carrying their arrows further, the Lancastrian defences broke and they fled, crushed in the scrum or drowning in the overflowing river, which reputedly ran red with blood. Edward had given the order that no mercy was to be shown and such was the carnage that as much as 1% of the country's entire population was lost on that single day. Among them was Margaret's stepfather, Lionel, Lord Welles.

Sir Henry Stafford was one of the lucky ones who returned home as Edward rode in triumph back to London to plan his coronation. With the opposition in tatters and King Henry VI having fled to Scotland, Stafford was wise to capitulate and make peace with his new ruler. Margaret had no choice but to fall in line. All those who had fought against Edward, who dated his reign from before the battle, were considered traitors, and ran the risk of forfeiting their lands, even their lives. Elizabeth's family fell into this category, as her father Richard and brothers Anthony and Richard had fought on the side of the Lancastrian regime. The Woodville men joined in offering their loyalty to the Yorkist King, who was keen to forgive all except those directly involved in the death of his father. Sir Richard was the first to receive his royal pardon, on 12 July 1461, with Anthony's issued eleven days later, although the younger Richard had to wait until the following February. That autumn, as *Warkworth's Chronicle* relates, Elizabeth's father was knighted as part of Edward's peace-making appointments: 'the Lord Rivers Earl Rivers ... and other gentlemen and yeomen he made knights and squires, as they had deserved.'[4] To all intents and purposes, the Stafford and Woodville families had come through the crisis of 1460-1 and had sworn to serve their new King. On a personal level, though, the dynasty into which Margaret had married, and for whom her cousins had fought, had been crushed.

Elizabeth Woodville had not only lost the father of her children. Her husband's reputation was lost too. While her father and brothers had survived to beg for their pardons, Sir John Grey had died fighting for the wrong side, making him a traitor to the new regime. His estates were forfeit to the crown, leaving Elizabeth without means of support, and her sons without an inheritance. In her distress, she hoped to rely upon the financial support of her husband's mother, Elizabeth Ferrers, Baroness Ferrers of Groby, but the older women's marital arrangements unexpectedly changed, as did her loyalties.

The Baroness had been widowed in 1457, when her first husband Edward died soon after John's marriage to Elizabeth. The first baron had made provision for his heirs by arranging for the income of three manors to be set aside, totalling 100 marks annually. This should have provided for Elizabeth's sons and in February 1461, when John lost his life at St Albans, she would have assumed they would be well looked after. Perhaps, initially, they were. However, at some point before May 1462, the Baroness remarried a much younger man, Sir John Bourchier, the son of York's sister Isabel, and thus a cousin of the new King Edward. This marriage allied the family with the Yorkist regime, and it would have been politically imprudent for either woman to have objected to Bourchier assuming the title of Baron with all its privileges, including the manors. It left Elizabeth in a difficult financial situation, dependent upon her parents, with her sons' futures uncertain.

Mothers, even aristocratic ones, had few rights over their children following the death of a spouse. At least Elizabeth Woodville was allowed to keep her boys at her side, even if providing for them was difficult. The death of a regime, though, was to prove more decisive for Margaret than the loss of her son's father had. As the nephew of a deposed king, five-year-old Henry Tudor's future could not be left to chance. On 12 February 1462, Edward IV awarded the boy's guardianship to William Herbert, Earl of Pembroke, the Yorkist Lord responsible for Edmund Tudor's death. Herself a product of this system, Margaret could not openly complain, no matter how much she bitterly resented the move, and especially the choice of the boy's new guardian. From this point, she experienced a significant and lasting separation from her son. Throughout his childhood at Raglan Castle, she could only maintain a correspondence and see him when permitted. The situation would not be remedied for another twenty-three years, when he became King. Initially, both Elizabeth and Margaret suffered as Lancastrian women when a Yorkist took the throne. Soon, though, it was to become the making of one of them.

The powerlessness of Margaret and Elizabeth at this point in their lives stands in strong contrast to the rise of influential women in Italy. In states like Florence, Milan and Venice, arguably the crucible of renaissance and reformative thought, aristocratic women's influence was decades ahead of that in England and would not cross the Channel in any lasting sense until the turn of the century, even when it came to reigning queens. Thus, Venice could produce Cristina Sanudo, who became a Dogaressa by marriage in 1462, and used her power to intervene in the textiles industry; Rimini had Isotta degli Atti, who governed on the excommunication of her husband and during the minority of her son; and the regency of Monaco was fought for by Pomellina Fregoso. In France, Lorraine was ruled by the Duchess Isabella whilst her husband was imprisoned, in Navarre, Eleanor was promoted to heir, ruler and regent by her father, and in Provence, Yolande of Aragon had fought for her husband's rights, acted as regent for her son and played a political role in wars against the English. In Spain, too, Maria of Aragon held her husband's lands during insurrection and personal illness, while Isabella, Queen of Castile, overcame her political enemies only to be banished from court during her widowhood, struggling with illness and depression as she raised the future queen who bore the same name and would be the mother of Catherine of Aragon. The closest England came to producing a comparable figure in the 1450s and 1460s was Margaret of Anjou, who found her political efforts were blocked by official channels. As Englishwomen born and bred, Elizabeth Woodville and Margaret Beaufort understood just how limited their positions were, and how little leeway they had to act within a male-dominated hierarchy. It would not be until the next century that two Renaissance queens would begin to redefine the nature of contributions open to a queen of England.

A Queen Is Made

1464–1469

The ideal of female beauty in the early 1460s is perhaps best captured in Paolo Uccello's *A Young Lady of Fashion*. Painted in profile, against a plain black background, the fair-skinned, golden-haired sitter appears to exist outside space and time, a suspended icon depicted with quasi-religious reverence. Pearls adorn her hair, headdress and throat, and a blue cloak, pinned at the shoulder, covers a red sleeve with gold floral patterns. Her neck is long and graceful, her brows plucked and arched, her hair scraped back to create a high forehead. The chin is pert and rounded, the nose straight and lips red and small. Perhaps what is most striking is the young woman's eyes, which look slightly glazed under heavy lids, as if she is looking away, unfocused, into the distance. With her backbone completely straight, her purity of colour and unattainable quality, she embodies the physical qualities attributed to Elizabeth Woodville.

If there was one characteristic on which all her contemporaries would agree, even her enemies, it was Elizabeth Woodville's beauty. Described in Hearne's *Fragment* as the 'most beautiful woman in the island of Britain', Elizabeth's 'constant womanhood, wisdom and beauty'[1] were extolled by all, including the Italian diplomat, Dominic Mancini, who recorded her 'beauty of person and charm of manner'[2] as late as 1483. Elizabeth's looks propelled her into the limelight whilst she was still at the height of her beauty and surviving contemporary portraits and images capture something of her appearance, partly as a means to justify exactly how she was able to captivate a king.

A coronation portrait of Elizabeth appears in the *Illuminated Books of the Fraternity of Our Lady's Assumption of the Skinners' Company*, one of the oldest and most prominent of London's medieval guilds. The illustration depicts Elizabeth in her coronation robes, an event which took place on 26 May 1465. She is dressed in a long royal blue gown with a gold trim, fastened at the neck with what look like two gold, flower-like clasps. Under this, she wears a long scarlet robe with a central panel of ermine extending over her hips, identifiable as white painted with tiny black flecks, and this also lines her cloak. The copious fabric lies in folds at her feet, hiding them entirely, as if she's floating. Elizabeth's eyes stare straight out at us. Her face is generic enough, but her golden hair hangs long loose and flowing, as a symbol of virginity, even though this queen was a widow with two small children. Another illustration of Elizabeth can be found in the *Luton Guild Book*, which depicts her among the founding members of the Fraternity of the Holy and Undivided Trinity and Blessed Virgin Mary. Here, she wears a long lilac-coloured cloak, edged with ermine, over a golden V-necked Burgundian gown, embroidered with blue flowers gathered in a high green waist band. Her hands are clasped in prayer and her eyes appear downcast and demure. Her features are regular and serene, her mouth small and eyebrows high, her hair scraped back under the double-pronged henin. In Lambeth Palace's copy of the *Dictes and Sayings of the Philosophers,* another illustration can be found of Elizabeth, who appears rather statue-like and abstract, seated slightly behind Edward to his left, holding the formal regalia of her queenship. Her hair is long, blonde and loose, her features small. She wears blue robes trimmed with ermine and an ermine collar, over which hangs a gold chain. She represents an ideal of contemporary beauty, and it was this quality, this aspect of her gender, that enabled her social advancement.

By 1464, Elizabeth Woodville had been widowed for three years. Living quietly at her parents' home at Grafton, and raising her boys, she and Jacquetta watched as their menfolk gradually assimilated their way into the Yorkist court. It was a pragmatic move. With Henry VI in Scotland and Margaret of Anjou raising support abroad, the Woodvilles were wise enough to bury any lingering Lancastrian sympathies. Instead, they presented themselves as true servants of the new King, especially as these years were marked by minor acts of failed rebellion that might easily have cost them dear. Reaching her mid-twenties, with many years of potential childrearing ahead, Elizabeth may have been considering remarriage, although it would have to be to a man of suitable rank, resources and political sympathies.

Exactly when Edward fell in love with Elizabeth is unclear. The King had stayed at Grafton in June 1461, but this may have been before Elizabeth's return to her parents, and so he could have missed her on that occasion. Early in his reign, he may also have been involved with other women, with later reports suggesting an informal betrothal, even a marriage, with an Eleanor Butler, née Talbot. His interest in Elizabeth appears to have been prompted by her attempts to enlist support in regaining the inheritance of her sons. She had been urging her boys' case in the local courts and in May 1463, Sir William Feilding, a knight of the shire for Leicestershire, took an interest. Like the Greys, Feilding had Lancastrian sympathies and would later lose his life fighting in the attempt to restore them to the throne. Feilding's report of Elizabeth's situation stressed that she had been 'wife of John Grey, knight, for life', and that her sons should have right of pasture to certain lands belonging to their maternal grandfather William Ferrers, who had died in 1445. Feilding appointed an attorney named William Brokwode to deliver seisin, or possession, of the lands, followed by more grants of access to the manor of Woodham Ferrers in Essex, delivered by David Malpas that November.[3]

Perhaps it was these small legal successes, asserting the rights of the boys to continue the use their grandfather had established, that encouraged Elizabeth further. Next time, she aimed higher. Her first recorded contact with Edward's court was on 13 April 1464, when she appealed to Edward's close friend, William, Lord Hastings, probably in his role as overseer of the Yorkist Midlands, for his assistance in her dispute with Baroness Ferrers. Hastings agreed to intervene so long as Elizabeth split the rents and profits of the Grey lands with him, and a marriage was arranged between one of Elizabeth's sons and any future daughter born to Hastings.

Driven by desire for a woman who was considered an unsuitable consort, Edward's wooing of Elizabeth took place in secret. He was also aware that the Earl of Warwick was currently in the middle of negotiations to win him a foreign bride, Bona of Savoy, sister to Queen Charlotte of France. The *Danzig Chronicle* describes how Edward fell in love with Elizabeth when he 'dined with her frequently'[4] implying regular visits to Grafton, which Hearne echoes, stating that he was there at 'divers times'.[5] John Hardyng, writing at the time of the marriage, expressed the opinion of many 'kynges and pryncs' that Edward had been 'led rather by blynde Cupide than by anye reason'.[6] According to Mancini's 1483 account, Edward fell in love with Elizabeth in spite of her comparatively humble background, because of her 'beauty of person and charm of manner' and his feelings strengthened when he realised 'he could not corrupt her virtue by gifts or menaces.' Legend has Elizabeth waiting for Edward under an oak in Whittlesbury Forest to petition him for assistance in the case against her mother-in-law, but this cannot be corroborated. Whatever her feelings and motivation, it was a game-changing marriage, based as it was upon attraction, perhaps even affection, opening the door for the companionate marriage model that would hold so much appeal for their grandchildren.

Edward and Elizabeth were married in secret, possibly on 1 May 1464, and certainly by September at the latest. Hearne, Gregory, Fabyan and other chroniclers pinpoint the day as 'the first of May... (when) our sovereign lord the King, Edward IV, was wedded to the Lord Rivers' daughter... and this marriage was kept full secretly long and many a day, that no man knew it,' while Warkworth tells us the wedding 'was privily in a secret place'.[7] More details about the wedding day come from chronicler Robert Fabyan[8] who describes how Edward made a detour on a hunting trip to the north and took Elizabeth's mother Jacquetta into their confidence, but not her father Richard. He adds that the ceremony was performed in a small priory, or hermitage, dedicated to St Michael, which stood on the edge of Woodville land near Shaw's Wood. The place was already in decline, after having merged with the nearby Abbey of St James, so the couple would have needed to supply a chaplain of their own to conduct the ceremony, no doubt a welcome factor in their desire for secrecy. After the ceremony, Fabyan relates, the couple consummated their union, staying in bed for three or four hours, before Edward rode back to Stony Stratford as if he had been out hunting.[9]

Elizabeth certainly understood the implications of undergoing a ceremony of marriage with a reigning king, even if she did not fully understand the political and international repercussions. The service itself may have been conducted in private, but the presence of witnesses and a priest, along with the mutual promises and subsequent consummation, made it legally binding. Elizabeth was a product of her time, which considered it a woman's duty to make the best match she could for the advancement of her family. By marrying the King, Elizabeth brought unimagined influence, power and wealth into the Woodville fold, with all the advantages this could bring to her sons, parents and siblings. Equally, a king was a difficult man to refuse.

Edward's personal attractions, let alone his position, made him a desirable husband for a widow who had been seeking protection against the legal injustice of the loss of her inheritance. In attracting Edward's serious attentions, Elizabeth had struck gold, and in the context of the late medieval world, she would have been a fool not to accept what he had to offer her.

*

Elizabeth's marriage now placed her on the opposing side to Margaret. After having made the Woodvilles' fortune, Edward's next act would destroy the Beauforts. From his new wife's bed, he hurried over three hundred miles north to Hexham in Northumberland. There he met Margaret's cousin Henry in battle, after the young Beaufort had taken a gamble to strike back and reclaim the throne for the Lancastrian line and Henry VI. It did not pay off: Henry clashed with Edward's army at Hedgeley Moor in April 1464 before their final, fatal confrontation on 15 May. Young Beaufort was captured after the battle, executed and buried in nearby Hexham Abbey. His traitors' death brought Margaret's family into the spotlight again, a reminder that they had formerly opposed the King and a warning of their potential to breed dissent. All property owned by Henry was confiscated by the crown, his brothers fled to Flanders, and their mother, the aged Duchess of Somerset, was imprisoned. Henry's actions, or rather, Henry's failure, brought all those who bore the Beaufort name under suspicion, reminding Margaret how important it was to appear to be a good subject of the Yorkist King; and now also, of the new Yorkist Queen.

That summer, Sir Henry Stafford was summoned to attend a session of Edward's second Parliament, which was meeting at Reading in September. The intention was to finalise the King's marriage to Bona of Savoy, sister of Charlotte, wife of Louis XI of France. Stafford attended in good faith and was stunned to hear the King interrupt the negotiations and make a surprise announcement. Five months after the secret ceremony, the King was forced to admit that he already had a wife, the widow of a Lancastrian knight, five years his elder, with two small children. Elizabeth was summoned to join her husband at Reading and face the thinly veiled disapproval of the Lords.

Elizabeth Woodville was not a suitable queen by any contemporary standards. The Croyland Chronicler noted how 'the nobility and chief men of the kingdom took amiss, seeing that he had with such immoderate haste promoted a person sprung from a comparatively humble lineage.'[10] Waurin added that while the Council recognised Elizabeth Woodville's charms, they rejected her background, telling the King that 'however good and fair she might be, he must know well that she was no wife for so high a prince as himself; she was not the daughter of a duke or earl but her mother ... had married a knight ... she was not, all things considered, a suitable wife for him, nor a woman of the kind who ought to belong to such a prince.'[11] The Earl of Warwick, chief negotiator for Bona's hand, was 'greatly displeased' and 'great dissension' arose between him and the King. Nor was he alone. A contemporary dispatch from Bruges, dated 5 October 1464, stated that the people of England were 'offended' by the union and the lords were 'very much dissatisfied at this' and were holding meetings 'for the sake of finding means to annul it'.[12] No doubt Stafford was among them, and Margaret was, at the very least, surprised by the news.

Elizabeth had to make a rapid adjustment to the demands of queenship. It cannot have been an easy rite of passage for a woman whose life had been predominantly spent in seclusion in the countryside. Yet it was done, Elizabeth was Edward's wife and Queen of England. Edward granted his new wife £466 13s 4d 'for the expenses of her chamber, wardrobe and stable against this feast of Christmas next coming' and over the next two years she received the palaces of Sheen and Greenwich, lands worth an annual £4,500 and numerous lordships and manors in England and Wales.[13] Edward was planning her coronation as early as October 1464, when safe conduct was granted for Elizabeth's Burgundian relatives to travel to England, in an attempt to stress her European pedigree, and their invitations for the event were issued the following January. The Mayor and Aldermen received summons to be present, suitably dressed, in mid-April. A month later, Margaret and Henry Stafford made their way to the capital in order to attend the new Queen.

*

26 May 1465 was one of the few days in their early lives which brought Margaret and Elizabeth together. The Staffords were a high-status couple, and Margaret's rank required her to attend the new queen at her coronation and subsequent ceremonials. It would also have been an important way for the Staffords to display their loyalty in the

wake of Henry Beaufort's defeat at Hexham. Pageants and songs were performed along the route, with the city guilds turning out their best performances and craftwork to honour the queen along streets that had been swept and decorated. Inside the abbey, Elizabeth was anointed before the assembled crowds, before being escorted to a feast in the Palace. Following the fashionable Burgundian etiquette, Elizabeth was distanced from most of the other female revellers, the thirteen duchesses in red velvet and ermine, fourteen baronesses in scarlet and miniver and twelve ladies in scarlet, among whose number Margaret would have been seated. Elizabeth was attended at table by Edward's sisters, Elizabeth and Margaret of York, and her cup was borne by her brother Anthony. Nothing suggests there was any sort of personal connection between Margaret and the new queen on this occasion and, with the spotlight falling definitively upon Elizabeth, it fell to Lady Stafford to observe the Yorkist pageantry and bite her tongue.

It was while Elizabeth and Edward were visiting Canterbury that July that news reached them of the capture of Henry VI. After the defeat at Towton, the Lancastrian royal family had fled to Scotland and since then Queen Margaret had travelled to France and Burgundy in attempts to raise support for their cause. Henry had remained hidden in various locations in the north until his arrest that summer, when he was betrayed by friends and taken during dinner near Clitheroe in Lancashire. The former King was conducted to London and established in the Tower, in his own suite of rooms, where he spent the next five years in quiet seclusion. Around the same time, Elizabeth realised that she had fallen pregnant. Her first child arrived on 11 February 1466, at Westminster Palace; a daughter who shared her mother's name and has come to be known to history as Elizabeth of York. Over the next few years, the Queen bore two more daughters, Mary in 1467 and Cecily in 1469. With the former King behind locked doors, all the couple needed now was a son to secure the succession.

In the second half of the 1460s, the Staffords followed the Yorkist line and more alliances were forged between Margaret and Elizabeth's families. Edward accepted their proffered loyalty and rewarded them for it: Henry Stafford's eleven-year-old nephew, the new Duke of Buckingham, was married to Elizabeth's younger sister Catherine Woodville in February 1466, and the same year, Margaret and Henry were granted the former Beaufort manor of Woking, which would become their chief home. Now standing in ruins, the house had been a royal residence since the thirteenth century, but upon taking it over the Staffords began the improvements that would develop it into a palace. The place was not ready to host them for the Christmas season, though, as they spent six weeks with Margaret's mother at Maxey Castle in Cambridgeshire, and did not move into Woking until the following March. In May 1467 Stafford attended a meeting of Edward's Council held at nearby Mortlake and the following May Margaret accompanied him to London by boat and stayed at the Mitre Inn, while he attended an important session of parliament to discuss Edward's plans for invading France. It was a further sign of royal trust that the army was to be led by Henry's stepfather, Walter, Lord Mountjoy, although subsequent events delayed the expedition until 1475. During these years, Margaret maintained close contact with her son by letter and in September 1467 she and her husband visited young Henry at Raglan, staying for a week. No doubt the Staffords were also guests on the occasion that Edward married his sister by proxy to Charles the Bold, Duke of Burgundy, when weeks of celebrations at court culminated in a long procession of the English nobility down to Dover, to wave the young bride goodbye.

By the end of 1468, the quiet obedience of the Staffords appeared to have won royal approval. In December, the couple entertained King Edward at Brookwood, their hunting lodge near Woking, with Stafford meeting the King at Guildford and accompanying him the seven miles to the lodge. Pewter dinner plates and glasses were purchased in London and culinary supplies from Guildford, including pike, lampreys, oysters and ale,[14] which were consumed under a purple canopy to music played by the royal minstrels. It is not clear whether Elizabeth was present on this occasion as Margaret's guest, but as the queen was entering the third trimester of her pregnancy with Princess Cecily, she may have chosen to remain closer to home.

Elizabeth's rise to power had been meteoric. By 1469, she had good reason to celebrate her successes, making the most lucrative marriage of her era, being crowned and bearing three more children, as well as having the love of her husband. Margaret had also found protection and fulfilment in her second marriage and had weathered considerable storms in order to retain her position, to the extent that the new King had consented to be her guest. Although the political climate currently favoured the Woodvilles over the Beauforts, both women had achieved an equilibrium in their private and personal lives. However, as a new decade approached, each was to be threatened with the loss of everything they held dear.

4

A Queen Is Unmade
1469–72

The year 1469 was one of change and new beginnings. That October, Ferdinand of Aragon and Isabella of Castile, future parents of Catherine of Aragon, were married at Valladolid, uniting the two most important kingdoms of Spain. Their future court painter, Michael Sittow, was born in Estonia, whose portrait of their daughter would become among the most iconic images of the Tudor age. Louis XI of France and Charles the Bold, Duke of Burgundy, were engaged in a feud that would define international relations in northern Europe for years to come. Louis' wife, Charlotte, had survived his abandonment of her in Burgundy, his neglect, serious illness and six pregnancies, and was compiling her collection of over 100 manuscripts that would form the basis of the National Library of France. Duke Charles was newly married to his second cousin, Edward IV's sister, Margaret of York. In July 1469, James III of Scotland took Margaret of Denmark as his wife, throwing off the influence of the powerful faction that had controlled his minority in order to rule independently.

The Madonna was still the most popular subject in art, depicted in 1469 by Andrea del Verracchio in *Madonna of the Milk*, and no fewer than four times by Botticelli since 1467. The momentum of the Renaissance was nevertheless shifting north from Florence and Venice to northern Europe, with more earthy, real, confrontational depictions of individuals, and greater focus on the grubby business of life. In 1466 Quentin Matsys arrived in Antwerp, painter of the iconic, even revolutionary *Grotesque Old Woman* and *The Money Changer and his Wife*. The year before saw the birth of Gerard Horenbout, future court painter to Henry VIII. In 1469, Petrus Christus, a student

41

of Van Eyck working in Bruges, produced his *Portrait of a Young Girl,* who stares out at the viewer with a confrontational complexity in her dark eyes that challenges as much as the Mona Lisa would, four decades later.

1469 also saw the birth of new thinkers. Niccolo Machiavelli, who would come to typify a new kind of politics in the emerging humanist age, was born in Florence. Having served as secretary to the Medici-run city republic, he would compose his most famous work of statecraft, *The Prince,* in exile. His argument that a leader should remain above religion whilst retaining it as a tool to ensure the compliance of his people fed into the pre-Reformation debate about the purposes and abuses of the Catholic church. Another notable arrival of 1469 was Laura Cereta, one of the greatest female humanists, who was born in Brescia that September. Cereta's public lectures, letters and essays championed the rights of women to access higher education and advocated an ideal marriage as a partnership of mutual respect, esteem and honesty, rather than the form of slavery she had witnessed. Born into an upper-class family and highly educated, Cereta actively sought fame and immortality, writing with the intention of being published, and opening a dialogue that would remain relevant into the twenty-first century.

It was an English marriage of 1469 that marked the moment when Elizabeth and Edward's peace began to unravel. Dissatisfied with the King's foreign policies and advancement of the Woodville family, the Earl of Warwick married his eldest daughter, Isabel Neville, to Edward's younger brother, George, Duke of Clarence. Until Elizabeth bore the King a son, any child George had by Isabel would automatically become heir to the throne. Then the pair launched a rebellion, which took the King by surprise, as he was dealing with an uprising in the north. Among those who fought for him were Elizabeth's father, Richard Woodville, and his second son, John, but after the battle turned against them they were taken prisoner. Conducted to Kenilworth Castle, the pair was hurried through a hasty trial, convicted and beheaded. The implications of this were political and personal: Elizabeth understood that this was a direct attack upon her family, whose rise Warwick resented, and their deaths were indicative of the lengths to which the Earl was prepared to go.

Another casualty of Edgecote was William Herbert, Earl of Pembroke, guardian of the twelve-year-old Henry Tudor, who had accompanied the Earl to the battlefield. Waiting at Woking, afraid for her son's life, Margaret was relieved to learn that he had been led to safety and for the time being remained with the widowed countess, Anne Herbert, at Pembroke Castle. Margaret and Henry Stafford arrived in London on 24 August 1469, keen to seize the advantage offered by Edward's captivity. Margaret met Anne at the Bell in Fleet Street[1] and then paid a visit to the residence of George, Duke of Clarence, who had been granted the honour of Richmond formerly owned by Edmund Tudor, the title she hoped to obtain for her son. It was a bold and daring move, after years of caution, indicating that Margaret saw the Warwick-Clarence alliance as potentially lasting, and as replacing Edward's rule. However, this hope quickly proved to be premature.

Edward IV had not been present at Edgecote, but Warwick's men apprehended him in the Midlands. He was imprisoned in one of Warwick's properties while the Earl briefly attempted to rule in his place and, for a while, it must have seemed as if Edward's life, or at least his reign, was in grave danger. However, Warwick stopped short of harming his cousin, and his attempts to rule were undermined by a lack of support among the nobility. That September he was forced to free the King, or to allow him to 'escape' during a hunting expedition. Edward rode south, gathering support in advance of his formal entry to London, the news of which must have gladdened Elizabeth but instilled fear into the hearts of the Staffords, who feared reprisals. Sir Henry hastily purchased a new hat, spurs and sixteen shafts of arrows, to be among those riding out to welcome the King's return. However, Stafford's health had deteriorated that year, and Margaret worked to ensure his provision of medicines and attendance by doctors and apothecaries. It has been suggested that Stafford suffered from the skin condition erysipelas, considered then to be a form of leprosy, perhaps explaining his and Margaret's choice to join the confraternity of Burton Lazars in 1467, her devotion to St Anthony, patron saint of lepers, and the instructions given to his chaplain to distribute alms to the afflicted when they travelled.

Edward IV had regained the throne more by default than victory and these events proved to his enemies that he was not unassailable. A shamefaced Warwick and Clarence received a pardon from the King and were welcomed back at his court. But Edward had forgiven them too readily, too quickly, or else underestimated the danger they posed to him. Just six months later, discontent was stirring again, and the rebel pair seized upon a feud within Margaret's family in order to strike against Edward. In the north, her stepbrother, Richard de Welles, was locked in a land dispute with Sir Thomas Burgh, the King's Master of the Horse. When Richard's son, Robert, attacked Burgh's house, it unleashed a wave of lawlessness that may have been stirred up by Warwick with the intention of distracting Edward from the capital. If this was the case, the Earl's efforts failed and he was forced to flee abroad, but the implications for Margaret could potentially have been severe. Henry Stafford hoped to avoid involvement, but a royal summons called him to join the King's forces, to march north and deal with the disruption. Unable to disobey, he arrived at Edward's side on 12 March, when the King clashed with the rebels at Losecote Field. There was nothing he could do to prevent the executions of Welles and his son, the latter having declared for Warwick and Clarence. Stafford was then given the task of riding to Maxey Castle to break the news to Margaret's mother. Once again, the taint of treason came close to Margaret, but through Stafford's wise actions she emerged from the crisis.

Yet Warwick and Clarence had not given up. Sulking in Calais, they planned their next attempt to depose Edward by forging an unexpected alliance with the exiled Lancastrian Queen, Margaret of Anjou. Having married his younger daughter, Anne, to Margaret's son, Edward, Prince of Wales, Warwick returned to England in September 1470, determined not to fail a third time. Margaret must have listened cautiously to news that the tide was turning in favour of the Lancastrians again as the rebels marched west, raising enough men to place Edward in serious danger. Soon, the King realised he was cornered. He had underestimated his relatives and, unprepared to meet them, was forced to flee into exile in the Netherlands leaving behind his wife and children. Those who had suppressed their loyalties in recent years, paying lip service to the Yorkists out of pragmatism, now came forward to support the Earl in his attempt to restore Henry VI.

*

Five years had passed since Elizabeth Woodville's coronation. She had borne three children and was eight months pregnant with her fourth, preparing to enter confinement in a suite of prepared rooms in the Tower, when news reached London of her husband's flight. With the country in Warwick's hands, and the Earl rapidly approaching the capital with the intention of freeing and restoring Henry VI, Elizabeth understood that she had to act swiftly. That night, she gathered a few possessions and fled with her three daughters and Jacquetta to the safety of Westminster Abbey, where they signed the register as 'sanctuary women'. From there, Elizabeth sent the Abbot of Westminster to the Mayor to inform him that she was surrendering the Tower, because if she did not, 'the said Kentishmen and others would invade the sanctuary of Westminster to despoil and kill her.'[2] It is impossible to know what might have happened to Elizabeth, had she remained, when the Tower surrendered two days later, but the chivalric code tended to shield women from acts of violence in such circumstances. No doubt the fear of falling into enemy hands was considerable. After the executions of her father and brother in the wake of Edgecote, Elizabeth had every reason to believe that Warwick held a personal grudge against her family, and that flight was her best option. Her condition made her more vulnerable and after her delivery on 2 October she had an infant prince to protect, the future hope of the Yorkist line. She named him Edward.

By the time Warwick and Clarence entered London, Elizabeth was safe. Her family was offered lodgings in three rooms of a house called Cheneygates, the residence of Abbot Millyng, surviving parts of which are now known as the Deanery. As a deposed queen, she had no way of knowing whether she would see her husband again, or what the future might hold for her and her children. Destitute and despairing, she was cared for by the Abbot and permitted the services of a visiting doctor, and loyal London tradesmen sent her provisions. The gates were barely closed behind them, though, when Warwick liberated Henry VI from his five years of confinement, installing him in the apartments that Elizabeth had prepared for her lying-in. At Woking, the news of this dramatic turn-around was received in quite a different manner from Westminster. Margaret learned that, against all apparent odds, the Yorkists had imploded and the Lancastrian dynasty had been restored. This brought her renewed hope for her son, for the future of the Beaufort and Tudor names. While the change in circumstances made Elizabeth into an outcast, it seemed to reward Margaret for her years of pragmatism, bringing her triumphantly to London.

On 13 October, Warwick orchestrated the restoration or 'readeption' of Henry VI, leading him through the streets to St Paul's Cathedral for a formal 'crown-wearing' ceremony. With Woking lying around thirty miles to the west, it is quite within the realms of possibility that Margaret and Stafford, setting out as soon as they heard the news, could have reached London in time to witness this event. There is also a chance that they were already in the capital. Loyal Lancastrians, especially those who had made concessions under Yorkist rule, would have flocked to the city in order to celebrate Henry's return and give assurances of their loyalty. Margaret may well have witnessed Warwick bearing the King's train and proclaiming him 'through all the town of London... to celebrate the greatest festivities and triumphs... so that it seems a miracle or a dream, yet it is so'.[3]

Soon afterwards, Margaret was reunited with her son. Jasper Tudor collected the boy from his temporary guardians in the west and brought him to London where he stayed with his mother, perhaps in their rooms at the Mitre Inn, the Staffords' habitual residence when visiting the city. On 27 October the three were rowed in the Stafford barge from London to Westminster, where they had an audience with Henry VI, young Henry's half-uncle. The meeting has been infused with symbolism by later chroniclers, who suggested that the King paid special attention to the boy and predicted that he would have a great future, although this is difficult to corroborate. It seems likely that the King would show interest in his relative, whom he may not have seen since Henry was a young boy, and especially given his personal responsibility for arranging the Tudor-Beaufort marriage in 1455. Vergil's claim that Henry VI foresaw his nephew's future kingship was made in hindsight, to strengthen the Lancastrian connection; but such sentiments cannot have been far from Margaret's mind, as she saw new opportunities unfolding before her boy. Henry Tudor remained with his mother and stepfather into November, leaving London and riding with them to Woking, from where they paid visits to nearby Guildford, Henley and Maidenhead. With an eye to his upbringing as a man of future importance, Margaret entrusted her son to his uncle Jasper Tudor and on 11 November, the pair returned to the west country.

In early March, Margaret was visited at Woking by her cousin Edmund Beaufort, brother of Henry who had died at Hexham in 1464. With the political situation still so volatile, he was procrastinating, refusing to commit until either side achieved a clear victory. In public, Margaret may have supported this stance, but other actions she took during this time suggest her willingness to take a stronger line in favour of the restored dynasty. Stafford was among those issued with a commission to recruit men on behalf of Henry VI, but when Edward reappeared in London, every inch the conquering hero, Stafford foresaw the likely outcome and rejoined the Yorkist cause. He hastily drew up a new will in favour of his 'most entire beloved wife' Margaret, and prepared to defend Edward in battle.

Hidden away in her Westminster sanctuary with their three daughters and six-month-old son, Queen Elizabeth prayed and waited for news. Upon his arrival in London, Edward went to the palace of the Bishop of London and took Henry VI back into custody, returning him to the Tower. He then headed to the Abbey, where he 'comforted the queen, that had a long time abided there… in right great trouble, sorrow and heaviness, which she sustained with all manner patience that belonged to any creature, and as constantly as hath been seen at any time so high estate to endure.'[4] Edward was able to meet his infant son for the first time, little Prince Edward, 'to his heart's singular comfort and gladness and to all them that truly loved and would serve'.[5] With Elizabeth and the children removed to his mother's London residence of Baynard's Castle, Edward headed north to meet Warwick, taking King Henry with him. They clashed at Barnet in the thick fog early on the morning of 14 April 1471.

On the same day that Margaret of Anjou and her party finally landed in Weymouth, the Battle of Barnet ended in defeat for the Lancastrians. Warwick was slain in the field and Henry Stafford was seriously wounded. Hearing that her husband was injured, Margaret travelled to London seeking news of him, arranging for him to be brought home. Henry came back to Woking to try to recuperate under the care of his wife. It was a grave reminder that no matter how neutral or pragmatic members of the nobility might aim to be, certain commitments were unavoidable. Had Stafford shirked the battle, his loyalty would have been called into question. In trying to prove that loyalty and ensure his survival, he had endangered his life. The wounds were serious. Margaret would have summoned surgeons, doctors and priests to minister to her husband's body and soul. As a result of his injuries, Henry Stafford was not present at the battle that eradicated the final hopes of the Lancastrian dynasty. For the moment, the Staffords were out of the game, but their allies in the west were preparing for a final confrontation.

The final Lancastrian force under Henry VI's son met the Yorkists at Tewkesbury on 4 May. At eighteen, with no experience of fighting in the field, Prince Edward, along with Margaret's Beaufort cousins, Edmund and John, were defeated and killed by the three Yorkist brothers, Edward IV, George and Richard. Upon hearing of the defeat, Queen Margaret of Anjou surrendered. She was taken to London in chains and imprisoned in the Tower where, on the same night, her husband Henry was murdered. Confined to Woking with her husband, Margaret Stafford understood the devastating significance of these events. The line of Henry VI had been snuffed out, leaving her own son, fourteen-year-old Henry Tudor, as the closest claimant to the Lancastrian throne. And Henry, along with his uncle Jasper, had fled the scene at Tewkesbury to make their way into exile in France. Margaret would have to resume the waiting game.

Finally reunited, Edward and Elizabeth staged a public reassertion of their power. At Westminster, they took part in a second coronation, with two re-crownings taking place on Christmas Day 1471 and Twelfth Night 1472 in the Abbey, although Elizabeth did not wear her crown on the second occasion as she was tired, being heavily pregnant. After the terrible months of fear and doubt, this was a magnificent reassertion of her position, and that of her children. As Elizabeth's fortunes rose, so Margaret Beaufort's plummeted. That October, Henry Stafford died from the wounds he had received at Barnet, and Margaret was widowed for the second time at the age of twenty-eight. She closed her household and went to her mother's property of Le Ryall in London, trusting the legal arrangements to her secretary.[6] There seems little reason to doubt that she sincerely mourned Henry, as their marriage was a successful haven for both against the storms of conflict, until such time that the conflict demanded Henry's ultimate sacrifice. Yet Margaret was shrewd enough to recognise the few options by which the realpolitik of her times allowed women to create their own security and advancement. If she had learned anything from her years with Stafford, it was that she needed the protection of a powerful husband, whose influence could balance the heritage of her Beaufort name and any risks she may undertake on behalf of her son. She chose carefully. On 2 June 1472, Margaret placed her Devon and Somerset lands in trust for her son and ten days later she married Sir Thomas Stanley, Steward to Edward IV, bringing her right into the heart of the Yorkist fold.

5

Elizabeth of York
1472–1485

Elizabeth of York's first memories were formed during turmoil and conflict. She was just three years old when her father was imprisoned by the Earl of Warwick, four when Edward fled abroad and her mother gave birth in sanctuary, five when he returned, liberated them and regained his throne. Born in February 1466, nine months after her mother's splendid coronation, Elizabeth was a symbol of hope; the first child to arrive under a Yorkist regime, the first to live through its dramatic changes in fortune, the first in line to the throne, although as a woman, she would not have expected to inherit in her own right. In the event that her mother did not bear a son, Elizabeth would have been married to the most likely candidate for kingship.

The Earl of Warwick's rebellion held particular significance for Elizabeth, as the Earl was her godfather and in 1469 she had been betrothed to his young son, George. Warwick's death was more of a personal than political event for the little girl, marking a change in direction for her future. After this upheaval, a period of comparative stability followed, corresponding with the next decade of the Princess's life. Her early years in the 1470s were spent at her father's dazzling court, filled with culture and foreign influences. Yet, the shadow of disruption cast its long pall, a constant reminder of how swiftly fortunes might change and that in a crisis, survival depended upon seizing power.

Edward and Elizabeth's growing brood of children was committed to the care of Margery, Lady Berners, during the calm of the 1470s. Increasingly, the court was located at Greenwich, Windsor and Eltham, although as heir to the throne, their eldest son Edward, born in sanctuary, was given his own establishment at Ludlow on the Welsh borders under the guidance of his uncle, Anthony Woodville. At the age of seven, the Princess would have said her goodbyes to her younger brother, who was then only three, and resumed her position as the most important child in the nursery. In 1472, Elizabeth was present at Windsor for the visit of Louis de Gruthuyse, a cultured Flemish nobleman from Bruges who had sheltered her father during his exile abroad. Gruthuyse was received by the royal family at Windsor Castle, where there were games, feasting and dancing, after which the Princess danced with the Duke of Buckingham, young nephew of Henry Stafford. As Elizabeth grew up, more siblings arrived, with the births of Margaret in 1472, Richard in 1473 and Anne in 1475.

In 1475, Edward nominated his wife as regent during his invasion of France. This was a significant indication of trust, closeness, and confidence in her abilities. It was unusual for such a role to be granted to a woman, especially one whose marriage had initially proved so controversial and who had received no formal education or training in statecraft. Elizabeth's contribution to the dynasty briefly shifted in perspective, from the domestic and maternal to one of national governance. It indicates a level of communication between the married couple, and that Elizabeth was privy to her husband's confidences regarding the kingdom and the nature of government. Such conversations would not have been recorded, nor would Elizabeth have featured in the formal documents of the Council's daily business, but clearly she was Edward's confidante, accustomed to offering advice and with a good grasp of their court and its requirements. Clearly, she was not intended to rule like a king, but she was to hold the metaphorical fort, the closest she might come to the defensive stance of warfare, whilst her husband was abroad. It was always intended to be a temporary measure, but Edward left careful instructions and a will that named Elizabeth among those to whom he committed the charge of their son and heir. He returned within months, after a bloodless campaign, having secured himself a considerable pension and a marriage treaty for his eldest daughter. For the next seven years, Princess Elizabeth was betrothed to the Dauphin, Charles, during which time she was referred to as My Lady the Dauphin, a future Queen of France. This gave her a special identity at court and a sense of personal destiny.

In 1476, a key event for the Yorkist dynasty brought together Queen Elizabeth, Princess Elizabeth and Margaret Beaufort, now Lady Stanley. Over fifteen years after the death of Richard, Duke of York, his sons arranged for his body to be brought from the Priory at Pontefract where it had rested since early 1461 to the family home of Fotheringhay. It was Edward's younger brother, Richard, Duke of York, who accompanied the body on its journey, as well as that of another York brother, Edmund, who had died with their father at Wakefield. The two bodies were exhumed in July and brought east on ceremonial hearses, draped with cloth of gold and decorated with the heraldic and dynastic symbols of York. An effigy of the Duke lay on top of his coffin, dressed in the deep blue velvet of royal mourning with ermine trim, his hands clasped in prayer. Above his carved wax head was the figure of an angel holding a crown, to symbolise his rightful descent and his position as an uncrowned king. The service of re-interment took place on 30 July, with York's black war horse ridden into the church and mourners making offerings of pennies as the coffins were lowered into the ground; York in the choir and Edmund in the Lady Chapel. Although attendance at the service was restricted, a reputed 20,000 guests participated in the huge feast afterwards, seated in makeshift tents.[1]

In 1477, the eleven-year-old Princess was one of three Elizabeths to be admitted as a Lady of the Garter at the annual ceremony at Windsor in April. Along with her mother and her paternal aunt, Elizabeth was dressed in the Yorkist colour of 'murrey', or plum colour, and admitted to the chivalric Order of the Garter founded by Edward III. It was an honour symbolic of her status and future elevation as the queen of France. The following January, Elizabeth attended a family marriage intended to bring the Yorkists a connection with one of the most powerful English dynasties, and one of the wealthiest. With the marriage of the heir, Edward, Prince of Wales, reserved for future negotiation, the honour fell to her younger brother, Richard of Shrewsbury, then four years old. His bride was Anne Mowbray, Countess of Norfolk, only surviving child of the fourth Duke of Norfolk, whose death in 1476 left her as sole heir to his fortune. The ceremony took place in St Stephen's Chapel at Westminster, where Elizabeth sat with her parents under a gold canopy surrounded by azure hangings decorated with fleur-de-lys. A tournament was held three days later, at which the Princess and her sisters distributed the prizes, with Elizabeth giving a golden 'E' set with a ruby to the winner, Sir Richard Haute. In 1480, Elizabeth was also present during the state visit to England of her aunt, Margaret of Burgundy. Her uncle Sir Edward Woodville brought her to England aboard his ship *The Falcon*, and the guest stayed at

Coldharbour House, residence of her mother Cecily, before visiting Greenwich, where a state banquet was held in her honour.

These years were not entirely without fears and challenges, especially those relating to close family. Elizabeth's errant uncle, the Duke of Clarence, may have been forgiven for his earlier treason, but when she was eleven his unruly behaviour caused more doubts to be raised over his loyalty. Suspecting that the death of his wife had been caused by witchcraft or poisoning, he hounded her former servants in an illegal manner, hanging one, causing riots, interrupting council meetings, making wild claims and spreading rumours about Edward's legitimacy. Such behaviour could not be tolerated, especially after Clarence had already been forgiven so much. His execution in February 1478 demonstrated to Elizabeth how decisively a monarch needed to act to quell insurrection, even when it was instigated by a brother. A second harsh lesson she learned during this period was from the breaking of her betrothal to the Dauphin of France, when her father planned to invade the territories of Louis XI in 1482. Stripped of the title that had defined her for the past seven years, her future path was again uncertain.

Queen Elizabeth Woodville's main preoccupation through these years was pregnancy, childbirth and child rearing. Once peace had been restored in 1471, she returned to a more domestic and symbolic sphere, filling the royal nursery and appearing as a hostess and figurehead on state occasions. After Margaret, Richard and Anne, she gave birth to George in 1477, Catherine in 1479 and Bridget in 1480. In total, she had borne twelve children, two by John Grey and ten during her marriage to Edward. Such a high birth rate was inevitably tainted with tragedy, and the family lost Margaret at six months, George at two and Mary at fourteen. The latter must have had the greatest impact upon Princess Elizabeth, as Mary was her closest sibling, with the pair sharing sanctuary and adversity together, as well as the stability and celebration that followed. By 1482, when it appeared that the Queen's child-bearing days were over, Queen Elizabeth was forty-five and her eldest daughter, Elizabeth, was sixteen.

In 1482, Margaret Beaufort was forty-one and had been married for a decade to Thomas, Lord Stanley, by which time she had become a familiar face at the Yorkist court. The Stanley family had particularly close connections with the Woodvilles in the management of lands in North Wales and Cheshire,[1] and her husband's trusted role at the King's side brought Margaret frequently to London, where she had stayed in October 1472, Christmas 1474 and witnessed preparations for the invasion of France in 1475. Stanley was one of the army captains to sail with the King, leaving his wife in charge of his home affairs, just as Edward had. Margaret intended that her obedience to the Yorkists would bear fruit for her son in exile. In 1469, she had been hoping that George, Duke of Clarence, would name him heir to the Earldom of Richmond and following Clarence's execution the King went as far as to draw up a draft of transfer, but it was never formalised. This may be because Edward saw Henry Tudor as a threat to his throne and the inheritance of his sons. Margaret understood the danger, and urged him, in 1476, not to return to England, even if Edward offered him the hand of one of his daughters.[2] In January 1482, Henry Tudor reached the age of twenty-five, having grown to manhood out of his mother's sight.

*

In April 1483, Elizabeth and Margaret's world changed again. At the age of forty, Edward IV was taken ill after travelling on the Thames and died soon afterwards. Elizabeth became a widow again, with the rights of her children to protect. Her queenship, and the charged political situation, plunged the Woodville family into danger. She was not simply fighting for their inheritance, she was fighting for their lives, and the accession of her twelve-year old son. It was a catastrophic event for Elizabeth: she lost her husband of almost twenty years, her home and income, her status and protection, and many more of her loved ones.

That spring, Edward V was only eighteen months away from his majority, an age when he would have been considered able to rule independently. His succession should have been a straightforward transfer of power facilitated by Yorkist family members, the Council and the former King's household. The boy was at Ludlow with his uncle, Anthony Woodville, Earl Rivers, when news arrived of the King's death. The solid border castle had been his home for years, formerly one of his father's childhood residences, and where Elizabeth's brother had been put in charge of his education. Her distance from her son at this point was concerning, so she urged him to come to London as soon as possible and petitioned the Council for a large armoured guard to accompany him, only for the Council to dismiss this as alarmist. The coronation was set for 4 May, almost three weeks ahead, and preparations in the capital began. However, on the night of 30 April, news reached London that the new King's party had been met by that of his uncle, Richard of Gloucester, who was travelling down from the north. Elizabeth's brother, Rivers, and Richard Grey, her son from her first marriage, had been arrested on charges of concealing weapons with the intent to attack Gloucester. Recalling the deaths of her father and brother in 1469, Elizabeth gathered her children and fled to the safest place she knew: the sanctuary of Westminster. There, she could do little but watch the unfolding drama.

Equally motivated to act as a protective mother, Margaret Stanley's response to the crisis was to attempt negotiations with Richard of Gloucester. The main difference was that Elizabeth's children were at Westminster, of vulnerable age and, potentially, in danger. At least Margaret's son was abroad, far from the scenes of chaos, and had reached adulthood, but although she could not protect his person, Margaret attempted to secure his inheritance. In a move that mirrored her overtures to Warwick in 1470, she approached Richard's closest ally, Henry Stafford, Duke of Buckingham, nephew of her former husband. With Buckingham acting as intermediary, Margaret hoped to negotiate with Richard and secure Henry Tudor's lands, and even bring about a marriage between Henry and Elizabeth of York. Initially, Margaret saw Richard as a potential new ally, rather than as a threat.

Then, on 13 June, when Richard gathered his Council at the Tower, an event took place that must have shaken Margaret and Stanley to the core. The Grafton Chronicle suggests that Margaret's husband already suspected that the meeting would end badly, sending word to his ally, Lord Hastings, by a 'trusty and secret messenger at midnight' urging him 'in all the haste... to rise and ride away with him'.[3] Whether this warning was actually sent, or taken seriously, both men still attended the meeting the following day. Richard absented himself soon after it had opened to liaise with other Council members meeting elsewhere, before returning and accusing Hastings of treason. Hastings was dragged outside for immediate execution; Stanley was violently attacked and narrowly avoided death himself. Thomas More's account of the day, most likely drawn from the memories of his mentor John Morton, an eye-witness, describes how one of the soldiers 'let flee at the lorde Stanley which shronke at the stroke and fell under the table or else his head had been clefte to the teethe, for as shortly as he shranke, yet ranne the blood about hys eares.'[4] Stanley was taken into custody, along with others present at the meeting, and although this was not for long, it must have marked a turning point for Margaret and her husband, who saw greater expediency in their need to placate Richard, but also increased their distrust of him. More than ever, their loyalty was a public show to conceal their private concerns.

In those same weeks at the end of June 1483, Elizabeth Woodville began to understand Richard's degree of determination to rid himself of his enemies. Young Edward's coronation was postponed again, and Elizabeth had been prevailed upon to send her younger son, Richard of Shrewsbury, to join his elder brother in the Tower. The terrible news reached her of the impromptu executions of her brother Anthony and son, Sir Richard Grey, along with Sir Robert Vaughan, Edward V's chamberlain, on 25 June at Pontefract Castle. The men had been in captivity since their arrest, and although Richard had wished to execute them at once, his Council had insisted there was no grounds or evidence to suggest their treason. The executions at the end of June were a measure of how confident Richard had become in his attempt to take the throne, and Elizabeth must have seen this as ominous at least. A day later, her own marriage was declared invalid and her children illegitimate, in a sermon delivered at St Paul's by Ralph Shaa, a theologian and half-brother of the Lord Mayor. The next day, Richard of Gloucester was declared King.

Once again, the fortunes of the two women seemed to be inversely related: as Elizabeth saw her offspring discredited, her reputation in tatters, even her life in danger, Margaret realised that her best chance of survival was to make a deal with the new rising power. On 5 July Margaret and her husband travelled to Westminster to meet Richard and his chief Justice, William Hussey, to secure their aid in a financial matter.[5] The following day, they both participated in the coronation of Richard III, Margaret carrying the train of the new Queen, Anne Neville, taking precedence over Richard's sister, the Duchess of Suffolk, and serving at the banquet that followed. As a sign of favour, she had been allocated ten yards of scarlet for her livery, one long gown made of six yards of crimson velvet, with six yards of white cloth of gold and a second gown of similar dimensions, this time cut from blue velvet and crimson cloth of gold.[6] If there was doubt in her heart, Margaret at least looked the part as she followed Queen Anne down the aisle. Stanley, presumably with his wound from the council meeting healing, took part in the ceremony as a new Knight of the Garter. He was restored to the Office of Steward of the Household and appointed Lord High Constable. It was a swift response to the realpolitik of the moment, and one which allowed the Stanleys to survive the transition between monarchs, choosing to back the powerful, adult Richard III instead of his displaced young nephew. However, with the situation changing day by day, it was a decision Margaret would quickly come to reassess.

*

By the end of July, a rebellion was being planned among Edward IV's former employees with the intention of restoring his son to the throne. This would have seen a restoration of the house of Woodville and grant Elizabeth the freedom to leave sanctuary as the Queen Mother. Nothing linked her directly to her plotters, but they acted in her interests, and it is highly likely she was at least aware of their intentions, if not their plans. Details and names of the leaders are given by the sixteenth-century chronicler John Stowe taken from an earlier manuscript that has since been lost.[7] Elizabeth may not have personally known Robert Russe, Sergeant of London, or William Davy, pardoner of Hounslow, but she would have been familiar with John Smith, Edward IV's groom, and perhaps Stephen Ireland, a royal wardrober, among others involved. They planned to start fires across London to distract attention from the Tower in order for them to 'steal away' Edward V and his younger brother Richard. However, for reasons that remain unclear, the plot failed. Around fifty conspirators were arrested; Russe, Davy, Smith and Ireland were executed and their heads set upon spikes at Tower Bridge.[8] The Princes were withdrawn into the inner recesses of the Tower, disappearing from view. Neither Margaret nor Elizabeth were censured or punished at this point, suggesting their involvement was initially distant or else Richard was not fully aware of their roles. By early autumn, as Thomas More and other chroniclers record, there was a widespread belief in London that the boys had been killed. Helpless in sanctuary, Elizabeth began to fear that she had lost her two young sons. As a result, the focus of the rebellion switched to Henry Tudor as the only figure who might restore justice.

Margaret needed little more encouragement to champion her son's cause. Less than three months after her meeting with the new King, she was dabbling in treason, becoming involved in a plot for Henry and Jasper Tudor to invade England.[9] Thus her purpose became allied with that of Elizabeth Woodville, and it is likely that Margaret initiated the contact that began between the two women. Messages were carried back and forth by Margaret's Welsh physician, Lewis Caerleon, while her servant Hugh Conway and chaplain Christopher Urswick took letters to Henry in Brittany. The steward of her household, Reginald Bray, liaised with Buckingham. Her motivation was personal. She acted as much for advancement of her son as for the removal of Richard, if not more. With the agreement of Elizabeth Woodville, Henry Tudor's reward was to be marriage to Elizabeth of York, a bold move designed to bring him home and into the heart of the English royal family.

The initial intention was not to place Henry Tudor on the throne. His role was to facilitate the restoration of Edward IV's line by rescuing and restoring Edward V, as hope still remained that the boy was alive. The original intention was that Edward V would rule, Elizabeth Woodville would be liberated as the King's mother, and Margaret would see her son married to the most eligible woman in the land. Also heavily involved by this stage was Margaret's former step-nephew, Henry Stafford, Duke of Buckingham. This represented another significant desertion of Richard III, as Buckingham had formerly assisted his rise to power, being present when the journey of Edward V was interrupted en route to London and the young King's household arrested. It was reputedly Buckingham who had been behind the sermon denouncing Elizabeth Woodville's marriage and offspring. Now, the Duke abandoned his friend and wrote to his cousin in exile on 24 September, urging him to launch a fleet at once. Tudor was already primed for action. Securing a loan of 10,000 crowns from Francis, Duke of Brittany, he hired 5,000 mercenaries and gathered his ships.

The first attempted invasion took place on 3 October 1483, with Henry hoping to meet Buckingham on English soil two weeks later, but storms forced him to return to port. Buckingham raised troops from Brecon, his base in Wales, as did Elizabeth's eldest son, Thomas Grey, Earl of Dorset in Exeter, and her brother, Lionel Woodville, in Salisbury. In Kent, the main centre of rebellion was at the original Woodville family home of The Mote, Maidstone, which illustrates the Beaufort-Woodville alliance at the heart of the network of conspirators. However, miscommunication or mistiming led the Maidstone men to rise too early, on 10 October, a whole week ahead of the intended date. The Kentish rebels were swiftly put down by the Duke of Norfolk, but their premature activity meant that the plan was exposed, making Richard aware of Buckingham's involvement. The Duke fled west with a price of £1,000 on his head, but the bad weather that had defeated Tudor's fleet prevented Buckingham from escaping across the River Severn, leading to his capture. By the time the weather allowed Henry Tudor to set sail again, this time successfully reaching the coast of Dorset, his English support had been decimated and Buckingham had been captured. The Duke was executed on 2 November, prompting Tudor to abort the mission and turn his ships around just off Plymouth.

Margaret and Elizabeth were now in the gravest danger. Margaret, certainly, had actively participated in the planning of treasonous acts and Elizabeth had supported her through secret messages conveyed between them. They were also suspect through association with the activities of their male relatives. The result was the same: both were guilty of treason. Elizabeth, at least, was as safe as she could be, in sanctuary, but Margaret and Stanley must have lived in fear of her arrest. When Richard summoned his parliament that January, Acts of Attainder were passed against Tudor, his allies and Margaret:

> Forasmuch as Margaret countesse of Richmond, mother to the kynges grete rebell and traytor Henry erle of Richmond, hath of late conspired, confedered and committed high treason ayenst our sovereign lord the king Richard the Third in dyvers and sundry wyses, and in especiall in sendyng writings, messages and tokens to the said Henry, desiring, procuring and stirring hym by the same to come into this roialme and make were ayenst oure said sovereign lord; to the which desyre, procuring and stirring, the said Henry applied himself... also the said countess made, by chevisancez (supplies/funding) of great somes of money, as well within the citee of London, as in other places of the roialme, to be employed to execution of the said treason and malicious purpose.[10]

Once again, just like through the Stafford years, Margaret was saved by the demonstrable loyalty of her husband. Because Stanley had remained steadfastly devoted to Richard III throughout the crisis, either unaware of her activities or, more likely, choosing to turn a blind eye, Margaret was given a reprieve. The King chose to recall 'the good and faithful service that Thomas, Lord Stanley, hath done and entendeth to doo to oure sovereigne Lorde, and for the good love and trust that the king hath in him, and for his sake, remitteth and woll forebere the grete punysshment of atteynder of the said countesse.'[11] Instead of being condemned, she was considered legally irresponsible, 'disabled in the law' like a naughty child. Her punishment was to be stripped of the assets she held in her own right, which were put into Stanley's hands, but her income, her right to inherit and the west country lands she had held in trust for her son were all confiscated. Stanley was instructed to keep her confined in some secret place without company or household staff so that she might not contact her son. She was as effectively a prisoner as Elizabeth and her daughters were in sanctuary. However, she was still alive. Whether or not she deliberately exploited it, Margaret's gender served as a tool to save her own skin, demonstrating implicit use of contemporary stereotypes of women as weak and easily swayed, and submitting to the authority of her husband. Had she been a man, she would undoubtedly gone the way of Rivers, Grey, Vaughn, Hastings and Buckingham. What saved Margaret's life in the autumn of 1483 was her gendered capitulation and Stanley's unblemished record.

Richard then turned to Margaret's co-conspirator, the dowager Queen Elizabeth. The sanctuary of Westminster placed her beyond physical harm, but it was powerless to prevent him unleashing the full power of the law against her. The new King's first Parliament passed the act Titulus Regis, which discredited Edward's character and rule, and the legitimacy of his marriage. Richard's assertion, drawn from a statement made by Bishop Stillington of Bath and Wells, was that Edward's precontract to an Eleanor Butler, née Talbot, was accepted by Parliament, meaning that Elizabeth had been no more than the King's mistress through their nineteen years together. It also meant that all her children by Edward, including Princess Elizabeth, were now ruled to be illegitimate. By rejecting her former status, the act deprived Elizabeth of her title as dowager queen and removed the dower payments she had been receiving as Edward's widow. Elizabeth had no formal voice to refute these charges, nor those that her husband had reigned by 'extortion and oppression', spilling the blood of Christian men, and that no woman had been safe from the fear of being 'ravished' and 'befouled' by him.[12]

*

In the light of Titulus Regis and the collapse of the Tudor-Buckingham invasion, capitulation was the also best course of action for Elizabeth Woodville. Early in 1484, in the knowledge that the King was aware of her involvement in the plot, and faced with the possibility that his reign might last for years, even decades, to come, Elizabeth had to act as a mother. There was little she could do to protect her lost sons, but she had five surviving daughters, two of whom were approaching marriageable age, and she could not remain in sanctuary forever. On 1 March she reached an agreement with Richard that must have come after weeks of cogitation, questions and doubts. Yet it was really the only move left to her. Pragmatically, Elizabeth agreed to leave the sanctuary of Westminster and enter into a secluded confinement similar to that which Margaret was experiencing. In the absence of a husband to be her keeper, as with the Stanleys, Elizabeth was assigned to Sir John Nesfield, Constable of Hertford Castle, who allocated her new quarterly allowance. In return, she insisted that Richard swear a public oath that he would not harm any of her daughters, but would 'put them in honest places of good name and fame' and treat them honestly and courteously, allow them income through annual rents of 200 marks and see that they 'bene mariable to gentilmen borne'.[13]

With Margaret and Elizabeth stripped of their power, hidden from sight, the spotlight fell upon the next generation. In December 1483, after limping back to Brittany following the failed invasion, Henry Tudor swore an oath at Rennes Cathedral to marry Elizabeth of York, to continue the plan established by their mothers. Just months later, the eighteen-year-old Elizabeth left sanctuary and made her debut at her uncle's court. With Henry miles away in exile, and more of her family submitting to Richard, including her uncle Richard Woodville, it may have seemed to the young Woodville girls that the moment for rebellion had passed. At some point in the late spring or summer 1484, Elizabeth and her sisters, conscious of their social demotion, entered the household of Queen Anne Neville. The younger daughter of the rebellious Earl of Warwick, Anne was then twenty-eight and had been married to Richard for around twelve years, with one son. Mere weeks after the Woodvilles emerged from Westminster, this son, Edward, died at the age of around ten. The loss of their only heir was a great blow to both parents, so it was amid a climate of intense grief that the girls joined their aunt's household, and followed her lead, probably dressing in the black of mourning.

Controversy has surrounded Elizabeth's time at her uncle's court. Much has been made by historians and novelists of a report describing the celebrations at Christmas 1484, which focuses on the details of Elizabeth of York's behaviour and clothing. The source of the rumours about this occasion was the Croyland Chronicler:

During this Christmas feast too much attention was paid to singing and dancing and vain exchanges of clothes between Queen Anne and Lady Elizabeth ... who were alike in complexion and figure. The people spoke against this and the magnates and prelates were greatly astonished; it was said by many that the king was applying his mind in every way to contracting a marriage with Elizabeth either after the death of the queen, or by means of a divorce for which he believed he had sufficient grounds.[14]

However, it is crucial to realise that this was written after April 1486, when Richard had been defeated in battle and the marriage of Elizabeth of York to Henry Tudor had taken place. The possibility of a love affair, or even an arranged marriage between Elizabeth and her uncle, has proven rich material for novelists, but the facts indicate that such a match was never Richard's intention. Anne Neville died in March 1485, following which Richard issued a statement that 'it never came into his thoughts or mind to marry in such manner-wise,' and instead took steps to arrange a joint match for him and Elizabeth with members of the Portuguese royal family.[15] The Croyland report was compiled with the intention to retrospectively blacken Richard's character, to accuse him of an incestuous match with a woman who had since been raised as a paragon of virtue to the English people. The likelihood that Elizabeth contemplated marriage to Richard is vanishingly small.

In the summer of 1485, when intelligence reached England that Henry Tudor was on the verge of relaunching his invasion fleet, Richard sent Elizabeth and her sisters north to his castle at Sheriff Hutton for their safety during the impending conflict. In separate locations, unable to influence the outcome, Margaret, Elizabeth Woodville and Elizabeth of York waited in anticipation of an event that would redefine their fortunes. Although Margaret was living in seclusion with her husband appointed as her keeper, Stanley allowed his wife to continue writing to her son during his exile and after Henry Tudor's successful landing in Wales on 7 August. This alone was sufficient to condemn Stanley for treason, and Richard already had his doubts when summoning him to engage under the royal banner. Stanley pleaded illness, claiming that he was suffering from the sweating sickness, but his son, Lord Strange, fell into the King's hands, and admitted that he and his uncle, William Stanley, had supported Tudor. With Strange's life offered as guarantee for his father's loyalty on the battlefield, the Stanley brothers took a position in neutral territory on the land outside the Leicestershire village of Market Bosworth, to see how the battle unfolded.

Margaret's location that August is unknown, but it is unlikely to have been near the battlefield. She may have been in Leicestershire or London, or at her property of Knowsley in Lancashire, where she would later display the hangings taken from Richard's Bosworth tent.[16] Elizabeth Woodville was at Sheen Palace in Richmond, her daughter even further north at Sheriff Hutton, but all three were caught in the passive trap of their gender; their activities behind the scenes had contributed to this outcome, but they were helpless to contribute to the male arena of the battlefield. Instead, they would have taken the only path available to them, by which they believed they could exert any influence. As the two armies clashed on the morning of 22 August 1485, Margaret, and the two Elizabeths would have been on their knees in prayer. Perhaps later that day, or early the following morning, they received the news that would transform their existences. Henry Tudor had won the field.

Henry's victory at the battle of Bosworth Field initiated the arrival of a new dynasty. After the struggles of Lancaster and York, the name of Tudor was a relative newcomer in the race for the throne, its success facilitated by the way other families had decimated their heirs through warfare, murder and betrayal. Henry could not trace his line through decades of royal descent, parliamentary acts or complex pedigrees. Neither his father nor grandfather had aspired to the throne, unlike the recent Yorkist and Lancastrian kings. It was only in the last two years that he had entered the race as a candidate, as a rank outsider, taking the throne by right of conquest owing to the support of Richard's enemies. He had formerly been something of a royal satellite, connected to the Lancastrian court but rarely present, never central to policy or pageantry, descended from kings amid a host of cousins of similar descent. Henry's long exile from England meant that he had been dependent upon the support of others, particularly of important women. The roles that Margaret Beaufort and Elizabeth Woodville played in his journey were limited by their gender and circumstances, but their promotion of his cause was symbolic and significant. It is highly doubtful that his invasion could have taken place without their support.

*

Studying the lives of Elizabeth Woodville and Margaret Beaufort across the five centuries after 1485 allows us to see the practical contributions they made to creating the Tudor dynasty. But they also highlight the problems of reconstructing alternative versions of mainstream history, of opposing the metanarrative and research conducted in mostly male-authored documents and accounts. Though Elizabeth and Margaret may have sometimes been on opposing sides, their interweaving narratives share themes and motives common to their status and gender, which allow for greater understanding of the essential questions arising from an analysis of women's contributions. As a starting point for the Tudor dynasty, they unveil the numerous cultural, legal and religious obstacles that barred even high-ranking females from closer involvement, and help expose the methods women used to gain influence. Their actions, and the consequences, remind the historian that the dangers faced by women were specifically gendered, and that the methods of uncovering their truths must deconstruct layers of patriarchal control.

Firstly, there is the question of material. The extent of our understanding is determined largely by the limited survival of records, which is itself an indicator of women's roles, the duration of their lives and male perceptions of their legal importance. It is also a measure of the nature of fame, and historiography, by which certain individuals are favoured, recorded and promoted above others. This can be as much by accident as by design. It is also important to recognise that the female personifications of the era, from real women such as Jeanne d'Arc and Margaret of Anjou to the much painted and sculpted Virgin Mary and Botticelli's idealised Venus, are atypical representations of femininity, surviving in forms of patriarchal construction, manipulated to serve the male narrative. Recovering the actual women behind famous surviving names is far more complex.

Secondly, the female sphere of influence was more tenuous, more fragile, than that of their male peers. Frequently, their lives were affected, even re-routed, by conflicts that were not of their making, in which they could not play a visible part or take a role of practical leadership. Not all of them understood this. When Queen Margaret of Anjou offered herself as Regent for her son in 1453, her rejection required no second thoughts from the King's Council, and her bravery was perceived as the dangerous audacity of a foreigner. It was Elizabeth Woodville, Elizabeth of York and Margaret's experiences as native-born English women that gave them an innate understanding of what roles were available to them, as opposed to the factional French politics of Margaret of Anjou's youth, where strong leading female figures and regional regents were valued. In order to succeed, even to survive, English women had to be sensitive observers of cultural nuances from an early age. Their goals were not to redefine the rights and position of women, but to promote and advance their dynasties as team players. Often, the only means available to them were indirect and subtle, established through conversations, example, personal influence, patronage and the cultivation of relationships. Even when they engaged directly with matters concerning dynastic conflict and war, the extent and scope of their influence varied and frequently went unrecorded.

Thirdly, women were largely accepting of the gender dynamic as the cultural norm, and accepted their perceived inferiority. Yet, they could play the gender card, and did, if it meant saving their own skin. Margaret's ambition on behalf of her son was explained, but not excused, by the stereotype of a woman's 'natural' feelings, and the belief that wives could be wayward and headstrong, requiring strict governance and correction from their husband. The birth of an heir, particularly that of a male, and the safeguarding of his inheritance, allowed women the only real opportunity to borrow 'masculine' behaviours and step outside expected gender patterns. The acceptable spaces for female activity were domestic, concerned with childbearing and rearing, providing emotional and material comfort, arranging marriages, piety and patronage. A woman could be excused almost anything when it came to acting on maternal instinct, as this fed the patriarchal dialogue about legitimate heirs and dynastic survival. Essentially, it was in men's best interests when women fought for their children. Thus, Margaret's inexhaustible efforts on behalf of her son, and Elizabeth's negotiations on behalf of her daughters, were considered understandable. Consciously or not, both women allowed male concepts of their gender to overlay their actions to their advantage, and chose to subvert them when it suited their cause better. This was a facet of their gender that would increase throughout the Tudor dynasty, when women were propelled into positions of power that did not accord with contemporary ideals of femininity.

On the whole though, women who displayed perceived 'masculine' qualities were condemned. As Margaret of Anjou found to her cost, England had traditionally been governed by active men with passive, ideally fertile wives, whose role in politics was minimal. They had been personifications of that most popular of medieval cults, the embodiment of the Virgin Mary on earth; pure, compassionate, suffering in silence, maternal and forgiving. As figures of piety and patronage, they had taken on a 'mother-of-the-nation' role. Women who had challenged their husbands, or become too politically minded, such as the Empress Matilda, Eleanor of Aquitaine and Isabella of France, were looked upon with horror. There was not a culture of female authority outside the private estate in England, as there was to some extent in Europe in the second half of the fifteenth century.

Fourthly, it is clear that the mid-fifteenth century Tudor mothers were not proto-feminists seeking to create a sisterhood based on equal rights. One of the most interesting questions arising from the events of 1483-5 is just how close Margaret Beaufort and Elizabeth Woodville were. A lack of surviving sources contributes to uncertainty about the extent of their involvement and friendship, and although their fortunes were often inversely related, Richard III's reign united them against a common enemy. It is not possible to state that they were friends, but as the mothers of two individuals at odds with the King between 1483 and 1485 there was a degree of understanding between them, upon which they chose to act. Sharing a common aim, each made the decision to trust the other, which must have had its roots in their contact under Edward IV, as well as their aspirations. Their alliance may have been born out of necessity, and the letters they exchanged to unite their children may have been few, but the bond of motherhood allowed them to extend trust.

Finally, it is clear that the historical reputations of Margaret Beaufort and Elizabeth Woodville have been shaped by their identities as women. The accounts of contemporary chroniclers, and those historians writing in the intervening centuries since their deaths, have attempted to interpret their behaviours as conforming, or failing to conform, to certain gender expectations. There is a truth in this: their identities cannot be separated from their biology, nor the way it dictated their paths, and the responses of their peer, but it has led to the drawing of some over-simplified conclusions, even the perpetuation of stereotypes, without allowing for each woman's specific enactment of their gender.

Thus, Elizabeth Woodville is frequently depicted as the beautiful, capricious woman using her luck to advance her family, the typical 'Eve' figure her contemporaries would have recognised. She is often drawn as passive and reactive, whilst her flight into sanctuary is 'running away' instead of a tactical withdrawal when faced by uncertainty and with the odds stacked against her. Conversely Margaret Beaufort is scheming and 'masculine', transcending her gender by being active and politically minded, much like her contemporary Margaret of Anjou, but where the Lancastrian Queen had failed, Margaret's efforts were validated by her son's success, even though that success had been influenced by luck. Margaret of Anjou's attempts to support her husband and promote her son in the 1450s and 1460s led her to be defined as greedy and grasping, war-like, bloodthirsty and deeply unfeminine, because her Lancastrian line was defeated, and she was largely described by pro-Yorkist chronicles. Women adopting 'masculine' characteristics of determination, ambition and initiative were only given credence when they were successful. This success was often dependent upon circumstances beyond their control, not as a function of their abilities or understanding. The most successful of all, Elizabeth of York, was deified by the Tudor chroniclers as the mother of Henry VIII, preserved as the perfect ideal of womanhood: fertile, beautiful and supportive. Yet her early years, defined by political turmoil and the uncertainty over which man to support, could equally have taken her down a different route.

It is clear from the lives of Margaret Beaufort and Elizabeth Woodville that upper class women did play active roles in personal and national events. However, they had to confine their activities to certain spheres, and they had to be careful not to give offence or be caught. They might possess great quantities of inner strength, character, morality, piety, vision and personal ambition, but these were exercised around the activities of men, which frequently removed them from events, or left them waiting for news. Their greatest abilities lay in their patience and commitment to causes that affected their children, and in finding solutions to challenges that allowed them to retain their positions. Women might display some similar characteristics to men but their long-term definition in relation to contemporary expectations of gender was by no means straightforward. Being a woman proved to be both a tool and a handicap in the continuing struggles for survival during the Wars of the Roses. Margaret and Elizabeth found ways to use their influence to preserve their children and plan the first Tudor royal marriage. Circumstances led to their lives converging on the same purpose. Their efforts, sometimes overt, sometimes behind the scenes, often personally dangerous, paved the way for the union of their children in January 1486. Without two such guiding, devoted mothers, Henry Tudor and Elizabeth of York may not have survived the turmoil of the 1470s to reach the altar.

PART TWO

The First Royal Tudors

1485–1509

6

The First Tudor Queen
1485–86

Within hours of his victory, Henry Tudor was thinking of Elizabeth. He dispatched Sir John Halewell and Sir Robert Willoughby to bring her in 'a noble company' and with 'all convenient speed' to be reunited with her mother in London. The messengers probably reached Sheriff Hutton on 24 or 25 August, riding as fast as possible, day and night, to traverse the one hundred and thirty miles of roads and tracks. The official Tudor historian, Bernard André,[1] later presented Elizabeth's delight and relief at the outcome, as did subsequent chroniclers and poems such as Nicholas Brereton's *The Song of Lady Bessie*,[2] which reflected events following the battle. Such sentiments were to be expected once the Tudor dynasty had been established, depicting the new King's wife and mother of his future heirs.

In 1485, Elizabeth's position was different than that of her mother or Margaret Beaufort, and not only due to their ages. She was nineteen, beautiful, healthy, eligible and heir to the Yorkist dynasty. In patriarchal terms, she was the prize to be plucked along with the English crown. Her adult life lay ahead of her, with the prospect of marriage, children and potentially, queenship. The victory at Bosworth defined her future, whereas it offered security and peace after a life of struggle to the women of the older generation. Margaret Beaufort, who had invested all her hopes in her heir, and Elizabeth Woodville, who believed Richard to be responsible for the deaths of her sons, could both have anticipated convictions for treason in the event of a Yorkist victory. After their complicity in the rebellion of 1483, life would have been very difficult for them under a Ricardian regime that survived Bosworth. A return to permanent imprisonment or exile seemed most likely. It would not be for another fifty years that Henry VIII would break the taboo of executing queens and aristocratic women on charges of treason, but Margaret and Elizabeth Woodville's situation was such that they would not have wished to try a victorious Richard's patience. Thus, the victory of Henry Tudor can be seen as one in which they had invested their lives.

In comparison with her mother and Margaret, Elizabeth of York's position in 1485 was one of strength. Her future was secure whatever the outcome of the battle, as was her life. She would either have become Queen of England, as her mother hoped, or Queen of Portugal, according to Richard's proposed marital alliance of spring 1485. Bosworth decided where her queenship would be located, rather than the fact that it would occur. As with all women, she had to be an opportunist and pragmatist, finding her place in an ever-shifting male world, ready to voice approval of the victor and condemn the loser. For a woman to do otherwise would have been to threaten the inheritance, liberty and lives of herself and all her relatives. As it happened, the Tudor victory facilitated the outcome that allowed Elizabeth not only to remain in England with her family but to become its Queen and secure the Woodvilles' futures. Equally, though, Elizabeth's hereditary claim to the throne made her a valuable commodity, as her gender meant she would pass that claim to any man she married. Potentially, any other husband she took could mount a legitimate challenge to Tudor, which would elicit Yorkist support. Thus, Henry and Elizabeth's marriage was desirable on both sides, for personal and national security.

Elizabeth was brought into London with a large entourage and conducted to Coldharbour House on the Thames. Margaret Beaufort was in residence when Elizabeth and her mother were reunited under its roof, orchestrating and hosting the event. Her path with her future daughter-in-law had already crossed on a number of occasions at the Yorkist court, probably for the duration of the young woman's life. The care of Elizabeth's sisters, Cecily, Anne, Catherine and Bridget, was handed over as a legal formality to Margaret, who was granted 'the keeping and guiding of the ladies daughter of King Edward IIII (sic)'[3] along with Edward Stafford, Margaret Plantagenet, and Ralph Neville, the young Earl of Westmorland.

The reunions of Margaret and her son, Elizabeth and her daughter, were symbolic and highly charged. Over fourteen years had elapsed since Margaret had seen Henry, who had been a mere youth on his departure from England under the guidance of his uncle Jasper. In the intervening years, she had managed a fine balance of promoting his inheritance and submission to the Yorkist regime, a policy of appeasement that now smoothed the way for her union with the Woodville women. If nothing else, the events of 1485 justified the risks she had taken. Now, Margaret was faced with a tall, slender man of twenty-seven, his eyes described by different chroniclers as blue or grey, his hair fine and yellow, his countenance 'cheerful and courageous'.⁴ Her son had become a man during their separation and now he was to become her King. Yet Margaret had experienced so much disappointment that she was still fearful, even on the verge of victory. As she welcomed the former queen and her daughter, Margaret trembled over the future vision unfolding before her, fearful that something would occur to prevent her success from coming to fruition. The account of her chaplain confirms that her experiences of fluctuating fortune and deep personal superstition filled her with apprehension about the dangers that lay ahead. Having waited so long for this moment, Margaret found it difficult to believe it had come true.

Emerging from the shadow of Richard's reign, Elizabeth Woodville could feel a rightful vindication of her former position and her husband's kingship. This did not restore the terrible family losses and dramatic privation she had endured, but it at least provided a neat dynastic answer to them. Her sons had disappeared, presumed murdered in the autumn of 1483, but the Yorkist bloodline would continue through the issue of her eldest daughter and the man who had dispatched the Princes' presumed killer. This was the greatest victory of the women who had not fought at Bosworth. Quietly at Coldharbour House, behind closed doors, their successes were consolidated, their many dangers recalled, and their lost loved ones honoured, as they planned the most significant marriage of their era. Their lives had been arduous, but their long-term prayers had been answered; now they held the aces. The future, the forging of a new family, a new dynasty and direction for England, was in the hands of the mothers. This match of the matriarchs was a different way of doing politics. The mood in the house overlooking the Thames that autumn must have been something like euphoria tempered with caution.

*

Yet Henry and Elizabeth were not married at once. Five more months would elapse before the ceremony took place. There were many reasons for this, but the most imortant is likely to have been Henry's desire to establish his power and be crowned independently of his wife's claim. Henry's preferential treatment of Elizabeth that autumn, bringing her to London by escort and lodging her with his mother, was certainly suggestive of her impending status, as were the legal steps he took to secure her reputation. There was also the pressing need to convene Parliament, required to overturn the act of Titulus Regis and reinstate her legitimacy in order for the marriage to go ahead, and to avoid any future doubts about her offspring. Everyone must have been keen to avoid a repeat of the slurs that had damaged the children of Edward IV in 1483. The new king's wardrobe ensured that Elizabeth was equipped for her new role, supplying her with yards of crimson velvet and russet damask, and expensive ermine to line her garments. Henry's coronation took place on 30 October, attended by his mother but not his future wife, who remained at Coldharbour.

Parliament assembled a week later, in early November, to suppress Titulus Regis for its 'falseness and shamefulness'.[5] The roll on which the act had been written was publicly burned by an official hangman, followed by a declaration that all existing copies be surrendered by the following Easter, on pain of fine and imprisonment. Bishop Robert Stillington, responsible for the Act's inception, was arrested and brought to York, but at his advanced age was considered too infirm to travel to London and received a merciful pardon. He would die in 1491. The slanders against Elizabeth Woodville and Elizabeth of York were thus legally and physically destroyed. Nor was Elizabeth Woodville's former position forgotten. As the act invalidated any doubts regarding the legitimacy of her marriage, it reinstated her as a rightful dowager queen and returned her to her former 'estate, dignity, pre-eminence and name'[6] along with her widow's rents and revenues. The reversal of the act, though, was a double-edged sword, as it acknowledged the legitimacy of her dead brothers, opening the door to potential future Yorkist claimants or pretenders. Perhaps this could be seen as indicative of Henry's belief that the boys were dead, but the absence of bodies made a definitive accusation of murder problematic. The reversal of the act went as far as to accuse Richard of unnatural crimes such as the 'shedding of infants' blood',[7] a conveniently unspecific crime intended to address the issue tangentially.

Parliament also restored to Margaret Beaufort all the lands, estates, properties, revenues and titles that had been confiscated from her in 1483, granted in her own right and not as the dependent of any husband. This gave her a unique status as a woman in England, affording her a level of legal equality with a man. Lord Stanley's decisive action at Bosworth was rewarded with the titles of Earl of Derby, steward of the Duchy of Lancaster and Constable of England. As an additional union between the two families, on 7 November Elizabeth Woodville's sister Katherine was married to Jasper Tudor, who was given the Dukedom of Bedford.

One of the first official uses of the union rose, the white rose of York juxtaposed onto the larger red of Lancaster, occurred with the minting of a new currency in November 1485. In Parliament that December, in the King's presence, the Speaker announced Henry's intention to marry Elizabeth in the hope that 'there would arise offspring from the race of kings for the comfort of the whole realm,' to unite 'two bloods of high renown' and 'one house would be made from two families that had once striven in mortal hatred.' This was received in the house with 'harmonious consent', to which Henry added that it would 'give him pleasure to comply with their request'. On 10 December, the wedding day was set, the rings were ordered and the arrangements began in earnest. This belied the rumours that Henry was considering marriage to Anne, Duchess of Brittany, or his childhood friend Katherine Herbert, and although there may be truth in the rumour that Maximilian of Austria saw Elizabeth as a potential bride, these connections faded in the face of the arrangements being made in London. The first Tudor marriage was moving closer to completion.

Almost a thousand miles to the south, in the sun-drenched plains of central Spain, the next piece of the Tudor jigsaw was about to fall into place. In the Archbishop's Palace of Alcala de Henares, just north of Madrid, Isabella of Castile went into labour with her seventh child. On the night of 16 December she gave birth to a red-haired daughter, who was named Catherine, after her English ancestor, her great grandmother, Catherine of Lancaster. She would come to be known to history as Catherine of Aragon, ascribed the title of her father rather than that of her more powerful, more famous mother. As a descendant of John of Gaunt's second marriage, the newborn was related to Margaret Beaufort, the descendant of his union with

Katherine Swynford, later his third wife. As the first Tudor queen prepared for marriage, the second lay in her cradle.

The reversal of Elizabeth of York's position could not have been more complete. In the space of two years, she had been cast down from her status as first Princess in the land, second only to her mother, and a potential bride for a foreign king, into the dangerous territory of illegitimacy. Now she was restored, her bloodline honoured, her father revered, and herself on the verge of becoming England's queen. The previous precarious situation, and her affinity to Henry by the fourth degree of relation, demanded that all doubts be removed regarding their union, so that no future challenges might be made to the rights of their children.

Henry had acquired his first papal dispensation to marry Elizabeth in March 1484, while he was still in exile. Now he petitioned the Pope a second time, to confirm that the ceremony might go ahead. In mid-January 1486, Giacamo Passarelli, Bishop of Imola, papal legate to England, acted upon the King's petition. It stated Henry's claim to the English throne by right of conquest, by God's providence, and that he had been 'asked by all the lords of his realm, both spiritual and temporal, and also by the general council of the said realm' to marry Elizabeth and that he, 'wishing to accede to the just petitions of his subjects, desires to take the said lady to wife'.[8] On 14 January, in the chapel of St Mary the Virgin at St Paul's Cathedral, the legate interviewed eight witnesses regarding their marriage, including Margaret's husband, Lord Stanley, posing questions to ensure the couple should receive their dispensation. No objections were raised to the match and just two days later, the necessary paperwork was issued. After years of turmoil and uncertainty, Elizabeth was to become Queen of England.

The wedding was held at Westminster, either in the Abbey itself or the smaller, more exclusive chapel of St Stephen. Henry was dazzlingly dressed in cloth of gold, while his young bride, a few weeks short of her twentieth birthday, wore a dress of silk damask and crimson satin, over a white kirtle with gold damask and matching mantle, furred with ermine. Elizabeth's wedding ring, made of pure gold, was heavy at two thirds of an ounce and cost 23s 4d. The ceremony was conducted by the ageing Archbishop of Canterbury, Thomas Bourchier, and followed, according to court poet Bernard André, with 'feasts, dances and tournaments'[9] along with liberal gift giving and prayers for the young couple's future. The chroniclers and poets celebrated the symbolism of the union as a final act of peace between the warring houses of York and Lancaster, with Elizabeth as an instrument of tranquility for the beleaguered nation, and this was the enduring image in which her queenship was to be cast.

Following the exchange of vows, Henry and Elizabeth presided over a huge feast at Westminster. According to long-standing tradition, the couple was served by members of the nobility, who took ceremonial roles in pouring their drinks, carving the meat, carrying tableware and linen, bearing and holding necessary items. The meal would have been announced by heralds, accompanied by champions on horseback, punctuated by readings and the presentation of decorative subtleties, or carvings made from sugar or marchpane (marzipan.) With the entire proceedings lasting several hours, the feast concluded with the ritual accompaniment of the bride and groom to their bedchamber. Henry and Elizabeth passed the night in the thirteenth-century painted chamber, possibly in the huge four-poster bed featuring elaborate carving of Adam and Eve, painted in bright colours. Their intimate guests followed them into the chamber, where the bed was checked for dangers and then blessed, while the onlookers partook of wine and spices. Then, one by one, they receded, some to travel home, some to their quarters in the palace, some even to sleep outside the door and, finally, Elizabeth was left alone with her new husband.

Elizabeth's first child was probably conceived on her wedding night, or very soon after. Although pregnancy dates and durations are not always an exact science, varying between women, the arrival of her son eight months later is still consistent with conception having taken place in mid-January. She would have been unaware of this at first, as she accustomed herself to the role of queenship and the new family dynamic that was being established. Elizabeth had not only married Henry, but also his formidable mother, with whom the rest of her life would be spent in close proximity, thrown together more often because of their gender. As the Queen's mother, Margaret was second only to Elizabeth in state ceremony, but her experience and energetic capabilities frequently gave Margaret greater influence. She would appear with her son in public when Elizabeth was unavailable, and her activity and organisation would contrast with her daughter-in-law's more passive, reactive style. However, the pair were united in their mutual interest and established their unity early in the marriage, when Henry issued them with a licence to jointly found a chantry in Guildford, Surrey, where priests would pray for their lives daily, and honour their souls after death.

Nor was Elizabeth Woodville forgotten, as on 3 April 1486 payments were made to 'Elizabeth, queen of England, late wife of King Edward IV, in full satisfaction of her dower, with arrears since Michaelmas last, for term of her life'.[10] She received an annual £102 raised from a Bristol farm, as well as the lordships of seven Essex villages, for the duration of her life. On 10 July, Elizabeth was also granted the lease of Cheneygates, Abbot's house at Westminster, where she had sought sanctuary in 1470[11] and where she had spent the first few months with her son Edward, awaiting the return of her husband. Perhaps she chose the building because it held memories for her of lost loved ones.

Soon after the wedding, preparations began for Elizabeth's coronation. In spring 1486, timber for chairs, scarlet cloth from Brittany, spurs for horses, ermines and other furs, were all listed as items 'against the Queen's coronation',[12] but the onset of her pregnancy delayed the event. Henry embarked upon a progress to the north, where a minor rebellion had broken out led by Humphrey Stafford, of the Grafton Staffords, distantly related to Margaret Beaufort's former husband. Elizabeth retreated to the familiarity of Greenwich Palace, one of her favourite childhood homes, in the company of her mother. The rebels were easily intimidated, Stafford was arrested and executed, but his younger brother Thomas and loyal friend of Richard III Francis Lovell escaped to Burgundy. At the end of May, when Henry returned south to be reunited with his wife, she would have greeted him open-laced, with her bodice loosened to accommodate her new girth. On 5 June, Elizabeth was at Henry's side as they took a barge to Westminster for the King's formal re-entry to the city. They remained close to London over the next few weeks, with Henry required to attend to formal business in Windsor, but the King did not intend for his first-born to arrive there. Towards the end of August, a month before Elizabeth's due date, they travelled south to Winchester in Hampshire.

Henry selected Winchester as a symbolic location because of its traditional association with the legends of King Arthur. Following the example of Edward I, and Elizabeth's own father, Edward IV, he believed the city to have been the old capital of England, the site of the fabled Camelot, and that a son born there would augur a new golden era for the country. Elizabeth was established in the Priory of St Swithin, which is now the Dean's house attached to the Cathedral. Her mother, Elizabeth Woodville, was present, as was Margaret Beaufort, overseeing the practical arrangements. The exhaustive and detailed Ordinances Margaret drew up to cater for her daughter-in-law's confinement were detailed even down to the number, size and material of the cushions in the bedchamber.[13] On the night of 19 and 20 September 1486, Elizabeth bore a son. Elizabeth Woodville played a central role at the christening, awaiting the child's arrival inside Winchester Cathedral, presenting him with a rich cup of gold, standing as his godmother. Margaret's husband, Thomas, Lord Stanley, was godfather. The child was named Arthur.

7

Dynasty in Danger

1487–92

Plans were in full swing for Elizabeth's coronation when news arrived at court of another crowning. In Dublin's Christ Church Cathedral, a ten-year-old boy had been anointed as Edward VI, with support from Lord Deputy, Gerald FitzGerald, eighth Earl of Kildare. The Yorkist cause still had a large following in the Irish capital since Richard, Duke of York's Lieutenancy of 1447-50, and now the Dubliners supported the boy's claim that he was Edward, Earl of Warwick, son of Richard's third son, George, Duke of Clarence. This would have made him Elizabeth's cousin, and a potentially damaging rival who could unite any residual anti-Tudor feeling following the Yorkist defeat at Bosworth. Henry and Elizabeth knew this claim to be false, as the real Warwick had been incarcerated in the Tower since 1485, reputedly 'feeble-minded'.

The imposter was a child of humble origins, known to history as Lambert Simnel, although contemporary records refer to him as John. His likeness to the York family men was spotted by an Oxfordshire priest who tutored him in suitable manners and behaviour in order to pass as the incarcerated Earl. To disprove the newly-crowned claimant in Dublin, Henry ordered the twelve-year-old real Earl of Warwick to be paraded through the London streets, where he was permitted to speak with various 'important people'.[1] The boy pretender was only a figurehead for the Yorkist rebels, and such displays did not deter them.

In early summer, England was invaded in the name of Edward VI by members of Elizabeth's own family and former court circle. Behind young Simnel was John de la Pole, Earl of Lincoln, Elizabeth's paternal cousin, with financial and military assistance from her aunt

77

Margaret, Duchess of Burgundy. Only seven years had elapsed since Margaret had visited England, enjoying the hospitality offered by her brother Edward, Queen Elizabeth Woodville and their daughters at Greenwich. Yet now she funded the shipment of 2,000 mercenaries to Ireland, with the intention of challenging her niece's position and installing an imposter on the English throne. She was persuaded to do so by Lincoln, who visited her in Burgundy, who lied to her that he had assisted in Warwick's escape from the Tower. A mixture of Flemish and Irish troops landed in Lancashire on 5 June where they were joined by further Yorkist supporters.

Henry hurried to face the rebels, making his headquarters at Kenilworth Castle, with its long Lancastrian associations. Elizabeth went to Farnham to collect the infant Arthur, in case he should become a target for the rebels, then travelled to join Henry, who had summoned his mother Margaret and 'dearest wife' Elizabeth to come to his side. For the two women, waiting after he had departed for battle, it may have seemed that the hard-won victories of recent years were on the verge of being lost. Perhaps Elizabeth thought of her mother's position in 1470, newly delivered of an infant prince and awaiting her husband's return. With the outcome of the battle still unknown, the devout Margaret would have encouraged her daughter-in-law to join her in prayer, hoping that her belief in his divine purpose for her son's rule was to be justified again. Margaret's deeply superstitious nature and propensity to tears in times of duress cannot have made the waiting easy for Elizabeth. While the new Queen is often considered by historians to have been somewhat overshadowed by her formidable mother-in-law, it may have been on occasions like this that Elizabeth summoned the patience in adversity she had learned from her own mother, and proved herself equally as strong.

On 16 June 1487, at around nine in the morning, the Tudor army met the rebels near the village of East Stoke in Nottinghamshire. With the other two flanks of his army commanded by Jasper Tudor and John de Vere, Earl of Oxford, more troops and better equipment, Henry engaged in fighting for three hours before the Yorkist defences crumbled. Lincoln, Fitzgerald and the leader of the Burgundian mercenaries were killed, and young Simnel was captured, pardoned and sent to work in the royal kitchens. Margaret of Burgundy was reported to be 'very sorye' at the failure of the plan and began to consider new ways to 'vexe and perturbe' Henry.[2] For the moment, though, nothing could detract from the victorious procession back to the capital. Margaret and Elizabeth occupied a house in St Mary Spittal in order to watch him parade through the streets, having confirmed the right of conquest by which he held the throne. Against those Irish prelates who had supported and crowned the pretender, Henry invoked papal censure, by writing to Innocent VIII and imploring him to 'proceed against them at law'[3]

Elizabeth Woodville was notably absent during the months of the Simnel rebellion, having retreated to Bermondsey Abbey earlier that year. On 12 February, she made the decision to leave her Westminster house of Cheneygates and signed the Abbey's register, occupying rooms that had been set aside for the descendants of their benefactor Richard de Clare, Earl of Gloucester. As the widow of Edward IV, the Clare family heir, Elizabeth would have been entitled to occupy those quarters, and pass her days in quiet contemplation amid the rituals of the monks. There was also an historical precedent for her retirement, as Catherine of Valois had made the same move at the end of her life, dying at the Abbey fifty years earlier. Situated across the Thames from the Tower of London, close to the site presently occupied by Bermondsey market, the monastery was then surrounded by countryside, with old illustrations showing its cloister, church, tower and entrance gate. On 1 May 1487, when Henry was at Coventry, he transferred all Elizabeth's sources of income to her daughter, although the dowager Queen would continue to receive monies for her day-to-day expenses and a grant at Christmas.[4]

Some historians have read significance into the timing of this move. Elizabeth's retreat, including the transference of her lands, has been interpreted as a punishment by Henry for her involvement in the Simnel rebellion. There is not a single shred of evidence to suggest that Elizabeth played any part in the plan to depose her daughter and disinherit her grandson. Having endured so much loss and danger, and fought so hard to achieve the Tudor marriage, with its national and dynastic stability, it is difficult to believe that Elizabeth would risk everything to support such a rebellion, especially given that Simnel was claiming to be Warwick, not one of her missing sons. Even if she had entertained the slightest hope of the survival of the princes in the Tower, the rebels of 1487 were not purporting to act on their behalf. They had initially proposed the identity of the younger prince, Richard of Shrewsbury, for Simnel, before switching to Warwick, an action unlikely to win Elizabeth's support, suggestive that the general feeling was against the possibility of Richard's survival.

Mourning her husband and sons, approaching the end of her life, it is far more plausible that Elizabeth sought the same peace and seclusion as many women of her age and class. She may even have been suffering from illness at this point, and the resurgence of rebellion in the country provoked memories of past suffering. It would seem logical, in those circumstances, that her retirement and the reassignment of her resources was an act of selflessness, even humility, which is reflected in the self-effacing arrangements she made in her will five years later. There is no evidence that Henry VII was displeased with Elizabeth either, as the payments he made to her in 1488, the grant of an annual 400 marks 'towards the maintenance of her estate' and the one-off £6 for a tunne of wine, were all made out to 'our dere moder' or our 'right dere moder'.[5] The previous November, as a further mark of trust, Henry even entered into marriage negotiations on Elizabeth's behalf, with none other than James III, King of Scotland, 'for the greater increase of the love and amity between them'. Whether or not the union was considered a serious option, it was thwarted by the death of James in June 1488 after his defeat at the Battle of Sauchieburn. Elizabeth did venture out of her retreat on important occasions. During the Queen's second confinement, at Westminster in late November 1489, she gave an audience in her chamber to the French Ambassadors, headed by her kinsman Francois de Luxembourg, at which Elizabeth Woodville and Margaret Beaufort were both present. The child was a daughter, who was named Margaret.

Only one detail suggests the potential complicity of Elizabeth Woodville, or her family, in the Simnel rebellion. When the news first reached the English court early in 1487, Henry moved to arrest Thomas Grey, Elizabeth's surviving son from her first marriage. This was around the same time that the dowager queen went to Bermondsey. Yet this is not sufficient to imply any guilt on Elizabeth's part, or even on Thomas's. The timing of the arrest does seem to marry with the start of the rebellion, but the nature of Grey's involvement cannot be assumed. Then in his early thirties, Grey had been made Marquis of Dorset by Edward IV and attempted to rise against Richard III in 1483, for which he was attainted. He inherited the title Lord Ferrers of Groby from his grandmother, and after Henry VII reversed his attainder, was restored to his titles and estates.

It is not impossible that Grey considered engaging with the rebels, or was interested to investigate their claims, or, equally, that he was approached by them as a potential insider. And perhaps his theoretical involvement was the final straw that encouraged his mother to withdraw. Any involvement he did have was certainly of brief duration, or simply suspected, as he was released after Henry's victory at Stoke. Five years later he accompanied Henry to France, but only after he had been obliged to demonstrate his loyalty in writing, to ensure he did not commit treason. His former arrest may have been sufficient justification for this, but it was also at the time when the second pretender of the reign, Perkin Warbeck, had been received by Charles VIII of France. Henry's mission resulted in the Treaty of Etaples, by which Charles agreed to expel the pretender, so the King's usual sensitivity to security would have been amplified. In 1487, though, Grey was released without charge and no evidence links his mother to the challenge to her daughter and son-in-law.

It is also true that Margaret Beaufort took something of a step back at this point. She retained Coldharbour House on the Thames and still attended court regularly, but her main residence was the manor of Collyweston in Northamptonshire. In addition to its extensive grounds, the Collyweston estate included its own chapel, almshouses, council building and prison, by which Margaret and Stanley oversaw local justice. It also contained the substantial library Margaret was building, much of which she would leave to Cambridge University. In the coming years, she would endow the foundation of Christ's and St John's Colleges, and commission translations of romances and devotional works from William Caxton's press. Her increasing interest in scholarship came out of her regret over her lack of early education in Latin and marks a shift away from the arena of politics into patronage. It may be that both Margaret and Elizabeth Woodville saw this period as having successfully transitioned power from one generation to another and, in their different ways, they stepped away from the limelight. Margaret, though, was never one to remain away for long.

*

Elizabeth of York's coronation took place on 25 November 1487. Accompanied by her mother-in-law, Margaret, and a host of other ladies, Elizabeth was carried down the Thames from Greenwich to the Tower, amid great pomp and ceremony. The barges must have created an impressive spectacle for those watching on the bank, alerted to their arrival by the notes of music drifting across the water. Each of the city's guilds had responsibility for decorating a barge in the Queen's honour, and one, known as the 'bachelor's barge', was adorned with a huge red dragon spouting real flames, adorned with silk banners and streamers, and announced by the blasts of trumpets and clarions.[6]

The following day, Elizabeth processed from the Tower to Westminster dressed in white cloth of gold with an ermine mantle, gold and silk laces and tassels. She wore a gold circlet on top of her headdress and was carried in a litter decorated in cloth of gold. Before her rode Jasper Tudor, Duke of Bedford, and now Constable of England, and behind came the important ladies in chariots, including her paternal grandmother, Cecily Neville, and her Yorkist great aunts. Her guardsmen's horses were draped in hangings embroidered with the white rose and sunburst symbols of her Yorkist heritage. The streets had been cleaned and hung with cloth of gold, silk and velvet, and choirs of children sang along the route. Inside Westminster Abbey, Margaret and Henry sat in a concealed balcony to watch as Elizabeth spoke her vows and was anointed with the sacred oil. Afterwards, the new Queen was conducted to the great hall for the coronation feast, where she was served by the Archbishop of Canterbury, Cecily Neville and her aunt, the Duchess of Bedford. Elizabeth Woodville did not attend.

Margaret and Elizabeth of York's relationship has attracted scrutiny from historians, especially after the comment made by a Spanish ambassador that the queen was 'kept in subjection' and did not like Margaret's influence over Henry.[7] No family relationships are entirely free from strain, especially under the pressures experienced by the Tudors in the first part of Henry's reign. Yet this is the only surviving comment of its type. It was made by a foreign observer, an outsider, used to the protocol of the Castile-Aragon court, with its dominant queen. Equally, the ambassador went on to dismiss the matter along music hall lines, adding that the Queen disliked her mother-in-law 'as is generally the case'.[8] There is no doubt that Margaret exerted a strong influence and may have been controlling at times, but Elizabeth was wise enough to appreciate her support, which allowed her to model a different kind of queenship. In fact, the styles of the two women complimented each other well, with Margaret taking the active, more traditionally 'masculine' role of organisation, political engagement and intellectual pursuits, while Elizabeth followed the gentler, more 'feminine' method of her mother, of patronage, piety and maternity.

Margaret and Elizabeth were often together in a public show of unity. The day after Elizabeth's coronation, Margaret accompanied her to hear Mass in St Stephen's Chapel and sat at her right hand in the Parliamentary chamber. Margaret remained at court until Christmas, dining with Elizabeth in her chamber. When Henry and Elizabeth walked crowned in procession to Matins, Margaret walked with them, wearing a rich coronet. At the Twelfth Night festivities of 1488, they appeared in co-ordinated costumes, in 'like mantle and surcoat', stressing their connection. In April, they were both issued with the miniver and red liveries of the Order of the Garter at Windsor Castle. Accounts list the family frequently travelling together and visiting each other, when Margaret's rooms would often be connected to those of her son. Margaret also played the role of hostess for important scholars and international guests, taking the part of ambassadress at Henry's side. In September 1490, she and Stanley welcomed a deputation from Spain whose negotiations with the King resulted in the signing of the Treaty of Woking, outlining the future marriage of Prince Arthur to Catherine of Aragon. The only reminder of past breaches may have arisen in December 1488, when Margaret's cousins, Edmund and John Beaufort, killed at the Battle of Tewkesbury in 1471, were reburied in the Abbey; but all the living could unite for the act of remembrance, whichever side they had formerly taken.

In June 1491, Queen Elizabeth entered her third confinement at Greenwich Palace. The birth of another prince, the future Henry VIII, coincided with a time of European redefinition, when philosophers, theologians, artists and writers were attempting to make sense of the world. In Milan, Da Vinci drew up his *Vitruvian Man* in pen and ink, a familiar, often-reproduced image of a man standing inside a square, inside a circle, to demonstrate the perfect proportions of a man according to geometry and the workings of the human body as an analogy for the workings of nature. In Florence, Sandro Botticelli drew up his *Chart of Hell* as an illustration for Dante's *Divine Comedy*, with its different layers descending in deep, tightening rings into the centre of the earth. A twelve- or thirteen-year-old Michelangelo completes his first masterpiece under the patronage of the Medicis.

His *Temptation of St Anthony* depicts the saint borne into the air (or ambushed) by a host of nightmarish devils, winged, grotesque, lewd, some reptilian. These images remind us of the clash between late medieval and emergent renaissance thinking, juxtaposing centuries-old beliefs in the tenets of Catholicism with the humanistic redefinition of man's purpose and place in the universe.

Henry's birth also coincided with the explosion in printed materials that would transform Europe in the following century and enable the dissemination of new ideas. The earliest printed books (those produced before 1501 known as incunabula) had encompassed a wide range of subject matters from presses in Westminster, Oxford, St Albans and in greater London. Increasingly these works were dedicated to Margaret or Queen Elizabeth, in the hope that this would gain patronage and increase sales, perhaps appealing to a more literate, educated female aristocracy. William Caxton had pioneered the industry with the first editions of *The Canterbury Tales*, *The Golden Legend*, *The Book of the Knight in the Tower*, *Le Morte d'Arthur* and the first translation into English of Ovid's *Metamorphoses*, but his death in late 1491 or early 1492 passed the mantle to the next generation of printers. The spread of the printing press marked a shift away from the painted image to the printed word, which would be central to Henry VIII's future struggles and the lives of his future wives, and to the Reformation.

*

On 10 April 1492, Elizabeth Woodville drew up her will at Bermondsey. She requested a simple, humble and plain funeral, with burial beside Edward in St George's Chapel, Windsor. It would seem likely that an advancing illness allowed her enough warning to record her final wishes, as she did not die until two months later, on 7 or 8 June, in her mid-fifties. As she desired, she was conveyed quietly to Windsor by river in a coffin draped simply in black cloth and buried privately at about 11pm without any dirge or Mass. Her tomb was visited by relatives, including some of her daughters, who made offerings of gold and silver coins and ordered that requiem masses be said for her soul. Elizabeth of York did not attend, as she was in confinement at Sheen Palace, awaiting the arrival of her fourth child. She may not have been informed of the loss until after the safe delivery of a daughter on 2 July, as bad news was thought to impact foetal and maternal well-being. The Queen named the little girl Elizabeth.

Elizabeth Woodville's death marked the end of the establishment of the Tudor dynasty. By 1492, she knew there were no guarantees, but she had come through the crisis of 1483-5, seen her daughter married and crowned as queen, and the birth of her first three grandchildren, including two boys to inherit the throne. Her life's path had brought her from the outskirts of a social elite into its very core by virtue of her marriage. With hindsight, it is possible to identify clear biographical turning points, and the effect of these upon the course of national events. To an extent, Elizabeth was independent in her decision-making, but she was also responsive to the actions of others and wider events. She able to exercise some personal choice within the perimeters of her gender, class, personal relations and politics. As a woman, a queen, a wife and a mother, the reach of her decision-making was sometimes national, sometimes personal.

When it comes to the key moments of Elizabeth's life, it was really only on one occasion that she was a passive agent of fate, faced by a situation over which she had no control. As a woman, she could not influence or prevent the death of her first husband, John Grey, in 1461, or the resulting change in her status. However, the financial and dynastic result of Grey's death may have spurred her to action as a mother. If the legends are true regarding her appeals to Feilding and Hastings, it was by Elizabeth's initiation that her case came to the King's notice. It is possible that she emphasised her dependent position as the widow of a knight, and exploited her beauty, as tools to achieve her aim, but she can hardly have anticipated attracting Edward's romantic attention, or his proposal of marriage.

In 1464, Elizabeth gave her consent to marry Edward, but just how much choice could she actually exert when faced by the desire of the new King? Elizabeth was aware of the difference in rank between them, the precarious truce between the Yorkist and her Lancastrian family, and the potential rank and wealth he offered. Nor could she forget she was his subject to command as he chose. Under those circumstances, and whatever her personal feelings might be, she would have been foolish to reject such an opportunity. It was the ultimate career marriage for women of her time. Yet, it was her choice to insist upon the promise of wedlock that highlights her character as either moral, or ambitious, or both. She did not immediately seize the prize on offer but exercised the little personal power she had as a woman; that of access by a man to her body, under canon and civil law. By imposing conditions to Edward's advances, she gained a means of control in an otherwise challenging situation and turned it to her advantage. Her shrewd and careful handling of events in 1464 paved the way for the establishment of one half of the future Tudor family and set a precedent for the second marriage of her grandson, Henry VIII.

Later, when faced with danger, Elizabeth showed herself able to act swiftly for her personal safety and that of her children. Her flight into sanctuary in 1470 was timely, as she left the Tower the evening before Warwick retook it, proving that this was a wise response to the danger he posed. She removed herself from falling into his power, but it was essentially a reaction under duress. Once secure in Westminster, she waited to be liberated by her husband, but could not influence this outcome. Fortune favoured her in 1471, as it had not in 1461. Her second flight, in 1483, was different. It was more of a political statement that Richard, Duke of Gloucester, could not be trusted and meant her harm, and was designed to demonstrably align his actions with those of her enemies in 1470. Without a political voice, and lacking the Council's support, her best option was decisive action. Her withdrawal to sanctuary that summer was an act of political protest as well as personal protection.

Yet although the act of entering sanctuary was one of empowerment, it ultimately limited Elizabeth's sphere of influence. She was unable to prevent the removal of the nine-year-old Richard of Shrewsbury, after Gloucester employed Thomas Bourchier, Archbishop of Canterbury, to argue on his behalf. It was pragmatism as a mother that prompted her to work with Margaret Beaufort for the union of their children and to leave Westminster in March 1484, even if this required striking a deal with her enemy. These choices were made in the best interests of her children, and it is in this light that her final major decision of 1487 must be read. Elizabeth's retirement and her relinquishment of her estates was her own choice, as much as her modest funeral was, in recognition that her moment had passed and in demonstration of her piety. Her mother-in-law, Cecily Neville, had retreated to live the quasi-secluded life of a vowess in 1485, and Elizabeth chose the same path. It was a typical act of late-medieval gendered recognition that they were no longer able to fulfil their roles as mothers, or offer their energies, and did not wish to be a burden upon their children.

Mourning the loss of loved ones, possibly ailing physically, and seeking spiritual retreat after years of turmoil, Elizabeth's choice is easy to understand. She recognised the time to relinquish her role in the dynasty she had helped created.

Elizabeth's personal qualities have often been summed up as a comparative, or a negative, by saying what she was not, or did not do, when placed alongside the example of Margaret Beaufort. Clearly, the two women had differing characters and followed different models of motherhood, but this was partly dictated by their circumstances. When it came to their commitment to their children's futures, their careful marital choices and their loyalty to the dynasty, Elizabeth and Margaret appear to have more in common than not. Elizabeth's specific contribution to the Tudor dynasty was a very feminine one, by the standards of the time. She was the gentle, compassionate counterpart to a warlike king, fulfilling the ideals of wife and mother, excelling in the domestic sphere and influencing behind the scenes. She was also a model of piety and patronage, particularly of family loyalty, although this was bitterly resented by those whose animosity towards the Woodvilles was too great to be overcome. For most of her life, she took a secondary role in politics, happy to excel in the traditional virtues of English queenship; but for a short period of time, 1483-5, national turmoil dictated that she become a player in the political arena. It was her perseverance as a mother that contributed to the inception of the Tudor dynasty.

8

Tudor Princesses
1489–1501

Elizabeth of York's daughters were born into a world that was rapidly re-evaluating the role of its royal women. After historian Joan Kelly-Gadol published an article in 1977 entitled 'Did women have a renaissance?'[1] extensive scholarship has unearthed examples that prove the changing nature of female education and cultural contributions at the turn of the fifteenth century. Traditionally, learned women had belonged to the cloister, excluded from all forms of higher education, dichotomising the roles of the female scholar and the mother. But the increase in the number of schools and universities which began to accept women as students, and even as teachers, brought a new level of intellectual engagement into the lives of aristocratic daughters. Increasingly, they had access to the texts and tenets of humanism alongside their cultural lessons about etiquette and manners. The effects of this were uneven, and slow to reach England, but the mother of the second Tudor queen was pioneering this change.

In the 1480s, Isabella of Castile founded a school of classics with separate classes for young women in grammar, logic, natural and moral philosophy, metaphysics, canon and civil law, and poetry. The female teachers included the philosopher and linguist Cecilia Marello, the mathematician Alvara des Alba and the classicist and disciple of Erasmus, Isabel de Vergara. Historians have recognised Isabella's patronage of education as a significant marker in the path of the Renaissance, as there had never before been 'such a numerous and select retinue of ladies under previous sovereigns' and that 'the fuller participation of women was one of the chief differences of the Spanish Renaissance.'[2] This sparked a trend for the establishment of *colegios de doncellas*, schools for girls, with Galíndz founding one in Madrid and Cardinal Ciseros starting another in Alcála de Henares.[3] Isabella was preparing her daughters to take leading roles in a changing world, where they needed to be at least the equals of their male peers, and perhaps even their superiors. Her youngest daughter, Catherine of Aragon, would bring this legacy with her upon her arrival in England in 1501.

At the French court in the 1480s and 1490s, Anne of France, sister of Charles VIII, was also an important figure in female education. In her early twenties, Anne acted as regent for her young brother, overcoming challenges and unrest and training up a number of aristocratic girls for future political roles, including Margaret of Savoy, later Duchess of Austria, Louise of Savoy, mother of the future Francis I, and Diane de Poitiers, later the mistress of Henry II. Anne oversaw the female teachers she employed at her Amboise home, including Hélène de Chambes, wife of diplomat and chronicler Philippe de Commines, and Madame de Ségre. Anne's instructional manual *Lessons for my Daughter*, written at a time that saw a surge in contemporary literature about etiquette, advocated humility as the most important of all the virtues, but underpinned by thorough scholarship. Anne presents an ideal of womanhood in the emerging Renaissance tradition, citing classical authors Ovid, Cato, Socrates and Aristotle, as well as those in the Christian tradition such as Augustine and Thomas Aquinas, referring her daughter to a long reading list for her spiritual edification. Anne's position was more influential than pioneering, as although she recommended key new texts, her writing did not so much engage with them as advocate them alongside former behavioural standards.

England would produce a handful of educated women during the early part of the sixteenth century, such as Thomas More's daughter Margaret, Jane Grey, Mary and Elizabeth Tudor, the Cooke sisters, Elizabeth, Anne and Mildred, and the women who contributed to the Devonshire manuscript, Mary Shelton, Mary Howard and Lady Margaret Douglas, but these were the exception rather than the rule. With a few notable exceptions, status, wealth and literacy levels determined the small elite group who had access to the new learning at this point. However, their experience of humanist texts was largely for their spiritual rather than practical benefit, and still occurred within the expectations of domesticity, with the approval of men. Their education was considered important in order to make their marriages stronger, rather than affording them any greater independence or academic standing. Some may have published translations of key texts, but few would yet create a work of their own as independent creative authors. Thus, their humanist education was a patriarchal investment in wives, daughters and future mothers by 'enlightened' men, which would not bear greater intellectual fruit until the second half of the sixteenth century. The education of Margaret and Mary Tudor straddled this change, designed to equip them for future queenship, but as the wives of foreign kings, rather than ruling or having autonomy in their own right.

*

Elizabeth of York had four daughters. Margaret, who arrived in 1489 and Mary, born in 1496, survived to adulthood while Elizabeth and Katherine died at the ages of three years, and eight days, respectively. The Tudor girls were established in a nursery at Eltham Palace, which included their younger brothers Henry and the short-lived Edmund, but not their elder brother Arthur who, as heir, had his own household at Ludlow. Set outside London, in the modern borough of Greenwich, Eltham Palace was sufficiently removed from the capital to be considered a country retreat. It was a place Elizabeth of York knew well, being an old favourite of her father's. Edward had built the Great Hall with its hammerbeam roof and hosted over 2,000 guests there at Christmas in 1482. Reconstructions based on detailed Elizabethan surveys of the estate suggest an outer courtyard with gatehouse and service buildings and an inner, moated complex, filled with imposing red-brick apartments centred around the great hall. Combining security, splendour and accessibility to the capital, it was a suitable home for the future royals.

The King and Queen were at Woodstock in late summer 1495, with Elizabeth three months pregnant with Mary, when they heard of the death of their second daughter. Only two months past her third birthday, Princess Elizabeth died at Eltham of a 'wasting disease' or 'atrophy', which might cover any number of possible causes, or reflect the symptoms of an underlying illness. Through Elizabeth's short life she was probably closest to her nurse and her older siblings, Margaret and Henry, then aged almost six and four. While Margaret was being considered as a future bride for the King of Scotland, negotiations had just begun for Elizabeth to marry Francis of Angoulême, later King Francis I. She was given a lavish funeral, processing from Eltham to Westminster Abbey where her body was laid to rest in St Edmund's Chapel, accompanied by 100 poor men in dark hooded gowns, at a cost of £318.[4] A tomb in Purbeck marble was built for her, topped by her effigy in copper gilt and inscriptions in her honour. Six months later, a future queen of France, Princess Mary, joined the establishment at Eltham.

The children's household was overseen between 1496 and 1499 by Elizabeth Denton, a Suffolk woman, who progressed to became lady-in-waiting and keeper of the wardrobe to Elizabeth of York. Her replacement was Anne Cromer, either the daughter of a gentleman usher or a Kentish knight, who retained her position until 1502, after which she received an annual pension of £10. There was also a Welsh nurse named Anne Davy and assistants Anne Mayland and Margaret Troughton, who received £3 3s each a year.[5] Within that structure, each child had their own smaller team of dedicated staff, including gentlewomen, physicians and teachers specific to their age and needs. Later, the girls' households came under the charge of Jane Guilford, née Vaux, known as 'Mother Guildford'. Originally a lady-in-waiting to Margaret Beaufort, Jane married Richard Guildford, the son of the former Comptroller of the Household to Edward IV, a figure who would have been well-known to Queen Elizabeth. Joan's own son, Henry, was born in the same year as Margaret Tudor, and likely to have been a regular fixture at Eltham.

The Tudor princesses' education covered the French and Latin essential for diplomatic relations and the courtly accomplishments of music and dancing, combined with the highly skilled art of needlework, essential for maintaining the tradition of embellishing their future husbands' shirts. It has been recently theorised by historians that samples of her children's handwriting suggest Elizabeth of York taught them to read herself, which would make her quite the exception among queens, but it is by no means impossible. Along with all the Tudors, they girls enjoyed their outdoor sports of hunting, hawking and archery. A young French woman, Jane Popincourt, was also placed in their household, perhaps to encourage the children's conversational skills in her native tongue. When the Dutch humanist scholar Erasmus paid his famous visit in 1499, he was deeply impressed by the abilities of young Prince Henry, as the student of his own protegé, William, Lord Blount, but paid less attention to the future King's sisters. He merely wrote that as well as Henry, he had seen 'Margaret, about eleven years old, afterwards married to James, King of Scots, and ... Mary, a child of four.'[6]

As the girls grew, Margaret Beaufort appointed a number of her humanist scholar friends to act as tutors. John Colet encountered the teachings of Erasmus, Savonarola and Guillaume Bude whilst in Paris in the 1490s, and established himself in Oxford from 1496, where his lectures addressed new methods of interpreting the scriptures. Thomas Linacre was a physician who studied Greek in Italy and brought his enthusiasm for the new learning, translating Aristotle and Galen, and Willian Grocyn's classical studies in Florence, Rome and Padua informed his lectures at Oxford and at St Paul's. In employing her forward-thinking humanist friends, Margaret Beaufort departed from the traditional model of instruction for princesses, which focused on etiquette, to expose her granddaughters to the intellectual debates of their day. Just how far Margaret and Mary engaged with these is unclear, but this set a precedent in the education of royal girls that would inform the raising of the next generation.

It is not difficult to visualise the Tudor princesses sitting at their lessons, or roaming the gardens at Eltham. Surviving accounts give an indication of the adult-style clothing in which the children appeared, as the nursery was also a location for the entertainment of dignitaries and foreign visitors, and the children were a powerful, visible indicator of the dynasty's future. In November 1495, Henry spent £7 on 'diverse yerdes of silk' for Henry and Margaret, while baby Mary the following year was clothed in kirtles of black silk and velvet, edged in ermine and mink.[7] The following year as she was beginning to walk, her dresses were made of baby buckram, a fine cotton, not like the stiff, modern version, and she required linen smocks, three pairs of hose, eight pairs of single-soled shoes and four pairs of double.[8] The children were frequent visitors to Windsor, Westminster, Greenwich, Sheen and Baynard's Castle, or wherever their parents might be, attending important events and festivities, expected to show themselves to best advantage in front of guests. No doubt the girls were also influenced by Margaret Beaufort's model of piety and were visible attendees at church on red letter days in the Catholic calendar, but they were also lively, energetic participants. One of Margaret's most notable public appearances as a small child was her fifth birthday in November

1494, on which occasion her younger brother Henry was elevated to the Dukedom of York. A tournament lasting three days was held at Westminster, after which Margaret handed out the prizes, dressed in a velvet and buckram gown trimmed in gold lace with a white, winged cap in the Dutch style. Afterwards, Margaret and her young brother danced to the delight of the court.[9]

At Eltham, Margaret and Mary were shielded from the dynastic struggles that their parents were experiencing in the 1490s. A second pretender, far more serious than the young Lambert Simnel, had emerged in Europe, and was being fêted by enemies of the Tudor regime. Claiming to be Richard of Shrewsbury, the younger of the Princes in the Tower, a young Flemish merchant by the name of Perkin Warbeck arrived at the Burgundian court, swiftly winning over Elizabeth's aunt Mary, who schooled him in the details and manners of the Yorkist court and encouraged him to distribute coins minted in his name. Warbeck was initially welcomed at the court of Charles VIII of France, until Charles ejected him under terms of the Treaty of Etaples he signed with England in 1492. The pretender returned to Burgundy, where he was invited to attend the funeral of the Holy Roman Emperor and recognised as Richard IV. However, after a failed attempt to invade England, and a brief flirtation with Ireland, Warbeck went north, towards the Scottish King with whom Henry had hoped to ally his eldest daughter.

Margaret had been considered as a potential bride for James IV since she was little, despite the unstable relations between the two countries (or perhaps because of it). As recently as 1482, Edward IV had waged war on James's father, resulting in the capture of Edinburgh, Berwick-upon-Tweed and the Scottish King himself. The new King, James IV, had seen Perkin Warbeck as an opportunity to gain international leverage and offered shelter to the pretender in 1496, furnishing him with clothes, armour, tournaments, and even a wife from among the nobility. Together, Warbeck and James made a half-hearted attempt to invade England that August, travelling four miles over the border before their supplies ran out and support failed to materialise. By the following July, James wanted rid of his new friend and dispatched him back to Ireland, in a ship ironically named the *Cuckoo*. Warbeck would be defeated by a royal army in Cornwall in 1497, brought to London and imprisoned in the Tower until he confessed that his claim was unfounded.

It was the Spanish ambassador to the Scottish court, Pedro de Ayala, who concluded the Treaty of Ayton between James and Henry in September 1497, establishing peace between the two countries. James was then twenty-six, and had previously sought an English wife with an engagement to Elizabeth of York's sister Cecily, as well as considering marriage to Maria of Aragon, sister of Catherine. He had been spurred to marriage by the death of his long-term lover, Margaret Drummond, and was also the father of several illegitimate children, the eldest being only four years younger than his potential bride, Margaret Tudor. James was clearly a fully-grown man, confident in his sexuality, but Margaret was still too young, as her father explained to the Spanish ambassador in 1498:

> A marriage between him [James] and my daughter has many inconveniences. She has not yet completed the ninth year of her age and is so delicate and weak that she must be married much later than other young ladies. [It would] be necessary to wait another nine years... The queen and my mother are very much against this marriage.[10]

It was feared that James would not be able to refrain from consummating the match and could injure his young bride. However, it was from this point until the conclusion of the marital treaty in 1502 that Margaret was aware that her future lay with the Stewart or Stuart dynasty, in a country traditionally considered by her countrymen to be barbaric. Now Margaret was to be the diplomatic tool by which a lasting peace was planned.

Mary received her first offer of marriage before she could have understood what the word meant. It came from a figure at the very heart of the European Reformation, from a country to which England did not have traditional marital ties, from a family whose reputation may have preceded them. Ultimately, the match was not considered good enough for a daughter of the King of England, but it would have represented a very different path for Mary, had Henry been more minded to opt for wealth alone and accept Maximilian Sforza as a son-in-law. Ludovico Sforza, Duke of Milan in 1494, had benefited from the enlightened education offered by his mother, Bianca Visconti, who ensured he was taught by humanist scholars to appreciate the visual arts as well as the arts of warfare. In 1491, he married Beatrice d'Este, who made their court a centre for the patronage of artists such a Leonardo da Vinci, and bore her eldest son, Maximilian, in January 1493. Sforza hoped to ally with England in order to gain Henry's assistance against the French, even though a state of peace currently existed between them. The ducal ambassador, Raimundo di Soncino, was dispatched to England in 1497, and although his proposal did not meet the King's approval, he was a witness to important news arriving in London, which he reported back to the Duke in August and December. The previous year, Henry had funded the Venetian explorer John Cabot to sail across the Atlantic. Soncino wrote of his discovery of the east coast of America, which was rich in spices, jewels, silk and fish. No doubt the Tudor princesses heard some of the traveller's tales too.

Seeking a more prestigious husband for Mary, Henry looked towards the mighty Hapsburg Empire that stretched across northern Europe. Relations with Burgundy had been predictably strained since the Duchess, formerly Margaret of York, supported both pretenders, Simnel and Warbeck, in their attempts to oust Henry in the 1490s. Now Henry appealed to Margaret's step-grandson, Philip the Handsome, recently married to Joanna, a sister of Catherine of Aragon, in the hopes that the Spanish martial alliance he was pursuing might influence the young Duke. It was a good move, which paid off in 1500 with a treaty of friendship between Henry and Philip. Two important marriages were proposed, that of Henry, Duke of York, to Philip's elder daughter Eleanor, and that of Mary to the four-month-old Charles Hapsburg. This also laid the foundation for a wider future alliance with Spain, as the deaths of Joanna's elder brother and sister meant that she and her husband had inherited Castile. In years to come, young Charles would inherit a massive territory encompassing Spain and the Netherlands.

Henry sought to create a lasting peace for the Tudor dynasty through the marriages of his children. Yet there remained two thorns in his side. Although the betrothal of Prince Arthur and Catherine of Aragon had already taken place on 26 March 1489, when the pair were aged just two and three, Ferdinand and Isabella were still uncomfortable about the existence of Warbeck at court and that of the Yorkist heir, Edward, Earl of Warwick, who had been imprisoned in the Tower shortly after Bosworth. Warbeck had been brought into the heart of Henry's court after admitting being an imposter, heavily guarded, but permitted to attend feasts. Here, he would have come face to face with Elizabeth of York, whose brother he had pretended to be, and whose throne he had attempted to usurp. It may have been with mixed emotions that Elizabeth looked upon the pretender, perhaps with dismissal, or curiosity, perhaps even with compassion, as she prayed for the forgiveness of his sins. She took his wife, Lady Catherine Gordon, into her household as a lady-in-waiting. This may have been under her husband's direction, or out of sympathy for a woman who had been deceived by the pretender. In June 1498, Warbeck attempted to escape from Richmond Palace, after which he was sent to the Tower. It proved decisive. Mary of Burgundy, Elizabeth's Yorkist aunt, issued Henry with an apology for backing the pretender and the Spanish Ambassador had a four-hour meeting with Henry, Elizabeth and Margaret that July.

Warbeck's arrest bore fruit for Henry's marital policy with Spain. On 19 May 1499, which fell upon Whit Sunday, the proxy marriage of Prince Arthur and Catherine of Aragon was held at Tickenhill Manor, near Bewdley, in Worcestershire. The Spanish ambassador, de Puebla, stood in for Catherine, repeating her vows and taking the seat of honour at the banquet that followed. From that moment forward, Catherine was officially styled 'Princess of Wales' but although she and Arthur were legally married, they were still in separate countries. Yet, that summer, Ferdinand and Isabella, wrote to Henry expressing concerns about the existence of another potential claimant to the English throne, the Earl of Warwick, Elizabeth of York's cousin, who had grown to manhood in captivity.

In summer 1499, Warwick and Warbeck were lodged one above the other in the Tower, and by exchange of letters became embroiled in a plan to escape. The intention was to release Warwick while the royal family were on progress, visiting the Isle of Wight, whereupon he would take the Tower and seize the treasury. Warbeck appears to have encouraged Warwick, who was to be the main claimant, although their exact roles are unclear. Probably initiated, or at least encouraged, by Henry from afar, the plan was observed at every stage by his agents, who moved in to arrest the pair in November. A week later, both were executed, Warbeck at Tyburn in the tradition of traitors and Warwick beheaded on Tower Hill, as befitted his royal blood. With both potential dangers removed in one sweep, the way was now clear. The Tudor dynasty was stronger as a result of the closure achieved in its patriarchal narrative, which now facilitated its female achievements.

The expected contribution of Tudor princesses in the 1490s was unequivocally marriage and motherhood. Margaret and Mary were given sufficient education to equip them as the wives of foreign kings, in terms of languages and accomplishments. They could anticipate holding court, producing children, representing an ideal of behaviour, piety and patronage, and perhaps even acting briefly as regent if the circumstances required it, until the arrival of the next adult male. They were not expected to rule in their own right, or to apply their minds to politics or international relations, merely to be fruitful ornaments to the men who did. As it happened, neither woman would settle for a passive role, opting to take their happiness into their own hands, although they were more motivated by love than political engagement. Soon, though, a new princess would arrive in England, a princess educated in the European humanist style, who would use her learning for her own defence, even when it conflicted with her husband's will. On 2 October 1501, Catherine of Aragon landed at Plymouth.

9

The Spanish Bride
1501–03

After a long journey to England, troubled by many delays, the fifteen-year-old Princess Catherine of Spain arrived to be married to Prince Arthur. Her safe conduct into the capital was entrusted to Edward Stafford, Duke of Buckingham, son of Margaret Beaufort's former nephew-in-law. On the morning of Friday 12 November, he brought the princess from her lodgings at Lambeth Palace to St George's Field, which was the meeting point for the entry into the city itself. Mayor Sir John Shaa was waiting to greet them, and the guests were lined up to be paired with an English courtier of equal rank. Here Catherine was to meet the person who was to have the greatest impact on her life. She cannot have known it, as the ten-year-old Prince Henry rode up, confident in the saddle, enthusiastic about his role in the day's proceedings. Catherine was short, with the red-gold hair inherited from her Lancastrian great-grandmother and namesake, Catherine of Lancaster. Her Spanish fashions, with the unusual headdress and stiffly hooped farthingale skirt, as well as her colourful entourage, featuring African and Moorish faces, looked strange and exotic to the spellbound Londoners.

The streets were full of elaborate pageants, reflecting Catherine's heritage, her virtues and English hopes for the fertility and stability she would bring. Finally, amid all the singing, speeches, spectacle, costume and colourful display, the entourage reached St Paul's Cathedral, at the central and highest point of the city. At the door, the Mayor, Aldermen and guildsmen presented Catherine with their traditional gifts, including 'basins and pots filled with coin to a great sum' and other treasures. Once inside, the Princess was blessed by the

Archbishop of Canterbury and left her own offering to St Erkenwald. She would also have given thanks for her safe arrival in the city; just like her mother, Catherine was used to the juxtaposition of lavish celebrations with piety, and the theatre of royalty in the church which served to enforce her majesty, and special relationship with God. Finally, she was led through a private door to the adjacent Bishop of London's Palace where she was to pass the night, disappearing for a while from the public gaze.

Catherine had learned how to be a queen from her mother, Isabella of Castile. Never less than regal and theatrical, Isabella framed herself in cloth of gold, jewels, imposing architecture and absolute dominance of the Spanish people. Her justification was that of a Christian crusader, a chosen one, enacting God's will, which gave her the same complete conviction in her actions that her daughter was to display. Travelling with her mother from a young age, witnessing her statecraft, her negotiating skills, her diplomacy and the planning that went into equipping her husband's campaigns, Catherine had imbibed her queenly example as much as the lessons and books from her humanist teachers. She had been betrothed at the age of three, a queen-in-waiting for most of her life, with an iron will and a sense of divine destiny. She was the first foreign bride to arrive in England since Margaret of Anjou in 1445 and, like her, came from the European tradition of strong, educated women, willing to take an active and influential role and with a sense that leadership was a partnership between king and queen, man and wife. With her first glimpse of her new country, her new husband and family, the fifteen-year-old Catherine took her place in the Tudor dynasty that she would help redefine through her future choices.

On the afternoon of 13 November, Catherine was conveyed to Baynard's Castle, where she was received by her future mother-in-law, Elizabeth of York. For the daughter of Isabella of Castile, Elizabeth offered a very different model of queenship to that with which the girl had grown up. Instead of the imposing figure of leadership, whose drive and fervour had led to the conquest of Granada and the expulsion of the Jews, the organiser behind Ferdinand's campaigns and the master of dramatic performance and dress, Elizabeth of York appeared placid and gentle; but her strength lay in this softness of approach. Henry was clearly the driving force in the relationship and Elizabeth deferred to him, forging her own identity as the face of compassion, piety and supplication. Hugely popular with the people, she was the recipient of their regular gifts, with surviving accounts from 1502-3 indicating a steady stream of fresh fruit, vegetables, eggs, meat, flowers and delicacies being brought to her palaces whenever she was in residence.[1] Through her motherhood, she was associated with the cult of the Virgin Mary, an earthly embodiment of divine maternity and a conduit to heaven by virtue of her anointed position. Her accounts reveal her warmth and charity, rewarding old servants, assisting those who were ill or in need, those who served her or who undertook pilgrimage on her behalf.[2] She was an accessible figure, submissive, obedient and passive, mild and self-effacing, personifying her motto 'humble and reverent', with daughters of her own just a couple of years younger than Catherine.

Elizabeth and Margaret Beaufort joined forces again to welcome their new daughter-in-law. Margaret hosted a feast for the Spanish party, and there may also have been a more intimate, personal note, if the women took the opportunity to try and speak to the girl, using translators, about their expectations of her. Just as Henry would describe himself as a new father figure for Catherine, it is quite in keeping with what is known about Elizabeth's character that she would adopt a maternal role towards her son's wife. Whether or not she recognised it at the time, Catherine had a potential ally in the Queen, who would have been a considerate and welcoming figure, a friend to the young girl so newly arrived in a foreign land, a sympathetic ear, even an advocate to steer her amid the male-dominated world of politics. At the least it is likely that Elizabeth outlined the arrangements for the following day, for the wedding itself, which was to be the costliest event of Henry's entire reign and the most significant for the Spanish visitors.

Princesses Margaret and Mary were to take prominent positions in the days that followed and both had new clothes suited to the occasion. The presence of the Scottish Ambassador throughout fuelled rumours that Margaret was on the verge of being betrothed to James IV, and the tawny gown of gold tissue trimmed with ermine she wore, followed by a purple velvet gown, crimson French hood and white cloth of gold sleeves confirmed her importance. Mary, at five years old, was dressed in russet velvet with ermine and miniver, a tawny satin kirtle and green satin sleeves. The court were also issued with new clothing for the occasion, with King Henry's henchmen in crimson cloaks edged with black satin, Prince Henry's in blue and yellow, and the royal guard in the Tudor colours of green and white. Catherine and Arthur both dressed in white satin, long before it was a traditional colour for the bride.[3]

On November 14, 1501, Catherine and Arthur were married in St Paul's Cathedral. They entered along a wooden platform, covered in red cloth and railed on each side, stretching the entire 350 feet from the choir door to the west door, standing four feet high and twelve feet wide. King Henry, Queen Elizabeth and Margaret Beaufort observed the ceremony from behind a screen, so they would not upstage the young pair in terms of precedence. Afterwards, they headed for the Palace's great hall, where the wedding feast was served to over a hundred guests. The theme for the feast was 'all the delicacies, dainties and curious meats that might be purveyed or got within the whole realm of England',[4] which were served up in three courses, of twelve, fifteen then eighteen dishes. As the honoured guest, Catherine sat at the high table with the 'Bishop of Spain' as the English termed Antonio de Rojas Manrique, Bishop of Mallorca, later Archbishop of Granada. Arthur was seated separately with his siblings, Henry, Margaret and Mary, surrounded by cupboards displaying gold plate and expensive hanging tapestries. As was the custom during such important events, they were waited on by the Lords of the English court, dressed in their finery, 'wonderful ... to behold'.[5] The feasting went on until four or five in the afternoon.

The wedding night that followed would prove a pivotal moment the rest of the Tudor dynasty. The question of whether or not Catherine's first marriage was consummated would return to haunt her two decades later, and redefine the monarchy in relation to Europe and the church. After the blessing and prayers recited by the Bishop, the guests withdrew and the pair were left alone. Catherine and Arthur might have spent their entire lives being trained to endure the public gaze but in private, how well equipped were they for the anticipated consummation of their marriage? To put it bluntly, the question that confounded England in the 1530s and has been wrangled over by historians ever since, is how likely is it that Catherine and Arthur had sex? The following morning, Arthur appeared flushed and thirsty, 'good and sanguine', calling for a drink as he had spent the night 'in the midst of Spain' and that it was a 'good pastime to have a wife'.[6]

Later, Catherine swore that they didn't have sex and she never wavered from this position all her life. The following morning, she was quiet and subdued, remaining with her ladies. Juan de Gamarra, a twelve-year-old boy, had slept in her antechamber on the wedding night, literally adjoining Catherine's bedroom, and stated that 'Prince Arthur got up very early, which surprised everyone a lot,' perhaps even before the Princess herself woke. When Gamarra went into her room, he found Catherine's dresser and confidante, Francesca de Carceres, appearing sad and informing the others that 'nothing had passed between Prince Arthur and his wife, which surprised everyone and made them laugh at him.'[7] Hence the need for Arthur's boast, perhaps. Catherine's first lady, Dona Elvira, was convinced that the Princess was still as pure as she had been when she left her mother's womb, and she imparted this belief to Ferdinand, who did not doubt her. In addition, Catherine's doctor later deposed that Arthur had not been capable of the act, having been 'denied the strength necessary to know a woman, as if he was a cold piece of stone, because he was in the final stages of phthisis (tuberculosis)' and he had never before seen a man whose limbs were so thin.[8] Convincing as this may sound, though, it does belong to a period of hindsight, from a man who treated the Prince on his deathbed. Whatever happened that night, the feasting and jousting continued for weeks, with the court leaving Westminster for the more private venue of Richmond. It was here that Duke Henry took to the floor with his sister Margaret and, 'perceiving himself to be accombred with his clothes, sodainly cast off his gown and daunced in his jackett' to the delight of his parents.[9]

It was unclear at first whether Catherine and Arthur should live together as man and wife. King Henry had concerns about the wisdom of allowing the couple to commence married life at once, which may or may not have been based on Arthur's health. Contemporary medical opinion was still divided when it came to sexual relations between young newly-weds. While a physical relationship was considered beneficial in general terms, with the denial of natural urges leading to health problems and temptation, the timing was critical. After all, there was no hurry. So far as they knew, the pair had the rest of their lives to perfect their union and produce children. Yet just before Christmas, Henry swung away from caution, ruling against the advice of the Spanish and much of his Council, that Catherine would accompany Arthur into Wales at once. They departed for Ludlow on 21 December, five days after the Princess turned sixteen.

Ludlow Castle sat at a high point along the River Teme, its solid stone walls encircling the outer bailey where artisans served the inhabitants and an inner bailey with apartments, hall and a free-standing round chapel. Away to the west, the Welsh hills were a purple ripple on the horizon and to the east lay the rolling green lands of Shropshire and Herefordshire. They would have approached through the walled town, entering through the Gladford Gate or Old Gate, progressing up the hill past the rows of timber-framed buildings into the wide market place, which gave access to the castle gatehouse. Catherine's rooms were clustered in a line to the north-west with the large thirteenth-century Solar block of around 11 feet, sitting over the castle's cellars. This gave onto to the great hall with its three trefoil windows and central hearth, which in turn led through to the first-floor chamber block, about 16 feet long, and a four-storey tower containing bed chambers and storerooms. Ludlow was built from a local red-grey limestone, developed piece by piece since the eleventh century, with some sections of the Solar and Great Hall finished in a hurry. To a Princess accustomed to the elegant, breathtaking complexity of the Alhambra, it may have seemed a little crude. With Arthur resuming his duties, Catherine's days passed quietly as she settled into her new home. They would have come together for meals but otherwise, the Prince's work required him to travel and undertake long days of work in the government of Wales.

*

With Arthur and Catherine settled, Margaret's turn came next. On 24 January 1502, the Treaty of Perpetual Peace was concluded at Richmond Palace, between England and Scotland. It was signed by Henry, Patrick Hepburn, Earl of Bothwell, Robert Blackadder, Archbishop of Glasgow and Andrew Forman, Bishop of Moray. The following day, Margaret was betrothed to James IV. The ceremony took place in Queen Elizabeth's presence chamber, a symbolic location signalling her endorsement of the match. Presiding over their vows, Blackadder asked whether the Tudor royal family knew of any impediment to prevent the alliance, to which Henry, Elizabeth and Margaret each replied, 'there is none.' Henry asked whether it was 'the very will and mind of the king of Scotland that the said earl Bothwell should in his name assure the said Princess?' The archbishop and earl confirmed that it was. Margaret was then asked whether she gave her consent to the marriage, without compulsion, and if she entered into it of her own free will, to which she replied, 'If it please my lord and father the king, and my lady mother the queen.' Henry affirmed that it was his 'will and pleasure' and Margaret knelt for her parents' blessing.[10]

After Bothwell had spoken his vows on behalf of James IV, Margaret made her promise;

> I, Margaret, the first begotten daughter of the right excellent, right high and mighty prince and princess, Henry by the Grace of God king of England, and Elizabeth queen of the same, wittingly and of deliberate mind, having twelve years complete in age in the month of November last past, contract matrimony with the right excellent, right high and mighty prince, James king of Scotland, and the person of whom, Patrick earl of Bothwell, procurator of the said prince, represents, and take the said James king of Scotland into and for my husband and spouse, and all other for him forsake, during his and mine lives natural, and thereto I plight and give to him, in your person as procurator aforesaid, my faith and troth.[11]

Then, trumpets blew and the minstrels played joyfully. Elizabeth of York took Margaret's hand and led her to the royal dais, where they sat side by side, equal as queens. The next few days were spent in celebratory tournaments and banquets at Westminster Hall, and Margaret was thereafter known as the Queen of Scotland.

The terms included that Margaret's marriage to James IV should take place before Candlemas next (2 February 1503) and that neither country should invade the other, or harbour traitors and rebels, on pain of excommunication. Henry promised to furnish his daughter with £10,000 as a dowry, and James promised her an annual cash payment of £1,000, plus £6,000 drawn from rents and a dowager's allowance of £2,000 in the event of his death.[12] A dispensation was also required, as James and Margaret were related through Margaret Beaufort's ancestor Joan Beaufort, granddaughter of John of Gaunt. Joan had married King James I in 1424, and survived the assassination attempt which killed him to become regent for their young son. If Margaret knew anything of Joan's history, it might have prepared her for the brutal struggles and factional in-fighting that lay ahead. The reality of her queenship was nothing like that portrayed in the allegorical poem 'The Thrissil and the Rois' (The Thistle and Rose) by William Dunbar, who was present in London to witness the arrangements.

Soon after the court celebrated Easter, a messenger arrived from Ludlow. Only three months since his departure from London, Prince Arthur had died of what his doctor diagnosed as 'phthisis', or pulmonary tuberculosis, possibly exacerbated by another infection. Catherine had also fallen ill but survived. The news was broken to Henry by his confessor early in the morning of Tuesday 5 April and the King sent for his wife, so that they might 'take the Painefull sorrows together'.[13] After comforting each other, Elizabeth concealed her pain long enough to remind Henry that they still had healthy children and were still young enough to create more. The loss was severe, and both parents felt it deeply, but their eldest son had been taken to God and the dynasty rested on the shoulders of a ten-year-old. Within weeks the Queen would fall pregnant again. This caused an unexpected shift in the family dynamic too, as it meant that Margaret was now the eldest, and technically the heir, even though she had a younger brother. However, with the Scottish arrangements concluded, Margaret's future was already conveniently directed elsewhere, and avoided any awkward circumstance by which she might contemplate inheriting the throne. In reality, as a boy, Prince Henry would always be the preferred candidate to take on the Tudor mantle. Henry VII and Elizabeth of York were fortunate to have produced a surviving spare heir; Elizabeth's reaction to Arthur's death underscores just how far the couple were focused upon safeguarding the dynasty.

Arthur's unexpected death left him no time to make provision for his sixteen-year-old widow. He left most of his possessions to his sister, an act which stands testament to how close the pair had been, and that his death was unexpected. Elizabeth despatched a litter of black velvet fringed with valance and ribbon to bring Catherine back to London. Her accounts for the end of May included a payment to Ellis Hilton for two and three-quarter yards of satin of Bruges black for the covering of a saddle for the Princess and a yard and a quarter of black velvet to trim it.[14] She was settled in Durham House, or Place, the thirteenth-century base of the Bishops of Durham, with its marble-pillared great hall abutting the river Thames, its chapel, solar and two-acre garden. For the next three years, this was to be Catherine's principal residence, sandwiched between the Thames and the Strand, flanked on either side by York House and Ivy Lane beside the Strand, in the parish of St Margaret.

The Privy Purse accounts of Elizabeth of York for 1502-3 give an insight into the life of the Tudor court shortly before Arthur's death, but they also represent the model of queenship espoused by Elizabeth, and her character. On Maundy Thursday, the Queen's almoner Richard Pain paid out 114 shillings for her to distribute among thirty-seven local women, one for each year of her life.[15] She also made offerings on Good Friday and every day of Easter week, along with gifts to locations associated with cult of the Virgin Mary, the particular favourite of English queens, and established a pattern of piety and patronage that Catherine was to follow. In terms of Elizabeth's life at court, a Robert Fairfax was paid for setting an anthem to music, minstrels were rewarded, as were the kitchens, scullery, porters and saucer. Payments were made to those who brought the queen gifts, such as a carp from her son Henry's fool, apples, pears and a sole brought to her at Richmond, and almond butter at Hampton Court. On March 31, she received the gift of some oranges from a 'servant of the prothonotarye of Spain'. The bill of a saddler named Nicholas Major was settled for £10, 'for making of certain stuff of his occupation against the marriage of the prince'.[16] The records also capture the change in mood. After the news of Arthur's death broke, the court went into mourning. Elizabeth's accounts contain payments to a William Botery for black tinsel satin for the 'making of an edge of a gown of blake velvet for the queen'.[17]

From the windows of Durham Place, Catherine might have seen Arthur's family being rowed past on their way to Greenwich or the Tower and back again past Westminster to Richmond or Windsor. There are no indications in the Privy Purse accounts of Catherine's seventeenth birthday being acknowledged that December, or that she was present at court at any time during the Christmas season. The year 1502, which had begun so auspiciously, drew to a close for Catherine in loneliness and uncertainty, possibly in neglect.

*

Queen Elizabeth had fallen pregnant swiftly after the death of Arthur, and was nearing the end of her term, when she went into labour 'suddenly' at the end of January 1503. She may have been caught unawares, with the child arriving early, as indications suggest she had planned her confinement to take place at Richmond, which was far quieter and more suitable than the Tower, where she found herself. With the exception of her first two labours, Elizabeth had favoured the countryside locations of Richmond and Greenwich with, historically, the Tower of London rarely ever being chosen by queens, unless under duress. Her accounts reveal the visits of nurses in the late autumn, perhaps as routine, but plausibly because of the concerns raised during her penultimate delivery when she bore a son named Edmund in 1499, who had lived only sixteen months. Elizabeth bore a daughter on Candlemas Day, 2 February, to whom she gave the name Katherine, perhaps as a favour to the princess, or in reference to the queen's own sister of the same name who features more frequently in her accounts. Doctors were summoned, but the Queen died nine days later, on her birthday, followed shortly afterwards by her infant. The loss of Elizabeth as a queen, wife and mother, as well as the gentle kindness which may have softened Catherine's hardship, was a severe blow. In terms of her family contribution, Margaret and Mary lost their mother, and Catherine lost a potential advocate, a model for queenship and a guide through the pitfalls of childbirth, as well as a relationship that the circumstances never allowed to develop into friendship.

Elizabeth was given a dramatic state funeral, in stark contrast to the quiet affair her mother had requested just over a decade before. Her black velvet coffin was surmounted by a cross of white cloth of gold and the corners were draped with white cloth, a symbolic custom to indicate the nature of her death. On top of that lay the effigy of the queen, painted and dressed to resemble her in life, of which the top portion survives in the Abbey still. It wore a wig under a jewelled crown, rings on its fingers and carried a sceptre. Virgins in white linen carrying lit tapers and wreaths of Tudor green and white lined her route to Westminster, where she was accompanied by eight ladies on white horses. Inside, hundreds of tapers burned and the interior was hung with black cloth. Work commissioned by Henry on the Lady Chapel, which he intended as the Tudor mausoleum, had only just begun. Elizabeth was temporarily laid to rest in one of the side chapels until the place was complete, when she would finally be buried under the Renaissance Italian-style tomb in black marble and gilt bronze.

A summary of Elizabeth of York's contribution to the Tudor dynasty could easily reach a reductive conclusion which places her in a series of gender boxes: daughter, wife and mother. Undoubtedly, her fulfilment of these roles is central to understanding her character, and their importance must not be denied, but these are roles which many of her contemporaries filled and do little to delineate her individual contribution. Moreover, they were roles over which she exerted little choice, and which she entered almost passively, as others dictated. As the daughter of a king, her status mattered, and she was raised and acted accordingly. She was a bigger symbol for England than just her descent, and the marriage her mother helped negotiate was of immense national significance, as were the children she bore. And yet, Elizabeth is in danger of slipping through the gaps. Of all the Tudor queens, she seems one of the most elusive, perhaps as the result of being judged alongside her more vocal mother-in-law, or overshadowed by her maternity, or simply less prominent due to certain elements of her character. Outside of fictional portrayals, it feels more difficult to 'know' Elizabeth, or to delineate her contribution beside the more strenuous actions of others.

As the first Tudor queen, Elizabeth's contributions must be judged in terms of her choices and the ways in which she chose to interpret, or enact, the roles that fate offered her. She was a queen more in the gentle, maternal model, like her mother, a more private, domestic, personal queen, than Margaret of Anjou before her, or than the model her mother-in-law Margaret Beaufort set. Yet all these women came to power in different circumstances, by different routes, which defined their enactments of power. Margaret Beaufort, through whose line her son's claim passed, was not actually a crowned queen, but asserted her heritage on her son's behalf by her activity, and occasions such as public crown-wearing on certain occasions. Elizabeth of York was the only one of these women who had been royal since birth, and raised in the entitlement and sense of divine favour that brought. When she had suffered privation and uncertainty, it had been passively, although no less agonisingly, awaiting the solutions and protections of her parents, her future husband and more persuasively, God. Throughout her life, each of Elizabeth's trials had been vindicated by subsequent success, from the readeption of 1470-1, the fall from power in 1483-5, her marriage, to the challenges of pretenders to the throne. If she had endured the slings and arrows of outrageous fortune with stoic patience, it was because her patience had always been rewarded. Just as much as Margaret Beaufort, Elizabeth must be understood as a woman devoted to her duty. Her words of comfort to her husband in 1502, about bearing another son, offer a telling insight into her character.

At the start of her reign, Elizabeth chose as her motto, 'humble and reverent' and she lived by this for the remainder of her life. By genetics, habit or design, her character was similar to that we might observe in the Elizabeth Woodville who stepped out of the limelight and retired to Bermondsey, and who made the humble funeral arrangements of 1492. For both women, service and duty mattered, along with a sense of their appropriate role at any given moment. Elizabeth of York displayed great strength in her gentle piety and the constancy of her devotion; once she had committed to the Tudor dynasty, her commitment was absolute. If she ever questioned that she was fulfilling God's plan for her, she never showed it, but accepted success and adversity with the equanimity of a true survivor. Records surviving from different phases of her life show the variety of outlets by which Elizabeth demonstrated her faith beyond her daily routine of services; pilgrimages, patronage, gifts, offerings, devotions, charitable grants, kindness to the sick and infirm and those in need, as well as the rewards of loyalty to those who had served her father and brother, or her current family. Her contribution to the Tudor dynasty, beyond the vital physical act of its creation, as wife and mother, undoubtedly lay in her example of piety, charity, humanity, and being the gentler half of a successful ruling partnership.

In this sense, though, Elizabeth was essentially a backward-looking queen. Although she gave everything she had, even her life, to ensure the future of the dynasty, she did not redefine the role of queen or adopt new ideas or beliefs by which she might have championed change. She cannot be claimed as a Renaissance queen but was rather a queen in the late-medieval model, just as her mother had been. Her role, her education, expectations, piety and deference were calculated to compliment the attributes of a husband, to comfort and support, not to engage in theological or philosophical debate about the new ideas coming from Europe. She benefited from Henry's forward thinking in reshaping and redefining aspects of his kingship, including finances and their household, and no doubt she enjoyed the cultural influences he introduced into the creation of Renaissance palaces such as Richmond, even to the extent of contributing to the design of a garden, but she was not the intellectual driving force behind such change. Although she had witnessed great upheaval with the replacement of one dynasty with another, she was a model for continuity, not change, extending the attributes of her mother into the next reign. Her queenship was to be the last in this style that England would experience. The new generation would be steeped in a new way of thinking, exposed to new ideas about the world and its potential and limits, critical of old ways of worshipping, recasting their roles, refashioning their images as they saw fit. The emergent Renaissance questioned the nature of the self in ways that would have conflicted with Elizabeth's sense of dynastic duty, bearing fruits that she would have found unacceptable.

Yet perhaps Elizabeth's greatest role, whether consciously chosen or not, was in her exemplification of contemporary female virtues. She was an iconic beauty, a figurehead of maternity, an earthly correlative with the popular cult of the Virgin Mary. Her subjects adored her and brought her gifts with the same devotion that they took to the Marian shrines and altars across the country. They brought whatever they could; flowers, fruit, rosewater, game, cheeses, eggs; the offerings they lay at the feet of their Queen were interchangeable with those by which they asked for saintly intercession, for better health, successful harvests, safe deliveries. In the 1980s, historian Anne Crawford came closest to identifying Elizabeth's appeal by writing that she was 'probably everything a fifteenth-century Englishman could have hoped for in his queen.'[18] The first Tudor queen was, indeed, the personification of an ideal, more so than any other queen, in pedigree, appearance, character, piety, fertility, loyalty and accomplishments. Even more than this, she fulfilled contemporary masculine concepts of perfect femininity, which was re-enforced by her unattainability, as the culmination of chivalric and courtly love fantasies. Elizabeth excelled in the position designated to her by men and never challenged the codes of perceived acceptable behaviour for her gender. She was uncomplaining, she adopted a behind-the-scenes role, she didn't interfere, upstage or overtly display any of the 'masculine' qualities that Margaret of Anjou, and even Margaret Beaufort, were criticised for. Elizabeth was by no means a proto-feminist, even if such a label was not so unsuitable for any women of her era. She was an ideal of Tudor womanhood, venerated by men and women alike, an aspirational standard, popular with the people, an early prototype of a 'national treasure'. Seemingly perfect, untouchable and unblemished, her death in childhood, in doing her duty to England, proved her humanity in a way that provoked genuine grief among her subjects. Such perfection would be difficult to replicate.

10

The Two Margarets

1503–09

The sixteenth century hovered like a sea change on the horizon. A contemporary belief that the year 1500 would mark the end of the world, had been extrapolated from a phrase in the Book of Revelation, stating that the apocalypse would come 'half-time after the time'. Despite this alarmism 1501 arrived, as did 1502, and the world remained intact. Across what was widely believed to be a spherical earth, a population of approximately 450 million continued about their business, of whom slightly under 3 million lived in England, and 60-70,000 dwelt between the King's bastions of Westminster in the west, and the Tower in the east.[1]

Yet the undercurrents of cultural and religious evolution were in motion. Albrecht Dürer completed his Christ-like self-portrait, Erasmus published his *Handbook of a Christian Knight*, Christopher Columbus began his fourth and final voyage to the New World, Michelangelo worked on his *David* and Da Vinci started painting the *Mona Lisa*. In Flanders, a baby girl named Susanna was born to Gerard Horenbout and his wife Margaret, who would become the first woman artist to work at the court of Henry VIII. Old Sheen Palace had burned to the ground and a new, fantasy Italian-style Richmond rose from the ground, with pepper-pot domes, huge windows, long galleries, octagonal towers and whimsical gardens. The values and practices of the medieval world were overlapping with those of Renaissance learning and redefinition, spreading across Europe, in books and essays, disputes and sermons. The spread of printing made a few books affordable in middle-class homes. It was the start of a century that would transform women's lives, through increased literacy, changes in cultural perception, and the redefinitions of gender and authority. On a Norfolk estate, a baby girl was born to Thomas and Elizabeth Boleyn, whose queenship would challenge the status quo of her age, and produce the greatest female monarch in England's history.

The traditional patriarchal narrative of the Tudor dynasty until 1500 was one of pacific and economic success. As a Venetian visitor to England that year remarked about Henry, 'no king has reigned more peaceably than he has,' and having won his title through combat rather than inheritance, his 'good fortune had been equal to his spirit, for he has never lost a battle.'[2] Having won his unlikely victory at Bosworth, the new King had seen off traitors and rebels, defeated challengers to his throne, beaten armies at Stoke and in Warbeck's south-west, made peace with foreign rulers, kept a potentially rebellious nobility in check, amassed wealth, married the ideal wife and fathered a number of children. Yet, as Henry was to discover, not all battles could be anticipated, carefully planned, or even fought.

The matriarchal narrative had been one of struggle and rewards. It differed in being a narrative of multiple voices, rather than the traditional masculine investment of power in one individual. Theirs had been a story of pragmatism, patience and compromise. Their tools were prayer, conversation, touch, letter-writing and the visible display of that elusive blend of softness and strength. Elizabeth Woodville had lived long enough to see her gamble pay off, her name restored and her surviving children promoted. Margaret Beaufort's years of faith and investments, her risks in the face of danger, and her faith in God's plan for her son, had borne fruit beyond anything she could have dreamed through the 1460s and 1470s. While the new Tudor King had been active and wise in his decision-making and defence of the realm, it had been his wife, Elizabeth, who had endured the pain of a string of pregnancies and the rigours of childbirth. Having borne seven, possibly eight, children in just over sixteen years, she had suffered agues and, as her doctor's bills suggest, ill-health and complications. The delivery of her penultimate child had been difficult but, at the age of thirty-six, she had been determined to present her husband with another son. It was in this personal, domestic sphere that the early tragedies of the Tudor dynasty struck.

As the new century dawned, death was lurking in the shadows of Tudor success. In June 1500, Prince Edmund died at the age of sixteen months, followed by Arthur, Prince of Wales in April 1502, then Elizabeth and her newly delivered daughter Catherine in February 1503. These devastating deaths, occurring so swiftly, one after the other, broke Henry. His character, his children's lives and the mood at court, changed permanently, exposing just how central this matriarchal contribution was to the dynasty. Without its essential core, Henry's achievements rang hollow. That women's world, created through sacrifice and childbearing, comfort and loyalty, was the foundation upon which he had constructed his achievements and his hopes for the future. The devastation was initially so intense that Henry shut himself away for weeks at Richmond, a most personal response from a man who had shifted the structure of government so that he held all the reins. In the wake of Elizabeth's death, he was so desperate to replace his domestic core that he considered marriage to the widowed Catherine of Aragon, then aged seventeen, and earmarked as a bride for young Henry, Prince of Wales. Catherine's mother, Isabella of Castile, wrote from Alcala de Henares, expressing her disgust at this 'very evil thing, one never before seen and the mere mention of which offends the ears ... we would not for anything in the world that it should take place.'[3] Determined to prevent the match, she commanded that the Princess should return home as soon as possible, even if it meant that Catherine should join a fleet of Spanish merchants then conducting business in Flanders. 'In this way,' Isabella wrote, 'the king will be deprived of his hope of marrying her' which was a 'barbarous and dishonest' act.[4] Henry abandoned his scheme, but Catherine also lost her protector, learning of the death of her mother the following year.

Margaret Beaufort suffered personal losses of her own during these years, with the death of her long-term friend, Lord Chancellor, Cardinal and Archbishop of Canterbury, John Morton, who had christened the royal children. Morton had been her staunch confidant and supporter through the most difficult years of the York-Lancaster struggles, opposing the usurpation of Richard III and working with Henry to build his financial strength. He was buried in Canterbury Cathedral under a painted, carved effigy and memorial brass in the crypt. Then, in 1504, Margaret's husband, Thomas Stanley, died at the age of sixty-nine, having successfully navigated his path through five decades of political drama and intrigue. The couple had increasingly lived apart in recent years, with Margaret based at her new home in Collyweston in Lancashire, in which she reserved rooms for her husband's frequent visits. As with all her marriages, it had been a dynastic choice rather than personal inclination, but it had proved a fruitful and amicable partnership.

Margaret had taken a vow of chastity in 1499 with Stanley's permission, which she renewed after his death, remaining politically active but aspiring to greater spiritual purity. It was usual for women to undertake such a promise in widowhood, as Elizabeth of York's paternal grandmother Cecily Neville had done, but to do so during a husband's lifetime was an exceptional elevation of piety and personal devotion over the duties Margaret had promised to fulfil in the marriage ceremony. Even the inventories of Margaret's clothing predating Stanley's death are full of black items, reflecting her pious lifestyle. She had also drawn up the Ordinances that dictated mourning wear and her household modelled this in 1504. Stanley's body was buried among his ancestors at Burscough Priory, but a memorial service was held for him at Stamford, just four miles from Collyweston. Seven hundred yards of fine say cloth were dyed black for the occasion, during which Margaret hosted Stanley's heir Thomas at her home.

*

In 1503, the focus shifted to the daughters of the Tudor dynasty. Margaret was thirteen and Mary seven, the latter very much still in the nursery while the elder approached womanhood. The most famous surviving portraits of Margaret and Mary date from later in their lives, in their maturity, or else were painted posthumously. It is only through a couple of fairly crude sketches that we come closest to a vision of the princesses in their youth. A drawing of a young woman, labelled in French as being of Margaret, sister of King Henry VIII of England, shows a slender girl in traditional late medieval-style costume and pose. She has the fashionably high forehead, perhaps plucked to emphasise its length, high eyebrows over hooded lids, a longish nose and small mouth. Outside the poetry created to celebrate her wedding, no descriptions survive extolling Margaret's beauty. The only detail that survives is her physical frailty; on the verge of puberty, she was considered slight and under-developed for her age, which led to the delaying of her marriage until she had grown a little more.

A pencil drawing of Mary a decade later, at around the same age, shows a young woman with narrowed eyes and a slightly long face and nose, failing to capture the charm conveyed by the pen portraits of her admirers. Another sketch labelled 'La Royne Marie' shows her in a similar aspect, with a rosebud mouth, demure, hooded eyes and the same longish nose. Considered the more attractive of the sisters, she was variously described by ambassadors, scholars and politicians as being a very nonpareil of beauty. The Austrian ambassador claimed that 'never man saw a more beautiful creature, nor one having so much grace and sweetness,' the Venetian ambassador called her 'a Paradise, tall, slender, grey-eyed, possessing an extreme pallor', while Erasmus wrote that 'nature never formed anything more beautiful, and she excels no less in goodness and wisdom.' One Italian chronicler, Pietro Martire d'Anghiera, commented that she was 'beautiful without artifice. (who) looked more like an angel than a human creature', while Venetian merchant Lorenzo Pasqualigo described her as 'very beautiful and has not her match in all England... tall, fair and of a light complexion, with a colour and most affable and graceful'.[5]

Margaret's marriage had already been delayed on account of her family's fears about her frailty and youth. In particular, her mother and grandmother had opposed her being sent into Scotland too soon, as she was still so small for her age, perhaps even prepubescent at this point. The transition to puberty varied in girls of different classes, as well as being influenced by genetic factors. The protein-rich diets of aristocratic young women brought on the onset of the menarche, or first menstrual period, earlier in comparison with the more fibre-based meals of the lower classes, based on pulses, grains and lacking in fat. Although the Tudor girls may have engaged in physical activities such as hunting, hawking and archery, they were not engaged in the daily grind of labour in the fields, or in the home, which also kept down body weight, below the necessary threshold to kickstart the process. However, if Margaret had inherited her paternal grandmother's constitution, it seems possible that genetic factors overrode dietary ones, suggesting that despite being described as small and slight, she commenced menstruating at the age of twelve. Girls might also fall pregnant just before the appearance of the menarche, without being aware of the impending change, and there was also the possibility of injury, during conception or delivery.

Henry explained their objections: 'If the marriage were concluded we should be obliged to send the Princess directly to Scotland, in which case they fear the King of Scots would not wait, but injure her, and endanger her health.'[6] Although he stated his own doubts, it is clear that Margaret's mother and grandmother were taking the lead in this matter. Margaret Beaufort was speaking from experience, not wishing her granddaughter to replicate the pregnancy and traumatic delivery she had undergone at such a young age. Yet, the Princess was only just past the age of thirteen when a proxy wedding was held between her and James on 15 January 1503 at Richmond Palace. The Earl of Bothwell stood in for James again, wearing a gown of cloth of gold. Celebrations and feasting followed, recorded by the herald, John Young, as including 'right notable jousts'. It may well have been the last public occasion attended by the heavily pregnant Elizabeth before she gave birth two weeks later.

The queen's death in February delayed Margaret's departure for Scotland. Henry retreated to Richmond and the English court went into mourning, dressed in heavy black cloth. As spring edged towards summer, preparations for the wedding began in earnest, with the seamstresses and embroiderers hard at work, orders being sent to the royal wardrobe. Margaret was provided for as befitted a queen, with a trousseau of beautiful clothes and linen, including state bed curtains of Italian sarcenet embroidered with red roses. James also sent his wife a dress worth around £160 and, in May, confirmed her possession of certain lands and estates she had been promised, including the castles of Linlithgow, Methven, Stirling, Newark and Doune. Margaret was to be accompanied by Catherine Gordon, widow of Perkin Warbeck, who had been received into the English court after his capture in 1497 as a lady-in-waiting to Elizabeth of York. Catherine was fifteen years older than Margaret, and only eight years younger than the former queen, so she may have filled a quasi-maternal role for Margaret. It is likely that she entered the Princess's household after the queen's death and this, combined with her Scottish nationality, made her an ideal figure to accompany Margaret to her new life. Also accompanying her were Lady Surrey, Lady Lisle, Lady Stanley, two Lady Nevilles, Lady Jane Guildford, currently the Lady Mistress to Henry VII's daughters, and Elizabeth Denton, her former governess.

Henry accompanied his daughter and her entourage on the first leg of their journey, departing from Richmond on 27 June 1503.

Their destination was Margaret Beaufort's house at Collyweston in Northamptonshire, which had become her main country residence since it came into the hands of her son in 1486. Significant improvements had been made to the property during the fifteenth century, so that it stood around two courtyards, with a presence chamber, great hall, withdrawing room, great tower, long gallery, sizeable chapel, library and bedrooms. In advance of the 1503 visit, Margaret ordered more additions, including new lodgings with bay windows overlooking the extensive estate and gardens. Accounts of the works that May indicate that repairs were undertaken in the chapel, the organ was fixed and a border of angels with images of the Virgin Mary and the Trinity were painted. Margaret recorded that a 'great multitude of lords and other persons'[7] arrived with the King and young bride on 5 July, to spend the next three weeks in residence under Margaret's roof. They were entertained by her choristers, dancers and actors in disguisings, and in the newly completed gardens. On 16 July the royal wedding party also celebrated another wedding in Margaret's private chapel, when her half cousin, Elizabeth Zouche, was married to Gerald Fitzgerald, heir to the Earl of Kildare. Fitzgerald had been hostage in England since his father's support of Lambert Simnel's revolt. This marriage marked his forgiveness. The final farewell ceremony was held in the great hall, at which Margaret only permitted those with a blood tie to the royal family. Henry said goodbye to his daughter and entrusted her to the care of Thomas Howard, Earl of Surrey, who accompanied her to the Scottish border.

On 1 August, Margaret Tudor crossed into Scotland at Berwick-upon-Tweed. The chronicler Richard Grafton describes how she was 'conveyed with a great company of lords, ladies, knights, esquires and gentlemen until she came to Berwick and from there to a village called Lambton Kirk ... where the king with the flower of Scotland was ready to receive her.'[8] However, it appears Margaret did not, in fact, meet her future husband on that occasion. She was welcomed by Richard Blackadder, Archbishop of Glasgow, and a large cohort of the Scottish court dressed in their great chains of office. Margaret passed her first night eighteen miles north along the coast at Fast Castle, and the following day covered twenty-five miles to St Mary's Cistercian nunnery at Haddington, the largest nunnery in Scotland. By the third night, she had travelled a further fourteen miles west and was playing cards in her chamber at Dalkeith Palace when James IV arrived, dressed in red velvet jacket, with a troop of horsemen.[9]

The man Margaret met was thirty years old to her thirteen, described five years before by the Spanish ambassador as 'of noble stature, neither tall nor short, and as handsome in complexion and shape as a man can be. His address is very agreeable ... he never cuts his hair or his beard. It becomes him very well.'[10] Equally, he was a charismatic, cultured man, with a Renaissance education and passion for science and new learning. He founded Scotland's first printing press in 1507, patronised poets, musicians and architects, established an alchemy workshop, funded research into aviation and could speak six languages. In every way, he was a fitting match for the King of England's daughter, and Margaret would not have been disappointed by the warmth of his greeting. She performed a basse dance for him, accompanied by Lady Surrey, to which James replied on his lute. On that occasion, he kissed her goodnight, then returned to comfort her the following day after a stable fire killed some of her horses. She left Dalkeith on 7 August, riding pillion for the seven miles north to Edinburgh at James's side, pausing to witness two noblemen enacting allegorical battles of chivalry.[11]

The poet William Dunbar, one of the Scottish Makars employed at James' court since 1500, wrote in celebration of Margaret's arrival. His short welcome to the new queen in the alliterative tradition, was generic enough in praise and imagery, drawing on the combined imagery of the red and white roses in the Tudor dynastic symbol:

Now fayre, fayrest of every fayre,
Princess most pleasant and preclare, (illustrious)
The lustiest (cheerfullest) one alive that byne: (is)
Welcum of Scotlond to be quene!

Younge tender plant of pulcritud (beauty)
Descendid of imperialle bloode,
Fresche fragrant floure of fayrehede shene: (fairness bright)
Welcum of Scotlond to be quene!

Sweet lusty lusum (lovely) lady clere, (bright)
Most myghty kyng's dochter dere, (daughter dear)
Borne of a princess most serene:
Welcum of Scotlond to be quene!

Welcum the rose bothe rede and whyte,
Welcum the floure of our delyte, (delight)
Oure spreit rejoysyng(spirit rejoicing) frome the sone beme
(sunbeam)
Welcum of Scotlond to be quene!
Welcum of Scotlonde to be quene!

Dunbar's much longer major work about the marriage, *The Thistle and the Rose* mentioned earlier, deliberately references Chaucer's *The Canterbury Tales* and the medieval tradition of dream poetry to praise the couple and their match. Likening Margaret to the red and white Tudor rose, he wrote that no other bloom was so perfect, so full of blissful angelic beauty, imperial birth, honour and dignity. She had come, fresh and young, of royal stock, without a blemish, blown there in joy, of renowned beauty, to be crowned with gems. Margaret's gentle beauty tamed the 'awful thistle' with its bush of spears, symbolic of the warlike Scottish King, and gave it a crown of rubies. In reality, the thirteen-year-old girl would not be able to tame her mature husband, and although their marriage would ultimately be a success, Margaret was homesick and the years ahead would not be easy.

On 8 August Margaret was married to James at Holyrood Abbey, where the service was conducted by the Archbishops of Glasgow and York. According to the Somerset Herald John Young, she was dressed in white and gold damask bordered in crimson velvet, lined with white sarcanet, a collar of precious stones and a crown atop her long, loose hair. James's clothing complimented hers in colour and fabric; a gold and white damask robe, a jacket slashed with crimson satin, a waistcoat of cloth of gold and scarlet hose.[12] The party left for James's new gothic palace of Holyroodhouse, adjoining the Abbey, and although work was still underway at the time of the ceremony, Margaret may have seen the images of the thistle and rose painted on the windows. The chronicler Richard Grafton relates how James 'feasted the English Lords and showed them jousts and other pastimes, very honourably, after the fashion of this rude country'. The twenty dishes began with a wild boar's head.[13] Dancing and games followed, only interrupted when James left to attend evensong. A supper was served afterwards, before all retired for bed and, according to John Young, 'the King led the Queen apart. They went away together.' It is unclear whether the match was consummated that night, as Margaret's relatives had feared, or whether the King waited. The next day, Young recorded that she was 'in good health and merry', although he did not see her in person.[14] Shortly after this, Margaret bade farewell to her English party, including the Duke of Surrey who had conducted her north in the absence of her father, and they departed. The next time Surrey would meet James would be on the battlefield at Flodden.

Margaret certainly did not conceive a child on her wedding night, nor would she do so for almost three years. Her first royal appointment, just two days later, was attending Mass in St Giles in Edinburgh, dressed in a rich gown of cloth of gold, with an altar of images before her and red, blue and green velvet curtains in her closet. After Mass, James made forty-one knights, then took Margaret by her hand and led her to her chamber, where they drank hippocras and were entertained. The next day, after more jousting, she danced with her husband, then appeared 'in great state, enthroned in the bay window' of her Holyrood chamber, with Scottish women around her.[15] It appeared that Margaret's reception in Scotland had been a success, with honour and reverence from her husband, great pomp and prosperity, and the ceremony taking place smoothly. However, all was not as it seemed.

Margaret, even at thirteen, demonstrated her ability to play the royal role with dignity, just as her mother had. The accounts of observers liken her on more than one occasion to Elizabeth of York, yet a letter that she wrote to her father soon afterwards allowed her a rare outlet for her contradictory feelings. The initial portion of the letter, conventional enough in its sentiments, had been dictated to a secretary, but Margaret wrote the final portion in her own hand.

> For God's sake, Sir, hold me excused that I write not myself to your Grace, for I have no leisure at this time; but with a wish I would I were with your grace now, and many times more. And for this that I have written to your Grace, it is very true, but I pray God I may find it well for my welfare hereafter. No more to your Grace at this time, but our Lord have you in his keeping. Written at the hand of your humble daughter.[16]

Margaret's coronation took place the following March, probably at Holyrood Abbey. That spring, she quickly learned that her new home country was volatile, after an uprising of lords in the Western

Isles forced James to head an army to suppress them. By the summer she was at Dunnottar, a highly fortified castle on the north-eastern coast, perhaps chosen as a location to ensure her safety. Through the next two years, James was continually engaged in the defence of his kingdom, on raids, progresses, and attempts to reduce the power of the border clans for their lawless activities. His presence in Edinburgh was ensured, though, by the establishment of his parliament there, consolidating the city as his capital. Margaret appears to have spent considerable time at Holyrood Palace, and it was the location she chose for the deliveries of most of her children. She first fell pregnant in May 1506, at the age of sixteen, and delivered a son, James, the following February, who only survived for a year. Nine months later, she gave birth to a daughter in July 1508, who died soon after birth. She also lost her third child, a son born in October 1509, at the age of nine months. This record, coupled with her homesickness and youth, must have made the early years of Margaret's marriage difficult. The existence of her husband's illegitimate children, who James actively advanced with titles, can only have emphasised her losses. Margaret's contribution to the Tudor dynasty had been achieved in 1503. She had left her homeland and family, to be the dynastic bride of the Treaty of Perpetual Peace, but as a woman, and as the queen of the Stewart royal family, she had yet to fulfil the ultimate achievement of bearing a surviving heir.

*

For the first three years following the death of Arthur, Catherine was officially based at Durham House. This did not prevent her from being a frequent visitor at court, even perhaps something of a favourite with Henry VII, as a substitute companion for the wife and elder daughter he had recently lost. In the summer of 1504, Catherine was invited by the King to stay at Greenwich, which was then in the process of being rebuilt. Afterwards they travelled to Richmond, Princess Mary's favourite residence, from where they took Mary to Windsor, staying 'twelve or thirteen days, going almost every day into the park and the forest to hunt deer and other game'.[17] Next, they returned to Richmond, where they saw Prince Henry, but the King and Catherine left him and Mary behind when they went on to Westminster and then back to Greenwich. While staying there, Catherine fell ill, with the undiagnosed malaise that overshadowed these years. Henry wrote to her father that 'the princess had been unwell for three days, suffering from ague and derangement of the stomach.' She retired to Durham House but was 'rather worse' when she got there, suffering alternately from sweating and chills, losing her appetite completely, developing a cough and her complexion changing 'completely'.[18] By the autumn, Catherine had returned to 'perfect health'. That November, she stayed at Westminster Palace and the attendants were ordered to treat her and the Princess Mary the same.[19]

It was at the end of November, or early in December, that Catherine learned of the death of her mother. Isabella of Castile had been the most powerful queen of the fifteenth century, modelling the sort of regal partnership that Catherine wished to replicate. In August, she had fallen ill from a fever at Medina del Campo, her breathing became difficult and her body began to swell with dropsy. Peter Martyr wrote on 3 October that 'the fever has not yet disappeared and seems to be in her very marrow. Day and night she has an insatiable thirst and loathes food. The deadly tumour is between her skin and her flesh.'[20] She signed her will nine days later. The Queen of Castile, who had forged her own marital and martial destinies, who had fought a crusade on her own territory and who had claimed much of the New World, the mother whose influence shaped the core of Catherine's belief, breathed her last at around noon on 26 November. She was buried in the Alhambra, later being moved into the Chapel Royal that was erected there by her grandson Charles. As a Crusader queen who followed her own path with absolute conviction, her influence upon the nature of female rule in Europe cannot be underestimated.

In June 1505, Prince Henry was approaching his fourteenth birthday, the age of legal majority when her could commit himself to the betrothal which had long been expected between him and Catherine. This would honour the alliance with Spain and allow Catherine, and her financial and diplomatic assets, to remain in England. However, on the eve of his birthday, just as the preparations should have been coming together, the groom repudiated his bride. In the 'eastern portion' of 'one of the lower chambers' of Richmond Palace, Henry made a declaration in front of Richard Foxe, Bishop of Winchester, protesting 'against his marriage with Princess Katharine (sic) of Spain'. As he stated, they had been 'contracted in marriage during his minority' but now that he was 'near the age of puberty' he would not 'ratify the said marriage contract, but, on the contrary, denounce(ed) it as null and void'.[21] As if there was to be any doubt, it was signed by six witnesses and, presumably, endorsed by the King, whose name is conspicuously absent from the paperwork. The declaration took place on 27 June. The following day, Henry celebrated his birthday.

This marked a turning point for Catherine. The King disbanded her household at Durham House and installed her in an out-of-the-way corner of Richmond Palace. Even before this change, though, she was in financial trouble, as she was not receiving enough income to provide her with a basic standard of living, let alone one worthy of her status as dowager Princess of Wales. Back in March, she had complained to de Puebla of 'the misery in which she lives', which will 'reflect dishonour' on Henry's character 'if he should entirely abandon his daughter.' She explained that if she had 'contracted debts for luxuries, the King might have reason not to pay them' but she had been 'forced to borrow, otherwise she would have had nothing to eat.'[22] That September she wrote to her father on behalf of her ladies. Six of them had come with her from Spain and 'have served her right well, without her giving them a single maravadi' and she had nothing to offer them as dowries.[23] By December, she was describing herself as 'destitute' and unable to buy clothing; 'each day her troubles increase' and she had 'lost her health'.[24]

In January 1506, Catherine learned that her sister had arrived in England. Sailing from Burgundy to Spain to claim the throne of Castile, Joanna and her husband Philip encountered a terrible storm which forced their fleet to shelter at Melcombe (now Weymouth) in Dorset. Undoubtedly, Catherine hoped that their presence must encourage Henry to improve her treatment and she was eager to see the brother-in-law she had never met, and the sister from whom she had been parted for years. Philip and Joanna travelled to Windsor separately. Catherine was invited to the castle on the day of Philip's arrival and waited with Princess Mary in an inner chamber, where their guest 'kissed them and communed with them'.[25] Then Catherine entertained her brother-in-law by performing a Spanish dance in national dress, before Princess Mary danced with one of her attendants in the English style. But when Catherine approached Philip and asked him to dance, he first made an excuse, then dismissed her brusquely. Her response was to withdraw quietly and sit with Mary, but neither her father-in-law nor he responded in Catherine's defence. Mary fared better during the encounter, playing the lute and clavichord, so that 'she was of all folks there greatly praised that in her youth in everything she behaved herself so very well.'[26] The implication could be that Catherine, at twice Mary's age, had not behaved herself so well by interrupting Philip and pushing him to dance. It was also a comparison reflective of their differing statuses and levels of sympathy at court.

Catherine had to wait longer to be reunited with her sister. Joanna arrived at Windsor on 10 February and Catherine was invited from Richmond to dine with her. In contrast with the lavish welcome mounted for Philip, Joanna was ushered in by a back door, entering 'secretly... by the backside of the castle unto the king's new tower'. The King was waiting to greet her 'and kissed and embraced her' and in spite of Philip's attempts to keep them apart, Joanna made a favourable impression upon Henry.[27] Then she was brought to Catherine, who would, undoubtedly, have found her much changed. Apart from having borne five children in the last seven years, Joanna's mental health had deteriorated and her relationship with Philip continued to be tempestuous. The sisters had only a little time together, during which they were supervised, before Joanna departed, seemingly of her own volition. She and Philip had quarrelled and while Catherine returned to Richmond, where her brother-in-law was to join them, her sister headed instead for the coast. Catherine was disappointed, writing later of the 'great pleasure it gave me to see you and the great distress which filled my soul, a few hours afterwards, on account of your hasty and sudden departure.'[28] Philip and Joanna left England on 23 April without seeing Catherine again. That September, shortly after having finally reached Castile, Philip died of suspected typhoid fever, although Joanna believed the rumours that he had been deliberately poisoned. The following year, Ferdinand of Aragon forced his daughter to sign over control of Castile, and Joanna spent most of the remainder of her life incarcerated at Tordesillas.

In the early summer of 1507, as Joanna was seeking to raise funds to support her queenship of Castile, a grand tournament was held in memory of her stay in England with Philip. Held at Kennington Manor in Lambeth, it was hosted by Prince Henry, then aged sixteen. Princess Mary took the role of Lady May, dressed in a green gown embroidered with spring flowers, inviting the participants to joust in her honour. In role, and in costume, the eleven-year-old Mary addressed the assembly, placing herself in the hands of the chivalric knights with their noble, courageous hearts. She oversaw proceedings seated in a pavilion decorated with flowers, beside a hawthorn tree in bloom, the emblem used by her father to signify his victory at Bosworth.[29] Queens and royal women had frequently taken symbolic roles during tournaments, as figureheads and inspiration, a nod to an older chivalric cult and the popularity of Arthurian legend, dressed in fine costume and distributing prizes. Under Arthurian and Burgundian influences, Edward IV had reintroduced this type of spectacle, but it was during the reign of Henry VIII that this would really become a complicated art form, and a new way for royal women to contribute. In 1507 Mary fulfilled a position by virtue of her youth, beauty and blood, that Catherine of Aragon would make her own in the years to come.

Later that year, Mary's betrothal to Charles, son of Philip and Joanna, was consolidated in a treaty at Calais. In December, both sides agreed to a joint military and marriage agreement, a martial and marital alliance, the latter being carefully explained in twenty points which allowed for any future disharmony, details of the dowry, jointure, inheritance and possessions. Almost a year later, on 1 December 1508, when Mary was twelve and a half, an Imperial delegation arrived headed by Jean de Sauviage, President of Flanders and Jean III de Glymes, Comte de Berghes, a nobleman from Brabant, who was Emperor Maximilian's Chamberlain. On 17 December, the proxy marriage took place in the great hall at Richmond, which was hung with silk, and where the best of the royal plate was displayed, in a show of the King's wealth. Mary was escorted into the hall by Catherine and a train of ladies, up to a dais covered by a gold canopy. The Comte de Berghes stood as proxy for the eight-year-old Charles, repeating the marriage vows related by the Archbishop of Canterbury and placing a gold ring on Mary's finger, in addition to the gift of a second ring, decorated with diamonds and pearls, engraved with a 'K' for Karolus. Mary impressed all with her 'regal courtesy', her 'noble and truly paternal gravity' and 'splendid royal virtues … like a most wise princess'.[30] Musicians played as the party entered the chapel for Mass, performed by the Bishop of London, and afterwards to the sumptuous feast. Three days of celebrations followed, including a joust that Mary and Catherine watched from a gallery, dancing, more feasting and the presentation of more gifts to Mary, including a large ruby and a diamond brooch.[31] From this point forward, Mary was

Princess of Castile, married but living in a different country to her child-husband, waiting until the time came for her to depart, as her elder sister had.

*

Margaret Beaufort's life as a widow from 1504 was spent devoted to books, charitable works, and her son. Perhaps even more than before, her thoughts were divided between the temporal and spiritual realms, as her increasing devoutness was balanced with concerns about Henry's health. In the year she lost her husband, Margaret was granted a papal licence to visit, debate and dine with religious figures in closed orders, to dispute points of theology and enjoy the peaceful retreat of monastic hospitality. The following year, she paid a pilgrim scholar, perhaps one of her monastic acquaintances, to travel to the Catholic heart of Rome and offer prayers for her. Margaret's intellectual pursuits also reflected her absorption in religious questions. Before Stanley's death, she had translated the fourth book of Thomas a Kempis's *Imitation of Christ*, published by Richard Pynson in 1504. Her next project was a translation into English of the French devotional book *Mirror of Gold for the Sinful Soul*, which she also helped to distribute, buying 100 copies in 1505 and 50 in 1506. Pynson had set up his press in the Inner Temple in 1501 and worked closely with Margaret, publishing her works and many dedicated to her, and becoming official printer to Henry VII in 1506. Margaret had also enjoyed long-standing associations with Oxford and Cambridge, endowing lectureships and professorships of divinity in each and in 1505 investing in one of the smaller Cambridge colleges, then called God's House, which she renamed Christ's. She attended its ceremony of hallowing in 1507.

From 1505, Margaret left Collyweston and lived in properties closer to her son, especially Hatfield, Coldharbour and borrowed houses along the Thames. This allowed her to travel easily by boat to his side, as Henry's health began to fail. The King had been ill for a number of years, suffering from a range of respiratory problems which usually manifested as bad coughs, worsening in the spring. He was 'very ill' at Wanstead in 1503 and the following year at Eltham, before becoming dangerously unwell in October 1507, with what seems to have been tuberculosis. He recovered, only to fall ill again the following February, with his condition being worsened by failing eyesight and gout. During

January and February of 1508, Margaret stayed at Henry's side at Richmond throughout his illness, when it was considered that he was dying. By March, it was necessary to erect temporary lodgings in the palace grounds to house her staff. That July, the Spanish had heard that he was 'in the last stage of consumption' and on 17 August 1508 a report reached Venice via a letter sent to Milan, that he 'was very ill and in extremis'.[32] The King might have been ill but he wasn't quite at death's door at that point, growing stronger through the autumn and spending Christmas at Greenwich and Richmond. On 6 March 1509, when ambassadors arrived from Burgundy, they did not even lay eyes on the King, being welcomed and hosted instead by the seventeen-year-old Prince Henry.[33]

It would appear that Margaret was also suffering from ill health, or some of the ailments associated with ageing. When she died, among the items listed in the inventory of her possessions were pots for medicinal powders kept at her bedside and a number of cramp rings, to which Fisher alluded later as being cures for the stiffness in her joints. These were traditionally made from silver or gold and blessed by the King in a special ceremony on Good Friday. Margaret also had, close by her bed, a small,l gilt, glazed shrine with relics, a little bag containing a heart of relics, and a silver and gilt plate with an image of the salutation of Our Lady. Prayer would have been as powerful a panacea for Margaret in her final years as the powders mixed by her doctors, or the cramp rings she wore.

Henry VII completed his thirty-seven-page will on the last day of March, 1509. Thousands of masses were being sung for him daily and Margaret was made chief executrix. Prince Henry was also at his father's bedside and, no doubt, during this time much passed between the three about the future, including the father urging the son to fulfil the Spanish treaty and marry Catherine of Aragon. Both Margaret and her grandson were present when Henry breathed his last at eleven at night, on 21 April. The death was kept secret for three days, with the business of court continuing as usual, with meals, fuel and linen being brought to the King's chamber, as if Henry was still clinging to life. This allowed for a smooth transition, with Margaret at the helm, before the news was announced after supper to the Knights of the Garter at their annual St George's Day Feast on 23 April and then to the public on 24 April. The funeral was held at St Paul's, with the sermon preached by Margaret's close friend John Fisher, Bishop of Rochester. Catherine and Mary were among the mourners riding in procession through the streets, having been granted an allowance of black cloth for mantles and kerchiefs, as well as payments for saddlery. Chief place in precedence was given to Margaret. She would live long enough to witness the handover of power, before she too died, at Elizabeth Woodville's former home of Cheneygates house, in the Westminster precincts, on 29 June.

Margaret's body was moved to the Abbey's refectory on 3 July, where candle-lit vigils were held, and masses were said for her soul. She was laid to rest in her son's Lady Chapel and, like his, her golden effigy was designed by Pietro Torrigiano, adorned with Beaufort and Tudor symbols, depicting her in her widow's weeds, with a hood and mantle, with her head resting on two pillows. Also carved on her tomb were the arms of Henry VIII and Catherine, as the new rulers and hopefully, the continuers of her bloodline. The inscription on the tomb, written by the Humanist scholar Erasmus, reads:

> Margaret of Richmond, mother of Henry VII, grandmother of Henry VIII, who gave a salary to three monks of this convent and founded a grammar school at Wimborne, and to a preacher throughout England, and to two interpreters of Scripture, one at Oxford, the other at Cambridge, where she likewise founded two colleges, one to Christ, and the other to St John, his disciple. Died A.D. 1509, III Kalends of June 29.

Margaret's chaplain, Bishop John Fisher, delivered a laudatory sermon which has helped to shape a sense of the King's mother's character for later historians. He compared her to the biblical Martha in four senses: in their nobleness of person, in the disciplining of their bodies, in the ordering of their souls to God and in the keeping of hospitals and giving charity to their neighbours. Fisher praised Margaret as 'bounteous and liberal to every person of her knowledge and acquaintance' and loathing 'avarice and covetousness'. He gave further descriptions of her character:

> She was also of syngular Easyness to be spoken unto, and full curtayse answere she would make to all that came unto her. Of mervayllous gentylenesse she was unto all folks, but specially unto her owne whom she trusted and loved ryghte tenderly. Unkynde

she wolde not be unto no creature, ne forgetfull of any kindness or service done to her before, which is no lytel part of veray nobleness. She was not venegable ne cruell but ready anone to forgete and to forgyve injuryes done unto her, at the leest desire or mocyon ... mercyfull also and pyteous she was unto such as were grevyed and wrongfully troubled and to them that were in poverty, or sekeness or any other mysery.[34]

According to Fisher, Margaret also wore a hair shirt beneath her clothing, made according to the traditional Catholic method of animal hair or coarse sackcloth, sometimes woven with twigs or thin wire to mortify the skin as a means of penance and repentance: 'As to harde clothes wearyne, she had her shertes and grydyls of here, which when she was in helthe, everi week she fayled not certain days to weare, sometimes the one, sometimes the other, that full often her skynne, as I heerd her say, was perced therewith.'[35]

Fisher also praised the organisation of her household, which was run 'with mervaylous dylygence and wysedom', writing ordinances quarterly to be read aloud by her officers, whom she would 'lovingly' encourage to do well, although she was prepared to deal with any dissent or factions within her house 'with great discretion'. She was a thoughtful and sensitive hostess:

> ...what payn, what labour, she of her veray gentleness wolde take with them, to bere them maner and Company and intrete every person, and entertayne them, according to their degree and haviour [behaviour] and provyde, by her own commandment, that nothynge sholde lack that might be convenient for them, wherein she had a wonderful redy remembraunce and perfyte knowledge.[36]

She took care of those suitors and the poor who came to petition her for justice and help:

> ...of her own charges provyded men lerned for the same purpose, evenly and indyfferently to here all causes and admynyster right and justyce to every party, which were in no small nombre and yet mete and drynke was denyed to none of them ... Poore folks to the nombre of twelve she dayly and nyghtly kepte in her House, gyvynge them lodginge, mete and drynke and clothynge ... and in their

sykenesse visytyng them and comfortynge them and mynystrynge unto them with her owne hands: and when it pleased God to call ony of them out of this wretched worlde, she wolde be present, to see them departe ... Suppose not ye, that yf she myghte have gotten our Savyour Jhesu in his owne Persone, but she wolde as desyrously and as fervently have mynystered unto hym?[37]

In spite of such glowing reports from her contemporaries, Margaret's reputation among later writers has been mixed. Poet and tutor to Henry VIII, Bernard André, described her as 'steadfast and more stable than the weakness in women suggests', which springs straight from contemporary gender perceptions but allows Margaret to be strong and constant as an exception to the stereotype. She was only allowed to be a strong woman by the admission that she had transcended expectations of her gender. Her nineteenth-century biographer Charles Henry Cooper[38] saw her as 'the brightest example of the strong devotional feeling and active charity of the age in which she lived', who 'stepped widely ... out of the usual sphere of her sex to encourage literature by her patronage and her bounty' and was 'united to the strictest piety the practice of all the moral virtues and ... chastened, while she properly cherished, the grandeur of royalty by the indulgence of domestic affections and the retired exercise of a mind at once philosophic and humble'. Cooper's contemporary Caroline Amelia Halsted[39] echoed his view of Margaret as a role model to whom 'the females of Britain look with duty and affection, with pride as women, with devotion as subjects', considering her the 'brightest ornament of her sex'. By contrast, David Starkey's assessment typifies a more critical modern reaction to Margaret's talents, referring to her as imperious and tight-fisted.[40] As Helen M. Jewell summarises, Margaret's most recent biographers have taken a 'shrewder perspective, crediting her with a calculating temperament and natural astuteness, a veteran of bruising political battles' whose life and work show 'a constant blend of the practical and the pious, which argues at least an active and disciplined will.'[41] Margaret was a dynamic and influential figure, who had a unique influence upon the Tudor dynasty, creating, shaping and supporting it from its earliest inception.

Margaret Beaufort's contribution to the Tudor dynasty is without parallel. In the second half of the fifteenth century, she *was* the Tudor dynasty. She bore the first Tudor king and continued to promote his claim to the throne through decades of uncertainty, even when to do so threatened her position and freedom. What separates her example from those set by Elizabeth Woodville and Elizabeth of York, and later, Margaret and Mary Tudor and Catherine of Aragon, is the different way she deployed her gender, applying it flexibly to avoid danger and to breach cultural stereotypes. She was enabled to do so by her male protectors and as her circumstances and wealth dictated. Thus, in the years before 1485, Margaret was industrious and proactive in political circles in ways that were usually considered masculine, constantly pushing her son's advancement whenever she could, generating meetings and seeking alliances. Often these were secret from necessity, as they were in opposition to the throne or the rising power. On the occasions when she was discovered, she sought refuge in her gender, by retreating behind the legal protection of her husbands, to whom her enemies entrusted her restraint. As a woman, she was shielded from the worst excesses of punishment, and she may well have played upon the 'misguided woman' trope to her own advantage, compliantly submitting in public to the husbands she knew would continue to facilitate her activities.

After 1485, her commitment to the dynasty could be more overt, through the organisational capacity demonstrated in her many, detailed ordinances, in her patronage of and engagement in intellectual and theological debate. Her position as the King's mother allowed her licence to transcend gendered expectations and enter more masculine realms of the royal Council and the universities. And it is in this gender distinction that the success of her relations with Henry and Elizabeth of York can be understood. Margaret took on both roles of mother and father to Henry, while her identification with what were considered more masculine spheres allowed Elizabeth of York to fulfil the feminine role in which she excelled. Instead of rivals or combatants, this made them perfectly complimentary. Between them, they carried the Tudor dynasty successfully through its first generation.

PART THREE

The Glittering Court
1509–1525

11

New Wives

1509–15

The year 1509 marked a new direction for the Tudor dynasty. The smooth succession of Henry VIII distanced the family further from the York-Lancaster turmoil, and England's peace and prosperity allowed for cultural change. And change was certainly coming; aesthetically, theologically, intellectually and in terms of gender roles and expectations.

While ambassadors and poets were describing the new King as a 'perfect model of manly beauty', that June saw the publication of Luca Pacioli's *Divina Proportione*, with illustrations by da Vinci, exploring the golden ratio, and proportions of the perfect human in relation to architecture. The same year, English copies appeared of Alexander Barclay's *Ship of Fools of the World* and Henry Watson's *Ship of Fools*, two translations of Sebastian Brant's 1494 allegorical satire inspired by Plato's ship manned by a dysfunctional crew. It had long been part of the English carnival tradition to mock those in power, but these works combined medieval humour with a new Renaissance questioning of established roles. A little more critical but using a similar trope, whilst staying for a week in August with Thomas More and his family, Erasmus wrote *In Praise of Folly*, an attack upon Catholic superstitions and wealth. The Dutch immigrant, Wynkyn de Worde, owner of a printing press in Fleet Street, published a translation of Antoine de Sale's *The Fyftene Joyes of Maryage*, perhaps in celebration of the new King's nuptials. A newly ordained priest named Martin Luther received his second degree in theology from Wittenberg University, while a young William Tyndale was studying for his degree at Oxford's Magdalen Hall (later Hertford College) and, on 10 July, the future reformer, John Calvin, was born at Noyon in France. In 1510 Levinia Teerlinc was born to the Bruges-based Bening family of artists, who would one day portray the court of Elizabeth I.

Across Europe, there was great disparity between the experiences of women in power, some of whom were taking on unprecedented roles whilst others were unable to exercise their inheritances. In 1509, their lives exposed the difficulties women faced in balancing the dual nature of their positions, contrasting public and private, leadership and motherhood. In France, Anne, Duchess of Brittany, had become queen for a second time upon marrying her dead husband's cousin. She had endured at least sixteen pregnancies in twenty years but produced only two surviving daughters, complicating the succession. Waiting in the wings, Louise of Savoy was named as regent of France with Anne, in the eventuality of the King's death and the succession of her son, Francis. Louise had raised her two children since being widowed at the age of 19, arranging an Italian humanist education and commissioning books for them. In 1509, her seventeen-year-old daughter Marguerite, future author of the *Heptameron*, was married to Charles Duke of Alençon. That August, Lucrezia Borgia gave birth to her fifth child, Ippolito d'Este, future Cardinal and creator of the Villa d'Este in Tivoli. She would bear nine children in ten years and die from complications arising from her final confinement. Powerful women fared better in the Netherlands, where the Assembly of Franche-Comte confirmed the election of its first female ruler, Margaret of Austria. Margaret had already been made Governor of the Netherlands in 1507 and helped negotiate the trade agreements of the League of Cambrai in 1508. However, Margaret's former sister-in-law, Joanna of Castile, was still incarcerated in the Spanish castle of Tordesillas, after her father had taken power out of her hands and sent away her household, leaving her with only a staff accountable to him. Some women's circumstances allowed them to help define and exercise power, whilst others were stripped of it. As the next generation of Tudor women would discover, this depended largely upon the facilitation of their close male relations.

*

The change of king yielded unexpected rewards for Catherine of Aragon. Learning of Henry VII's death, her Spanish ambassador had advised her to start packing her effects in order to return home.

However, perhaps out of a final promise to his father, or personal inclination, or a sense of chivalric duty, Henry VIII decided to make Catherine his wife. The marriage took place at Greenwich on 11 June, overseen by the Archbishop of Canterbury, William Warham. Two weeks later, they were jointly crowned at Westminster amid symbolic pageantry and pomp. On around 4pm on the afternoon of Saturday, 23 June, Catherine and Henry left the Tower of London for the coronation procession to the Abbey. The streets were railed and barred, hung with tapestries and cloth of Arras, even with cloth of gold along Cornhill and Cheapside. Henry rode before Catherine on a horse draped in damask gold, under a canopy of gold, dressed in a crimson velvet robe edged in ermine, a placard studded with gems, a jacket of raised gold and a necklace of rubies. He was 'much more handsome than any other sovereign in Christendom' and 'most invincible', with such qualities that the Venetian ambassador considered him to 'excel all who ever wore a crown', making the country 'blessed and happy (in) having as its lord so worthy and eminent a sovereign'.[1] The queen's retinue came next, with 'lords, knights, esquires and gentle menne in their degrees, well mounted and richly apparelled in tissues, cloth of gold, of silver, tinsels and velvets, embroidered, fresh and goodly to behold'.[2] A total of £1,536 16s 2d had been spent on preparations for Catherine's coronation, only a little less than the £1,749 8s 4d required by the King for the same ceremony.[3]

Catherine was borne through the streets in a litter drawn by two white palfreys trapped in cloth of gold. She was dressed in white embroidered satin, with a 'rich mantle of cloth of tissue',[4] her red-gold hair loose 'hangyng donne to her backe, of a very great length, bewtefull and goodly to behold' and a coronet set on her head, made from 'rich orient stones'.[5] From the Tower, they rode west, but as Catherine passed the well-known tavern called The Cardinal's Hat in Gracechurch Street, a sudden summer shower almost destroyed the silken canopy over her litter and sent her hurrying for cover under the awning of a draper's stall. Once the rain had cleared, they pressed on into Cheapside, where representatives of all the guilds had gathered, along with the mayor and aldermen and virgins in white carrying white wax tapers, and out of the city gate towards the distant towers of Westminster Abbey.

At eight in the morning on Midsummer's Day, Henry and Catherine were dressed in crimson robes and took their place in the long procession from the Palace to the Abbey along a striped ray cloth strewn with flowers. Two empty thrones awaited them inside, elevated on a platform before the altar. Henry swore his coronation oath first and was anointed by Archbishop Warham, before the crown of Edward the Confessor was lowered onto his head. Catherine's ceremony was shorter, and her crown was lighter, being a golden coronet set with rubies, pearls and sapphires.[6] She was anointed on the head and chest and given a ring to wear on the fourth finger of her right hand, a sort of inversion of the marital ring, as a mark of her marriage to her country. A contemporary woodcut depicts them seated side by side, looking into each other's eyes and smiling as the crowns were lowered onto their heads, a poignant image of the moment, suggestive of a couple in love, as equals, embarking on a journey together. Above Henry's head was a huge Tudor rose, a reminder of his heritage and England's recent conflicts while Catherine's image was topped by her chosen device of the pomegranate, symbolic of the expectations of all Tudor wives and queens in the model of Elizabeth of York: fertility and childbirth.

Feasting followed, and the ensuing days were devoted to tournaments and jousts. Catherine was immediately thrown into a symbolic role of queenship and womanhood, as the presiding figure over the ceremonies, and its focus. She was placed inside a 'faire house', covered with tapestries and hung with rich cloth, outside of which a castle was erected over a fountain topped with a royal crown, alluding to the heraldic device of Castile, the battlements covered with gilded roses and pomegranates and the castle wound about by a vine with golden leaves and grapes. The sides of the castle were painted in white and green lozenges, each featuring a different image; a rose, pomegranate, sheaf of arrows, an H or a K for Kateryn. Here, the champions and challengers came to address her, explaining they had 'come to do feats of arms for the love of ladies'. their leader, Cupid, presented Catherine with his spear and asked her permission for their tournament to proceed.[7] The following day, 28 June, was Henry's eighteenth birthday. More celebrations followed, including a pageant during which Catherine was asked to give permission for the hunters to accept a challenge, but Catherine passed the question to Henry, who gave his permission. The question of permission, even in the context of such highly stylized and allegorical play, would underpin Catherine's world, and that of her successor, Anne Boleyn. Although the pageant honoured Catherine, and placed the granting of permission in her hands, this was little more than a convention. No one expected her to refuse to grant it, and her return of power to Henry on his birthday was symbolic of her understanding that she only had it in the first place by his assent.

These coronation celebrations established a pattern of deference and symbolism towards Catherine as queen that was to persist for the next two decades. In the elaborate play of court ritual, she was the chivalric focus of male aspiration, the earthly personification of inspiration, whose favour was always the central part of any regal event. The extent of her involvement was limited. She was an observer rather than a participant, the presiding goddess over the arena of masculine strength and violence and, by implication, the figure with authority over life and death, at the feet of whom offerings were made. This tells us much about concepts of queenship in 1509. In one sense, Catherine was still something of a medieval icon, harking back to troubadour stories of courtly love, symbolic as a figurehead almost in the way that the statues of the Virgin Mary were the passive recipients of prayers and offerings at shrines across the nation. Henry would soon adopt the name 'Sir Loyal Heart' in the lists, declaring his devotion to his wife and leading the way for the worship of Catherine by his courtiers. The presence of Catherine was sufficient, dressed in velvets, gold cloth and jewels, just as she had been the passive audience to the pageants of her first wedding day; she was metonymic for queenship, for loyalty, for England. In this way, it was an impersonal, distant sort of queenship, similar to that pursued by Elizabeth Woodville and his mother, Elizabeth of York. But Catherine was to break this model. She would not be content to be the silent beauty at her husband's side, worshipped for her femininity and royal blood. She was an educated humanist princess, a scholar who had read the classics, who had grown up at a court that prioritised Renaissance debates, an expert in canon law and soon to prove herself a warrior queen, like her mother. She was not a woman to keep her mouth shut when it came to matters of state or to accept such a passive, ceremonial role for long. Catherine understood the importance of ceremony and accepted the deference of the knights as her due; but after the long years of waiting, she was to fully and actively embrace her role as queen.

What remained for Catherine to achieve was the fulfilment of her maternal role. She conceived quickly, perhaps even on her wedding night, or soon after, and the court expected her to be confined in March. Her second trimester had begun when news arrived from Scotland that Margaret had been delivered of a boy. She had experienced poor health after former confinements, and had undertaken pilgrimages upon her recovery, so was relieved when Arthur Stewart had arrived at Holyrood on 20 October. Margaret named him after his dead uncle, as a reminder of his connection to the English throne, and she requested the goods bequested to her in Prince Arthur's will, although these were not sent. No doubt Catherine was encouraged by the birth of a boy to the Scottish Queen, and hopeful of emulating her achievement. On November 26, Henry issued a warrant to the Great Wardrobe on behalf of 'our most dear wife the queen' to send to her at Greenwich 'these parcels' containing eight fine pillows.[8] Catherine had chosen this favourite location as the place of her lying-in and her apartments there were prepared according to the guidelines set down by Margaret Beaufort in 1486.

At the end of January, when Catherine would have been around seven months pregnant, she felt a little ache in one knee, which seemed innocuous enough, but the following day she went into premature labour. The pain was so intense that she made a vow to make an offering of a rich headdress she owned to the shrine of St Peter the Martyr of the Franciscan Order, but she miscarried her child, which appears to have been a daughter. However, her swollen stomach convinced her doctor that she was still bearing the surviving twin of a double pregnancy, and that she could carry this second child to term. As March progressed, there was no sign that her labour was beginning. April arrived and Catherine may have assumed her baby was late, praying for the onset of delivery and taking herbal remedies to trigger contractions. Still, no baby came, and by May, she was probably confused and ashamed, embarrassed about the misdiagnosis and having to return to court without having produced the expected child.

Whilst awaiting a birth that never happened, in May 1510 Catherine conceived again. Her pregnancy was straightforward and she delivered a son, Prince Henry, on 1 January 1511. For a time, euphoria reigned at the English and Scottish courts, in response to the arrivals of two male heirs, two future cousin-kings, Henry and Arthur, who could rule in peace. It was the ultimate achievement of a Tudor queen, to secure the continuation of the dynastic line, as Elizabeth of York had done. Yet issues of still-birth and infant mortality were to plague the second Tudor generation in a way that has never been fully explained by science. Perhaps it was a particular gene, an inherited problem like McLeod syndrome,[9] or environmental conditions that affected the siblings' ability to father, or bear, children that survived beyond infancy. Margaret lost Arthur in July 1510, and Catherine lost Henry in February 1511. Both mothers were reported by contemporaries to be distraught as a result. Margaret would have three more pregnancies, resulting in one surviving son, James, whilst Catherine experienced three more stillbirths or short-lived children, and produced one daughter, Mary.

*

Early in 1512, a comet appeared in the skies above Scotland. Visible for twenty-one days, it reputedly cast beams like the sun. Ancient superstitions still lingered that natural phenomena like this were omens, or harbingers of doom, and the strength and duration of this comet instilled fear into Margaret and James. They may have recalled the 'great erd quak'[10] that had hit Scotland less than three years before, in September 1509, and related this to the losses of their three children so far. Such connections were commonly made at the time, interpreting divine commentary upon personal decisions and events, as individuals sought clarity for circumstances science had yet to explain.

Margaret's response was to undertake a pilgrimage to the shrine of St Duthac, an eleventh-century Scottish holy man. Situated almost two hundred miles north of Edinburgh, his shrine at Tain was an important national site of pilgrimage, attracting visitors to pray and ask for intercession at the repository of the saint's relics. James had been a frequent visitor, making the journey at least once a year throughout his reign, although the residence of one of his mistresses nearby may also have provided motivation. Margaret would have prayed, and possibly touched, his bones, shirt and bell, in the hope that his healing powers would have blessed her and assisted her fertility. She took her time over the journey, setting out from Dunfermline on 1 May and returning to Edinburgh on 20 July.[11]

Anglo-Scots relations had been warm since Margaret's marriage. In 1508, Henry VII had sent a gift of horses to James, which were presented to him on 1 October, and James reciprocated by sending him

Scottish horses in return, to 'maintain' and 'nourish' the love between the two, 'as between the father and the son'.[12] Upon the succession of Henry VIII, James sent an embassy to London to congratulate him and confirm the Treaty of Perpetual Peace. Then, in June 1512, Edmund and Thomas Howard, sons of the Earl of Surrey, attacked a Portuguese ship that sought shelter in a Scottish harbour. The incident sparked angry letters between James and Henry, with the Scots King seeking redress for the deaths and destruction incurred, and Henry replying that because the ship concerned had carried pirates, it was not a breach of the peace between the two nations. The Scottish historian, John Lesley, writing in the 1570s, described this as 'the first motion of the great troubles' that unfolded between the two countries, which he explained as arising because 'King Henry the eighth of England, being a young man left by his father with great wealth and riches was very desirous to have wars wherein he might exercise his youth.'[13]

It was international developments and allegiances that ultimately undermined the Anglo-Scots peace. Henry had joined the Catholic League, sworn to defend Italy and the Pope from invasion by the French, whilst James was committed to the Auld Alliance of Scotland and France. Encouraged by his father-in-law, Ferdinand of Aragon, and the Pope, Henry sought the French throne if Louis XII could be defeated and was also promised the title of 'Most Christian King of France' by Pope Julius II. James despatched an ambassador to the English court, desiring Henry, in a 'brotherly and loving manner,' to 'live in peace and quietness' and not to invade his allies, 'being tender as they were in blood and friendship to him' and offering to be negotiator between them.[14] An English ambassador, Dr West, arrived at the border, hoping to convene talks to redress all controversies between the two countries but, as Lesley recorded, no redress was made.[15] Margaret received him, despite being ill, gave him tokens for her brother, Catherine, and Princess Mary, and composed a letter for Dr West to carry back to Henry, pleading the Scottish case:

> Right excellent, right high and mighty Prince, our dearest and best beloved brother.
>
> We commend us unto you in our most heartly wise. Your ambassador, Dr West, delivered us, your most loving letters, in which ye show us that, when ye heard of our sickness, ye took great heaviness.

Dearest brother, we are greatly rejoiced that we see ye have respect to our disease; we give ye our hearty thanks, and your writing is to us a good comfort.

We can not believe that of your mind, or by your command, we are so unfriendly dealt with in our Father's legacy, whereof we would not have spoken or written, had not the doctor spoken to us of the same in his credence. Our husband knows it is withholden for his sake, and will recompense us so far as the Doctor shows him. We are ashamed therewith and would God never word had been thereof. It is not worth such estimation as is in your divers letters of the same. And we lack nothing: our husband is ever the longer the better to us, as knows God; who, right high and mighty prince, our dearest and best beloved brother, have you in governance,

Given under our signet, at our palace of Linlithgow, the 9th day of April.[16]

Initially, the response was positive. Henry wrote to James asking for the return of certain items 'pertaining to a prince' which Prince Arthur had left to Margaret in 1502, and promising upon his return to make James 'Duke of York and Governor of England to my homecoming', as he had no son yet of his own, 'for heirs of England must come either of him or me, and I have none yet lawfully.' At this point, Henry foresaw the potential joint alliance of England and Scotland, arising from his sister's marriage, adding 'but I hear say that Margaret, my sister, hath a pretty boy, likely to grow a man of estimation. I pray God to bless him and keep him from his enemies and give me grace to see him in honour when he cometh of age that I may entertain him according to my honour and duty.'[17] However, Henry had no intention of abandoning his plans to invade France.

*

On 11 June, Henry appointed Catherine 'Regent and Governess of England, Wales and Ireland during the King's absence in his expedition against France, for the preservation of the Catholic religion and recovery of his rights'. Although she would still be supervised by the Council, headed by Archbishop Warham, she was given 'power to issue commissions of muster', to give assent to Church elections, to 'appoint sheriffs, to issue warrants under her sign manual' and other powers. John Heron, Treasurer of the Chamber, was instructed to pay 'any sums of money ordered by the Queen ... to whatever persons she may appoint for defence of the kingdom'. Her servants were exempted from service in order for her to be 'suitably attended' with her chamberlain and chancellor both being mentioned,[18] which was especially important as she was by now four months pregnant. Catherine had the seasoned veteran, Thomas Howard, Earl of Surrey, who had fought at Bosworth and quashed rebellions in the north, in the event of any invasion or rebellion. She also approached the Venetian Ambassador in the hope of hiring Italian ships for the purpose, being 'very warm in favour of this expedition... (and) would fain to have four large galleasses and two bastard galleys from the Signory, and enquired of him the monthly cost of a galley afloat'.[19]

On 15 June, Catherine left Greenwich with Henry at the head of a train of 600 guards dressed in liveries of white and green with silver spangles and embroidery.[20] They made a slow procession through Kent, reaching Canterbury five days later, where they stayed in the royal forest of Blean, on a hill overlooking the city, before heading down to make their offerings at the Cathedral's shrine of St Thomas Becket, where Catherine was presented with a cup of silver and gilt. Five days later, on Henry's twenty-second birthday, they arrived at Dover Castle, set high on a windswept hill overlooking the Channel. Henry sailed the following morning and Catherine returned to the capital. When news of his departure reached Scotland, James dispatched his ships, the *Margaret*, the *James*, the *Great St Michael* and a fleet of smaller vessels, full of supplies, in support of Louis XII. He also sent a messenger to meet Henry at Thérouanne to announce that Scotland had declared war on England.

Young and keen for glory, Henry invaded France on 30 June 1513, defeating the French at the Battle of the Spurs and taking Thérouanne and Tournai. In his absence, urged on by Louis, who sent ships full of artillery, powder and wine, James reluctantly prepared to invade England. The King of Denmark also sent supplies across the North Sea to fund his campaign, and the Irish pledged their support. For Margaret in Scotland, seeing the planned invasion of her home country, and her husband pitted against her brother, her status as a native Englishwoman put her in an uncomfortable position. She also fell pregnant again, conceiving in July, as James was preparing his ships, including the *Margaret*. It was on 13 August, while Henry was still in France, that Scotland declared war on England.

Catherine put the country on alert, writing to Henry's almoner, Thomas Wolsey, that she was 'very glad to be busy with the Scots, for they take it for pastime. My heart is very good to it ... and I am horribly busy with making standards, banners, and badges.'[21] She met with her Council to discuss England's defences and the plan to repel the Scots, as part of which levies were imposed and sanctions threatened against anyone who disobeyed. In addition, all Scots men living in England were to be deemed enemies, but those married to Englishwomen might remain at the cost of half their possessions; all others were to 'have their goods seized and their persons banished, under penalty of their lives'. For good measure, all French people living near the coast were thrown into prison.[22] On 2 September Catherine wrote to Wolsey from Richmond Palace that she was sending the Duc de Longueville to the Tower for now, 'especially the Scots being so busy as they now be, and I am looking for my departing every hour.' Mindful of the paraphernalia of war that her mother had employed, she requested the Great Wardrobe to release certain banners and standards, including those bearing the arms of England and Spain, the lion, the cross imperial and the cross of St George.[23]

The mood between the Scottish King and Queen was less positive. Margaret's nineteenth-century biographer, Agnes Strickland, suggests that Margaret attempted to persuade James not to fight by exploiting his superstitious nature and relating nightmares as omens, or employing supposed prophetic figures to warn him of impending doom. Consistently unsympathetic to her subject, Strickland claims that arguments had taken place between the two due to the appeals made to James by Anne, Queen of France, who had sent him a ring in thanks for his support, and that Margaret had allied herself with the controversial Douglas clan out of jealousy of James's mistress, Janet Kennedy, who bore him three children. Whether or not the details of this are true, it may be indicative of Margaret's superstitious nature, inherited from her grandmother, and her attempts to use the only channels available to her to prevent her husband and brother from going to war: personal ones. Such disagreements were superficial though, as James drew up his will naming Margaret as executrix to their son, so long as she remained a widow, and passing his French endowment and various valuables on to the boy. In the last week of August, Margaret said farewell to her husband for the last time. She was also newly pregnant.

On 3 September Catherine learned that the Scots had already crossed the border and captured Norham Castle, the property of Thomas Ruthal, Bishop of Durham, who was absent in France as Henry's secretary. Surrey's troops, including his sons Edmund and Thomas, were ready and waiting at Newcastle; in the Earl's absence, as a Marshal of England, Catherine gave a commission of array to Thomas Lovell to raise troops in the Midlands and to hear the legal cases of murder, treason and other crimes committed during this period.[24] Catherine travelled north from Richmond Palace to Buckinghamshire and it is likely that this was where she addressed assembled troops, much as her mother had used to, 'making a splendid oration to the English captains' reminding them that 'the Lord smiled upon those who stood in defence of their own' and that 'English courage excelled that of all other nations.'[25] She certainly looked the part, as the royal goldsmith, Robert Amadas, was paid for 'garnishing a head piece with a golden crown'.[26] It was not quite thirty years since Bosworth, and Catherine had only been England's queen for four, but she intended to defend the Tudor dynasty with everything she had.

The armies clashed near the village of Branxton in Northumberland on 9 September, with the Scots and their considerable artillery meeting the vanguard led by Surrey, his Howard sons, Lord Darcy and Edward Stanley, Margaret Beaufort's stepson. The fighting was fierce but noble, with James refusing to fire his guns at the English whilst they were in a vulnerable position. The Scottish ambassador, Andrew Brounhill, also identified critical differences in technique between the two sides, the English generals remaining behind the lines in the new Renaissance style of warfare, while the Scots deployed their leaders, including their King, on the front line as was common in medieval combat. Though Thomas Howard appears to have fought on foot right at the front of the English lines, beside his father, so that James was able to get within a spear's length of them. The English bill, a polearm with a hooked blade, proved more successful than the Scottish pike in reach and impact.

Catherine was at Woburn Abbey in Bedfordshire, when the Red Cross herald, Thomas Hawley, brought her the 'rent surcoat of the King of Scots stained with blood'. She wrote to Henry from there on 16 September, sending the bloodstained coat, although she refrained from allowing James's body to accompany it, as 'Englishmen's hearts would not suffer it:'

> My Lord Howard hath sent me a letter, open, to your Grace, within one of mine, by the which ye shall see at length the great victory that our Lord hath sent your subjects in your absence. Thinks the victory the greatest honor that could be. The King will not forget to thank God for it. Could not, for haste, send by Rouge Cross 'the piece of the King of Scots coat which John Glyn now bringeth. In this your Grace shall see how I can keep my promise, sending you for your banners a King's coat. I thought to send himself unto you, but our Englishmen's hearts would not suffer it. It should have been better for him to have been in peace than have this reward. All that God sendeth is for the best. Surrey wishes to know the King's pleasure as to burying the King of Scots' body. Prays for his return; and for the same is going to our Lady at Walsingham, that I promised so long ago to see.[27]

To give thanks for the victory, Catherine travelled a hundred miles from Woburn Abbey to the north Norfolk town of Walsingham. She arrived on 23 September. Shortly after this time, it is possible that she miscarried. The child she had been reported to be carrying earlier that summer is mentioned no more in the records. When Henry returned to England at the end of October, he headed to Richmond to be reunited with his wife. Their meeting was 'so loving' that the bystanders 'rejoiced' to see it.[28] Flodden was a great personal victory for Catherine. Although Surrey had won the battle, in her husband's absence she had steered the country through a crisis, taking over practical arrangements and making critical decisions, acting to preserve the Tudor dynasty.

The news was brought to Margaret at Linlithgow Palace. Her role as queen was over, but her important new position of guarding over her eighteen-month-old son, the heir to both the Scottish and English thrones, was just beginning. Parliament met on 19 September at Stirling, to establish a General Council to rule in the names of Margaret and the new James V. Margaret hurried to her son, who was at Perth, and wrote to her brother, imploring him not to injure 'her little king' who was so 'very small and tender'.[29] Instead of injuring him, Henry considered taking control of the child, instructing Lord Dacre to inform Margaret of his plans:

The Queen of Scots, being ordered by the King's highness, may the rather cause the said young King to be also ordered and ruled by the King's grace, and his grace to set such protectors and rulers as he shall think good.' The 'said Lord Dacres' shall endeavour what he can to have the young King of Scots placed in the hands of the King of England, who is his natural guardian. In the above Dacres shall be careful to give the Scots no reason to remove the young King into any out isles or other parts, where he shall be in further danger and more difficult for the King to attain. Is to inform the Lord Chamberlain that the Queen of England, for the love she bears to the Queen of Scots, would gladly send a servant to comfort her.[30]

Such unwelcome sentiments may have prompted the rapid coronation of young James in Stirling's Chapel Royal on 21 September. The regency was granted to Margaret, with the assistance of a group of leading nobles: James Beaton, Archbishop of Glasgow, and the Earls of Arran, Angus and Huntley, with Stirling appointed as their main residence. Catherine also spared time to think of her sister-in-law, sending a Friar Langley north to comfort her in her hour of need.[31] Margaret replied on 11 November, thanking Catherine 'for her sympathy in the misfortune fallen upon her', following the arrival of the friar, and hoping that Catherine would 'keep her brother in remembrance of her, that his kindness may be known.'[32]

The following April, Margaret gave birth to a posthumous son, Alexander, who would live for eighteen months. In July 1514, she managed to repel calls for her to be replaced by John Stewart, Duke of Albany, who represented the pro-French alliance, and to make peace with England. However, her position was still precarious. As queen dowager, the sister of an enemy king, and as a young woman of twenty-four, she faced the long-standing allegiances of the Scottish nobility and the division between the English and French factions. Then Margaret made the extraordinary, life-changing decision that would bring her regency to a close, divide her from her children, and turn the majority of her former allies against her. Remarkably, for a queen, she chose to marry for love.

12

Widows

1513–1515

In 1514 and 1515, both Tudor princesses, Margaret and her younger sister, Mary, broke the rules by marrying for love. Without seeking advice or approval, they each selected what their contemporaries considered an unsuitable husband and became his wife in secret. There were precedents of kings doing this, specifically their grandfather, Edward IV, but it was unprecedented for princesses of their stature. Service must come before passion, especially for women who had to tread carefully when it came to the paternity of heirs and inheritance. Margaret and Mary had been raised with one aim: to make a successful international alliance, to leave their home country to become the wife of a stranger and to do their duty, all for the glory of their dynasty. Their education and childhoods, their activities and public appearances, the reception of ambassadors, the completion of treaties, betrothals, letters, proxy weddings, vows, titles and gifts, had defined their identities from their earliest years as foreign brides. And at first, they complied. Margaret became Queen of Scotland upon marrying James IV, a man old enough to be her father, and when Mary's long-standing alliance with Prince Charles of Burgundy was rejected by her brother in 1514, she went ahead and married Louis XII of France when she was eighteen and he was fifty-two. However, when both were widowed young, they considered their duty to have been done. Prioritising romantic love over dynasty, at a time when women's roles were undergoing redefinition, they made their bold statements.

What created this sea-change in the lives of the next Tudor generation? Not only Margaret and Mary but also their brother Henry VIII married for love in 1509, and he expected to be able to do so again in the 1520s. Was there some correlation between the rise of the individual and the advancement of Renaissance thinking? Was it the comparative security of the second generation of a dynasty? Or, for the women, the toll of having done one's duty and feeling abandoned in a foreign country? Was it a need for love, indicative of the loneliness of royalty and the tension between public duty and private emotion? Certainly, at Henry VIII's court it is possible to identify a flowering of chivalric activity, employing elements of fantasy, escapism, disguise, poetry and romance. The early years of his reign witnessed the rise of poets, the birth of masques and elaborate pageantry, the seeds of which had been sown in the celebrations for the reception of Catherine of Aragon in 1501.

From 1509, the theme of love was dominant at court. It began with the jousts at Catherine and Henry's wedding, when the knights of Diana, led by Cupid, asked her permission 'to do feats of arms for the love of ladies'.[1] Henry would personify this theme by adopting the name 'Sir Loyal Heart', when jousting in his wife's honour, and presiding over a young, passionate court of newlyweds. Love, romance and dalliance set the tone, with seven out of Catherine's eight ladies-in-waiting getting married between 1503 and 1509. In January 1510, Henry's men dressed in the green of outlaws to stage a surprise wooing of the queen and her ladies. In February he danced in costumes featuring Catherine's motifs and devices, and in October he fought a giant in her honour. The annual May Day celebrations saw more staged scenes from courtly love tales, with Henry wooing his wife in the woods with flowers, music and surprise feasts. Princess Mary frequently played a prominent role in these activities, witnessing the cultural veneration of the very real love and physical passion that existed between Henry and Catherine at this stage. After enacting so many romances as part of courtly play, Mary would step dangerously from fantasy into reality in 1515.

In February 1514, Mary was seventeen and her fiancé Charles Hapsburg, son of Philip and Joanna of Castile, had just reached his fourteenth birthday. After a long engagement reflecting the Anglo-Spanish alliance, their wedding date was finally set. That May, she would become his wife in person, in Calais, where elaborate jousts and celebrations were being planned as late as 21 March. But May arrived, then June, and no wedding took place. On 19 June, Mary was being considered as a potential bride by the General of

Normandy, a man 'said to be a great lord' as she was 'promised to the Prince of Castile but is still here unmarried.'[2] Pedro Martir (Peter Martyr) summed up the root of the problem in a letter written from Valladolid on June 8:

> The sister of the King of England was betrothed to Prince Charles on condition that he should marry her when he passed the age of fourteen. Henry is urgent to have the marriage completed, as the Prince was of the age required on the 24 Feb. last. Maximilian and Ferdinand require its postponement, as Charles is naturally of a feeble constitution. Henry is exceedingly angry, and threatens to make terms with France.[3]

In a fit of pique against Ferdinand, Henry threw away an excellent alliance for his sister and for England. He ignored the letter from Charles's aunt, Margaret of Savoy, on June 20, explaining that the moon was prolonging the boy's illness, but that he was improving.[4] Breaking with Spain and allying himself instead with France, Henry chose the ageing Louis XII, a newly widowed fifty-two-year-old, as his sister's bridegroom. Mary and Catherine must have been disappointed not just at the personal dimension, as large age gaps were not uncommon in dynastic matches, but at the rejection of such a powerful and significant political alliance. Having anticipated being Charles's wife from a young age, Mary had no say over the change. On 30 July 1514 at the manor of Wanstead, in the presence of witnesses, Mary formally renounced her marriage to Charles. The dowry was to be 200,000 crowns and Louis was to pay Henry an annual 50,000, as well as to permit him to keep Tournai.[5]

On 13 August, the proxy marriage between Mary and Louis took place in the Great Hall at Greenwich. The Duc de Longueville acted as proxy, taking Mary's hand and speaking the vows of the French King in front of William Warham, Archbishop of Canterbury. Then Mary took the hand of the Duke and repeated her promise in return, after which both signed their names and Mary accepted a gold ring for the fourth finger of her right hand. A formal bedding ceremony followed, at which the Duke allowed his bare leg to touch that of Mary as she lay in bed, signifying the consummation of the match. Afterwards, the Queen of France attended Mass with Henry, Catherine and Longueville. Mary obediently wrote to her new husband, promising to 'love him as cordially as she can' and claiming she had heard his vows 'with great pleasure'.[6]

Preparations were stepped up for Mary to leave England as soon as possible. Louis was keen to see his bride, sending coffers of gifts, including huge diamonds and love letters. The royal wardrobe and an army of seamstresses worked on an impressive array of dresses for Mary's trousseau, in the latest English, French and Milanese styles. The treasury yielded up jewellery and ornaments, tapestries and hangings. New beds were ordered and a cradle covered with scarlet. Mary's new great seal bore the motto *La volonte de Dieu me suffit,* 'the will of God is sufficient for me,' indicative of her devotion to duty, even in such an arrangement as this. A number of ladies were appointed to the new Queen's household, some to accompany the wedding party across the Channel and return, others to remain in France and serve her after the festivities were over.

The French were eagerly anticipating Mary's arrival. Having sent a number of gifts and loving letters, referring to her as his 'beloved consort', Louis travelled to Abbeville from Paris on 22 September, where a tournament was held in her honour. In such displays of courtly and chivalric devotion, a Queen did not even need to be present; the idea of her, as an abstract, aspirational symbol, was sufficient. In this way, the early Tudor Queens who presided over such occasions, in person or in absentia, fulfilled a similar purpose to the Virgin Mary with her all-pervasive pre-Reformation cult, and the figures of other female saints: a blend of devotion and distant encouragement from a pedestal, all wrapped up in the strange oxymoron of pure, platonic eroticism. It was a role dictated entirely by gender, which would find its fullest expression in the queen-bee-and-hive atmosphere of the court of Elizabeth I.

Mary left Greenwich the following day, travelling down to Dover amid a huge company that included Henry, Catherine, and most of their court, estimated at the time to be around 2,000 people.[7] The pregnant Catherine travelled behind in a litter, while Henry and his sister rode ahead, arriving in Dover as a storm was breaking. Mary's departure was delayed a little, but while she waited, she extracted a promise from Henry that after her marriage to Louis, she might choose her second husband for herself. It was an extraordinary bargain, Mary drawing on her personal relationship with Henry to ensure his recognition that she was doing her duty, but that he would allow for her own romantic inclination. He clearly agreed, as she would remind him in a letter of 1515, but cannot have anticipated just how soon Mary would be in a position to exercise her will:

> I beseech your Grace that you will keep all the promises that you promised me when I took my leave of you by the water side. Sir, your grace knoweth well that I did marry for your pleasure at this time, and now I trust that you will suffer me to marry as me liketh for to do.[8]

*

The weather finally allowed Mary to sail on 2 October, although conditions in the Channel were still stormy. Two days later, four out of the fourteen ships that left Dover finally reached land, while one was lost, and the others blown north along the coast of Flanders. Soaking wet, Mary was carried ashore and conducted to the home of Madame de Moncaverel at Montreuil to recover. Two days later she departed for Abbeville, where her husband was waiting.

The impatient Louis, however, could not wait to cast eyes upon his new bride. He headed north with a hunting party, ostensibly to hawk, but expressly to meet Mary 'by accident'. He despatched his heir and son-in-law, Francis of Angoulême, to delay her, and inform her of his approach, so that she might change into suitable clothing. Her dress of gold and crimson checks was mirrored by Louis' own costume, to allow the pair to instantly recognise each other. As he approached, Mary blew him a kiss and he rode alongside her, taking her in his arms and kissing her in person. After the meeting, Mary made her grand entrance into Abbeville behind a guard of fifty, the noblemen, ambassadors, heralds and trumpeters, all in gold collars. Mary rode behind them, accompanied by Francis, followed by her litter of cloth of gold, worked with the device of the Tudor rose and the fleur-de-lys of France, then thirty ladies wearing cloth of gold, and 300 archers. She was met by a large civic party, who conducted her to Mass, then into the Hôtel de la Gruuthuse where she was formally introduced to Louis, before retiring to the queen's lodgings.[9] This building had significance for Mary, as it had been the location for the death in 1512 of Jean de Bruges, also de Gruuthuse, son of the Louis de Gruuthuse who had sheltered her grandfather Edward IV during his exile in 1470-1.

The wedding took place on 9 October, a day when the whole of France was en fête in celebration of their patron saint, St Denis. After dressing from head to foot in gold, Mary with her party crossed through the gardens that separated her lodgings from the main palace for the ceremony in the Great Hall, which took place at nine in the morning. She was led by twenty-six knights, heralds and musicians, and followed by the leading English nobility dressed in their finest clothes and jewels, with Mary's ladies at the end of the procession. Louis was dressed in gold to echo his bride and bowed low at her approach. The service was conducted by Cardinal René de Prie, Bishop of Bayeux, including communion and the exchange of promises before the royal pair kissed before the assembled crowd. Later, a ball was held, during which Louis remained attentively at Mary's side, before leading her off to bed at around eight o'clock. In the morning, in a show of sexual prowess, he reported that 'thrice did he cross the river last night, and would have done more, had he chosen.'[10]

Mary's brief spell as Queen of France lasted less than three months. Days after the wedding, she was distressed when almost all her ladies were sent back to England, writing to implore her brother and Thomas Wolsey for help, but to no avail. To soften the blow, Louis showered his young wife with gifts, huge rubies, diamonds and pearls, and preparations were made for her imminent coronation. From Abbeville, they moved towards Paris, travelling slowly to accommodate Louis' attack of gout. On the way, they were intercepted by Sir Charles Brandon, one of Henry VIII's oldest and closest friends, whom he had dispatched to try and convince Louis to unite with England in an attack upon Spain. He met the royal party on 25 October at Beauvais, being admitted to the chamber where Louis was lying in bed, with Mary sitting at the side.

Mary had known Brandon all her life. Twelve years her senior, he was the son of Sir William Brandon, her father's standard bearer, who had been killed at Bosworth. Attractive and athletic, he had been raised at the Tudor court, a keen jouster who played a leading part in the high-spirited escapades of Henry's early reign. He had been married once before, fathering two daughters, although he had deserted his pregnant fiancée for financial gain, creating a scandal by marrying her wealthy aunt. Although he had enemies at court who resented his rise, he remained a great favourite of the King, who appointed him as Master of the Horse, Viscount Lisle, by virtue of his betrothal to his ward, and Duke of Suffolk. Henry thought so highly of him that in 1513 he encouraged his friend to woo Margaret of Austria, Regent of the Netherlands, daughter of the Emperor, a prize far out of Brandon's reach no matter what his personal charms may have been. The contrast between him and her new, infirm husband, must have been painfully apparent to Mary. Whether she had already favoured him, or these feelings developed subsequently, it was Brandon on whom Mary began to lean.

Mary fulfilled her obligations as Queen of France admirably. She played the role of the loving wife to Louis, welcoming him into her bed, returning his affection, sitting by his bedside through his suffering, and negotiating with her brother on behalf of her husband. To keep up Louis' spirits, she sang and played on the lute, prompting the English ambassadors to praise her to her brother. Henry wrote to Louis of his 'very great joy, pleasure and comfort' in hearing 'how she conducts herself towards you,' and did not doubt that 'you will, day by day, find her more and more all that she ought to be with you, and that she will do everything which will be to your will, pleasure and contentment.'[11] Mary acquitted herself equally well during her coronation at the Cathedral of St Denis on 5 November, and her state entrance into Paris, dressed in cloth of gold and riding in a gold carriage through streets hung with tapestries, lilies and roses. Seven pageants marked her route to Nôtre Dame, where she heard Mass, before a formal welcome from the Archbishop of Paris. That evening, a state banquet was held in the Grande Salle of the Palais Royale, where Mary sat at a marble table flanked by the women of her new family. She met her stepdaughter Claude, married since May to Francis, and his mother and sister, Louise of Savoy and Marguerite of Angoulême. Three more days of tournaments followed in Paris, before the court repaired to Abbeville again for further celebrations.[12]

It was in the tiltyard at Abbeville that Charles Brandon came into his own. He had arrived equipped with an allowance of £1,000 from Henry[13] to dress himself, his horses and entourage suitably to lead the jousting, along with Mary's cousin, Thomas Grey, Marquis of Dorset. Considered to be the best athlete, along with Francis, Brandon easily unseated his opponent and ran an impressive number of courses before Francis's jealousy provoked him to pit a German giant against his rival. The pair jousted and fought with spears and blunt swords before Brandon emerged as the victor again, so that the event was awarded to the English. He rode into Paris before Mary on 24 November, when she made her first formal appearance as Queen of France, before the court moved on to St. Germain-en-Laye. Brandon remained in attendance until mid-December, whereupon he returned to England, reaching Henry's side in time for the Christmas festivities.

Soon after the merrymaking came to an end, news arrived at court of the death of Louis of France on 1 January. Just four days earlier, the King had written to Henry that his 'satisfaction with the queen his wife was such that Henry might be sure of his treating her to her own and to his satisfaction.'[14] As a beautiful widow of eighteen, and a queen of France, Mary was potentially prey to the advances of potential suitors, including the new King, Francis, who already had something of a reputation for his love of women. Mary could not leave until it had been firmly established that she was not pregnant so she sat out the weeks in close confinement, considering her fate. Wolsey wrote to her on 10 January, sounding a note of caution, for as she found herself 'during her heaviness ... among strangers' she should not forget that Henry 'would not forsake her' and she should 'do nothing without the advice of his grace' and listen to no offers of marriage.[15] Henry and Catherine had moved from Eltham to Greenwich before Henry wrote formally to congratulate the new King of France on 14 January, at the same time as he sent Sir Charles Brandon to fetch his sister home.

Yet Henry had not reckoned with the promise Mary had extracted from him at Dover the previous October. She chose Charles Brandon, and persuaded him, with promises, seduction and tears, to marry her in secret. Brandon was unpopular with the royal Council and Mary predicted, correctly, that they would oppose the match, and that she might be married again for dynastic gain. Aware that he would incur the King's wrath, in particular in jeopardising the dower payments he had been sent to collect, Brandon wrote to Wolsey for help in early March. Apparently, Mary had been insistent and had 'never let (him) be in rest till (he) had granted her to be married.' They had lain together so much, Brandon added, that he feared that 'she be with child'. Knowing the King well, Wolsey suggested that Mary send him 'the Mirror of Naples', a French diamond with a big pearl, to smooth their return to England. Wolsey went straight to the King. Henry was furious when he learned what had taken place, unable to believe it at first, then taking it 'grievously and displeasantly';.but Mary was clearly in love, having 'always been of a good mind' towards Brandon, as she expected the King to know, and was now 'so bound to him that for no earthly cause could she change.'[16] She was also aware that Henry might go back on his promise and try to make a match for her elsewhere, or revive her previous match with Prince Charles. As the chronicler Edward Hall wrote, 'against this marriage many men grudged and said it was a great loss to the realm that she was not married to the Prince of Castile.'[17]

Mary had done her duty, and now begged for her brother's good will for her love match. Taking Wolsey's hint, she made a public gift to Henry of 'all such plate and vessel of clean gold' and jewels that Louis had given her. Did Catherine speak on her sister-in-law's behalf, or was she as horrified and disappointed as her husband at this rash match of affection? It was the duty of those born into the royal line to make advantageous marriages, not to follow their hearts. If they were lucky, like Henry and Catherine, or Ferdinand and Isabella, love might grow between them, but otherwise, there was a clear division between the destinies of princesses and the secrets of their hearts.

Mary and Brandon arrived at Dover on 2 May. Wolsey met them and conducted them to the home of Lord Abergavenny, where Henry was waiting. An agreement was reached whereby Mary would repay her brother £2,000 a year until her debt was paid, after which the couple were married again at Greenwich. Catherine had been at Richmond at the end of April but travelled down the river to Greenwich to be reunited with her sister-in-law and to attend the ceremony on 13 May 1515.

*

As one errant bride came home, so a second was also planning to return. In August 1514, Margaret had broken the terms of her late husband's will and secretly married Archibald Douglas, Sixth Earl of Angus. Born in the same year as Margaret, Douglas had lost his wife in 1513, his father at Flodden, and his grandfather soon after, from whom he inherited his title. As part of her Regency Council, Angus had drawn close to the Queen, who found his advances impossible to resist, although he was not held in high regard by his contemporaries. Margaret's decision was remarkable for being driven by passion and conducted in secrecy.

Predictably, her choice enraged the Scottish nobility, who withdrew her regency in favour of the Earl of Albany, to whom they granted the care of her children. Pregnant by Angus, Margaret sought permission from the Council to retire to Linlithgow, but instead fled south to throw herself on the mercy of her brother in England. On 8 October 1515, Margaret had reached the remote Harbottle Castle in Northumberland, just ten miles from the border. There, she gave birth to a daughter, Margaret Douglas. It was a difficult delivery and Margaret suffered from poor health as a result, detaining her at Harbottle. As she wrote to Henry, she was suffering from a 'great infirmity' with 'intolerable pain' in her right thigh, 'at the seat of sciatica', unable to stir, and only capable of eating broth, pottage, almond milk and boiled meats.[18] Reports arrived that Albany was marching on the castle with an army of 40,000 men, although he was also writing to Margaret, entreating her to return of her own free will. Margaret refused.

That November, as soon as she was well enough, Margaret moved south to Morpeth, but although she was safer, her personal situation rapidly worsened. Her younger son Alexander, whom she had left behind with his brother, grew ill and died before reaching the age of two. After that, Angus decided to come to terms with Albany and deserted Margaret at Morpeth as she lay ill with typhus, in despair of her life. The dowager queen may have bitterly resented her choice, which had brought her to the worst possible outcome and possibly the lowest point in her life. The former cherished daughter of the Tudor court was an abandoned fugitive on the verge of death.

The Tudor sisters had different experiences of queenship because of the comparative duration of their rule. Both had fulfilled the duty for which they were raised, serving the dynastic need, leaving their home country in order to marry a stranger. While Margaret's decade of queenship had encompassed dynastic highs and personal lows, Mary's brief months had not embedded her in her new country to the same degree. The death of Louis left her free to walk away and pursue her own choice, with the grudging indulgence of her brother. By contrast, Margaret was left with one surviving child, and anticipating the arrival of another, so her position as queen dowager was defined in relation to the needs of the country's heir. She could not simply desert Scotland and return home, even had she wished to. Both women's queenship was of the traditional kind, as figureheads, symbols, ornaments to the court and as the foci of cultural events, but beyond that, their experiences are not really comparable: Margaret was put to the test as Regent in circumstances when her nationality made her an enemy alien, while Mary returned home. The difference was that Margaret had borne children, who were heirs to her adoptive country, while Mary had not. What both women brought to the early modern debate about queenship was a new element of personal choice. As dowager queens, they made the controversial decision to pursue their own inclination, although this may have been as much about protection than it was about passion. Lacking a husband in a foreign country, Mary and Margaret both sought out an alliance with a male protector, rather than standing independently, even when that man was their social inferior. This was a recognition of the way the world operated, requiring women's definition through a husband's identity, even if those women were former queens, and the daughters of kings. Mary and Margaret still believed that the role of wife superseded all others, and this would not begin to change in England until the late 1550s.

Margaret and Mary's choices expose the true nature of queenship in the late fifteenth and early sixteenth centuries. As their grandmother Elizabeth Woodville discovered, a queen's power was always a function of that exercised by their men and could be as swiftly withdrawn as it was bestowed. The Tudor princesses were born into royalty but achieved their queenship through marriage, with the duration of their power determined by the lifespan of their husband, even if they were granted the role of regent. When their queenship was withdrawn, they actively sought a new position through alliance with another man. In this aspect, they were similar to their paternal grandmother, Margaret Beaufort, in their observance of the particular paths dictated by their gender, but unlike her, their choices were made for love, not political advancement. This was unusual in the context of their peers, whose choices were largely dynastic and designed to avoid further submission to men once they were free.

Across the Channel, women were pursuing their own independence after they had lost power. Joan, Duchess of Berry, was Queen of France for six months in 1498, before her marriage was annulled after a reputed lack of consummation due to physical deformities. Joan was 34 at the time, and fought the case, but the Pope granted her husband's wish for the furtherance of the Valois line. Joan could have attempted to remarry, especially to counteract such claims, but instead she founded a monastic order, of which she became Abbess and remained so until her death. Margaret of Austria was widowed at the age of eighteen after the death of the Spanish heir, Juan, Prince of Asturias, and entered another advantageous marriage three years later. When she was widowed again at the age of twenty-four and childless. Her intense grief led her to throw herself out of a window, but she survived and vowed never to marry again. Instead, she rejected all offers, even prestigious ones, and became ruler of the Netherlands. In Italy, Lucrezia Borgia submitted to the three marriages which were arranged for her, according to the aspirations of her father, but followed her own inclination by choosing her own lovers, perhaps even bearing an illegitimate child, while her sister-in-law, Charlotte of Albret, was widowed at twenty-seven and acted as regent for her daughter without remarrying.

Catherine of Aragon and her sisters represent a different example of companionate marriage, set by their mother, of seeking a husband who represented both a dynastic achievement and a love match. How this 'love' was defined, and how it developed, may well have resulted from the credentials of their spouse, their long-standing engagements, a sense of destiny and the parity of age and status between the couple. Joanna of Castile had fallen deeply in love with Philip the Handsome despite his cruel and controlling nature. By the time she was widowed in 1506, her emotional reactions had created her reputation for 'madness', which led to her being deprived of her Castilian inheritance and imprisoned by her father. As Queen of Castile, and still in her twenties, Joanna could have found a new husband to fight her case and reclaim Castile, but any political astuteness she possessed was overshadowed by her intense personal grief. Thus, she lost control of her inheritance and her queenship became merely nominal. Joanna's elder sister, Isabella of Portugal, was grief stricken and refused to marry again after the death of her first husband, Alfonso. It took six years for her parents to persuade her to accept another husband, and she agreed only after the death of her brother made her their heir. She finally agreed to marry her former husband's uncle, Manuel of Portugal. When she died in childbirth a year later, her younger sister Maria became Manuel's wife.

Margaret and Mary's queenships were of short duration, but their marriages created alliances in the service of the Tudor dynasty. Both bore children whose descendants would sit on the English throne, Margaret with James (James I) and Mary with Charles Brandon (Jane Grey). It was the personal nature of their decision making that was most controversial, by introducing the dangerous element of self into the equation, in line with new Renaissance thinking about the importance of the individual. Mary and Margaret pursued their individual desires after serving their dynasty, with wildly differing results. Men had done this for centuries, especially royal men, but it was an unusual path for a queen, and had historically led to scandal. The Tudor sisters broadened the queenly narrative to encompass the new debate about the emergence of individualism, visible in the portraiture of da Vinci and his contemporaries and writings of Machiavelli, Castiglione, della Mirandola and others. The old beliefs about the subjection of the self to one's God, country and family were shifting in favour of a new sort of self-actualisation, in which the individual mattered, and had a duty or right to self-fulfilment and achieving an optimum state of secular being. This isn't to suggest that Mary and Margaret were directly influenced by Renaissance texts, or even aware of the spreading dialogue, but more that they were responsive to a wider cultural change, a change in the mood, a shift in focus, part of a wider sea change of Renaissance self-fashioning.

13

Legacies of Love
1516–1520

At the end of January 1516, Catherine of Aragon made a ceremonial withdrawal into confinement at Greenwich Palace. Heavily pregnant with her fifth child, her dress open-laced, she led a procession into her chamber, where she was blessed, took part in prayers and partook of wine and spices, before her household withdrew. Symbolically enclosed, removed from male eyes, she would remain enclosed with her women until the process was over. Having experienced two miscarriages, one stillbirth and one child lost in infancy, the thirty-year-old Catherine was under considerable pressure to produce a male heir. Just before dawn on 18 February, she gave birth to a daughter, a healthy child whom she named Mary. Henry was so relieved that he stated hopefully that he and Catherine were both still young and that 'if it was a daughter this time, by the grace of God, the sons would follow.' The new Princess was christened on Wednesday, 21 February in the church of the Friars Observant at Greenwich, where her aunt and namesake, Mary, now Duchess of Suffolk, presented her with a gold pomander.

The first woman to oversee baby Mary's upbringing was Elizabeth Denton, who had been Henry's nurse back in the 1490s and had accompanied Margaret into Scotland, but her death in 1517 led to Lady Margaret Bryan being awarded her annuity of forty pounds for 'services to the princess'.[1] Catherine paid close attention to her daughter's upbringing from the start, even though she was not permitted to breastfeed her, as this would have interfered with her ability to conceive again. She liaised closely with Lady Bryan about the choice of wet nurse for her daughter, and her diet once she was weaned. Lady Catherine, wife of Leonard Poole, was appointed for the former task, as 'nutrici Marie filie Regis', being awarded an annuity of £20 on 2 July 1517, suggesting the Princess had been weaned at around sixteen months.[2]

Less than a month after Catherine had given birth in 1516, Mary, Duchess of Suffolk, went into labour with her first child at Bath Place. On 11 March, between ten and eleven at night, Mary delivered a son, Henry. Why she lay-in at the house owned by Thomas Wolsey, instead of at home at Suffolk Place, is unclear. Wolsey had been a friend to Brandon and his new wife, encouraging Henry to forgive them and facilitating their return, so they were probably frequent visitors to his property. Bath Place was in the west of the city, outside the city walls, along the Strand in the direction of Westminster. The Brandon's home was situated on the Southbank, in Southwark, close to London Bridge in the east. If the onset of labour had taken Mary by surprise at Bath Place, it is understandable that she did not wish to risk the journey home. There is also the possibility that Wolsey, with his great wealth, made his convenient, accessible home available to Mary at his expense. Suffolk Place was also undergoing building works, so Mary may have appreciated the offer to escape from noise and disruption. Soon after his arrival, baby Henry was swiftly brought back to Suffolk Place for his christening. While Mary was still recovering, Henry, Catherine and Wolsey stood as godparents among the guests in the great hall, which was hung with tapestries depicting red and white roses. The ceremony was performed by John Fisher, Bishop of Rochester, and Thomas Ruthall, Bishop of Durham. Baby Henry was carried back to his nursery by Mary's cousin Anne Grey, wife of Sir Edward Grey, grandson of Elizabeth Woodville.

After Mary had risen from confinement and been churched, she returned to her son at Suffolk Place, which became the family's main London home. Drawn by Dutch visitor Anton van der Wyngaerde in the late 1540s, the house was in the process of being transformed into a red-brick mansion with onion domes, Renaissance roundels, decorative carvings and friezes worked into the design. Set around two courtyards, it contained the requisite great hall, chapel, private apartments, extensive kitchens, gardens and deer park for the pursuit of a royal lifestyle. The Brandons also used Westhorpe Hall as their country retreat, a large moated house set around a courtyard to the east of Bury St Edmunds in Suffolk, and Donnington Castle, a formidable medieval fortress in

Berkshire. By early May, Mary had sufficiently recovered to return to court in order to welcome her sister upon her return.

*

In spring 1516, Margaret, dowager Queen of Scots, returned to London for the first time since her departure as a bride in 1503. She had been thirteen years old and Mary just seven when the pair last met, and both women had undergone queenship, widowhood, remarriage and maternity since that time. Margaret had taken several months to recover from the ill-health following her own confinement, and travelled south without the errant Angus, who had deserted her to join the new regent, the Earl of Albany. Hall relates how Henry sent William Blacknall, the clerk of his spicery, north with 'silver vessel, plate and other things necessary for the conveyance of her, and sent to her all manner of officers.' Margaret was 'well received' on the way south and wrote to her brother from Stony Stratford, thanking him, as she had been so 'comforted of you in my journey in many and sundry ways ... that I am in right good health and as joyous of my said journey toward you as any woman may be in coming to her brother.'[3]

Margaret rode into London on 3 May on a white palfrey sent to her by Queen Catherine, led by Sir Thomas Parr. She was met by Henry and a large retinue at Tottenham Cross, where they rested at Sir William Compton's house before resuming the journey, arriving at Baynard's Castle just before six. From there she was conveyed by river to Greenwich, 'and received joyously of the king, the queen, the French queen her sister and highly was she feasted.'[4] It was a significant reunion for this unusual triumvirate of queens, of England, France and Scotland, all strong women who had been widowed young, remarried and borne a child. This was an unprecedented moment in the history of the Tudor dynasty, with the presence in London of three royal cousins, Margaret, Mary and Catherine's infant children: Margaret Douglas, Henry Brandon and Mary Tudor, whose births heralded the dynasty's next generation.

On 19 and 20 May, Henry held a tournament in honour of his sister's return. He, Brandon, the Earl of Essex and Nicholas Carew answered all challengers in the lists, dressed in black velvet covered with embroidered honeysuckle made from fine, flat gold damask, 'cunning and sumptuous', with every leaf moving. The challengers were dressed alike in blue velvet and cloth of gold as they vied to outdo their rivals in front of the women. The next morning, the King and his party appeared in purple velvet costumes with rose leaves of gold, with their attendants in yellow velvet and satin, edged with gold, the challengers in white satin. When the knights had exhausted themselves, they retired to a banquet in honour of Margaret held in Catherine's chamber.[5]

The reunion of the three queens began a new phase of harmony for the Tudor dynasty. That September, Henry visited Mary and Brandon at Donnington Castle, leading Mary to thank her brother profusely for the favour he bestowed in forgiving and supporting their marriage. Mary, Margaret and Catherine were the guests of honour at the festivities held to celebrate Twelfth Night at Greenwich, when a garden of hope was wheeled into the great hall, surrounded by railings connecting four towers in the corners. Upon the artificial banks inside were flowers made of silk, gold and green satin, all around a golden pillar of the antique style, topped with an arbour from which sprouted red and white roses and a pomegranate bush. Twelve knights and twelve ladies appeared from the garden and danced a ballet to conclude the evening.[6] The presence of the trio also offered a shift in focus, a powerful reminder of how central women were to the family's success, and had always been. Between them, Catherine, Mary and Margaret were the daughters, sisters and wives of kings and related to Imperial royalty. The dynasty had been more successful in its production of girls who reached maturity, and the creation of female alliances, than in the birth of males. Whilst figures like Henry VII and Henry VIII would possess disproportionate power due to their kingship, the influence of the many Tudor women behind the scenes would be just as significant, if not more so.

After Christmas, Henry moved Margaret into lodgings at Scotland Yard, the traditional residence of the Scots Ambassadors in London. Conscious of the expense she was creating for her brother, she wrote to Wolsey asking to borrow £200 so she might afford New Years' presents for her family.[7] Wolsey obliged, but as heir to the throne the focus of attention was firmly upon Princess Mary and, at New Year, she received gifts from a number of those close to Catherine: Cardinal Wolsey gave her a cup of gold, her aunt Mary a golden pomander and the Duchess of Devonshire a gold spoon, while the Duchess of Norfolk gave her a primer, Lady Mountjoy a smock and Lady Darrell some pears.[8] Her household was based at Enfield, but at Christmas she was moved to Datchet, just over the Thames from where her parents were celebrating at Windsor, presumably to allow for visiting.

The following March, Catherine undertook another pilgrimage to Our Lady of Walsingham in Norfolk, a favourite shrine of the royal couple, which Henry had previously visited to give thanks for her safe delivery in 1511, and she had attended in the aftermath of Flodden. At the age of thirty-one, and with only one surviving child to show for five pregnancies, Catherine's journey is likely to have been prompted by the desire to conceive again, to leave offerings and ask the Virgin and saints to intercede on her behalf. It was a ritual that many women of all ranks undertook before the Reformation, at shrines all across the country, an established rite of passage that fuelled a considerable industry of hospitality, merchandise and services. On this occasion, Catherine was accompanied part of the way by Mary and Brandon, although Mary was then six months pregnant with her second child. After her visit, Catherine stayed with the Suffolks to break her journey back to London.

The tide was starting to turn when it came to shrines, even if they were being patronised by queens. Less than two decades later Catherine's husband would dismantle their wealth and break up their images and statues, destroying centuries-old rhythms of life and methods of worship. In 1517, the royal family were still devoutly, demonstrably Catholic, following its tenets, celebrating its festivals and feast days, enacting its rituals as an extension of their own majesty, unyielding when it came to challenging those perceived as heretics. Voices of dissent were comparatively slow to reach England, but they were already present at this point, including that of Desiderius Erasmus, the recent visitor to Eltham, who had written *The Handbook of a Christian Knight* in 1501,[9] exhorting the faithful to act in accordance with the spirit of Christianity rather than simply going through the motions of meaningless rituals. In 1513, Erasmus visited the shrines at Walsingham and Canterbury, using satire in his second volume of *Colloquies*[10] to expose what he perceived to be the follies of blind, unquestioning faith. He used the device of a fictional pilgrim's visit to St. James, Compostela, who thought that the saint had responded to him by giving a smile and nod of the head, and described Walsingham, where the glittering jewels, gold and silver were as 'conducive' to religion as the darkness and scent. The canons were not permitted to show themselves for fear that 'while they are serving the Virgin, they lose their virginity,' but the pilgrims were less likely to give donations if there was not someone watching over them, while some even stole from the shrine without retribution. Erasmus's character noted a great many abuses, such as holy water and milk of the Virgin being 'forged for the sake of getting money', the milk looking remarkably like beaten chalk, tempered with egg white. At the shrine of St Thomas, the pilgrim was shown the special relics of Canterbury Cathedral because of his friendship with the archbishop and his friend caused general embarrassment by asking why the treasures of the generous saint were not being shared among the poor.[11]

It was in this year that Martin Luther would nail his ninety-five theses to the door of All Saint's Church, in Wittenberg, sparking the discontent in Germany that snowballed into the German Reformation. Deeply devout and raised by parents on whom Pope Alexander VI had bestowed the titles of the most 'Catholic King and Queen' for their defence of the realm, Catherine's faith was more than a matter of conviction for her. It was a question of salvation and identity. Erasmus and his ilk posed a direct challenge to every aspect of her being. She would continue to worship in the 'old' ways, seeing these changes as imperilling the souls of new thinkers, and coming to represent something of a Catholic figurehead in England. Over the challenging years ahead, it was to become a defining aspect of her queenship.

By May 1517, Margaret had been resident at court and at Baynard's Castle for an entire year, and was 'richly appointed of all things meet (fitting) to her estate both of jewels, plate, carpets, Arras (hangings), coin, horses and all things of the king's gift and liberality'.[12] Henry, Wolsey and Albany had agreed terms for Margaret's return and just as arrangements were being made, rioting broke out among the London apprentices. After the insurrection was quelled, the young men were arrested and brought before the King at Greenwich, where Margaret, Catherine and Mary pleaded with their brother for mercy, resulting in a pardon being granted. This was as theatrical and staged as courtly pageants or tournaments, with the accused being paraded in chains, while the women knelt before Henry, symbolic figures of mercy. The performance was designed to create maximum impact, a show remarkable for its strange mixture of passionate emotion and detachment, of which the outcome had already been decided. The women were as much representatives of the chivalric ideal here as they were when awarding prizes to the jousters, with their gender placing them above the dirty business of fighting or crime, as interventional figures.

At the end of the month, Margaret bade her family goodbye and taking her daughter travelled north along the same route as her bridal departure, reaching York on 3 June. From there, she wrote to Henry requesting that the initial peace between England and Scotland be extended beyond its deadline of the end of November. Margaret waited until Albany had departed Scotland before riding into Berwick. Her husband, Angus, was waiting to meet her, but as Hall relates, 'Englishmen... hardly regarded him.'[13] She was less pleased to discover that he had appropriated some of her income and had since fathered a child with a woman he had been betrothed to before their marriage. At Craigmillar Castle, Margaret was reunited with her five-year-old son, James, but her frequent visits led to concerns that she would try and remove him to England, so he was moved into central Edinburgh and Margaret was forbidden from seeing him. At the end of June, she wrote in protest to Wolsey, thinking it 'right strange' that she was kept from her boy, but that she had otherwise been well received.[14]

On 16 July 1517, Mary Brandon delivered her second child at Bishop's Hatfield in Hertfordshire. It was a girl whom she named Frances. Henry and Catherine declined to attend the christening due to an outbreak of the sweating sickness but sent their representative instead; a woman who had been in Catherine's household since her early queenship, the wife of one of the diplomatic stars of Henry's court, recently foreign ambassador to the Netherlands and the mother of three children in their teens. Her name was Elizabeth Boleyn. Together with her husband Thomas, Elizabeth's name appears with increasing frequency at court entertainments and in official capacities in the Tudor records, often alongside Charles and Mary Brandon. In the spring of 1518, Catherine realised that she had conceived again. She was now thirty-two and had high hopes of delivering a son.

That July, while Henry and Catherine kept on the move to escape the sweat, there was a scare when one of the women in Mary's household fell ill 'of a hot ague'. Henry summoned his daughter to be brought to Bisham Abbey and on to further seclusion at the Manor of the More in Rickmansworth, Hertfordshire. The woman had already recovered but the King wished 'the Princess to be removed, notwithstanding' until her household heard his further pleasure.[15] Henry was known for such caution regarding his family's health, but this was balanced with the need to display the healthy child to the world. It was only a short while before that an ambassador had seen Princess Mary at court, and was able to draw near as she was carried in her nurse's arms.

After this, Princess Mary, who is two years old, was brought in. The Cardinal and Sebastian kissed her hand, the greatest marks of honor being paid her, universally, more than to the Queen herself. The moment she cast her eyes on the Reverend Dionisius Memo, who was there at a little distance, she commenced calling out in English 'Priest!' and he was obliged to go and play for her.[16]

*

In July 1518, a negotiation was underway between Henry and Francis I of France for a match between Princess Mary and his new-born son. Catherine would have hoped for an alliance with a prince of Spain or the Empire, but she had embraced England and Henry's wishes as thirty-four leading clerics and councillors signed the Treaty of London on 2 October. The terms were proclaimed at St Paul's, after which Henry hosted entertainments at Catherine's old home of Durham House, including twenty-four masked mummers led by Henry and his sister Mary in a banqueting hall decorated with huge vases of gold and silver. There followed a mummery of twelve female and twelve male actors, also masked and sumptuously dressed, led by Mary and Charles Brandon, after came 'countless dishes of confections and other delicacies' and then ducats, dice and dancing.[17]

Two days later, Princess Mary was betrothed to the little Dauphin Francis, who had been born that February. The ceremony took place in the Queen's Great Chamber at Greenwich on 5 October, as the Admiral of France took the hand of the Princess and espoused her in the name of the Dauphin of France, giving her a small ring set with a large diamond. The Princess was dressed in cloth of gold, with a black velvet cap and many jewels, and the church where they went to hear Mass was also hung with cloth of gold, in 'such rich array' that the ambassador 'never saw the like, either here or elsewhere'.[18] Mary was only four months off her third birthday and the prince was only seven months old, so Catherine may have taken heart from the fact that the wedding would not take place for at least fourteen years, during which much could change. She and Henry were also taking a risk, as while Mary remained their only heir, in line to inherit the throne, any husband she took would have become King of England, so this match opened up the possibility of the country being united with France under one pair of rulers, effectively conceding England to the French. It may be that they were counting on the hope that Catherine was about to deliver a son.

Further celebrations for Mary's marriage were held at Wolsey's residence of York Place, but Catherine retired early, in an advanced stage of pregnancy, leaving a masked Henry to partner one of her young maids of honour, Bessie Blount. It was around this time that the unmarried Bessie, then aged about nineteen, conceived the King's child. Catherine may have noticed that she disappeared from court soon afterwards, although she had plenty to occupy herself with her own approaching confinement. Her apartments at Greenwich were ready, with her bed draped in purple tissue edged in ermine. On 25 October, the Venetian ambassador Sebastian Giustinian observed that 'the Queen is near her delivery, which is anxiously looked for.' He hoped she 'would have a son, that the king may be at liberty to embark in any great undertaking.'[19] On the night of November 9-10, Catherine lost her child. 'This night the Queen was delivered of a daughter, to the vexation of as many as knows it,' Giustinian wrote, as 'the entire nation looked for a prince.' The baby was either stillborn or died soon after birth. It must have been a terrible disappointment for the Queen, when such losses were attributed to female negligence or sin. It is likely that this loss was the catalyst for her adopting a hair shirt.[20]

The following June, Bessie Blount gave birth to a baby boy at St Laurence's Priory, in Blackmore, Essex. The process was overseen by Wolsey who made all the arrangements with such discretion that none of the ambassadors commented on the child's existence and Catherine herself may not even have known at this stage. That summer, she accompanied Henry to stay in two of their Essex properties, Havering-atte-Bower, where Catherine hosted a banquet for which Henry 'thanked her hartely,' then Beaulieu, later called New Hall.[21] Both were conveniently within ten or twelve miles of Blackmore, so Henry could hear news of the baby's arrival and progress, and perhaps even visit on the pretext of hunting. The boy was christened Henry Fitzroy (an old French term meaning son of the king), which left no doubt about his paternity. It must have been very painful for Catherine that another woman had succeeded in the one task that she so desired to fulfil. Henry Fitzroy's existence was a constant reminder of the queen's perceived failure, and it gave the King cause to think. As the months turned into years it became apparent that the queen would not bear another child, but another woman might. The arrival of his son by Bessie convinced Henry that the problem lay with Catherine, not with him.

Four hundred miles north, Margaret was feeling increasingly isolated from her brother in England, and mistreated by the Scots. In April, she wrote that young James, then celebrating his seventh birthday, was in good health, but that she had 'been badly treated since leaving him' but did 'not wish to trouble him'. She was entitled to an annual income of £9,000 but had only been given £2,000 so far, which did not allow her to live in honour, and asked Henry to 'see to it, and not to believe the fair words of the Scotch lords.' Like Catherine in her widowhood, she felt obliged to give away the jewels and other gifts given her by Henry, and asked permission to come to visit him again. She had not seen Angus for half a year, who was causing her trouble and had confiscated one of her properties, which should have brought her considerable income. She even suggested that Henry might 'reasonably cause Scotch ships to be taken' as she had suffered so long, and was not loved there, and would never 'get good from Scotland by fair means'. She reaffirmed that her commitment was to the Tudor dynasty and not to her adopted land, promising that she would 'not marry but where (Henry) wishes, and will never part from him'.[22]

Thomas Dacre, Lord Warden of the Borders, who had discovered the body of James IV on the battlefield at Flodden, wrote to Margaret sternly in response that July. He reminded her that on her last visit to England, she had 'made urgent request...for the recovery of her authority, according to the will of her late husband, desiring that endeavours should be made that Albany might be sent to France for the security of herself and her son.'[23] It had been a condition of the 1518 Treaty of London, signed with France, that the regent, Albany, should not return to Scotland. Now, Dacre wrote, they had discovered Margaret had herself written to Louis XII asking him to release the regent and demanded to know if it was true. If so, Henry would 'take less aspect' to her causes and be less cordial.[24]

Margaret replied, in some distress, that the removal of Albany had not helped her cause, and she was 'never so evil answered of her lands as since her last coming to Scotland'. She had 'often written to the King and Cardinal but got no remedy' and was 'on the point of pawning her jewels' and could not pay her household expenses. She felt Henry's 'unkindness more than anything' and perceived she would 'get nothing but fair words from any quarter'.[25] It was ironic that while Margaret was struggling to make ends meet in Scotland, Henry was planning the biggest and most extravagant venture of his entire reign.

14

Gold

1520–25

The years 1520-22 saw Catherine and Mary, Duchess of Suffolk, playing a bigger role in international affairs. Charles, Prince of Castile, had been elected Holy Roman Emperor the previous summer, causing Henry to rapidly re-evaluate his European allegiances and invite Catherine's nephew to England. Charles had inherited a huge legacy from his grandfather and parents, which stretched across northern Europe and into Spain, making him the most influential new figure in the international game. If Henry was regretting breaking off the new Emperor's former engagement to his sister, in favour of France, he now hurried to rebuild that alliance.

Catherine was delighted at the prospect of meeting her nephew. 'Clasping her hands and raising her eyes unto heaven, (she) gave laud unto God ... that she might behold (Charles), saying it was her greatest desire in the world.'[1] She was 'gratified at his success' but there was also the option that Princess Mary's recent French alliance, conducted 'against the will of the Queen and all the nobles' would be replaced by one with Spain.[2] Although there was a large age gap, with Mary just four and Charles now twenty, Catherine hoped that one day her daughter might marry her cousin and join the kingdoms of England and Spain under one crown.

The new Emperor arrived at Dover on 26 May, where Henry was waiting in the castle, 'under the cloth of his estate of the black eagle all splayed on rich cloth of gold'.[3] The next morning Henry and Charles rode into Canterbury and attended Mass in the Cathedral to celebrate the feast of Pentecost, before processing along a purple carpet into the Archbishop's Palace, where Catherine and Mary were staying. They were greeted by twenty-five of the 'handsomest and best apparelled' court ladies and twenty of the queen's pages dressed in 'gold brocade and crimson satin in chequers'. It was Charles's intent 'specially to see queen of England his aunt' and Catherine waited theatrically for her nephew at the top of a flight of fifteen marble steps and wept as they met.[4] Charles also met Princess Mary who, but for the quirks of diplomacy six years before, might have been his Empress. The Elizabethan chronicler Holinshed adds 'peradventure the sight of the Lady Mary troubled him, whome he had sometime loved, and yet through fortunes evill hap might not have her to wife.'[5] Charles would have been aware that the 'evill hap' was more down to Henry than fortune, but their new relationship meant that was a thing of the past. After four days of festivities, on 31 May Charles bade farewell to his hosts and departed for Sandwich, from where he sailed to Flanders. That same day, Henry and Catherine headed for Dover, where they boarded ship for Calais, arriving at eleven o'clock that night.

A huge painting in the royal collection, measuring 169cm by 347cm, depicts a stylised version of what happened next. The Field of Cloth of Gold, so-called after the abundance of material used to make the tents and hangings, was a magnificent ceremony lasting from 7 until 24 June 1520, created by the kings of England and France. The picture depicts the temporary palace at the English camp at Guisnes, the village of tents, the tournament, feasts and fountains flowing with wine. Henry is featured prominently, but if his wife is depicted, it is only in tiny form, barely visible, with no personalised details. This may be because the work was completed or updated in 1545, long after Henry and Catherine were no longer married, but it is also indicative of the behind-the-scenes formal role that both queens adopted. Catherine and Claude, wife of Francis I, were not present at the initial encounters between the two Kings, who met and banqueted in a tent between the two camps. Hall gives us a glimpse of Henry as 'the moost goodliest Prince that ever reigned over the Realm of England,' dressed in cloth of silver of damask, ribbed with cloth of gold, 'marvellous to behold' and riding a horse likewise trapped in gold.[6]

The Queens finally met on 1 June, in a field that was decorated with a pageant of two trees. With the marital agreement between their children still fresh, Catherine and Claude met as mothers, saluted each other 'right honourably' and took their places on a stage to watch the men engage in a tournament 'so valiantly that the beholders had great joy'. The women sat in a 'glazed gallery, hung with tapestry and talked about the tourney'. Many in their company were obliged to use the services of translators, as they could not understand each other.[7] One of these translators may well have been the nineteen-year-old Anne Boleyn, the diplomat's daughter, who had entered the service of the French Queen in 1514 or 15. While Henry dined with Claude, it was Catherine and Mary, Duchess of Suffolk, received Francis on June 17, 'with all honour that was according'. On display were silver and gold plates and vessels and the finest ingredients had been sourced from local 'forests, parks, field, salt sea, rivers, moats and ponds'; men were well rewarded for finding great delicacies.[8] When the plates were cleared away, masked dancers performed and women acting as mummers.

Catherine, Claude and Mary were again present on 23 June, when a chapel was erected on the field which had hosted the tournaments, where Wolsey sang High Mass and issued an indulgence, a pardon for any sins, to all present, including both sets of kings and queens. Part-way through, a huge artificial dragon appeared in the sky from the direction of Ardres, four fathoms long and full of fire, which scared many of those assembled. It passed over the chapel 'as fast as a footman can go'[9] and while some thought it a comet or a monster, it was part of the festivities, either as some huge firework or balloon, recorded for posterity in the corner of the 1545 painting. Following this, the three women dined together before retiring for the night when guns were fired to mark the vigil of St John the Baptist.[10]

*

After her return home at the end of June Catherine wrote to Queen Claude, in response to her 'good and affectionate letters'. She had been 'very greatly consoled' to hear the 'good news, health, estate and prosperity in (which is my) very dear and most beloved good son, and yours, the dauphin.' She expressed the 'good love, friendship and fraternal intelligence and alliance which is now between the two kings our husbands and their kingdoms, which I hold inseparable and pray God that it may continue.'[11] Catherine learned that during her absence, the French ambassadors who visited Richmond were received by Princess Mary in her presence chamber, with 'the most goodly countenance, proper communication and pleasant pastime in playing at the virginals, that they greatly marvelled and rejoiced at the same, her young and tender age considered.'[12] They were treated to a banquet of strawberries, cherries, apples, wafers, wine and hippocras. The Princess had acquitted herself well.

Mary was still very much Henry's card to play when the occasion suited him. Just six months after the Field of Cloth of Gold, Mary's French betrothal was formally broken in favour of a marriage to her cousin Emperor Charles, who was then twenty to her four years of age. As Henry explained to Bishop Cuthbert Tunstall, 'our daughter will be of age before the French king's, and will be a more advantageous match than the other, by possibility of succession.'[13] Mary could conceivably be married at the age of twelve, in just eight years' time, instead of having to wait for the Dauphin to come of age. In opening the Imperial negotiations, Henry was mindful of his daughter's worth: 'It is to be considered that she is now our sole heir, and may succeed to the crown; so that we ought rather to receive from the Emperor as large a sum as we should give with her if she were not our heir.'[14] The main concern with a female heir was the authority that her husband would be able to wield over her: a queen's husband would, in effect, be King of England, so he must be chosen wisely.

On Valentine's Day 1521, the six-year-old Princess was given a brooch of gold and jewels bearing her fiancé's name, which was noted by the Imperial Ambassadors and reported back to Charles, along with Mary's 'beauty and charms'.[15] She also performed a dance, twirling 'so prettily that no woman in the world could do better... then she played two or three songs on the spinet' with the 'grace and skill... and self-command a woman of twenty might wish for.'[16] The following summer, Mary had a chance to meet Charles when he visited England again, this time at more leisure. He arrived at Dover on the afternoon of 27 May and Henry, who had been awaiting him at Canterbury, went to greet him and conduct him to London via Sittingbourne, Rochester and Gravesend. From there, on 2 June, they took a barge to Greenwich, arriving at around 6pm.[17] At the entrance to the great hall, Charles was reunited with Catherine and met Princess Mary, expressing 'great joy' to see the pair of them, especially the Princess. He was lodged in Henry's apartments by the river, which were so richly hung with tapestries that the visitors marvelled at them. Jousting, feasting and disguisings followed, in which a masked Henry was among those who 'toke ladies and daunsed' and rode in the lists among those dressed in gold and silver, with plumes on their heads.[18] On 16 June, Henry and Charles signed the Treaty of Windsor, committing Charles to marry Mary within eight years and that once she had reached her twelfth birthday, in 1528, the Emperor, who would then be twenty-eight, would send a proxy to London for the first formal wedding ceremony. Wolsey sealed the deal with his authority as a papal legate by adding the condition that if either man broke it, they would automatically be excommunicated.

And yet, Henry was still playing the diplomatic game of considering other matches. Margaret's situation in Scotland was difficult, and relations with England were still strained, but when her ambassadors suggested a marriage between James V and Princess Mary, Henry responded with enthusiasm. With Mary as a card in his hand, he asked his sister to keep their plan secret and sent his nephew a coat of cloth of gold and a sword. Such a marriage would have created an unprecedented union between England and Scotland, producing a single heir to both thrones, well before this finally occurred in 1603. But Henry infinitely preferred retaining his daughter as a bargaining chip to committing her to a foreign prince. During this time, he maintained separate agreements concerning Mary's marriage with France, Scotland and Spain, keeping his daughter close and giving his allies hope.

*

Margaret's own marital situation was less than happy. As early as October 1518, she had written to Henry raising the possibility of a divorce from Angus:

> I am sore troubled with my Lord of Angus since my last coming into Scotland, and every day more and more, so that we have not been together this half year... I am so minded that, an I may by law of God and to my honour, to part with him, for I wit well he loves me not, as he shows me daily.[19]

Henry and Catherine both tried to convince Margaret that divorce was not an acceptable action, with Catherine despatching a Father Bonaventura north to counsel her and sending her own advice not to make these matters public. Henry added his own representative, Friar Henry Chadworth from the Greyfriars at Greenwich, to tell his sister 'her ideas for divorce were wicked delusions, inspired by the father of evil, whose malice alone could prompt her to blame her husband ... or unnaturally stigmatise the fair daughter she had had by him.'[20]

With hindsight, these words feel deeply ironic, but Henry was far from the position he would adopt a decade later.

For a time, this strategy appears to have yielded results, with Angus writing to Henry in gratitude in October 1519:

> Friar Henry Chaidworth, minister of the Observant Friars in England, has arrived with letters from Henry to the Queen his sister. He has discharged his mission so well that the Queen is willing to remain with Angus her husband. Cannot express his gratitude to Henry for the result. Will be always ready to do him service, even if Henry commanded him to go on foot to Jerusalem and fight with the Turks. His brother, George Douglas, has been two years detained in France by the duke of Albany. Begs Henry to write to the king of France and the governor for his deliverance. Dalkeith, 19 Oct.[21]

The situation between husband and wife soon worsened, however. Prevented from seeing her son and even more determined to divorce Angus, Margaret stopped confiding in her brother and turned instead to the absent Regent, Albany. When he returned to Scotland in November 1521, after an absence of five years, Margaret received the Earl at Linlithgow and they made a state entry together into Edinburgh, where she presented him with the keys of the castle. Rumours reached England that she was intending to divorce only to marry Albany, but these were spread by her enemies. With her husband having fled to the Borders, Margaret's intention was to gain power for herself and her son, not to submit to the governance of a new husband. In 1524, while Albany was absent in France, Margaret drew on Angus's enemies to help her bring James to Edinburgh from Stirling. As the boy was now twelve years old, it was announced that the regency was over and the new King would rule alone. In practice though, it was Margaret who guided him, silencing any opponents and being recognised by Parliament that November as her son's chief advisor. Although the last decade had proved difficult and unpredictable for Margaret, she had been patient and used Scottish factional politics to draw support when she required it. Her coup of 1524 gained her control of her son. When she was reprimanded by English ambassadors for firing cannons to prevent her husband's approach, she told them to 'go home and not meddle with Scottish matters.'[22]

*

For Catherine, Margaret and Mary, the mid 1520s marked the end of their fertility. In 1522, Mary had lost her son Henry at the age of six, but bore a final child, another boy, in 1523, to whom she gave the same name. The two-year old Henry Brandon was invested as Earl of Lincoln in 1525, in a ceremony alongside the elevation of his illegitimate cousin Henry Fitzroy to the dukedoms of Richmond and Somerset. Bessie Blount's son was now six years old and this step has been interpreted as the King's recognition of him as his heir, in the knowledge that Catherine would bear no more children. The Queen's last pregnancy had been in 1518 and seven years later, as she approached forty, her erratic menstruation developed into the menopause. Spending long periods living separately from her husband, the details of Margaret's fertility are unclear, but by 1525, when she was thirty-six, her youngest child was ten years old. She would marry again, to a younger man, but would bear no more babies.

This moment marks a significant shift for the three queens. The main task of queenship, of wives, was the production of heirs, and they had experienced varying degrees of success. Catherine had a single surviving daughter, Mary, from six pregnancies. Margaret had a son, James and daughter, Margaret, from two different marriages and seven pregnancies. Mary had two daughters and a son from four pregnancies that we know of. That gives a survival rate of six children from seventeen pregnancies, almost one in three. Of the eleven children that were lost, three were miscarried or stillborn, three died at birth or very soon after, two died before their first birthday and three more were lost before they reached the age of seven. Suggested rates of infant mortality for the time offer a figure of 20-25% dying before their first birthday, with an additional 40-50% dying before the age of five, equating to an overall infant mortality rate of 30%.[23]

Catherine, Margaret and Mary had been fortunate to survive the process of delivery and its aftermath, which claimed the lives of many of their contemporaries, but their maternal experiences were very different. Mary fared best of the three, with the lowest rate of loss, at 25%, and not experiencing any stillbirths or miscarriages that have been recorded. Charles Brandon had already fathered two children before their marriage and would father two more after Mary's death, indicative of his robust reproductive health. Margaret lost two children at birth, two more before their first birthday and one aged eighteen months, giving her a rate of loss of five out of seven. Yet her statistics suggest the greater problem was keeping children alive in infancy, rather than issues of pregnancy and delivery. By contrast, Catherine experienced three miscarriages or stillbirths, one lost during or soon after delivery and one before the age of one.

Exactly why Catherine and Margaret experienced such difficulties in bearing and rearing live children is unclear. There may be no underlying pattern, or explanation for these losses, which may simply have been unfortunate; no doubt a host of contributing factors influenced genetic and physical circumstances which are not recoverable today. Catherine's record seems to suggest some inherited problem, which historians have laid more recently at the feet of her husband, potentially a carrier of Kell's blood antigens, a recessive genetic disorder resulting in McLeod's syndrome.[24] Given the long list of Elizabeth Woodville's children and grandchildren, it is plausible that the strain was passed down through the paternal line, although Margaret Beaufort's fertility was not subsequently put to the test. It has also been suggested in recent years that Catherine's extreme regime of fasting and prayer contributed to her losses, but her problem was carrying, not conceiving, and once pregnant she would have avoided any risks to her child, so far as she perceived them. The deaths of Margaret's children at an early age are more indicative of environmental factors, given her higher rate of live births, but her babies might equally have been born with some invisible genetic weakness, as much as being prey to infantile illness or conditions in the nursery. It is just not possible to know.

There was an implicit divine sanction in the conception and delivery of heirs that was reassuring for a family so recently come to power, which promised there would be no repeat of the inheritance struggles of the preceding century. But this was also a measure of failure, as Margaret did produce a surviving son but Catherine did not. By this single criterion, Margaret was a successful queen but Catherine was not. Their experiences illustrate the random nature of the female lot, with little control over their fertility and success rates, no matter how much care they may have taken, how many pilgrimages they undertook, or how much they wanted a child.

Catherine and Margaret made significant advances in the nature of early sixteenth century queenship. As Mary's tenure on the French throne lasted only a few months, and she acted swiftly to prevent any further dynastic marriage, she had no opportunity to demonstrate her queenship under pressure. But her personal choice was, in itself, significant. As Queen of France, Mary had been regal in behaviour, beautiful, loving and supportive to an infirm husband, the symbolic, majestic token bride in her mother's mould. Her second marriage, made whilst she was still young and childless, represented a significant shift in behaviour. By asserting her own preference and acting before her return home, she denied her brother, and her dynasty, her future service in the capacity as queen. The promise she had extracted from Henry at Dover in autumn 1514 could easily have been considered invalid or not binding in light of the brevity of her first marriage. At the age of twenty, her former engagement to Charles V could have been revived, but her self-assertion placed her individualism above her dynasty, for the sake of love.

After her marriage, Mary balanced her private life as a duchess with her continuing contributions as a Tudor princess. She was a popular figurehead at jousts and ceremonial occasions, as a hostess, meeting ambassadors, representing her dynasty in cultural, international and religious contexts. She was an active member of the royal family, but she was also off the marriage market and could slip more easily from her public role into domestic seclusion at Westhorpe Hall. She had greater control over the education of her children and their comparative obscurity reflects the more private nature of their upbringing. Mary also raised Brandon's daughters from his first marriage alongside her own three children in the Suffolk countryside, insisting that the elder, Anne Brandon, was brought home from the court of Margaret of Savoy, and would have had a hand in making the marriages of both girls in the mid-1520s.

The queenship of Margaret and Catherine lasted longer, with Margaret reigning in Scotland for a decade, and Catherine having been married for sixteen years by 1525. Both acted as regent during the absence of their husbands in 1513, and Margaret also did so for her son James. For half her marriage, Margaret was essentially a child in modern eyes, united to a much older man, with established relationships, allegiances, lovers, and even illegitimate children. It was challenging for her to enter this world, as a girl of thirteen, and negotiate the complex history of the Scottish court. She had to project her image of supportive queenship and majesty from the first day of her arrival, but whether or not she 'loved' James is a far more complex issue. When Mary crossed to France in 1514, she was at least a young woman of eighteen, better able to navigate her new situation. It is doubtful whether 'love' existed between Mary and Louis, Margaret and James, in the romantic sense of the word, in the sense that it did between Henry and Catherine. But 'love' might be a misleading concept, given our post-modern, post-romantic sentiments. 'Love' between a king and queen, in an arranged marriage, was an entirely different construct, part duty, part loyalty, respect, mutual protection and service to one's dynasty and country. Mary appears to have conducted herself 'lovingly' towards Louis, in playing her role, but history has long considered that she was 'in love' with Brandon. This may have been the case, or it might be that she experienced a similar construct of emotions towards him, as her protector and rescuer from an alternative fate. And of course, he was younger than Louis, an international jousting champion and reputedly good-looking.

Catherine's marriage to Henry VIII was the ultimate royal love-match of the early sixteenth century. This was one of her most significant contributions to the dynasty. It represented a similarly companionate marriage as that of Edward IV and Elizabeth Woodville, but with greater parity between the partners. Catherine had been born to be a queen, educated as a queen since her early years, absorbing the lesson of her mother's example and her parents' marriage; and she was older, and wiser, than Henry. In 1509, she was an active and intellectual support to the new young King, being Henry's equal in education and understanding, enabling her to engage in disputes, discuss strategies and international relations, to act as an ambassador and fulfil her role in pageantry and ceremony. Catherine's organisation and contribution to the Flodden campaign made England's success possible and stirred national pride. She was also outstanding in her communications with Henry and Wolsey in France, but also with her father and extended family, as an ambassador for England, and as a hostess during the visits of her nephew Charles and at the Field of Cloth of Gold. Erasmus even considered Catherine to be Henry's intellectual superior. She was a model of Catholic queenship in everything save her unfortunate childbearing record, something over which she had no control. The romance and devotion visible between King and Queen during the 1510s contributed as much to the celebration of love as Mary and Margaret's second marriages did.

PART FOUR

Fleeting Queenship
1525–1549

15

Breaking the Queenship Model
1525–1533

In 1525, Henry's fears about the succession were clarified. Catherine's menopause, following the birth of only one surviving daughter, convinced him that he was on the verge of a dynastic crisis. Realising that he could no longer remain married to Catherine if he wanted a male heir, he began to question why this had occurred, and how he might solve the problem. In line with the limits of medical and cultural understanding, he assigned their reproductive failure to Catherine and to the disapproval of God.

Over the next two decades, Henry fell in love, appealed for an annulment, broke with Rome and remarried, all of which scandalised Europe. In the minds of their contemporaries, Henry's actions would cast Catherine as a martyr to the old faith and a figure of popular sympathy among the conservative faction, and his new love Anne Boleyn as a representative of reform, iconoclasm and dangerous femininity. Henry's second marriage necessitated the reform and rejection of Catholic practices, the alteration of English churches, even a change to the countryside itself, and the pursuit of a brave new path independent of centuries-old cultural mores. Anne's legacy was not her deliberate policy: it was driven by Henry and ran concurrently with her queenship, but she was both the catalyst and the fuel for change. Anne may only have worn the crown for a little over her legendary thousand days, and battled to have her queenship recognised, but her cultural and religious legacies far outweigh that of any other of Henry's queens. Because Henry desired her queenship, England was changed forever.

Anne Boleyn came from a family with an established position at the Tudor court. Her father, Thomas, was the grandson of a former Mayor of London, and had built on the commercial success of his forebears to educate and advance himself, making an advantageous marriage to the daughter of the Duke of Norfolk. Boleyn had been a member of Prince Arthur's wedding party, accompanied Margaret into Scotland in 1503, a courtier to Henry, and ambassador to the Netherlands, France and the Empire. His proficiency in languages and easy manners had facilitated his rise, and the placement of his elder daughter in the retinue of Mary, Queen of France, and his younger daughter in the household of Margaret, Regent of the Netherlands. Anne's mother, Elizabeth Howard, had been sent to live in the household of Queen Elizabeth of York after Bosworth, and her beauty was praised, at the age of fourteen or fifteen, in a poem dedicated to her by court poet John Skelton. The couple married in around 1498, and had three surviving children, Mary in 1499, Anne in 1501 and George in 1503 or 1504.

Anne was raised at Blickling House in Norfolk until February 1506, when the family moved to Hever Castle in Kent, which they had inherited from Thomas's father. She received a quiet country upbringing suitable to her class, with the intention of equipping her for an advantageous marriage, although it would never have crossed her parents' minds to prepare her for queenship. At the age of twelve she was sent to Margaret's household in Mechelen, Belgium, which was one of the best 'finishing schools' for young ladies, where she was exposed to the intricacies of a great European dynasty, to international diplomacy, Reformation culture, Renaissance art and an extensive library. In 1514, when her sister accompanied Princess Mary to France, Anne was withdrawn from the Netherlands and sent to the French court, where she entered the service of Queen Claude. She spent the next seven years in the sophisticated surroundings of the Italianate chateaux of Blois and Amboise, where Leonardo da Vinci was a guest for the last three years of his life and where the discourse of reform was tolerated at court. Anne was being shaped into a forward-looking woman of the early modern era, open to challenging ideas and to change.

One of the most important lessons Anne learned in her years abroad concerned the exercise of power by women. In the Netherlands and France, she encountered female role models who broke gender rules to offer real leadership in political, religious and cultural spheres. The examples of Margaret of Austria, the French King's mother Louise of Savoy and sister Marguerite d'Alençon, showed Anne that women could play significant roles as politically astute, international figures.

She learned that exceptional high-born women could take leading positions on the international stage, but that the ceiling to their powers remained, as even Margaret was guided by her father Maximilian and brother Charles, while Louise and Marguerite were unable to prevent Francis embarking upon a war they regretted. Anne also saw how Queen Claude underwent a string of pregnancies that left her weakened and exposed to danger, whilst Francis entertained himself with his mistresses. Being the wife of a king was not the same as being an active queen, and Anne glimpsed what women might achieve when they were unfettered, as well as the types of restrictions and controls to which they were subjected. Late in 1521, at the age of twenty, she was recalled to England in preparation for marriage into the Irish Butler family, but after her return the plans fell through. By March 1522, Anne was at court; but she was not the Boleyn sister in Henry's favour.

*

On the night of 4 March Wolsey hosted a splendid entertainment at York Place, a symbolic masque featuring many of the leading figures of Henry's court, in which Anne took the role of Perseverance, alongside her sister Mary, who was portraying Kindness. Mary, former queen of France, played the part of Beauty, with the other roles filled by prominent women of the court. An elaborate castle was built in the great hall, painted green and decorated with leaves, where banners hung from three towers; the first bore the image of three hearts, torn in half; the second showed a lady's hand gripping a man's heart and the third showed another female hand 'turning' a man's heart.[1] The pageant was entitled the *Chateau Vert*, or, most aptly, *The Assault on the Castle of Virtue*, and from underneath the castle more figures appeared, but these were a grotesque parody of the courtly women trapped within. Played by choristers of the Chapel Royal, attired 'like to women of Inde' (India), they represented the negative qualities of lovers: Danger, Disdain, Jealousy, Unkindness, Scorn, Strangeness and Malbouche, or bad (harsh) tongue. Then eight lords entered the hall, dressed in blue capes and golden caps, yet not so dazzling as their leader, who took the role of Ardent Desire in a costume of crimson satin adorned with burning flames of gold.[2] A mock battle followed, an allegory for the overcoming of a lover's scruples, in which the ladies wished to yield to Ardent Desire but were dissuaded by Scorn and

Disdain. In their defence, the women threw rose water and comfits, whilst the men replied with dates and oranges and the suggestive 'other fruits made for pleasure'.[3]

This pageant was Anne's debut at the English court, but it made little impact upon Henry. Since 1520, he had been conducting an affair with her elder sister Mary. On 4 February 1520 Mary had been married to William Carey, a gentleman of the Privy Chamber, close to the King. He was a direct descendent of John of Gaunt, albeit through the female line, making him a distant royal cousin on the Lancastrian side. Henry had attended their wedding at the royal chapel at Greenwich and made an altar offering of 6 shillings and 8 pence, indicating his approval, perhaps even having had a hand in organising it. It may have been a reward and a cover for him enjoying the bride's favours. Very little is known about their relationship, even the duration of it, whether days, weeks, months or years. The paternity of Mary's two children, Catherine born in 1524 and Henry born in 1526, has sometimes been attributed to the King, but this was never publicly admitted, and both were acknowledged by Carey as his own. The affair is only public knowledge because Anne's enemies later attempted to use it to discredit her, otherwise it would have been lost to history. The Boleyn family continued to benefit from the connection, with appointments for Carey, Boleyn and George. No doubt the connection also helped Anne establish herself at the English court, perhaps in the household of Mary, Duchess of Suffolk.

Beginning a new phase of her life in England, Anne was perhaps more aware than many young women her age of the need to seek out opportunities that may present themselves for her family's advancement and turn them to her advantage. This quality has been subject to harsh criticisms by later historians, deconstructed and defined in the tradition of the male gaze as an unattractive ruthlessness, unbecoming to a woman, but such assessments are as anachronistic as they are simplistic, and miss the essence of Anne's character. As Henry's attraction to Anne would prove, there was nothing less feminine or appealing about her for her ability to understand the operations of the court, ride the waves of Tudor patronage and enter negotiations at the appropriate moment. It was shrewdness, a kind of intelligence, part innate, part developed from her experiences and observations abroad. Her French style and manners, her very different background and European polish made her desirable in a world where everyone, regardless of gender, wanted to be desirable in the eyes of the King.

The Tudor court was a giant wheel of fortune, a game of chance, of pot luck, and Anne was adept at the game. This made her an unusual figure at the English court, exotic, different and challenging to men who were used to taking wives from their neighbourhood circle or the small, known aristocratic gene pool.

Yet it was not an Irish Earl or the King himself who stole Anne's heart. Against her family's wishes, tradition and royal expectations, she did what Mary and Margaret had done a decade before. She chose her own husband for love. Henry Percy is thought to have been born in around 1502, making him a few months younger than Anne, and aged around twenty at the time of their meeting. He was a first cousin of Anne's brother-in-law, William Carey, and had been raised in the north before being sent to join Wolsey's household, where he did well, being knighted in 1519. A marriage had been planned for him with the heiress Mary Talbot, daughter of the Earl of Shrewsbury, in 1516, but the pair had reputedly disliked each other on sight. No image survives of him in his youth, but a later medallion shows him in middle age, in profile, with a prominent nose and full beard. The romance progressed through the end of 1522, into 1523. It was probably that spring or early summer that the pair reached an understanding that they would like to be married. Anne would have been aware that it was not the match her father had intended for her, and it did nothing to settle the Irish inheritance that motivated the Butler negotiations, but it was an equal match in terms of status. With Percy being the heir to his father's Northumberland title and estates, Anne would have become a countess in due course. If Boleyn could set aside his Ormond ambitions, or settle them in another way, Anne had every reason to hope her father might agree to her choice, especially if vows had been exchanged, making the liaison semi-official.

Somehow, the couple's secret came to light. It may have been that they naively took the step of formally requesting permission to marry, or that their preference was observed, or their confidences betrayed. Aristocratic marriages were not simply family matters, they had to be politically and practically viable and receive royal support. Cardinal Wolsey intervened, calling Percy before him and berating him in front of the servants of his chamber:

> I marvel not a little of thy peevish folly that thou wouldst tangle and
> ensure thye self with a foolish girl yonder in the court. I mean Anne

Boleyn. Dost thou not consider the estate that God hathe called thee unto in this world for after the death thy noble father thou art most like to inherit and possess one of the most worthiest Earldoms of this realm and therefore it had been most meet and convenient for thee to have sued for the consent of thy father in that behalf.[4]

Percy had been already matched 'according to your estate and honour, whereby you might have grown so by your wisdom and honourable behaviour in to the King's high estimation that it should have been much to your increase of honour. But now behold what you have done through your wilfulness, you have not only offended your natural father but also your most gracious sovereign.'[5] Anne was sent away to cool her ardour at Hever.

*

1525 was a watershed year for Catherine. Approaching her fortieth birthday and having not conceived for six years, she sat for the Flemish artist Lucas Horenbout, and was depicted by him holding a monkey. Horenbout had arrived in England in 1522, with his father Gerard and younger sister Susanna, both of whom were also artists; Gerard previously having been court painter to Margaret of Austria, and Susanna would become a favourite miniaturist at Henry's court, in competition with Levinia Teerlinc.

In Gerard's portrait, Catherine is dressed in the fashion of the day, opting for an archaic English gable hood, gold and studded with gems, with a thick red lappet sewn with diamond, or diaper, shapes, pinned up at either side, and the traditional thick black hood. Not an inch of her hair shows except for the shadow, a suggestion at the very top of her head. It was a conservative choice, favoured by older ladies over the lighter, smaller version or the round French hood Catherine had favoured as a young widow when she had sat for Michael Sittow. It marks the change in the woman, and the times, as this year of Gerard Horenbout's ascendancy also marked Sittow's demise.

Catherine wears a brown velvet bodice, with the entire length of the square neckline sewn with pearls and gold ornaments, revealing the very edge of her smock, which appears to be embroidered in blackwork. Her wide over-sleeves are folded back at the elbow to reveal the delicately patterned golden sleeves beneath, with their lace cuff. Her hands are bare and white; she wears no rings but in her right one she clasps a cluster of brown-grey feathers or a bunch of herbs. On a gold chain around her neck hangs a five-part pendant, with three drop pearls dangling below. Her face is fleshy, her nose and chin heavy, her mouth small and eyes almost stern. It is a regal portrait, but one of a woman past her physical prime. Henry was only thirty-four and he had no legitimate son.

At the same time, Antonio de Correggio of Parma, completed his *Venus with Mercury and Cupid,* or *The School of Love,* depicting the voluptuous, full bodies that represented the contemporary ideal of beauty, while Bartolomeo Veneto painted the nubile, golden-haired *Flora,* or the *Idealised Portrait of a Courtesan.* Henry's court, or rather, Catherine's household, was full of young, beautiful women, and although the King had previously strayed, he now began to question whether they might offer him more than just sexual satisfaction. Fertility was equated with youth and an outward physical beauty was considered to be a good indicator of moral character, which was passed from mother to child. Childbearing manuals from the first part of the sixteenth century, authored by men, attributed problems in conception, pregnancy and birth to women.

It was also around this time that Henry stopped visiting Catherine's bed. The poet Lydgate's *Dietary* advised, 'with women agyd, flesschly have not to do.' Canon law still advised post-menopausal wives to yield up the marital debt, to prevent their husbands straying into sin.[6] The idea of the conjugal debt in canon law related to the husband as well as the wife, but Henry wanted to free himself from this obligation. Apostle Paul stated that: 'You must not refuse each other, except perhaps by consent, for a time, that you may give yourself to prayer, and return together again lest Satan tempt you for you lack self-control.' Catherine had taken her marriage vows with sincerity and endured those of Henry's humiliating infidelities that she had been aware of. Setting aside the question of her queenship, and the rights of her daughter, she was not about to give her consent that Henry might refuse his marital obligations. Sterility or old age were not considered valid impediments to a marriage in medieval law, although the case of a king in need of a male heir was more complicated. Henry began to question why his marriage had not been blessed with healthy children, seeking out some impediment and debating the possible cause in secret with his confessor, John Longland, Bishop of Lincoln.

The year 1525 was also decisive for the English succession. The elevation of Henry Fitzroy to the Dukedoms of Richmond and Somerset was Henry's response to his failure to father a son with Catherine. The nine-year-old Mary was sent to Ludlow, the home of two former Princes of Wales, in a move that equated to a tacit recognition of her status as the legitimate heir. In early August, the Venetian ambassador reported that 'on Saturday last, the Princess went to her principality of Wales, with a suitable and honourable escort, and she will reside there until the time of her marriage.' About Mary's character, he commented, 'she is a rare person and singularly accomplished, most particularly in music, playing on every instrument, especially on the lute and harpsichord.'[7] Mary seemed to be in no hurry to arrive at Ludlow. Her journey took her from Woburn to Reading Abbey, then west to Thornbury Castle and Gloucester, before settling at Tickenhill for Christmas. Then she moved on to Worcester and continued travelling in that vicinity for the first half of 1526, escaping accounts of plague in the area, until she met Henry that summer and travelled with him on progress in Oxfordshire and Buckinghamshire.

The delay in Mary's arrival at Ludlow may have been caused by the improvements that were reported on in early September and mid-October 1525, overseen by Richard Sydnour, Dean of Totnes, Mary's surveyor general, and Walter Rogers who directed the work. Substantial repairs were made, as payments were made to masons, plumbers, tilers and labourers.

A thousand tiles were used, soldered on in lead by three plumbers, a carpenter 'winded and daubed' the walls of the chapel for two days. The diggers at the quarry received 3½d each a day. It cost 8d to make a new key for the great gate. Mary's room was 'soldered', new floors were laid, locks were created for the cellar and chapel and the old boiling house walls were stripped.[8] With the fate of her uncle Arthur in mind, there was also great emphasis placed on the importance of Mary taking exercise in 'gardens, sweet and wholesome places' and that she was kept away from anything 'noisome or displeasant'. Other necessaries provided for her new household included kitchen equipment and napery for her table, items for the laundry and stables, blue and green damask to dress all her staff in her personal livery colours, furnishing for her chapel including gold and crimson cushions, and ordnance and artillery for her defence.[9]

Mary's early education had largely been overseen by her mother, appointing tutors in foreign languages such as the Frenchman Giles Duwes and using texts specifically written for her: Thomas Linacre's *Rudimenta Grammatices* of 1523 and Juan Luis Vives' *De Ratione Studii Puerilis* of 1524. She also read works by Erasmus and Thomas More, who was well-known for teaching his daughters Latin and Greek and giving them the humanist education usually reserved for aristocratic young men. In his 1516 tract *Utopia*, More had called for the education of women, and in 1524 Martin Luther advocated the establishment of schools for girls. And yet, for Mary, the ultimate goal was still a good marriage, to the right man, rather than independent rule in her own right. She was educated to be a wife, not for leadership. In 1520 her great-aunt, Margaret Pole, Countess of Salisbury, had been appointed as her governess, with an interval in 1521 when the connection between her sons and the Duke of Buckingham was investigated. On Mary's departure in 1525, Margaret was dismissed, even though she begged to be allowed to continue her service without a salary. Henry appointed Richard Fetherston as her main tutor, Catherine of Aragon's former Chaplain and Archdeacon of Brecon. Her council were instructed to discuss her 'virtuous education' and health at least monthly. Mary did suffer from some ill-health as a child, especially poor eyesight and headaches, and sinus conditions, but she was otherwise well, or her parents would not have sent her to Ludlow. Just to be certain, though, Henry's trusted physician, Dr William Butts, was appointed to care for her.

*

It was late in 1525 or early in 1526 that Anne Boleyn returned to court. In her mid-twenties, she was slender, dark haired and elegant, dressed in clothes influenced by the recent fashions of France, skilled in dancing and conversation. It seems to have been the consensus among her contemporaries that she was not a conventional beauty, as Catherine had been in her youth, but that she exerted a compelling fascination that made her irresistible to men. Her best feature, according to the Venetian diplomat Sanuto, was her 'black and beautiful' eyes, but apart from these, he described her as having a 'swarthy complexion, long neck, wide mouth, bosom not much raised and in fact has nothing but the King's great appetite and her eyes, which are black and beautiful and take great effect...'[10] The French diplomat de Carles agreed that her eyes were 'most attractive' and that she knew how to use them, to send flirtatious messages, so that 'many a man paid his allegiance.' He found her beautiful, 'with an elegant figure... so graceful that you would never have taken her for an Englishwoman but for a Frenchwoman born.'[11] Anne's physical attraction lay in her exotic difference from the English concept of curvaceous, blue-eyed, blonde or red-golden-haired beauty typified by Catherine of Aragon. As the Queen had introduced a new style in 1501 when she wore the first hooped farthingale skirt in England, Anne was also a trend-setter. According to French chronicler Brantôme, she set a new fashion with her French style, devising new clothes that were copied by other ladies at court, and was 'the fairest and most bewitching of all the lovely dames'.[12]

Henry may have fallen in love with Anne in or around February 1526. At the Shrovetide jousts held at Greenwich, he dressed in embroidered gold and silver, bearing the device of a 'mannes harte in a presse, with flames about it' with the motto 'declare, I dare not.' His opponents were dressed in green and red velvet, decorated with the image of burning hearts, over which was a woman's hand 'commyng out of a cloud, holdyng a garden water pot, which dropped silver drops on the harte'.[13] The symbolism revealed a new object of affection, the pain of concealed love and the remedy, within the power of the right woman. Henry 'did service' to the Queen and her ladies, which possibly included Anne, to whom his cryptic message may have been directed. It is likely that by this time she was aware of the situation, although Catherine may not have been. The passionate love letters he wrote her, attempting to persuade her to be his mistress, and ending with a promise of marriage, date from 1526-7.

The year 1525 also saw a realignment of international relations, with implications for Princess Mary's future and her father's impending marital aspirations. That February, Francis had been defeated by Charles at the Battle of Pavia, ending France's efforts to reclaim parts of Italy, and resulting in the imprisonment of the French King. Henry had immediately seen the opportunity to benefit from his former friend's failure, siding with Charles and asking for the kingdom of France to be divided up between them. This irritated the Emperor, who preferred to come to terms with Francis, and the following March he ended all hopes of an English marriage by taking Isabella of Portugal as his wife.

Perhaps it was also Anne's influence that saw Henry return to his union with France, seeking an alternative husband for Mary, even considering the newly widowed Francis himself for a considerable dowry. In April 1526, the French ambassadors were entertained at Greenwich, meeting Catherine and Mary after dinner, where the eleven-year-old Princess conversed in Latin, French and Italian, played the virginals, and convinced the visitors that she was the most accomplished child they had ever seen.[14] The following month, Mary played a central role in the great masque held in her mother's apartments, hiding in a cave made of cloth of gold, from which she descended to the sound of trumpets to dance.[15] However, Henry was not prepared to meet their demand of sending Mary to be raised at the Valois court, as her youth and diminutive size meant she was 'not yet ripe' for 'carnali copula'. During the ambassadors' visit, Queen Catherine sat beside Henry under the 'goodly' cloth of estate, hung with the royal motto 'dieu et mon droit', but it was Anne whom the King deliberately selected as his dance partner. 'We were in the Queen's apartments where there was dancing,' reported the ambassador, 'and the king (danced) with Mistress Boulan who was brought up in France with the late queen.'[16]

In March 1527, Pope Clement VII granted Margaret Tudor a divorce from her second husband, the Earl of Angus. A year later, she married Henry Stewart, a distant cousin of James IV and Master of the Scottish Artillery. As with her choice of Angus, this second love match provoked a negative response from the nobility, headed by Lord Erskine and her son James V, who besieged Margaret and her new husband at Stirling Castle and imprisoned Henry. In England, her brother was quick to remark upon her folly. In the opinion of Henry VIII, the Pope's judgement was 'shameless', the marriage was 'divinely ordained ... inseparable' and 'first instituted in Paradise'. She had been 'seduced by flatterers to an unlawful divorce ... upon untrue and insufficient allegations.' He expressed much concern about 'the wealth of her soul and her own repute' and hoped she would 'turn to God's word, the true doctrine of Jesus Christ, the only ground for Salvation.' He urged her to avoid 'the inevitable damnation threatened against adulterers' and to reconcile with Angus 'as her true husband, or out of mere natural affection for her daughter'.[17] Henry then turned his attentions to setting aside Catherine, his wife of nineteen years, in order to marry Anne Boleyn.

Adam and Eve. (British Library)

Christine de Pisan and the goddess
Minerva. (British Library)

The coronation of an Amazon queen
in Christine de Pisan's *Book of the
City of Ladies*. (British Library)

Elizabeth Woodville. (Ripon Cathedral)

Margaret Beaufort.

St John's College, Cambridge,
founded by Margaret Beaufort.
(Courtesy of Beth Camp)

A celebration of Elizabeth of York's 1486 marriage to Henry VII. (British Library)

Young Margaret, Henry and Mary Tudor. (Wellcome Collection)

The Great Hall of Eltham Palace.

Ludlow Castle. (Courtesy of Ben Salter)

Henry VII's Chapel. (Author's collection)

Holyrood Abbey. (Courtesy of Brian Holsclaw)

Alcala de Henares, birthplace of Catherine of Aragon. (Courtesy of M. Peinado)

KATHERINA VXOR HENRICI . viii.

Catherine of Aragon. (Ripon Cathedral)

Above: Hever Castle. (Author's collection)

Below left: Mary Boleyn.

Below right: Anne Boleyn. (Ripon Cathedral)

The Blackfriars Trial,
from *Cassell's History*.

Initials on Anne Boleyn's
gateway at Hampton
Court. (Courtesy of Gail
Frederick)

The Tower Green site of
Anne Boleyn's execution.
(Courtesy of Justin
Ennis)

Above: Bradgate House.

Left: The execution of Lady Jane Grey. (Wellcome Collection)

Below left: Jane's carving in the Beauchamp Tower.

Jane Seymour.

Anne of Cleves.

Catherine Howard as the
Queen of Sheba.

Catherine Parr.

Above left: Mary I. (Ripon Cathedral)

Above right: A depiction of the burnings sanctioned by Mary, from Foxe's 1558 *Book of Martyrs*.

Framlingham Castle. (Courtesy of Squeezyboy)

Elizabeth I. (Rijksmuseum)

Mary, Queen of Scots.
(Metropolitan Museum of
Art)

Hatfield House. (Courtesy of Esther Westerveldt)

Above left: A medal from 1562 marking Elizabeth's recovery from smallpox. (Wellcome Collection)

Above right: Elizabeth as depicted in the nineteenth century. (Wellcome Collection)

Kenilworth Elizabethan Garden. (Courtesy of Elliot Brown)

Elizabeth in later life. (Rijksmuseum)

In June 1527, Henry had an interview with Catherine, during which he told her their marriage was over and that he wished her to retire to a nunnery. She reacted with shock and disbelief, although her advisors had warned her that this was coming, and even perhaps, that her own waiting-woman, Anne Boleyn, was the new wife Henry sought. Catherine's conviction that she had been born and raised with the destiny of queenship, coupled with her desire to protect her daughter, and her husband's soul, made her insist upon her rights and refuse to acknowledge any impediment. Henry had hoped to appeal to the Pope on the grounds of a text in Leviticus, which stated that any man taking his sister-in-law to wife would be punished. After all, only that March, Clement had granted Margaret the divorce she wished from Angus; with the same treatment, Henry might be married to Anne Boleyn by the end of the year, and fathering sons. But the next six weeks redefined everything. On 6 May, the troops of Catherine's nephew, Emperor Charles V, sacked Rome and took Clement VII hostage. There would be no swift divorce.

The weeks turned into months. Catherine remained hopeful that Henry would recover his senses and return to her, while Anne held out against consummating their relationship, swearing only to submit to the King as his lawful wife. The three were frequently resident at the same palace, although the sprawling nature of royal properties meant they could maintain independent establishments. When Vives visited at the end of December 1528, he travelled to meet Catherine at Greenwich, where both the King and Queen were keeping open house 'as it used to be in former years,' except that 'Mademoiselle de Boulan is there also, having her establishment (*son cas*) apart, as, I imagine, she does not like to meet with the Queen.'[18]

The impasse continued until 1529, when the Pope sent Cardinal Campeggio to sit alongside Wolsey in a legatine court, to try the validity of the marriage. On 31 May, the two cardinals assembled in the Parliament Chambers at Blackfriars Priory, to the east of Bridewell Palace. On the last day of May, the proceedings were begun by John Longland, Bishop of Lincoln, the confessor in whom Henry had confided his first doubts about his marriage and one of the most driven advocates of its annulment. Longland presented the Papal commission, in which Clement declared that it had 'frequently been related to him by trustworthy persons that there was a question about the validity of the marriage' between Henry and Catherine and 'because of the importance of the matter a rapid judgement was required.'[19] The two Cardinals then appointed Longland and John Clerk, Bishop of Bath and Wells, to summon the King and Queen to appear before the court on the morning of 18 June, between the hours of nine and ten.

Catherine knew what she had to do, and she gave the performance of her life. Rising from her seat, she knelt before Henry, addressing him only, appealing to him as her husband and as the only other person in the court of equal rank:

Sir, I beseech you for all the love that hath been between us, and for the love of God, let me have justice. Take of me some pity and compassion, for I am a poor woman, and a stranger born out of your dominion. I have here no assured friends, and much less impartial counsel. Alas! Sir, wherein have I offended you, or what occasion of displeasure have I deserved? I have been to you a true, humble and obedient wife, ever comfortable to your will and pleasure, that never said or did any thing to the contrary thereof, being always well pleased and contented with all things wherein you had any delight or dalliance, whether it were in little or much. I never grudged in word or countenance, or showed a visage or spark of discontent. I loved all those whom ye loved, only for your sake, whether I had cause or no, and whether they were my friends or enemies. This twenty years or more I have been your true wife and by me ye have had divers children, although it hath pleased God to call them out of this world, which hath been no default in me. And when ye had me at first, I take God to my judge, I was a true maid, without touch of man, and whether it be true or no, I put it to your conscience. If there be any just cause by the law that ye can allege against me either of dishonesty or any other impediment to banish and put me from you, I am well content to depart to my great shame and dishonour and if there be none, then here, I most lowly beseech you, let me remain in my former estate and receive justice at your hands. The King your father...and my father, Ferdinand, King of Spain... thought then the marriage between you and me good and lawful. Therefore, it is a wonder to hear what new inventions are now invented against me, that never intended by honesty... I most humbly require you, in the way of charity and for the love of God, who is the just judge, to spare me the extremity of this new court, until I may be advised what way and order my friends in Spain will advise me to take. And if ye will not extend to me so much impartial favour, your pleasure then be fulfilled, and to God I commit my cause![20]

Henry attempted to raise Catherine from her knees, but she would not move. Finally, she rose, curtseyed, and turned to walk straight out of the court room. An official called to her to return, but she responded that 'it makes no matter, for it is no impartial court for me, therefore I will not tarry. Go on!'[21] With her head held high, she swept out, never to return to the court room. Henry, moved by her performance, echoed that she had indeed 'been to me as true, as obedient, and as conformable a wife as I could in my fantasy wish or desire. She hath all the virtuous qualities that ought to be in a woman of her dignity ... she is also a noble woman born.'[22] But he went on to outline his suspicions, after 'all such male issue as I have received of the queen died incontinent after they were born, so that I doubt the punishment of God in that behalf.' He explained that he wished to 'take another wife in case that my first copulation with this gentlewoman were not lawful, which I intend not for any carnal concupiscence, nor for any displeasure or mislike of the queen's person or age, with whom I could be as well content to continue during my life, if our marriage may stand with God's laws, as with any woman alive.'[23]

Catherine's performance left an impact, but it did little to change Henry's mind. Anne's influence over him grew stronger, although she too was frustrated with the situation. Now at the age of thirty, she was concerned that her most fertile years had passed her by, when she might have been married well and borne several children. With the importance Henry placed upon siring an heir, this was a reasonable fear, and frustrated hopes put their relationship under strain as the Pope continued to prevaricate and avoid making a decision. The Imperial Ambassador Eustace Chapuys reported that 'the King received letters from Rome ... which did not please him much, nor the Lady either,'[24] and even more explicitly, 'I hear the King was never in greater perplexity than since the last news from Rome, and that neither he nor the Lady sleeps at nights.'[25] In addition, as the ambassador reported, Martin Luther had come out against the divorce, 'which has increased the King's headache and restlessness'.[26] The unwelcome news may even have led to tension and sharp words between Henry and Anne, as ambassador Micer Mai reported that Henry 'has quarrelled with his Lady, Mistress Anne, but that they afterwards reconciled themselves with each other. According to what happens generally in such cases,' Mai added, 'their love will be greater than before.'[27] The impasse was finally broken in July 1531, when Henry and Anne rode away from Windsor leaving Catherine behind. She would never see her husband again.

*

In rejecting his wife and seeking to marry Anne, Henry was redefining Tudor queenship. European kings had cast off unwanted wives and remarried before, with Louis XII divorcing the supposedly 'deformed' Joan of France upon his succession in 1498, in order to marry Anne of Brittany, and Catherine's great-uncle Henry IV of Castile divorcing Blanche of Navarre in favour of Joan of Portugal in 1453. Both divorces were granted on the basis of sexual incompatibility and the imperative to father heirs. Yet in both cases, the new wife had been of high or equal rank: Anne ruled Brittany in her own right and was a former queen of France, while Joan was sister of the King of Portugal. They had royalty as a precedent, educated and raised in the expectation of power, and brought lands, titles, status or foreign connections to the match. Henry's choice of Anne Boleyn, the daughter of a nobleman, broke the strictly defined class lines and proved as controversial as Edward IV's choice of Elizabeth Woodville.

Edward had been unmarried, though. Henry was rejecting a daughter of the Spanish power couple Isabella and Ferdinand, and the aunt of the Emperor, in order to marry Anne. He also broke with the Pope and Church of Rome, setting himself up as Head of the Church of England, answerable only to God. The roles his first two wives played in this process were to broadly symbolise the increasing divide in the country. Catherine was the symbol of the 'old religion,' a Catholicism and conservatism that rejected the new, reformed thinking and simplification of worship. One of Anne's greatest contribution to Tudor queenship was that she represented religious change and an iconoclastic questioning of the old mores that reflected England's transition to the early modern era. But one ought not to overstate their roles. Neither woman chose her position or had the power to engineer change alone; this dichotomy was necessitated by Henry's needs and action, struggling to achieve his own autonomy and the freedom that granted him.

In 1532, Henry and Anne planned to visit Francis I at Calais. Acceptance by a foreign king would offer validation to their relationship, ahead of the pair taking their marriage vows. Henry gave Anne jewels from the royal coffers forcibly removed from Catherine's possession, and ennobled her to Marchioness, or Marquis, of Pembroke. At Windsor, on 1 September, Anne wore a crimson surcoat with straight sleeves, edged with royal ermine, and with her hair traditionally loose, as she was conveyed into the King's presence to receive her formal papers, with the process mirroring the rituals of a coronation. This appointment broke tradition in making her the first woman to be elevated to the hereditary peerage, marking a significant manipulation of gender roles, and establishing Anne upon a degree of equality that a number of men at Henry's court would find difficult to accept.

Later that month, just before they were due to depart, Anne and Henry were walking in the countryside when they came across Princess Mary. Imperial Ambassador Chapuys related the incident for the eyes of the Emperor, Mary's cousin. His bias against Anne reflects the degree of feeling against her in the pro-Marian, pro-Catholic faction:

> Eight days ago the King met the Princess in the fields, but did not say much to her, except to ask how she was, and assure her that in future he would see her more often. It is certain that the King dares [not] bring her where the Lady is, for she does not wish to see her or hear of her. Thinks he would have talked with the Princess longer and more familiarly, if the Lady had not sent two of her people to listen. There is no likelihood of a treaty of marriage between the duke of Orleans and the Princess, as the King did not speak of it to her. The Princess will be at Windsor during the King's absence. The arrangements for the Queen are not known. The Queen was very much afraid that the King would marry the Lady at this meeting; but the Lady has assured some person in whom she trusts, that, even if the King wished, she would not consent, for she wishes it to be done here in the place where queens are wont to be married and crowned.[28]

Anne and Henry crossed the Channel on 11 October 1532, but Anne had to wait two weeks more before her reunion with Francis. The French Queen, Eleanor of Castile, Emperor Charles' sister, had known Anne during their year in the Netherlands, but now refused to meet her, as did Francis's sister Marguerite, in a deliberate snub to her aspirant queenship. On Sunday 27 October, when the Kings' business was concluded, Anne finally made her international debut as Henry's partner. That night, Francis came to dine with Henry in a chamber hung alternately with panels of silver and gold tissue, with seams covered with embroidered gold, full of pearls and gems. Three courses were served, a hundred and fifty dishes of 'costly and pleasant' food, with the meat dressed in the French style for Francis and in the English style for Henry. Anne entered the chamber with seven ladies including her sister Mary Carey and her sister-in-law, Jane Boleyn, all masked, wearing crimson tinsel satin with cloth of silver 'lying lose' and caught up in gold laces. Every lady 'took a Lord', with Anne partnering Francis, before her mask was removed.[29] The pair had not seen each other since Anne's departure at the end of 1521, but, clearly the French King now met with her on a different footing. The account tells us that they talked 'for a space' before Francis retired for the night, without revealing the subject of their conversation.[30]

On 29 October, after exchanging gifts, Henry and Anne said goodbye to Francis and prepared to leave Calais. The weather though, was terrible, with storms making it dangerous to cross the Channel and 'such a winde, tempest and thunder that no man could conveniently stir in the streets of Calais.'[31] Waiting for two weeks at the Exchequer in their fine rooms, linked by a connecting door, this may well have been the moment that Henry and Anne consummated their love. If they had not slept together before, this event had been eagerly anticipated for seven years and a lot depended on it. If Anne had successfully held Henry at bay all that time, protecting the virginity she now yielded to her experienced lover, it must have signified that she felt certain of their future. They finally left Calais at midnight on 12 November and after a terrible crossing sailed into Dover early in the morning of 14 November, St Erkenwald's day. (Ironically enough, the seventh-century Bishop of London, Erkenwald, won special privileges for the church from the king.)

According to chroniclers Hall and Sanders, the couple were married secretly the same day, probably in the chapel or their apartments at Dover Castle. Most other sources cite 25 January 1533 as their marriage day, officiated by Rowland Lee, Bishop of Coventry and Lichfield, in the king's chapel at Whitehall. If so, the second ceremony may have been provoked by Anne's discovery that she was pregnant. Her queenship was finally within reach.

16

Wives and Daughters

1533–34

1533 was a year of tremendous change in England. A new queen was crowned whilst a former one lived, a new archbishop of Canterbury made judgements formerly reserved for the Pope and a sentence of excommunication was passed against Henry VIII. It was a time of tension between old values and new reforms, of controversy and reaction, the rise of the individual and factionalism. After centuries of dominance by a small, genetically circumscribed elite, the court was being infiltrated by those who had risen on merit. A butcher's son might become a cardinal, a blacksmith's son may aspire to be chancellor of the exchequer and a diplomat's daughter could be anointed queen. The world was changing very quickly.

Anne Boleyn's father, Thomas, commissioned Erasmus to write *A Plain and Godly exposition, or Declaration, of the Common Creed*, published in 1533, a Catholic explanation in response to Luther's reforms. Hans Holbein painted *The Ambassadors*, a profoundly rich double portrait displaying the status of the sitters, full of social and cultural signifiers, and the famous anamorphic skull, combining the playful and intellectual aspects of the Renaissance in its clever use of perspective. In the same year, Holbein produced a portrait of Thomas Cromwell, the self-made man, watchful and cautious, who played a key role in removing Catherine from Henry, and Anne's head from her shoulders. It was the year that tracts were published on sundials, the solar quadrant and other astronomical instruments, a subject which was echoed in the subject matter of one of the first Tudor interludes performed at court, *The Play of the Weather*. Also enacted at court that year, amid the real dramatic triangle between Henry, Catherine and Anne, was *The Play of Love*, indicative of the culture of romance and uncompromising idealism. While Henry had turned his back upon the protection of Rome, breaking one of the oldest, holiest alliances, the Hapsburg Charles V followed the example of Francis I and signed a peace treaty with the Infidel Turks. As the Renaissance and Reformation advanced through England, separately, overlapping, and at varied speeds, the impetus more than ever was upon new ways of seeing, of measuring, assessing and defining the world, as a way for the individual to navigate a path through the complex web of religious and cultural expectations. Amid this, Anne had risen like a meteor, high above what her initial social rank promised, based upon her personal qualities. The exaggerated pageantry of her coronation procession drew heavily upon classical mythology, learning, symbolism, music and poetry, in true Renaissance style.

On Saturday 31 May 1533, Anne left the Tower to process across London to Westminster. Dressed in silver tissue, with her hair loose over her shoulders and a coronet upon her head, she sat in a chair of cloth of gold under a silver canopy, between two mules that were trapped in silver damask.[1] One Venetian observer described how she was accompanied by 'the greater part of the nobility of this kingdom, with the utmost order and tranquillity' through the decorated streets where the houses were 'crowded with persons of every condition, in number truly marvellous.'[2] Her rounded belly and loosened clothing showed that she was six months pregnant with the heir that the city pageantry was designed to validate.

Upon leaving the Tower, Anne's route lay along Tower Hill and north-west up to Fenchurch Street, where the first pageant in her honour awaited her, with children dressed as merchants singing verses of welcome in English and French. After this, Anne headed west, and at Gracechurch Corner was a mountain of white marble flowed with four streams running with Rhenish wine, where Apollo and Calliope sat on Mount Parnassus surrounded by the nine muses playing music and praising Anne in epigrams. This was the 'marvellous and cunning'[3] work of the Merchants of the Steelyard, who had commissioned Holbein to design it for them. The surviving sketches give an impression of the imposing majesty of the finished product, placed atop a triumphal arch. Awaiting Anne at Leadenhall was a mountain under a gold canopy, set with red and white roses, where her badge was displayed as a falcon landing on a stump, being crowned by an angel in armour. St Anne, mother of the Virgin, sat below the stump and a child 'made a goodly oration to the Queen about the fruitfulness of St Anne ... trusting that like fruit should come of her.'[4] Here, Anne was addressed in verses written by antiquarian John Leland and Nicholas Udall, describing her symbol, the white falcon shining bright and incomparable, courageous and worthy.

In the centre of Cornhill sat the main Conduit, where the three graces Juno, Pallas and Venus were waiting to greet Anne in a pageant of The Judgement of Paris. A child declaimed that Anne, 'most excellent that ever was,' should receive the 'crown imperial... to your joy, honour and glory immortal'.[5] The next stop was at St Paul's Gate, where Cheapside divided in two, either side of the church of St Michael le Querne. Above Anne's head, wafers inscribed with welcome messages rained down upon her, chimes sounded and the boys from the newly founded St Paul's school sang. Just inside the precincts, at St Paul's Cross, Anne was greeted by two angels bearing a crown and was presented by Master Baker, the recorder, with a purse of gold containing a thousand marks, 'which she thankfully accepted with many goodly words.'[6] Three ladies held tablets, speaking a prophecy that Anne would one day bear a son who would bring 'a golden world unto her people'.[7] Next, St Martin's Church hosted a choir who sang ballads to Anne from the rooftops before she rode out of the city and crossed the Fleet River. The final pageant of a tower with four turrets had been erected upon the Fleet's conduit, where the figures of different virtues were positioned, each promising that they would not desert Anne. Music was played from within on 'solemne instruments ... a heavenly noise'.[8] Further along, where the road split at Temple Bar, another choir greeted Anne before she headed along the Strand, through the newly built Whitehall and down towards Westminster. The hall there was hung with cloth of arras and newly glazed, and she was conducted to a spot under a cloth of estate and given wine and spices.[9] The following day, 1 June, she was crowned in the Abbey.

*

Catherine and Mary were informed of Henry's new marriage in the spring. By this point, they had not been allowed to see each other for two years, although they wrote frequently. In July, Catherine was moved to Ampthill in Bedfordshire, in an attempt to break her will and distance her from her supporters, and letters to and from her daughter were forbidden. Arriving to assist her departure, William Blount, Lord Mountjoy, her Chamberlain, found her 'lying on a pallet' as she had 'pricked her foot with a pin and could not stand,' and was also suffering from a cough.[10] He informed Catherine that she was no longer to be referred to as Queen, because Anne was Queen, but must revert to the title of Princess Dowager, her status on the death of Arthur. Catherine refused, repeating that her marriage was valid and her proper status was that of Henry's legitimate wife and Queen. Mary was also informed of the change in her status, and defied the ruling, refusing to defer to Anne and insisting that she still be treated as a Princess.[11] Mary was given new staff, with Sir John Hussey being charged with removing her jewels and plate, and his wife becoming her attendant. The Husseys were sympathetic to Mary's plight though, and refused to counter her obstinacy with any serious sanctions. Lady Hussey's persistence in calling her Princess cost her her position, and her liberty for six months. The situation prompted Mary's health to suffer, as she began to experience pains in her head and stomach, during which she was unable to eat and constantly vomited. Catherine sent her own physician, who diagnosed 'strangulation of the womb', which appears to have been linked to her monthly cycle.

However, Anne's coronation prompted Catherine and Mary's position to be validated by the Catholic church. In July 1533, Pope Clement issued a sentence against Henry's actions, declaring that his separation from Catherine and the marriage to Anne were both invalid. On 8 August, he further published a bull commanding Henry to restore Catherine to her former position and to 'put away Anne, in ten days, on pain of excommunication.'[12] This confirmed for Catherine that her new mission was greater than her queenship. Henry had gone astray, imperilling his soul, and she was the chosen instrument to bring him back to the true path of religion and the vows of their marriage. It was also essential for the future of their only surviving heir, for whose position Catherine had struggled for so long. For the final three years of her life, moved between isolated and unsuitable accommodation and increasingly unwell, she would never relinquish the battle.

One person who supported Catherine entirely was Henry's sister Mary, Duchess of Suffolk. The former French queen was then in her mid-30s, a mother of three, passing most of her days quietly in the countryside. Her long-standing affection for her sister-in-law, predating Henry's accession, and the devout Catholicism she had imbibed from her mother and paternal grandmother, made Mary reject Henry's decisions to marry Anne and break from Rome. Also in the Brandon's household since 1528 was their ward Katherine Willoughby, the daughter of Queen Catherine's close friend Maria de Salinas, who had accompanied her from Spain in 1501. For eight months in 1530, Mary had also given a home to her sister's daughter. The fifteen-year-old Margaret Douglas had been invited to the English court by Henry VIII, but instead of being given lodgings in a London palace, she stayed at Westhorpe Hall, perhaps in a move designed to keep her away from the influence of Anne Boleyn. That December, Margaret entered the household of her cousin, Princess Mary, as chief lady of her privy chamber. Mary's loyalties lay with those she had known and loved for years. By 1532, she was unable to hold her tongue about her brother's treatment of his wife and daughter, which led to a violent quarrel between Brandon and Anne's uncle, the Duke of Norfolk. It was reported by one ambassador that 'I am assured it was owing to opprobrious language uttered against Madam Anne by his Majesty's sister, the Duchess of Suffolk.'[13]

In May 1533, Mary and Brandon's elder daughter, Frances, was married to her cousin, Henry Grey, Marquis of Dorset. Both were the great-grandchildren of Elizabeth Woodville, Henry by her first marriage and Frances by her second. The bride was fifteen, the groom sixteen. The wedding was held at Suffolk Place in Southwark, and attended by the King, although Frances' closeness to her aunt Catherine and cousin Mary probably prevented Anne from attending. A short while later, Mary returned to their Suffolk home, but Charles Brandon was obliged to attend Anne Boleyn's coronation in his capacity as Constable and Lord High Steward. Mary did not attend, which accorded with her personal inclination, but also because she was unwell, having never fully recovered from the sweating sickness that she contracted in 1528. She wrote to Henry that she had been 'very sick and ill at ease' and had not wished to 'send for Master Peter the physician but was rather worse than better.' She intended to return to London soon with Brandon, and would be pleased to see her brother, 'as she has been a great while out of his sight and hopes not to be so long again.' Mary also blamed the countryside for her illness, stating that if she 'tarried' there, she would never escape the sickness.[14] She was more unwell than she realised, or than she chose to communicate. A few days later, on 25 June 1533, Mary died at the age of 37, the same age as her mother.

Mary had been popular in her home county of Suffolk, putting in regular appearances at nearby Bury St Edmunds, where the local church bells proclaimed her death at eight that evening. Her body lay in state at Westhorpe for three weeks, and Henry held a requiem Mass in her honour at Westminster Abbey on 10 July. A delegation from France arrived to attend her funeral ten days later, in the Abbey of Bury St Edmunds, where her coffin was topped by a life-size effigy in robes of state, gold crown and carrying a sceptre. It was remarked by one chronicler that Mary had been 'so much attached' to Catherine that 'the sight of her brother leaving his wife brought on an illness from which she died,'[15] but this was fanciful speculation. Mary was upset at the treatment of Catherine, but it was a real, visceral condition that caused her death, perhaps cancer or some complication arising from her previous illness.

After her early position as the ornament of her father and brother's court, much of Mary's later life had been spent in privacy, as a wife and mother. Her companionate marriage pushed her out of the spotlight into a more domestic sphere, and although she appeared at court on occasions of personal relevance, it was in a symbolic capacity, as an adornment to the dynasty. Mary was the Tudor jewel, an incomparable beauty to be displayed to ambassadors just as Henry might order out his best plate or tapestries, an indication of good genes and divine blessing. She played her part to perfection, as a gracious, fairy-tale princess, dancing, conversing, parading in her finery, overseeing jousts, distributing prizes, and was popular as a result. In this respect, she was very like her mother. Her two main contributions to the Tudor dynasty were that she defied her brother and married for love, paving the way for others to do the same, and she epitomised the dynasty at its best. Setting aside her second marriage, her approach was one of conservatism and conformity, a devout Catholic and respecter of marriage and class. Her love match, made with an attractive protector while she was young, adrift and widowed in a foreign land, has parallels with that of her great-grandparents, Jacquetta of Luxembourg and Richard Woodville. Although Jacquetta was not of English royal blood, her status as Henry VI's aunt meant that her remarriage and dower were of political significance, and subject to the approval of King and Council. It was the loyal, trusted servant Woodville who was sent to convey her to England, just as Brandon was dispatched to France to bring Mary home. Both matches were conducted in secret, and both couples forgiven fairly soon after being subject to financial penalties. Of course, Jacquetta's sister-in-law, Catherine of Valois, had made a similarly secret match to Owen Tudor only a few years earlier.

Had she chosen a different path, Mary might have made an even greater political contribution to the Tudor dynasty. If she had not wed Brandon and returned to England still widowed in 1515, her former betrothal to Charles V may have been salvaged, with the ceremony taking place the same year, or the next, when he attained the age of 16. Three years later, she would have become Queen of Castile and Empress over a vast realm. Her power would have been far greater than she, or Henry, could have anticipated, and when it came to Henry's marital struggles in 1527, she would have been in a position of influence. However, the direction in which she may have exerted that influence cannot be stated with certainty. Had she persuaded Charles and the Pope to grant Henry's annulment then, England may well have remained under the church of Rome and resisted the extremes of the reforming influences. Equally, she may have resisted Henry's wishes out of loyalty to her sister-in-law, who would also have been her aunt-in-law by marriage. It is possible to imagine an alternative path, coloured by modern hindsight. What matters is that Mary did not choose this direction. She chose her own way based on personal inclination, quickly asserting her own preference before she was reclaimed as an international pawn, and that was her specific contribution to the dynasty: a Tudor princess was not simply a slave to marital expectation.

However, marital expectation was exactly what would prove Anne Boleyn's undoing. Just as Catherine saw her new role as being the saviour of Henry's endangered soul, Anne considered that she had been sent to provide the Tudor King with an heir. The subtext of this, echoed in her coronation imagery, was that Anne's youth and fertility could offer new hope, that she would be the salvation the Tudor dynasty so desperately needed. The lack of a male heir was nothing less than a crisis, inviting invasion and challenges of the kind Henry VII had endured, or a return to the chaos of the Yorkist and

Lancastrian struggles. Chapuys reported that Henry's view of the female succession was still very traditional, with princesses like Mary being married off to husbands by whom they would be led, and men inheriting the throne:

> The King said that he wished to ensure the succession to his kingdom by having children, which he had not at present, and upon my remarking to him that he had one daughter, the most virtuous and accomplished that could be thought of, just of suitable age to be married and get children, and that it seemed as if Nature had decided that the succession to the English throne should be through the female line, as he himself had obtained it, and therefore, that he could by marrying the Princess to some one secure the succession he was so anxious for, he replied that he knew better than that.[6]

Through the summer of 1533, Anne's pregnancy advanced and her defining moment approached. Supplies were ordered and preparations made for her suite of rooms at Greenwich. On 26 August she heard Mass and made her formal retreat into confinement. The huge French bed borrowed from the treasury dominated her chamber, which was hung with tapestries depicting the life of St Ursula and decorated with gold and silver plate. Between three and four o'clock on the afternoon of Thursday 7 September, she delivered a healthy child. Contrary to all the predictions, it was a girl. At least mother and baby had survived the process and Anne had proven to Henry that she was capable of bearing healthy children. Still, the mood of disappointment lingered at court. The celebratory jousts were cancelled and the paperwork announcing the birth was altered from 'Prince' to 'Princess'. Chapuys reported somewhat harshly that the baby had arrived 'to the great regret both of him and the lady', but he was correct that it was also 'to the great reproach of the physicians, astrologers, sorcerers, and sorceresses, who affirmed that it would be a male child.'[17] The girl was named Elizabeth.

*

At the end of October 1533, another important marriage took place on the international stage. After his dramatic defeat at the battle of Pavia in 1525, Francis I had bought his freedom at the expense of sending his two sons into captivity in his place. The dauphin, 'born the most beautiful and strong child one could imagine', was incarcerated between the ages of eight and eleven, and became sombre and solitary as a result, broken in health and spirit by his ordeal. He would die at the age of eighteen, reputedly poisoned, but more likely as the result of tuberculosis or some weakness contracted from the unhealthy conditions of his prison cell. In 1533, his younger brother Henry, then still the second son, was married at the age of fourteen to Catherine, daughter of Lorenzo de Medici of Florence. This marriage, set to be one of the most significant unions of the century, echoed similar questions about fertility and inheritance to those which were being asked in England. The French Henry and Catherine also struggled to produce heirs. For a decade, Catherine did not conceive, but Henry fathered at least one illegitimate child, thus proving his fertility and increasing his impatience. Their story had a different ending though, as following advice from her doctor to correct some slight abnormalities, Catherine went on to bear ten children. Her eldest son Francis would later become the husband of James V of Scotland's daughter, Mary.

In November 1533, another young woman married into the Tudor dynasty. It was an unusual marriage, controversial to some, considered risky by others, uniting the young bride with the King's only surviving son. While there were only daughters in the royal nursery, speculation was rife about the future of the illegitimate Henry Fitzroy, and what his father's intentions concerning his future might be. The King had already moved heaven and earth to achieve his desires. After Henry had broken with Rome, it was not too fanciful to imagine that some act of legitimacy might place the young man above his sisters in the order of succession. In which case, the young woman who became his wife might one day find herself wearing a crown.

Mary Howard was the second daughter of the Duke of Norfolk, making her a cousin to the new queen, Anne Boleyn, who had reputedly promoted the match. Born in 1519, Mary had grown up in the shadow of scandal. Her mother, Elizabeth Stafford, is reputed to have been the lover of Henry VIII in 1510, until their trysts were discovered by Catherine, prompting the royal couple's first major row. Elizabeth had been removed from court by her brother Edward, Duke of Buckingham, who was then the most powerful peer in England, and a claimant to the throne through his descent from Edward III. However, when Mary was just two years old, her uncle Edward was executed by the King on charges of treason, for hearing prophecies of Henry's death and even plotting to kill him. All his wealth was confiscated by the crown and his children were prevented from inheriting anything. His sister Elizabeth's marriage to Norfolk was notoriously stormy, having been arranged after she had already been betrothed to Ralph Neville, which appears to have been a genuine love match. Norfolk overrode her feelings and insisted on taking her as his wife, fathering five children with her. Elizabeth was a regular attendee at court and an ally of Queen Catherine, until Norfolk took a mistress in 1527, with whom he lived openly, after which the marriage quickly disintegrated. In 1531, Anne Boleyn banished Elizabeth from court because of her continuing vocal support of Catherine. Two years later, Lady Howard refused to attend Anne's coronation 'from the love she bore to the previous queen,' so when Anne and Henry proposed that her daughter Mary be married to Henry Fitzroy, Elizabeth Howard objected but was overridden.

Mary was not the first proposed bride for the King's illegitimate son, nor the most controversial. In 1528, there had been rumours of a plan to marry Henry Fitzroy to his half-sister Princess Mary. To the medieval church, this would not have been as scandalous as it appears today. Sex between half-siblings, even full siblings, for purposes of procreation only, was considered preferable to fornication between two unrelated individuals. Dispensations could be obtained, although obviously these could not protect against possible health problems inherited by their children. The dynastic inbreeding the Hapsburgs was evident in the physical defects of a jutting jaw, thick lower lip, extreme underbite and thick tongue, but Henry considered the risk worth taking in the interests of his succession. Pope Clement was even prepared to issue the necessary paperwork, if it would produce an heir and prevent England from breaking with Rome. But such a match was not ideal and perhaps speaks more of Henry's desperation at the lack of progress towards an annulment than any real intention. The scheme was quickly dropped.

Henry Fitzroy and Mary Howard were married in November 1533, when he was fourteen and she fifteen. The Duke's new wife was reputed to be very beautiful, but a sketch of her by Holbein is disappointingly unfinished, giving her merely the ghost of features, lightly drawn in a pale face. The eyes are cast down, the mouth small and expression demure, the forehead is wide and the chin somewhat pointed. Beneath the black hat with its matching feather, a little of her red-gold hair is visible and the collar of her chemise covers her throat and neck. There is little to denote any personality beyond the conventions of the time. She was also intelligent, as her involvement with the Devonshire manuscript reveals. Playing a role in Anne Boleyn's court, Mary was one of three women who collected poetry reproduced in the manuscript, including extracts of famous works, translations and new compositions.

For a King's son, few details survive about the wedding or any subsequent festivities that were held to mark the occasion. Ambassador Chapuys only remarks on the fact that it was taking place. Nor does it seem that the pair consummated their match, according to the debate that arose upon Fitzroy's death, after which Mary was denied the dower lands to which she would otherwise have been entitled. They lived apart at first, with Fitzroy remaining at Windsor, perhaps out of concern that consummating the marriage too young would be harmful. However, in 1534, Henry granted his son Baynard's Castle and the pair moved in together.

A new household was being established for the infant Princess Elizabeth at Hatfield House, under the watchful eye of Margaret, Lady Bryan. Then in her mid-sixties, Margaret (née Bourchier) the mother of Sir Francis Bryan and the half-sister of Elizabeth Boleyn, making her Anne's aunt. Also appointed was Anne's aunt, Lady Anne Shelton and her sister, Alice. Chapuys made noises of dissatisfaction about the plan to disband Princess Mary's household and install her as a 'lady's maid'[18] to Elizabeth, but Henry was keen to establish Elizabeth's new precedent over her sister. That December, the Duke of Norfolk was sent to break the news to the recalcitrant Mary, and to remove her 'principal jewels and ornaments ... in consequence of her refusal to pay her respects to the lady'.[19] When the time came for Elizabeth's household to move, Mary had to be carried by force into the litter with Lady Shelton. When she and Catherine persisted in challenging Anne's marriage, Norfolk's reply was that 'it was needless to discuss the case of the marriage further since the thing was done, or to impugn the validity of their statutes, which they would defend to the last drop of their blood.'[20]

Soon after, Henry went to visit the uncomfortable ménage at Hatfield. With little Elizabeth established as the reigning Princess, the newly bastardised Mary was forced to show her half-sister deference and even serve her, to emphasise their difference in station. Henry's intention by visiting had been to persuade Mary to renounce her title, but according to Chapuys, Anne feared that Mary would be able to influence her father and that he would be lenient towards her. Despite her reduced status, no one doubted Henry's love for his elder daughter. Reputedly, Anne sent messengers after the King, 'to prevent him from seeing or speaking with Mary'. The result was that he visited Elizabeth's chamber but sent Cromwell to deal with Mary, refusing her request to come and kiss his hand. As he was departing, Mary appeared on a terrace at the top of the house, kneeling with her hands clasped, as if in prayer. Henry had 'either been told of it, or by chance, turned round,' saw her and bowed.[22]

Justly or unjustly, Anne gained a reputation for unkindness to Mary. The hostile Chapuys related that, 'having heard of the prudent replies of the Princess,' Anne 'complained to the King that he did not keep her close enough, and that she was badly advised, as her answers could not have been made without the suggestion of others, and that he had promised that no one should speak to her without his knowing it.'[23] On other occasions, the ambassador believed, Anne was threatened by Mary's beauty and virtue, so refused to allow her to come to court, as 'she would win the hearts of all.'[24] Apparently Anne told Lady Shelton to 'box her ears as a cursed bastard' if she did not conform, and not to allow Mary to dine in the privacy of her own chamber.[25] Norfolk and George Boleyn had also 'reprimanded' Anne Shelton for treating Mary 'with too much respect and kindness, saying that she ought only to be treated as a bastard.'[26] Of course, Chapuys' reports are always coloured, and far as Anne was concerned, Catherine and Mary's continuing refusal to accept the demotion in their status was not only a direct challenge to her position and that of her daughter but provided a rallying point for supporters of the Empire and Catholicism. It was Henry, however, who was most enraged by his daughter's refusal to submit after she requested his blessing as Princess of Wales, prompting his comment that 'he would soon find the means of humiliating her and subduing her temper.'[27]

When Anne next visited Elizabeth at Hatfield, on 7 March, she attempted to make a gesture of friendship to Mary. Urging the young woman to accept the change in her circumstances and recognise Anne as queen, she offered to intercede with Henry and try and bring about a reconciliation. Mary might come to court and be 'as well or better treated than ever'.[28] Anne may have been playing a cunning game, as some supposed, trying to keep her enemies close, but this incident could represent a genuine attempt to win her stepdaughter over and return her to her father, which Anne knew would greatly please Henry. There was nothing to be gained by Anne making overtures to Catherine, but Mary's youth and popularity made it a shrewd move to establish good will between her and the girl. Mary, though, rejected Anne's effort with cool politeness. She knew no queen in England except her mother and 'if madame Anne de Bolans would do her that favour with her father she would be much obliged.'[29]

The same month, Parliament passed the Act of Succession, which declared Mary to be illegitimate and Princess Elizabeth to be Henry's heir. All subjects, if commanded, were obliged to swear an oath affirming that Anne's marriage was valid and the supremacy of the King over the English church. To refuse to do so was made a capital offence under the Treasons Act, which followed immediately after, when it became high treason to

> ...maliciously wish, will or desire, by words or writing, or by craft imagine, invent, practise, or attempt any bodily harm to be done or committed to the king's most royal person, the queen's, or their heirs apparent, or to deprive them or any of them of their dignity, title, or name of their royal estates, or slanderously and maliciously publish and pronounce, by express writing or words, that the king our sovereign lord should be heretic, schismatic, tyrant, infidel or usurper of the crown.30

Subjects had to swear that 'all the issue had and procreate, or after to be had and procreate, between your Highness and your said most dearly and entirely beloved wife Queen Anne, shall be your lawful children, and be inheritable and inherit.' Henry was anticipating the arrival of Anne's child, which he hoped would be a son, whose rights along with those of any future male siblings were clearly established in terms of future rule. Anyone speaking critically of the marriage, or of Henry and Anne in person, was liable to be imprisoned, have all their goods, lands and properties confiscated, and to suffer death.[31] In addition, Anne was named regent and absolute governess of her children and the kingdom in the event of Henry's absence abroad or his death. Pregnant and hoping to deliver a son, Anne's power was now at its pinnacle.

17

Queen, Interrupted

1534–36

The preparations for Anne's second confinement began in April 1534, with a nursery being planned 'against the coming of the Prince' at Eltham Palace, the location where Henry had spent much of his childhood. This planning would be triggered by Anne's child quickening, at around four or five months, suggesting all was on track. At the end of that month, an observer wrote that 'the king and queen are merry and in good health' and that 'the queen hath a goodly belly, praying our Lord to send us a Prince.' Henry was considering visiting France again and was 'very desirous of it, and in wonderful haste to go,' wishing Anne to go with him 'notwithstanding she is enceinte.'[1] This plan was still going ahead on 3 June, when he requested that the streets of Calais be cleaned and cleared of any infested individuals in advance of his arrival.[2] Henry also ordered a cradle fit for a prince, which was made by his goldsmith Cornelius Hayes, with images painted by Hans Holbein. A medal depicting the new queen, with her motto 'The Moost Happi' and initials A.R., for Anna Regina, was commissioned in advance of the event, of which the original survives in the British Museum. As late as 27 July, Chapuys was still able to write of Anne's 'condition'[3] indicating that there was still a general anticipation of her imminent confinement. Yet no child came. There are no records of Anne entering confinement, nor are there any surviving reports of a miscarriage or stillbirth, although this is the most likely explanation of what happened. The much-anticipated male heir Anne had promised Henry had not appeared. The 'Moost Happi' medal was decommissioned.

As if this was not bad enough for Anne, Henry's attentions were already straying. It was rumoured in France was that she 'was in disfavour with the King, who had fallen in love with another lady' and Chapuys later clarified that Henry had 'renewed and increased the love which he formerly bore to another very handsome young lady of his court,' and that Anne had reputedly 'attempted to dismiss the damsel from her service.' He also related how Jane Rochford, Anne's sister-in-law, had been banished from court because she conspired with the queen 'to procure the withdrawal from Court of the young lady whom this king has been accustomed to serve, whose influence increases daily, while that of the Concubine (Anne) diminishes.'[4] This mysterious lady, sometimes referred to as the Imperial Lady on account of her sympathies, reputedly told Mary to be 'of good cheer, and that her troubles would sooner come to an end than she supposed, and that when the opportunity occurred she would show herself her true and devoted servant.' This might be an early reference to Henry's third wife, Jane Seymour, who was a member of Anne's household, and a devout Catholic and supporter of Mary. Or it may be another, unknown woman. Henry also was involved with Anne's cousin, Madge Shelton, for around six months, in the early part of 1535. Chapuys recorded that the 'young lady who was lately in the King's favour is so no longer,' but had been replaced by 'a cousin german of the concubine, daughter of the present gouvernante of the Princess.'[5] This did not bode well for Anne, and when she reacted in anger, Henry told her to hold her tongue as her betters had done before her.

In September 1534, Mary Boleyn's secret marriage was exposed. After the death of William Carey from the sweating sickness in 1528, Mary had followed the example of Henry's sisters and chosen her second husband for love, and she had not told her family. The exact date of her remarriage is unknown but Anne's change in status now meant that Mary was the queen's sister. William Stafford was the son of an Essex landowner, distantly related to the family of the former Duke of Buckingham, but too far to give him any significant social position or influence. Mary had been at Anne's side through her early queenship, attending her coronation and appearing on the list of New Year's gifts for 1534, but by September, Mary was pregnant and unable to conceal the fact any longer. Anne was not sympathetic. Not only was Mary's successful pregnancy an untimely reminder of her own recent failure but she had breached protocol in a way that her ambitious family could not forgive, and she was banished from court. Despite appeals for her return, Mary would not see her sister again, and there is no indication that her child survived. She would live in obscurity until her death in 1543. Ironically, the Boleyn family were less able to accept a marriage for love than Henry had been with his own sisters.

By the end of 1535, Anne and Henry's marriage was volatile but apparently not under threat. There were passionate arguments and moments of happiness, but nothing suggests the catastrophic events that were to follow. On their summer progress, Anne had conceived again, and could anticipate delivering her son the following June. While the court was spending Christmas at Eltham Palace, news arrived that Catherine of Aragon was seriously ill. Shut away at Kimbolton Castle in Cambridgeshire, her health deteriorating rapidly, the former queen lingered over the festive period and rallied briefly before breathing her last on 7 January. She was fifty, neglected, and probably suffering from some form of cancer. Distanced from her friends and daughter, not glimpsed at court since the summer of 1531, Catherine been stripped of her individuality, reducing her to a symbol, an obstacle to Henry's will, that had now been removed. She was sincerely mourned by those who had loved her, who now swiftly transferred their allegiance to Princess Mary.

Aware of the regrouping around Mary, Anne made a gesture of friendship on 21 January, declaring she would be the 'best friend to her in the world and be like another mother' to her. If Mary set aside her obstinacy, Anne promised that she might have anything she asked, and if she came to court, she would be exempt from holding the tail of Anne's gown. Reputedly, Anne Shelton delivered this message 'with hot tears' and implored her charge to 'consider these matters.'[6] Heartfelt perhaps; but equally, this may have been a politically shrewd act on Anne's part, a recognition that her opponents would be more concentrated by their grief and were now backing a far more dangerous figure, a young woman of almost twenty, an adult with an hereditary claim to the throne. With her own daughter, Elizabeth, not yet three, Anne must have hoped to avoid potential conflict between the two, with the intention of securing Elizabeth's succession. Perhaps Anne considered that Mary's youth and her recent loss might dispose her to compromise, as part of a longer-term strategy to obtain her stepdaughter's obedience.

Anne may not have anticipated that Catherine's death would give Henry a sense of freedom. He was no longer bound by any obligation to return to his first wife if he found fault with his second. Soon afterwards, Anne discovered Jane Seymour sitting on Henry's knee and, although Henry told her 'peace be, sweetheart and all will be well with thee,'[7] Anne became hysterical. Worse still, on 24 January, Henry was thrown from his horse whilst taking place in a tournament at Greenwich. Dressed in full armour, he was pinned under his horse and lay unconscious for two hours, whilst rumours flew around the court that his injuries were fatal. The news was broken to Anne by her uncle Norfolk, in a way that she later described as having been rather abrupt. Although Henry recovered, this incident gave Anne a shock and raised the question of the succession. Had Henry died that January, statesmen and courtiers would have had to decide whether to back the adult Mary, the 'legitimate' 2-year-old Elizabeth, or wait until the birth of Anne's child in the hope that it would prove male. It would have created a succession crisis, and the Council understood just how volatile that situation would have been.

*

On 29 January 1536, Catherine of Aragon was laid to rest in Peterborough Cathedral with the honours due to a dowager Princess of Wales, but not as a queen of England. Details of the occasion were recorded in the 'Remembrance for th'enterrement of the right excellent and noble Princesse the Lady Catherin, Doughter to the right highe and mighty Prince Ferdinand, late King of Castle, and late Wief to the noble and excellent prince Arthur, Brother to our Soveraign Lorde King Henry the viijth.' Torches were lit in all the towns through which her body passed, and nine lights burned inside the cathedral. The body was attended by three mutes and various noblemen, four knights bore a canopy over it, while six knights bore the coffin, assisted by six barons. Catherine was represented by a 'puffed image of a princess', but no wooden effigy like those which had topped the coffins of Elizabeth of York and Henry VII and their predecessors. The chief mourner was her niece Frances Brandon, who was almost the same age as Princess Mary, who had not been permitted to see her mother since 1531, nor attend her funeral.

On the same day, Anne miscarried the child she was carrying. The foetus had the appearance of being a male of around fifteen weeks development. According to Chapuys, this caused Henry 'great distress' and Anne attempted to 'lay the blame on the Duke of Norfolk, whom she hates,' saying he frightened her by bringing the news of the fall the king had.'[8] However, Chapuys added, it was 'well known that is not the cause, for it was told her in a way that she should not be alarmed or attach much importance to it.' Court speculation suggested it was 'owing to her own incapacity to bear children' or due to 'fear that the King would treat her like the late queen',[9] especially in the light of his recent favouritism to Jane Seymour. The rumours extended to Elizabeth's nursery, where Anne Shelton and her daughters and niece were concerned that if Elizabeth knew of the loss, they 'would not for the world that she knew the rest,' which Chapuys interpreted to mean danger to Anne, or 'some fear the King might take another wife.'[10] Likewise, the Emperor's sources repeated rumours that reached the continent that 'La Ana fears now that the King will leave her to make another marriage.'[11] Anne was right to be afraid.

The new mother was still recovering when Henry left Greenwich on 4 February, travelling to York Place, now Whitehall, where he kept Shrovetide. He may also have left in order to attend the final session of the Reformation Parliament. He sent presents and messages to Jane Seymour before summoning Anne to his side on 24 February. Throughout March, there were intermittent signs of royal favour being invested in the Seymour family, although this was not yet at the cost of the Boleyns. An official inventory drawn up on 3 March of all grants made to Thomas and George Boleyn is difficult to interpret. It was probably too early for Henry to have been considering depriving them of positions, as he would add to them at the end of the month, and it may have simply been routine. Of greater concern for Anne, though, was Henry's decision to evict Cromwell from his rooms at Greenwich, so that Edward Seymour and his wife could move into them. This certainly was sinister, as a private corridor gave them access to the King's chamber, in a move that was reminiscent of Henry moving Anne into position in 1528 whilst under the same roof as Catherine. Chapuys reported that 'the new amours' of Henry and Jane continued, 'to the intense rage of the concubine'. Jane had rejected Henry's gift of a purse full of gold coins, which only served to increase his desire for her, and Anne's enemies were soon canvassing members of the court, trying to increase the Seymours' backing.[12] Given the nature of court life, with its intrigues, rumour and counter-rumours, it is likely that Anne had some awareness that Henry's relationship with Jane had changed.

As late as 20 April, Anne's position still outwardly appeared to be secure. Her trip to Calais with Henry, scheduled for 4 May, was still being spoken of as assured. George Boleyn had written to Lord Lisle three days earlier to confirm that 'the King intends to be at Dover within this fortnight' and asking for assistance for his servant 'to such thing as he shall need for my provision.'[13] The trip was referred to again as a certainty on 25 April, just days before the intended date of departure, with plans for Anne's reception in the town by Lady Lisle; and again on 28 April. Yet this may all have been a cover, as on 20 April, Henry's most trusted minister, Thomas Cromwell, withdrew from court at the King's request, perhaps to investigate claims about Anne's behaviour. He returned on 23 April, maybe with a strategy or with new information, and approached the King along with Thomas Wriothesley, in whom he appears to have confided. An eye-witness, the Scotsman Alexander Aless, observed that the King was 'furious' but quickly 'dissembled his wrath'. However, the following day, Henry signed a commission presented by Cromwell to investigate 'unknown treasonable conspiracies'. Around 26 April, Anne sought out her chaplain Matthew Parker and begged him to ensure that two-year-old Elizabeth was looked after if anything happened to her. A few days later, Alexander Aless witnessed the couple arguing through a window, with Anne holding her daughter in her arms, appearing to be begging something of Henry. Halfway through the May Day joust held at Greenwich, Henry rose abruptly and rode away. The next day, 2 May 1536, Anne was arrested and taken to the Tower.

Anne's fate has attracted a vast amount of historical investigation, which has successfully proved that the majority of the instances Cromwell cited of Anne's alleged adultery are impossible, as either she, or the man accused, was not present at the named location on that day. Whilst forces at court were clearly moving against her, Anne did not help her own cause by being indiscreet and pushing boundaries. On 30 April, she was overheard conversing with Henry Norris, foolishly asserting that he sought 'dead men's shoes', or wished to marry her once the King was dead.[14] It was an ill-advised comment, but that is probably all that Anne was guilty of. Now that Catherine was out of the way, it was easier to get rid of Anne. Since Henry had coldly put aside the first wife he had once loved, he had fewer scruples about removing his second. It was done for the same reason: to enable him to father a legitimate son.

The charges against Anne are well-known. She was accused of adultery with five men, including her brother, and after a show-trial which could only produce supposition and rumour, George Boleyn, Henry Norris, Francis Weston, Nicholas Brereton and her lutist Mark Smeaton were beheaded by axe on 17 May. Anne was killed by the single blow from a special French executioner's sword, two days later, on the morning of 19 May. It was a shocking and brutal departure from the long-standing chivalric tradition of mercy towards women. It was Anne's unfortunate contribution to the Tudor dynasty that she was the first queen to be tried and executed, losing her life to a more vicious type of factional politics. Aristocratic women actively engaged in treason, like Margaret Beaufort, Cecily Neville and Elizabeth Woodville, had formerly been attainted, deprived of all their goods, even incarcerated, but the gender rules prescribed that they never lost their heads, as their male counterparts did. Anne's death broke this taboo and established a precedent from which her cousin, and other female members of court, would suffer. Her body was buried in an unmarked grave in the chapel of St Peter ad Vincula, within the Tower of London.

*

The reigns of Catherine and Anne redefined Tudor queenship. The twelve years from 1525 to 1537 realigned the monarchy's focus and brought about its painful transition from medieval to early modern, Catholic to Church of England, traditional to reformist, conservative to reactionary. The King's great matter was the crucible in which three important new elements were formed. Firstly, it set a dangerous new precedent in the treatment of anointed queens. Catherine, the proud daughter of Isabella of Castile, resisted her marginalisation with everything she had, but old age, illness and her husband's greater strength proved too much for her. Anne's end was so rapid, accelerating at such a rate, that she was scarcely able to process events as they unfolded. From 1536, onwards, the beheading of a queen was acceptable if the circumstances were right, and the fabricated charges against Anne showed that this was not the consequence of sin, bad rule or evil character. A sentence of death was not merely the appropriate punishment for a wicked queen, but a political act implemented by her enemies. From this period forward, queenship was more dangerous and queens became more vulnerable.

Secondly, the Catherine-Anne stalemate precipitated religious changes that may not have occurred in England until later, if at all, or to a different degree. By breaking with Rome and establishing himself as head of the Church of England in order to validate his choices, Henry created a climate in which reformers could influence his son and younger daughter. Had the Papal ties remained, it is unthinkable that the monasteries would have been dissolved, their wealth sequestrated and their architecture destroyed. Catherine and Anne were not agents of the Reformation: Catherine found it an abhorrent indication of her husband's impending damnation and even Anne's role as a reformed thinker was intellectual, or ideological, as she sought to support religious institutions late in her marriage, making her less ardent for the iconoclasm that drove Henry.

Thirdly, neither Catherine or Anne could have anticipated that their conflict and their struggles to produce a son would result in two queens regnant. Their daughters, Mary and Elizabeth, suffered as the result of their mothers' fates, being declared illegitimate and experiencing difficult relations with their father and uncertainty about their own succession. Still, though, they came from a tradition that earmarked them for foreign marriage in the footsteps of their aunts. But succeed they did, switching the male dynastic narrative over to a female one, with all the changes in voice, focus and methods that this brought. This centralised the female experience of rule, rather than as the wives of rulers, with the commensurate autonomy this brought. Yet this shift was almost incidental to the experiences of Catherine and Anne. None of these three important new elements had been actively created, anticipated or sought by them. Their cruel treatment, the establishment of the Church of England and the female succession were the by-products of their situations, borne out of the dynastic crisis, where their personal narratives intersected with wider historical currents beyond their control.

Catherine and Anne's contributions to Tudor queenship differed greatly. The contrasting circumstances of their births show Anne's trajectory as meteoric. Catherine was the daughter of a reigning king and queen, a princess destined for foreign queenship as the result of a dynastic marriage, while Anne was the daughter of a knight in the king's service. Catherine's education was full and enlightened, giving her insights into the classics as well as the greatest philosophical debates of the new learning, but also equipping her with the skills of monarchy, while Anne's years spent abroad exposed her to reformist thinking and the cultural influences of the French court. With their vastly differing marital prospects, Catherine's two marriages fulfilled her parents' expectations, while Anne's arose out of a specific dynastic need and the increased social mobility and elements of meritocracy at Henry's court. She elevated her family's standing beyond their wildest dreams, only for their fortunes to plummet equally as dramatically.

Anne's tenure on the throne was brief and troubled. Her queenship was deeply divisive even before her marriage and coronation, so she was faced with the difficult task of establishing herself in a potentially hostile situation, both at court and among her subjects, with all the volatility and insecurity that entailed. She was not welcomed and fêted as Catherine was, or allowed to enjoy her position. She was not trained and prepared for queenship, as Catherine had been. Anne had to find her feet as a queen and a wife in the gaze of a public who were holding up Catherine's example for comparison. Her queenship experienced its highs and lows, from her magnificent coronation to the lost pregnancy of 1534 and the birth of Elizabeth, and the reformed, Renaissance model of womanhood she offered. Anne had great potential to be a transformative queen, capable of taking England through the challenges of the Reformation, a symbol for cultural change. Her experiences in Europe, her exposure to debate and Renaissance thought, and the iconoclastic drives that were concurrent with her rise, could have made for an exciting, unprecedented style of queenship, had she been granted the opportunity. This would have involved her continued patronage of individual figures, writers, thinkers, artists and religious figures, and the support of sympathetic, reformist figures in positions of authority at church and court. But her potential was sunk by the personal narrative of her relations with Henry and her gynaecological record, which was doomed too early, because of its similarities to Catherine's. Anne gave birth to possibly the greatest Tudor monarch of all, but her personal dynastic contribution was one of tragedy and lost potential. The show trial that convicted her in order for Henry to pursue his next queen introduced a terrifying new potential danger for queens, and exposed just how fragile her position had always been, dependent as it was upon her husband's whim. Just as he had promised, Henry had made her, and he destroyed her. Her queenship served to foreground the King's ruthless absolutism and cruelty in an unprecedented way.

There is no doubt that Catherine of Aragon committed every fibre of her being to the Tudor dynasty. Her style of queenship was full-blooded, enthused with energy, commitment and passion, and it was a queenship she had been anticipating since the age of three, modelled in the Spanish style, of crusaders, conquistadors and absolutism. As Henry's equal and helpmeet, she acted as ambassador, hostess, figurehead, negotiator, communicator, wife and mother, through the years of partnership, and endured her husband's rejection with a complete conviction as to her rightful position and with the absolute faith of a martyr. Early on, she helped set the tone of Henry's new court, with its fantasy and romance elements, balanced with her theatrical piety, which epitomised the pre-Reformation 'merry England' style of monarchy. She was equally at home dancing in gold, hawking in the fields, or prostrate before a saint's shrine or handing out the prizes at a joust. In spite of her childbearing difficulties, there was a joy about her early queenship, the glow of a woman who had found her place, which makes the contrast with her later years all the more painful.

Catherine was Regent during Flodden, engaged in preparations, organisation, communications, possibly marking her finest moment. She was a popular symbol from her welcome in 1501, as a focus of pageantry, ceremony, supplication, patronage and piety among her subjects. Her visible devotion to the Catholic church, which she continued even after Henry's rejection of her and it, made her a champion of the old practices for those resistant to reform. Her marital strife with Henry brought her a lot of sympathy, especially after she was exiled from court. People turned out to cheer her in the streets as she was moved from one property to the next. Catherine had what is called the 'human touch' and her subjects responded to her as a young wife and widow, as a woman and a mother, following the twists and turns of her heart-breaking story. Apart from giving birth to a future monarch, Catherine's personal contribution to the Tudor dynasty was her absolute, unflinching commitment. She made it her personal mission. But for her childbearing difficulties, she might have remained its revered, devoted queen until her death. It was her and Henry's personal tragedy that he saw their failure to produce a son as reason to treat her with such cruelty. If any woman deserved the honour of a great state funeral reserved for a queen, it was Catherine of Aragon.

18

The Search for Love

1533–37

The 1533 Tudor interlude, *The Play of Love*, has been attributed to composer, musician and playwright John Heywood, a favourite of Henry VIII. As a prolonged discourse between the allegorical characters 'Loving not Loved' and 'Loved not Loving', it marks the flourishing of a theme which had been developing at court since 1509. The theme of romantic love had been gaining momentum since the chivalric pageants and jousts of Henry's early years, with the symbolic lovers' gifts, costumes embroidered with coded messages and knights seeking ladies' favours, through to the marriages of Mary and Margaret, and the King's choice of Anne Boleyn. Anne's own behaviour can be understood in this context, in her secret engagement to Henry Percy, and Thomas Wyatt's poems in celebration of her beauty, and her ill-judged flirtation with Henry Norris. In the second half of Henry's reign, a significant number of women contributed to the Tudor dynasty in this way, either by submitting to the King's romantic desires, or seeking an ideal lover of their own. Yet this courtly culture, epitomised in poetry and revels, and the increasing numbers of secret affairs, rapidly proved that this apparent freedom in love was deceptive. More so, it was to prove deadly for some. Romantic love at the Tudor court was a pleasant pastime, or fantasy, but only when it concurred with the King's will.

Margaret Douglas was seventeen when Anne Boleyn was crowned queen in 1533. As the daughter of the Scottish queen, the niece of Henry VIII, young, beautiful and with something of her mother's temperament, her turbulent childhood made her a romantic figure, a significant prize to be won on the marriage market. On the majority of James V, Margaret Tudor had regained her power, as she and her new husband became the chief advisors to the young King. His mother was keen to negotiate peace with England and to plan a meeting of monarchs to rival the Field of Cloth of Gold. Young Margaret was sent to England, to the uncle who seemed very fond of her, perhaps as a gesture to cement the alliance. Initially she entered the household of Cardinal Wolsey, but after his fall in 1529 she joined her cousin Princess Mary's household at Beaulieu. Margaret remained in the heart of her English family, present for the Christmas festivities at Greenwich in 1530, 1531 and 1532, receiving generous gifts from the King and observing a court in transition between two queens. Upon Anne's succession in 1533, she was placed in the new queen's household.

It was during her service to Anne that Margaret met the new queen's uncle, Thomas Howard, Thomas was a younger son of the second Duke of Norfolk by his second marriage, and was then in his early twenties. Little is known about the young man, then four years Margaret's senior, who carried the canopy at Princess Elizabeth's christening in September 1533. No portrait survives of him, and he has often been confused with his elder half-brother, the third Duke. During the early part of Anne's queenship, a number of love affairs were conducted in her household, often prompted by the interaction of the queen's ladies and the king's gentlemen in their frequent enactment of allegorical love roles, dancing and entertainments. The atmosphere of courtly love was captured in the poetry of Thomas Wyatt, himself an ardent admirer of the queen, who understood the delicate balance of play and more serious flirtation. His most famous line about Anne, or 'brunet,' as he called her, 'noli me tangere, for Caesar's I am,' demonstrates the inherent dangers of young men getting too close to well-born, or even well-married, ladies of the court. It was in this heady atmosphere that Margaret and Thomas fell in love, as Anne and Henry Percy had done, and became secretly engaged in 1535.

After Anne's fall in May 1536, the change in succession changed Margaret's status. Now that Henry had declared both his daughters illegitimate, Margaret was next in line to the English throne after the childless James V, making any husband of her choosing a potential future king. That July, when Henry discovered that his niece was betrothed, and that her fiancé was a member of Anne's family, he showed Margaret as little mercy as he had others he had formerly loved. Both Margaret and Thomas were arrested and imprisoned in the Tower on a charge of treason. With Anne's body newly at rest in the chapel, the young lovers must have been terrified about their fate. The succession question became more serious five days later, when Henry Fitzroy died of a lingering illness at the age of seventeen, removing the King's fall-back option.

Thomas was examined by Thomas Wriothesley, Earl of Southampton, who had previously been charged with questioning witnesses to enable Henry's separation from Catherine. When asked how long he had loved Margaret, Thomas replied 'about a twelvemonth,' and that he had given her a cramp ring as a token, and received a small picture and a diamond from her in return.[1] They had become engaged at Easter that year and, as far as Thomas was aware, Margaret had confided in the wife of Lord William, and that Lord had informed Hastings, the servant of Thomas's mother, the Duchess of Norfolk. A Thomas Smyth was also examined, and swore that he had 'never carried any tokens between them' nor had he ever been made 'of counsel by either party'. He was asked whether he had seen Howard 'resort unto' Margaret when his niece, Henry's daughter-in-law, Mary, Duchess of Richmond, was present, to which Smyth replied he had seen it 'divers times' and that Howard would 'watch till my lady Boleyn was gone, and then steal into her chamber.'[2] On 18 July, an act of attainder was passed accusing Thomas of 'attempting to interrupt, impedit and let the said succession of the crown', and a sentence of death was pronounced. All members of Henry's family were forbidden from marrying without his permission.

Upon hearing the news in Scotland, Margaret Tudor wrote to her brother in alarm. She could not believe Henry intended to punish her daughter for her betrothal and hoped he would 'have compassion and pardon her'. A desperate Margaret renounced the connection and wrote to Thomas Cromwell:

Is under great obligation to him for getting her the King's favor. Desires to know how to avoid again incurring his Grace's displeasure. Has only two more servants than when she was in Court, who were indeed servants of my lord Thomas [Howard], and whom she will dismiss, since she is to keep none that belonged to him, though she took them in consideration of their poverty. Desires Cromwell 'not to thynk that eny fancy doth remayn in me towchyng hym.' Has only a gentleman and a groom that keeps her apparel, another that keeps her chamber, and a chaplain that was with her in the Court. My Lord's servants are but a small charge, 'for they have nothing but the reversion of my board.' Has no visitors except gentlewomen; it would not become her, a maid, to keep company with gentlemen.[3]

Both Margaret and Thomas fell ill whilst incarcerated in the Tower. He was shown no clemency, but in November she was removed to Syon Abbey, to be nursed, fuelling speculation that she was concealing a pregnancy and underwent a confinement some time later that year or early in 1537. That October, Thomas died in the Tower 'from an ague', whereupon Margaret was released from captivity. Tragedy had befallen the young pair who had dared to fall in love amid an atmosphere of courtly romance. Margaret's youthful idealism and naivety had led her to believe that her personal preference might override her bloodline. The example of Margaret and Mary Tudor, and even Anne Boleyn's relationship with Henry, might have led her to speculate about a rosy future, but the mood at court was darkening. As Margaret, Queen of Scotland, found her attempts to divorce her third husband blocked, Anne Boleyn went to the scaffold, and Henry remarried in unprecedented haste, the King was far less likely to tolerate scandals of the heart. The only person permitted to fall in love outside their familial duties was Henry himself. And yet, just three years later, Margaret would fall in love and make exactly the same mistake again.

*

Henry VIII chose his next wife 'for love', but more in the hope that she would bear him a son. Jane Seymour became his third queen on 30 May 1536, just eleven days after Anne's execution. She had been born at Wulf Hall in Wiltshire in around 1507, where Henry and Anne had been entertained on their progress into the west country in the autumn of 1535. Her background was conservative, Catholic and sympathetic to the plight of the former queen Catherine and her daughter, Princess Mary. Her father, John, had fought the rebel army of Perkin Warbeck in 1497 and been knighted by Henry VII in gratitude. He had campaigned with Henry VIII in France in 1513, being present at the sieges of Therouanne and Tournai, and attended the Field of Cloth of Gold. In 1532, he had been made a Groom of the Bedchamber, one of the most important roles safeguarding access to the King and allowing for a closer relationship between monarch and subject. Jane's mother, Margery Wentworth, was a descendant of Edward III, making Jane related to Henry in the third degree of affinity.

Jane's education stands in contrast to that of Anne Boleyn and Catherine of Aragon. She had experienced a quiet upbringing in the countryside, raised as an obedient daughter and future wife, trained in domestic and household skills such as needlework, untouched by the shifts towards European humanism and reform that had transformed Anne from a country girl into a figure who could hold her own on the international stage. Chapuys tactfully described Queen Jane as not having 'a great wit, but she may have had good understanding.' She represented a pre-Reformation style of English noblewoman, raised with the intention of securing a suitable husband and bearing sons. In the ambassador's eyes, she was 'of middle stature and no great beauty, so fair that one would call her pale than otherwise.'[4]

Jane probably came to court in the late 1520s as part of Catherine's household and witnessed the disintegration of her marriage. In many ways, Jane was Anne's opposite, fair where Anne was dark, quiet where she was outspoken, demure where she was bold, and towards the end of Anne's reign, this is precisely what drew the King to Jane. In the autumn of 1535, whilst Henry and Anne were on progress in the west, they spent a week in early September at Wulf Hall, and if Jane had not yet caught the King's eye this would have proved a significant moment. Anne's subsequent pregnancy secured her position in Henry's affections again, but that had not prevented his attentions straying, nor Anne expressing her displeasure. It was January 1536 when she surprised Jane sitting on Henry's knee, and there may have been further rivalries, including an apocryphal story where Anne discovered Jane wearing a locket that Henry had given her. The Seymours were on the rise, with Jane's brother Edward appointed to the Privy Chamber on 3 March and the influential Thomas Cromwell allying himself with the family in April. Chapuys reported rumours that Henry and Jane discussed marriage long before Anne's arrest, and that Jane had shown concern for the King's treatment of his daughter Mary, upon which Henry had told her 'she was a fool, and ought to solicit the advancement of the children they would have between them, and not any others.' Jane's reply shows her diplomacy and tact, as in seeking the 'restoration of the princess, she conceived she was seeking the rest and tranquillity of the king, herself, her future children, and the whole realm; for, without that, neither (Henry) nor this people would ever been content.'[5]

In the spring, Henry had removed Jane from court and placed her at Beddington Park, Croydon, the home of Nicholas Carew, his Master of the Horse and long-term friend. Carew was a cousin of Anne Boleyn, but their estrangement marked the turning tide against her, and he joined the pro-Catherine faction, transferring his support to Mary after the former Queen's death. This move was intended to distance Jane from any scandal arising from Anne's arrest and subsequent trial, and also to give the appearance that her fall had not been prompted by Henry's desire to be with Jane. On 14 May, she was brought closer to court, to Thomas More's old house at Chelsea, where she was 'splendidly served by the king's cook and other officers' and 'splendidly dressed'.[6] On the day of Anne's execution, 19 May, a dispensation was issued by Thomas Cranmer, Archbishop of Canterbury, for Henry and Jane to marry without publishing their banns. The very next day they were betrothed, and ten days later, on 30 May, they were married in the Queen's closet at York Place. On 3 June, Jane's household servants were sworn in and she made her public debut the next day, when her brother Edward became Viscount Beauchamp. On 7 June, a water pageant was held in her honour on the Thames outside York Place, and the following morning Cranmer pronounced Henry's marriage to Anne unlawful, having pronounced in its favour three years before.

Jane's rise to queenship took place with unprecedented speed. Henry was forty-five and unwilling to endure the years of agonised waiting that had accompanied his transition from Catherine to Anne. She had been propelled from relative obscurity into the limelight and, as Chapuys recorded, appeared to be quickly overwhelmed and needed to be 'rescued' from speaking to ambassadors. If Anne had been unprepared for queenship, Jane was even less so. If Anne had been raised above her rank, she had at least spent a decade living amid European royalty. In March, Jane had been a gentlewoman of the queen's chamber and by the end of May, she was queen. Henry's intention to father a son was the primary motive, as he began placing his hand on Jane's belly as early as that summer, saying 'Edward, Edward,' a full six months before she conceived. His actions, and the rapidity of her rise, cannot have misled Jane about her purpose. Henry's 'love' for his new wife was not inspired so much by her personal charms as by the functioning of her womb. If Chapuys is to be believed, the King even confided to him soon after the wedding that he had recently seen two beautiful new women arrive at court and wished he had waited a little longer before remarrying.[7] Jane was never to have her moment of regal glory, though, as the magnificent coronation Henry planned for her, intended to outstrip those of Catherine and Anne, was postponed due to the religious discontent that erupted in the north that summer.

The death of Henry Fitzroy that July made Jane's delivery of a son even more crucial. Whereas the King previously had one illegitimate male heir, he now had none, and only two illegitimate daughters. There was also the presence at court of Fitzroy's young widow, Mary, a close friend of the disgraced Margaret Douglas, whose future remained unsettled. As events transpired, Mary's contribution to the Tudor dynasty had been a very slight one. She had undergone a marriage ceremony with Fitzroy, and briefly lived with him at Baynard's Castle, although the young man was mostly at Windsor and St. James' Palace, and she insisted it had not been consummated. When Mary petitioned Henry for her dower lands, he refused to grant her the full widow's entitlement, as she had never been Fitzroy's wife in the fullest sense. Had Fitzroy lived, or fathered a child himself, the future of the Tudor dynasty might have been very different. In 1538 and 1546, Mary's father Thomas Howard, 3rd Duke of Norfolk, attempted to arrange a marriage for her to Jane's brother, Thomas Seymour, but either Mary or her brother, Henry, Earl of Surrey – or both – objected strongly and the match was dropped, despite having the support of the King. Mary remained at Henry's court until his death, then retired to a quiet life in the country, without ever remarrying. She died in 1557.

Mary represents one of the most significant of the many 'what-ifs' of the Tudor story. Had her husband lived, instead of Jane's son, she may have found herself at the head of a movement to make her queen of England and making a far greater dynastic contribution than she could have anticipated. But her opportunity was dependent upon the duration of her husband's life. For a brief time, she represented the next Tudor generation, and her future reign would have set a precedent in the succession of an illegitimate son.

*

For another Mary, the events of summer 1536 failed to bring about the momentous change they seemed to have promised. With Anne Boleyn's marriage declared invalid and her influence over the King gone, Princess Mary had high hopes that she and her father might be reconciled, the former relation with Rome restored, and even her illegitimacy overturned. Her treatment recently had been brutal, with Lady Shelton resorting to forcing her bodily into her carriage when she refused to move properties, and increased threats to 'box her ears' or impose the ultimate sentence for her failure to swear the oath of succession or acknowledge her changed status. Yet Mary had clung to the belief that Anne lay behind this treatment, rather than Henry's stubborn will in opposition to hers. She wrote to Cromwell as early as 26 May, saying that she would have approached him before, 'but I perceived that nobody durst speak for me as long as that woman lived, which is now gone.'[8] The one consolation she had been allowed was the presence of Mary Scrope, Lady Kingston, formerly in the service of Queen Catherine as Mary Jerningham. It was only with her help that Mary was now able to write in May, asking permission to contact her father. When Cromwell replied, stating that her obedience was expected as a condition of reinstatement, she promised to be 'as obedient to the King as can reasonably be expected,' and hoped her father would 'not only withdraw his displeasure but license her to come to his presence.'[9]

Mary wrote directly to her father on 1 June, begging 'as humbly as child can for his daily blessing,' which was her 'chief desire in this world'. She asked forgiveness for 'all her offences since she had first discretion to offend till this hour' and promised to 'submit to him in all things next to God.'[10] She rejoiced to hear of her father's new marriage, desired leave to wait upon the new Queen and prayed God to send them a prince. However, it was clear from her words that Mary considered her duty to God was greater than her duty to her father, so Henry drew up a list of articles to which she must submit. Again, Mary asked Henry for some token or message of forgiveness, whilst pleading with Cromwell for tolerance, that she might not be asked to swear that which went against her conscience: 'I desire you, for Christ's passion, to find means that I be not moved to any further entry in this matter than I have done; for I assure you I have done the utmost my conscience will suffer me, and I neither desire nor intend to do less than I have done.'[11] But Henry was implacable.

On 15 June, a delegation arrived at Mary's home at Hunsdon, in Hertfordshire. Headed by Thomas, Duke of Norfolk, Anne Boleyn's uncle, who had been part of the group who convicted her, it presented the Princess with two questions. Would she reject the Pope and accept her father as head of the Church of England, and would she accept that her mother's marriage had been invalid? She refused. Her situation was delicate, unprecedented and potentially dangerous. More and Fisher had gone to the block for their refusal to submit, and now an anointed queen had lost her head: but would Henry inflict the same sentence upon his own daughter? Late the same night, Mary wrote to Henry as 'your most humble, faithful, and obedient subject, which hath so extremely offended your most gracious Highness that mine heavy and fear full heart dare not presume to call you father, deserving of nothing from your majesty, save that the kindness of your most blessed nature does surmount all evils, offences and trespasses, and is ever merciful and ready to accept the penitent calling for grace, at any fitting time.'[12] She had received letters from Cromwell advising her to make an immediate submission, and admitted to having 'most unkindly and unnaturally offended him by not submitting to his just laws.' She 'put her soul in his direction' and committed 'her body to his mercy and fatherly pity, desiring no state or manner of living except what he shall appoint her; it cannot be so vile as her offences have deserved.'[13]

Shortly after this, Mary made this submission to her father in writing:

> The confession of me, the lady Mary, made upon certain points and articles under written, in the which, as I do now plainly and with all mine heart confess and declare mine inward sentence, belief, and judgment, with a due conformity of obedience to the laws of the realm; so minding for ever to persist and continue in this determination, without change, alteration, or variance, I do most humbly beseech the King's Highness, my father, whom I have obstinately and inobediently offended in the denial of the same heretofore, to forgive mine offences therein, and to take me to his most gracious mercy.[14]

On all three points of previous contention, Mary relinquished her former position. She acknowledged the King as her sovereign, promising to submit to all his laws like a true subject, and maintain them to her power. Secondly, she acknowledged him as Supreme Head of the Church of England under Christ and repudiated the pretended authority of the bishop of Rom, (the Pope) renouncing every advantage she may claim thereby. Thirdly, she acknowledged the marriage between the King and her mother, the late Princess Dowager, to have been 'by God's law and man's law incestuous and unlawful'.[15] It must have been very painful for Mary to accede this last point, in fact Chapuys describes her as 'prostrate with grief and remorse', but she did so in the recognition that this was the only way to repair her relationship with her father and protect her own position. She requested Chapuys to write secretly on her behalf to Rome, to procure a 'secret absolution' for herself, or else her 'conscience could not be at perfect ease.'[16] Yet her actions bore fruit, when the commissioners returned to beg her forgiveness and offer their allegiance, after which Henry and Jane visited Mary at Hundson on 6 July. That summer, talks were even renewed concerning Mary's marriage, with a Prince of Portugal or France, and Mary made her first visit to court in years that October.

There could be no doubt in anyone's mind that Jane's primary function was to deliver a son. The likelihood of this was the subject of European gossip. Dr Pedro Ortiz wrote to the Empress in September that no children were expected 'on account of the complexion and disposition of the king'.[17] Chapuys reported in October that Jane's coronation had been delayed until the following summer, due to the Pilgrimage of Grace in the north, 'and some doubt it will not take place at all.' This statement was immediately followed in his letter by 'there is no appearance that she will have children,' suggesting a correlation between the two statements.[18] However, after eight months of marriage Jane conceived, with her condition being made public in April. In May, Jane appeared at Hampton Court, dressed in an open-laced gown, to announce her quickening and special masses were conducted at Westminster for her health and that of her child. She remained there throughout the summer to avoid the outbreaks of plague in London, and her suite of rooms was prepared for her confinement at the end of September.

At two in the morning, on 12 October 1537, Jane finally delivered her son after a long and difficult labour of two nights and three days. It was the eve of St Edward's day, auspicious timing, although the couple may have already chosen this name. The proclamations of his arrival led to widespread rejoicing, no less, wrote Hugh Latimer, than if John the Baptist had been born. Three days later, the baby was christened in the Hampton Court chapel, attended by his two half-sisters, Mary and the four-year-old Elizabeth, who had seen her life change dramatically, although she was too young to understand the full implications of it. She was carried by Lord Beauchamp, and held the 'richly garnished' chrisom cloth ahead of her brother in the procession, while Mary followed the canopy, standing as the baby's godmother. Mary's gift was a gold cup, and she, Elizabeth and Anne Seymour, Jane's sister-in-law, bore the train as Edward was carried back to his parents. In delight, Henry 'gave great largess'; he raised Edward Seymour to the Earldom of Hertford, knighted his brother Thomas and planned Jane's churching and return to court.[19]

Days later, Jane's condition suddenly worsened. It was reported that 'all this nyght she hath bene very syck,' prompting Henry to dispatch six doctors to her side.[20] On the night of 23-24 October, she suffered what the Bishop of Carlisle described as a 'natural laxe',[21] which was probably a heavy bleed caused by a post-partum haemorrhage as the result of internal injury or the retention of a portion of the placenta. At eight that evening, the Duke of Norfolk urged Cromwell to keep an eye on Henry, praying him 'to be here tomorrow early to comfort our good master, for as for our mistress there is no likelihood of her life, the more pity, and I fear she shall not be on lyve at the time ye shall read this.'[22] Prayers were said in St Paul's Cathedral and Jane's confessor was summoned. However, the complications arising after her delivery were too powerful for prayer or medicine and the last rites were administered. Queen Jane had given the Tudor dynasty the one thing it most needed in Henry's eyes, but she gave her life as a result, dying on 24 October at the age of twenty-eight.

Jane was given a magnificent state funeral and burial in St George's Chapel, Windsor, in stark contrast to the lack of appropriate ritual surrounding the final journey of Catherine of Aragon and the indecent haste with which Anne Boleyn's body was disposed of. This was a measure of the difference Henry perceived in their contributions to the dynasty. As the mother of his healthy son, Jane automatically retained the trump card, prompting Henry to direct that his own remains should be laid to rest beside her upon his death. Whether or not Henry had been 'in love' with Jane as much as he had with Catherine or Anne at various points, mattered less than her contribution of her child. Her death in the process, reminiscent of that of Henry's own mother, Elizabeth of York, added the touch of sacrifice that ensured her memorial had that added edge of pathos. Henry 'retired to a solitary place to pass his sorrows,'[23] whilst Sir William Paulet planned the funeral based on plans drawn up for Elizabeth in 1503.

After the process of embalming, Jane's body lay in state in the presence chamber at Hampton Court, surrounded by burning tapers and her ladies and watchmen in constant prayer. On 1 November, she was conveyed to the chapel on a hearse hung with banner roles, along a route lined with black drapes, for eleven days of masses and prayers. The final procession departed Hampton Court on 11 November, the casket topped by a wax effigy of the queen resting on a gold pillow, dressed in state robes, jewels and gold shoes, bearing a sceptre. Princess Mary was chief mourner with Margaret Douglas and Frances Brandon following in one of the five chariots along the route. They were met at Eton by two hundred poor men carrying lit tapers, and at the bridge across the Thames, the mayor and aldermen of Windsor were waiting to convey them up to the castle.[24] The following day, Jane's body was laid to rest, with her ladies laying expensive cloth over her coffin.

Jane Seymour was Queen of England for seventeen months. The final five or six months of that were spent nursing her long-anticipated pregnancy, taking her focus off her duties and into increasing retirement. Her role as Queen in those final months was to ensure the health and safety of her child as it grew in her womb. During the brief period before that, she had little time to assert much of her own style, exercise her power or establish a strong identity as Queen. Her identity was presented at the time, and has been understood by historians since, as a construct of opposites. Just as Anne attracted Henry through her difference in relation to Catherine, Jane's charms lay in the contrast she offered to Anne's character, in her modest, conservative and traditional nature. There was also her Catholicism, but this could only offer a symbolic position. Jane represented the old ways, but while adherents of those practices might find hope in her leadership, or anticipate her clemency, in reality, she was powerless to stop the dissolution of the monasteries or soften the severity with which Henry dealt with the Pilgrimage of Grace. When she pleaded with him to pardon the rebels of 1536, the King harshly reminded her of the fates of those who had formerly 'meddled in his affairs'. This must have been a chilling conversation for the newlywed Jane fresh on the heels of Anne Boleyn's execution, and a warning that her role of wife would always come first with Henry, not that of queen. No doubt Jane swiftly learned that lesson, and by the following summer, the Duke of Norfolk could describe her as 'in every condition of that loving inclination and reverend conformity that she can in all thing well content, satisfy and quiet herself with that thing that we shall think expedient and determine.'[25] If Catholics looked to her as a means to restore the church to its pre-1529 position, they were disappointed. However, realising this was not within her power, Jane was able to direct her influence in another direction.

Henry's rebuke refocussed Jane's contributions onto the domestic sphere. Her household was modest and chaste. The extravagant French fashions and gaiety of Anne's court were replaced by a restrained family model, and it was in her construction of this unit that Jane's influence was most felt. Since before her marriage, she had attempted to reconcile Henry with Princess Mary, and once she was Queen, brought her stepdaughter back to court and was responsible for significant improvement in the young woman's life. Although Jane could not get Mary reinstated, she reconciled father and daughter, with Mary ranked first after the Queen in courtly precedence and being invited to spend Christmas. The following spring and summer, Mary enjoyed greater freedom of movement, staying at Greenwich and Westminster as well as Hatfield and New Hall (formerly Beaulieu). The process of Mary's reintegration at court also provided hope for her future influence, as a devout Catholic with much popular sympathy, especially before the birth of her brother Edward and during his infancy. In turn, Mary wrote to her father about the sister she had previously refused to acknowledge, praising Elizabeth's abilities. Jane's influence was pacific and domestic. She was submissive and loving, helping to pour balm on the wounds of recent years.

In dynastic terms, Jane is of course remembered as the wife who gave Henry a son. She gave her life in the process, and those two facts undoubtedly determined the path which the Tudor line followed. Additionally, she gave Henry validation, that his recent actions in condemning Anne and rejecting the Pope had received divine approval, with Prince Edward as the incorporation of God's blessing. In confirming for Henry that he could father a surviving son, Jane's significance extends beyond the birth of Edward to the King's sense of identity, and its direct correlation with dynasty. This was the personal boost that ended Henry's religious and personal doubts of the 1520s and 1530s, and strengthened him in his conviction in pursuing the dissolution; and that his word, and his interpretation, were absolute, and deserved complete submission from his subjects. It was a fragile security, bound up in the health of a baby, but as Edward grew and survived childhood illnesses, it was a greater security than Henry had ever known. It may be misleading to imagine the path her queenship would have taken had Jane lived to help raise her son, as one in which she bore more children in the role of demure, quiet, loving wife and mother. But even if her gynaecological record had gone on to match that of Catherine and Anne, including miscarriages and stillbirths, the existence of her first-born would have always provided her with security. Jane's main contribution to the Tudor dynasty must always be the delivery of a future king, followed by her role as a pacifying influence within the royal family. Henry appears to have been genuine in his grief at her loss, writing to Francis I that 'divine providence has mingled (his) joy with the bitternes of the death of her who brought me this happiness.'[26] Although negotiations were reopened fairly soon after Jane's death, Henry was in no rush to remarry for another two and a half years.

19

Changing Times
1537–40

Relations between Henry and his sister, Margaret, Queen of Scots, had been shaken by his treatment of Catherine and Princess Mary. Having condemned his sister's divorce from Angus, Henry's own efforts to take a new wife and break with Rome had met with little sympathy in Catholic Scotland. In an attempt to repair the damage, he sent Anne's uncle, Lord William Howard, north as ambassador in 1534. Margaret wrote in response, 'your Grace is our only brother and us your only sister, and since so it be, let no divorce or contrary have place, nor no report of ill advice alter our conceits, but brotherly and sisterly love ever to endure.'[1] She also received a letter and token from Anne, to whom she referred as her 'dearest sister', and wrote to Cromwell, wishing him to pass on her regard for the new Queen.[2] The Scottish clergy had 'submitted in silence' to the report of Henry's new marriage, Margaret told Cromwell, but had sent one of the Blackfriars to condemn it in a sermon to James V. Margaret was not content with this, as part of the sermon had 'concerned our dearest brother and his realm'[3] and she assured Cromwell that her son took no heed of it. She was keen to arrange a meeting between her son and his uncle, envisioning something along the lines of the splendid Field of the Cloth of Gold, but the young James had recently recovered from smallpox and fever, and the plan came to nothing.

Instead, Scotland bound itself more closely to France. In March 1536, James was betrothed to Madeleine of Valois, daughter of Francis I, despite her father's insistence that her health should not permit her to become a wife. James refused to heed these warnings and went in person to collect her that September. They were married in Nôtre

Dame Cathedral the following January and returned to Scotland that spring, landing at Leith in May. Margaret was present to give her daughter-in-law a warm welcome, but the cordiality faded when it became clear that James would not grant her a divorce from her third husband, Henry Stewart, now Lord Methven, whose treatment of her had been worse than that of Angus, with his financial irresponsibility and adultery. Methven had the ear of the young King, who withheld his permission for the divorce out of concerns that Margaret would travel to England and remarry her second husband. She complained bitterly to Henry, stating she would enter 'some house of religion if she gets no remedy.'[4]

True to her father's prediction, Madeleine's health deteriorated and she died in July 1537. She was not yet sixteen. The following year, James married Mary of Guise, a widow with two small sons. Mary bore James two more sons, but both died in infancy. Then, on 8 December 1542, she delivered a daughter, whom they named Mary.

Margaret did not live to see the arrival of the most famous queen of Scots. In the autumn of 1541, she was at Methven Castle when she suffered a palsy, a kind of paralysis, which was possibly a stroke or heart attack. She sent for her son but did not make a will, in the belief that she would soon recover. However, Margaret's condition deteriorated, and she died on 18 October. Her body was laid to rest at the Carthusian Priory in Perth. Margaret's death removed a key figure in maintaining the peace between England and Scotland, and war soon erupted. Just four days after her death, James was writing to Henry complaining that 'the English have raised fire and made slaughter in the Middle Marches of Scotland.' He prayed 'that like hasty redress be made for this.'[5] The Scots won a skirmish against the English in August 1542, prompting Henry to raise an army to meet them as they travelled south. James was reputedly already ill with a fever before the battle, but news of the resounding defeat his men suffered at Solway Moss on 24 November finished him off. He died at Falkland Palace at the age of thirty. He was succeeded by his six-day-old daughter.

Margaret's contribution to the Tudor dynasty after her marriage is more fruitfully understood through her contribution to its future replacement, the Stuart dynasty. Before 1503, she had played her role as a Tudor princess making a foreign marriage, and afterwards, she chose to marry a second time for love, giving Henry hope of achieving his own swift divorce. Her later marital history, though, gave her something of a reputation for inconstancy, as her brother's did, pursuing one divorce after another at whim. As Queen, and then dowager queen and the King's mother, she did play an important role in Anglo-Scots relations, attempting to secure peace, although her relations with her brother were not smooth and she frequently felt she was being treated unfairly by him. Yet her very existence provided a buffer that prevented the countries going to war, as it was only a few weeks after her death in 1541 that hostilities broke out again. Margaret had been an essential bridge between the two countries, based on her Tudor blood and shared childhood with Henry. Her role as an English ambassador in Scotland was not always a successful one, but it succeeded in that one crucial fact. Margaret's most significant dynastic contribution to both the Tudor and Stuart families was the inheritance of her great grandson of both thrones, uniting the kingdom over 60 years after her death. Once again, it was a woman's reproductive function, undergoing the dangerous challenge of childbirth and delivering a healthy baby who survived the odds, which allowed the dynasty to continue for another generation. As James V was reputed to have said on his deathbed, 'It came wi a lass, it'll gang wi a lass,' meaning that the dynasty had been created, and would end, with women. However, there is a wider truth to his words about the centrality of women to dynastic survival. As the birth history of the Tudor family would dictate in the coming generation, women were to play transformative roles at the heart of the dynasty in unprecedented ways. After the arrival of Edward in 1537, there would be no more Tudor sons, and many of those, male and female, who shared the royal blood would find themselves marked by tragedy and heartbreak.

*

Through the latter decade of her brother's reign, Mary Tudor's daughters and granddaughters continued to thrive. Mary survived long enough to witness the marriage of Frances to Henry Grey in 1533, but not to see the birth of her first grandchild, Jane Grey, who arrived in 1537. After that, Frances also bore Katherine in 1540 and Mary in 1545. It was Henry's father Thomas, a grandson of Elizabeth Woodville, who built the family a home in the middle of Bradgate Park, a twelfth-century deer park in Leicestershire, three miles north of the Woodville family home at Groby. He added the two towers, either side of the main gatehouse, which still stand, but he died before completion, so his son took over. The project was most likely completed in 1520 and is cited as the birthplace of the couple's daughters and their main residence in childhood, although other research suggests they may have been born at Dorset House, the family residence in London. It was expensive to build such a large house as Bradgate out of red brick, and the lack of fortifications indicates a new phase in the Tudor dynasty, of comparative peace and prosperity for its junior branches.

The Grey sisters spent their early years between London and Leicestershire. Dorset House, formerly known as Salisbury House, was on the bank of the Thames between Bridewell and Whitefriars, just outside the city wall, south of Fleet Street. They also maintained the usual aristocratic series of visits to relatives: to Princess Mary at Newhall; to the Lady Frances's stepmother, Katherine, Duchess of Suffolk, at Wollaton; to Dorset's sister, the Lady Audley, at Walden; to his orphan wards and cousins the Willoughbys, at Tylsey; and to Lady Jane's paternal grandmother, the Dowager Marchioness of Dorset, either at her house at Croydon or at Tylsey. Whilst resident at Bradgate, they also travelled the short distance to nearby Leicester, where they received a warm welcome from the local mayor and dignitaries. The city archives record that in 1540 there was a charge of 'two shillings and sixpence for strawberries and wine for my Lady Marchioness's Grace, for Mistress Mayoress and her sisters'.[6] Also, on the occasion of another visit, 'four shillings' were paid 'to the pothicary for making a gallon of Ippocras, that was given to my Lady's Grace, Mistress Mayoress and her sisters, and to the wives of the Aldermen of Leicester, who gave the said ladies, moreover, wafers, apples, pears, and walnuts at the same time.' When the family travelled north, they were frequently accommodated at the White Hall Inn, with their expenses paid by the town.[7]

Much has been written about the education received by Jane, which presumably was similar to that of her sisters in the 1540s. Half a decade had passed since Margaret and Mary Tudor's upbringing which, for intended future queens, had certainly not been as full or as forward-thinking as that of Catherine of Aragon. Yet while Catherine gave her daughter Mary a mixed training, humanist ideals coupled with preparation for the role of wife and mother, her first cousin once removed, Jane Grey, benefitted from a very progressive approach. The three decades between the 1510s and the 1540s, had witnessed such dramatic cultural change in England, affecting faith, female literacy, education and the availability of published material, that the experience of the Grey girls marked a sea-change in thinking. There was an increasing acceptance, in England and Scotland, of women's ability for independent thought, as well as rule. Jane's cousins on her father's side, Jane and Mary Fitzalan, also received a remarkable education, with Jane translating Isocrates' works from Greek into Latin and Euripides' *Iphigenia and Aulis* from Greek to English. Jane was encouraged in this by her husband, a translator, book collector and scholar, who validated her intelligence and abilities far beyond the expected duties of a wife.

The dramatist Nicholas Udall relates in his translation of Erasmus's *Paraphrase on the Four Gospels* that 'a great number of noble women in that time in England were given to the study of human sciences and strange tongues.' Jane's peers were no longer being educated simply to be wives and mothers, even if this was at the highest level, they were being educated to think for themselves, and the young Jane Grey promised to be one of the outstanding female thinkers of her generation. Their lessons began with Dr Harding, the chaplain at Bradgate, who educated them in Greek, Latin, Italian and French. In 1547, the Grey sisters made their first formal debut when Elizabeth, or Bess, of Hardwick, married her second husband, William Cavendish, at Bradgate Hall. The unusual ceremony, which took place at two in the morning, was hosted by Frances and Henry as friends of the couple. If Jane, Katherine and Mary were not permitted to stay up to witness the exchange of vows, no doubt they would have taken part in any festivities that occurred at a more reasonable hour.

Jane's cousin, Elizabeth, four years her elder, was also embarking upon her education after the shock of her mother's fall. Based at Hundson House in Hertfordshire, Elizabeth may have been too young initially to understand the change in her status in 1536, occupied as she was with her toys and her daily routine. A surviving inventory from her infancy includes a number of dolls of all sizes, of which one or two were mechanical 'that could speke' and another imported from Italy, which could walk, a wooden rocking horse, a set of marionettes, cooking utensils and an ark, 'containing beasts and Noah with his family'.[8] Although her mother no longer came to visit, Elizabeth remained in the care of Lady Margaret Bryan, who described her as 'toward a child and as gentle of condition as any I have known.' In August 1536, Lady Bryan wrote to Cromwell requiring his help, as she was uncertain about Elizabeth's status and the child sorely lacked necessary provision: 'Now, as my lady Elizabeth is put from that degree she was in, and what degree she is at now I know not but by hearsay, I know not how to order her or myself, or her women or grooms. I beg you to be good lord to her and hers, and that she may have raiment, for she has neither gown nor kirtle nor petticoat, nor linen for smocks, nor kerchiefs, sleeves, rails, bodystychets, handkerchiefs, mufflers, nor 'begens."[9]

At almost three years old, Elizabeth was suffering from teething, as her teeth came through 'very slowly' and she was given 'her own way'[10] by her Governess a little more than she should. Lady Bryan was also concerned about the instruction of Sir John Shelton, Elizabeth's Governor and great-uncle, regarding Elizabeth's routine at mealtimes:

Mr. Shelton would have my lady Elizabeth to dine and sup every day at the board of estate. It is not meet for a child of her age to keep such rule. If she do, I dare not take it upon me to keep her Grace in health; for she will see divers meats, fruits, and wine, that it will be hard for me to refrain her from. 'Ye know, my lord, there is no place of correction there; and she is too young to correct greatly.' I beg she may have a good mess of meat to her own lodging, with a good dish or two meet for her to eat of; and the reversion of the mess shall satisfy her women, a gentleman usher, and a groom; 'which been eleven persons on her side.' This will also be more economical.[11]

Blanche Milborne, Lady Troy, was also a member of Elizabeth's household, as Lady Mistress, but upon the birth of Edward she and Lady Bryan were transferred into the Prince's household, leaving Elizabeth with her new Governess, Katherine, or Kat, Champernowne. Kat was possibly the daughter of Sir Philip Champernowne of Modbury in Devon, in her mid-thirties and unmarried by 1537, but had received a forward-looking education. Her influence upon Elizabeth as an educator and mother figure was significant, teaching her charge from a humanist academic curriculum including Flemish, French, Italian and Spanish, as well as history, geography, mathematics and astronomy, and the more traditional feminine skills of embroidery, decorating cambric shirts for Edward, deportment and dancing. As Elizabeth later explained, Kat took 'great labour and pain in bringing of me up in learning and honesty.'[12] In 1545, Kat married Sir John Ashley, then a senior gentleman of Elizabeth's household, and a cousin of Anne Boleyn through their mothers. While Kat remained a constant influence, Elizabeth's Greek education was taken over by William Grindal, and Giovanni Battista Castiglione was appointed to further her Italian. After Grindal died of the plague in 1548, his position was taken by Roger Ascham, one of the leading Greek scholars of his day, who infused Elizabeth with a lifelong passion for the language.

Elizabeth and Jane Grey had other cousins born in the 1530s and 1540s, as a result of the marriage of Eleanor Brandon, younger daughter of Mary, formerly Queen of France, and Charles, Duke of Suffolk. Born in 1519, Eleanor passed a quiet childhood, and little is known about the upbringing she and her sister Frances shared. Her marriage contract was drawn up in 1533, to Henry Clifford, son and heir of the Earl of Cumberland, but her mother's death delayed the ceremony. The wedding finally took place in 1537, in London, either at Brandon House in Bridewell, or the Duke of Suffolk's Palace in Southwark, and was attended by the King. The couple were fourth cousins on his mother's side. He was twenty, she was eighteen. Eleanor spent her married life in the Clifford ancestral home at Brougham Castle, in Cumbria, which her husband inherited after the death of his father in 1542, as well as Skipton Castle in north Yorkshire. Eleanor bore two sons, Henry and Charles, who died in infancy and a daughter, Margaret Clifford, who arrived in 1540.

Eleanor does not appear to have experienced good health. A sole surviving letter written to her husband relates how she had been 'very sick' and passing blood in her urine: 'at this present my water is very red, whereby I suppose I have the jaundice and the ague both.' She had no appetite for meat and was suffering from pains in her side and towards her back, as she had once experienced before. Knowing that the pain would increase if left untreated, Eleanor implored her husband to help her see a physician, in order to find a 'good remedy.' She asked specifically for a Dr Stephens, 'for he knoweth best my complexion for such causes.'[13] It is impossible to know, now, what recurring condition Eleanor was suffering from, as indicated by her gross hematuria and corresponding pain. It may have resulted from a bladder or kidney infection, or a more serious kidney condition.

Perhaps this illness was a contributing factor to her early death in 1547, at the age of twenty-eight.

In 1547, according to the Third Succession Act, which Henry had passed three years earlier, the Tudor dynastic line was seven-eighths female. After Prince Edward, the positions of Mary and Elizabeth were restored, and then the crown was designated to Frances Brandon, followed by her three daughters, and Eleanor's daughter Margaret. The nine-year-old Prince was the slender buffer at the top, keeping the dynasty from descent into the uncertainty of female inheritance. The only English precedent for a woman succeeding was the anarchy arising from the dispute between Empress Matilda and her cousin Stephen, and the expectation of a royal woman to marry and produce heirs generated concern about any potential husband's influence. Religion was also a significant factor in the debate concerning inheritance of the throne. England had undergone seismic change during the 1530s, the polarity of which was represented in the candidacy of Henry's children and nieces. The eldest, Mary, was a staunch Catholic in the model of her mother, but Edward and the Grey girls had been raised in the Protestant faith. The influence of Henry's final wife, Catherine Parr, would also be a significant factor in determining the path of their development and the cohesion of the Tudor family.

*

The nature of female dynastic contributions underwent significant change in the century from 1437 to 1537, between the births of Margaret Beaufort and Elizabeth Woodville, and the birth of Prince Edward. This was mostly because the dynasty had evolved from being a private family to a ruling one, but was also due to cultural change. After three generations, the methods of influence available to the Tudor women had widened. They moved out from behind the scenes, where they had risked their lives to challenge established authority, to the most direct and open acts of queenship, as ambassadors and individuals. The founding mothers helped shape the dynasty as a concept. They had to fight for the advancement of their children, even for their survival, while being dependent upon the good will of hostile rulers and enemies. Their gender limited their sphere of influence, but the cultural construct of 'femininity' also gave them, paradoxically, a shield behind which to retreat. No doubt this saved their lives on occasion.

Elizabeth and Margaret's granddaughters found themselves in a completely different position. They were born into established royalty, the second generation of reigning Tudors, with expectations of international marriages, greater influence and with far more resources at their disposal. As the first Tudor daughters, they had a new purpose and influence, to help embed the dynasty and establish stronger foreign ties; and with this came a new sense of privilege. This was the generation of women that asserted their needs as private individuals, partly as the result of their comparative security, but also due to the changing tides of the Renaissance, with its focus on the self, and the Tudor veneration of romantic love. Mary and Margaret both secretly chose their own second husbands, in the belief that they had already done their dynastic duty. Thus, they foregrounded the tension between public and private, self and state, which would characterise the women of Tudor blood for the next century.

The women who married Henry VIII had different expectations and influence. Marriage was a far more volatile guarantee of authority than birth, and Henry's reign was to reveal the catastrophic results when this power was misjudged or diverged from the wishes of the King. Despite experiencing disagreements with his sisters, a mutual respect rooted in birth and a shared heritage prevailed between them and Henry. When it came to his wives, though royal birth still mattered, the sanctity of marriage did not provide them with as strong a hold upon power. A change in the exercise of queenship resulted from Henry's break with Rome and reform of the English church. If the priority for a queen had been the production of an heir, Henry's lack of a son created an imperative redefinition of queenliness. This necessitated one woman of royal blood being set aside, the daughter of a knight becoming queen, two anointed queens being tried and executed, two marriages being annulled and one ten-day betrothal. Henry's marital dilemmas marked a change of status and expectations in a queen, from the stately pedigree of Catherine to the Renaissance culture and intellectual challenge of Anne, to the quiet, fertile domesticity of Jane. He was seeking a son from each, but their individual appeal and sphere of influence varied greatly.

For the next generation of Tudor women, the nieces and great nieces of Henry VIII, positioned at one or two removes from the throne, the challenges were different again. Mary's daughters, Frances and Eleanor Brandon, their daughters Jane, Catherine, Mary Grey and Margaret Clifford, and Margaret Tudor's daughter, Margaret Douglas, were born into the royal family but were unlikely to rule. With the exception of Margaret Douglas, whom circumstances placed at court, the others lived quietly, often in retirement, as daughters, wives and mothers. They had no need to strive for their position, instead, the battle was for their own autonomy, to be able to make decisions about their futures for themselves. Three of the younger generation would follow the example set by Mary and Margaret in the 1510s and choose their own secret husbands for love. However, the political climate had changed significantly, and they did not find the forgiveness experienced by Henry VIII's sisters. In fact, the cost of their choices was frequently their liberty and, in the cases of their husbands, sometimes their lives. The realpolitik of the mid-sixteenth century exposed just how dangerous it was to be any woman in the Tudor dynasty, not just one actively engaged in its advancement. Times were changing rapidly and queenship being was forced to change with it.

20

Women in Danger

1540–42

Recent years had witnessed the dramatic redefinition of England's place on the international stage, its religion, practices and culture. While the ripple effects of this continued to be felt, the first wave of the storm had receded by 1540. Catherine, Anne and Jane were dead, Henry had his son, and the dissolution of Waltham Abbey in March 1540 marked the end of the process of closures. However, with the setting of new, dangerous precedents, the wives Henry chose next needed to consider very carefully just how they exercised their queenship.

It was in 1540, that royal physician Thomas Elyot produced his book, *The Defence of Good Women*, praising women as good governors and rulers. With the fortunes and status of Princesses Mary and Elizabeth fluctuating, and one young boy between them and the succession, it was a topical work, but one which Elyot was careful to place at a remove, setting it in third-century Rome. His ideal female ruler received a suitable education and reformed laws, which she was certain to first implement in her own household, travelled through her realm to meet her subjects, and waited to speak in the council chamber until others had expressed their views. This last recommendation shows that Elyot's model of female rule was still a passive, receptive one, based on deference and example, rather than a more masculine, assertive shaping of rules. However, his book established a cultural expectation that female rule may be inevitable and was not something to be feared. Its timing was unfortunate though, in that he dedicated it to Anne of Cleves, whose tenure on the throne was to be the briefest of them all.

The reign of Henry's fourth wife lasted only six months, and made no significant immediate or long-term contribution to the Tudor dynasty, beyond her survival of it. It was swiftly made and swiftly undone, although not without deadly cost to its architect, Thomas Cromwell. Anne fared better, and after the marriage was annulled, she became a substitute sister to the King, an additional Princess, a royal presence at court who was fortunate to have escaped with her life. If anything, her experience confirms the dangerous nature of the path walked by all the women close to the King, either through marriage or blood. Whether by design or naivety, it was only Anne's complete capitulation that ensured her personal survival.

The negotiations for Anne's marriage began in June 1539. Henry's ambassadors visited Duren, in North Germany, midway between Aachen and Cologne, with the aim of securing a marriage alliance between Henry and a daughter of the Duke of Cleves. Henry told them to approach her mother first and use 'all their wisdom and dexterity to kindle them to the desire of this matter' for a 'speedy conclusion' and to examine the appearance of both daughters, Anne and Amalia, in order to assess their personal charms.[1] Although the custom of Cleves only permitted the ladies to appear heavily veiled, it was reputed that Anne's beauty eclipsed that of others 'as the golden sun did the silver moon' and that everyone at court 'praised her beauty'.[2] Court painter Hans Holbein was dispatched to capture her likeness and when his portrait arrived back in England that August, it met with the King's approval. The ambassadors from Cleves arrived in London on 16 September and by early October, the marriage contract had been drawn up.

Anne had been born in 1515, the second of the three daughters of John III and Maria, Duchess of Julich-Berg, and raised at the Schloss Berg, near Solingen. At the age of eleven, she was betrothed to Francis, son of the Duke of Lorraine, which arrangement lasted almost ten years until it was broken off in 1535; it had, however, dictated the content of her education. Destined to become a Duchess, she only spoke German and lacked the ability to sing, dance, play an instrument, games or sport, skills which were so valued by the Tudors. The court of Cleves, with its heavily moral tone and Catholicism tempered by Erasmian theories, did not encourage the sort of merrymaking, masques and lavish celebrations that had set the tone of Henry's court since his succession.

Early in the morning on 27 December, Anne's fleet set sail from Calais, arriving in Deal, just down the coast from Dover on the Kent coast, at around five in the evening. According to Charles Brandon, Duke of Suffolk, who was awaiting her, 'The day was foule and wynde with muche hayle ... contynuelly in her face,' but Anne was 'desirous to make haste' to her husband.[3] Suffolk rode with Anne to Dover Castle, which would have been far more on the scale of the European castles she was used to. After resting at Dover, Anne's retinue headed north-west over the seventeen miles to Canterbury, where forty or fifty 'gentlewomen of the town' awaited her in the newly furbished King's Palace, once part of St Augustine's Abbey. Anne took this 'very joyously, and was so glad to see the King's subjects resorting so lovingly to her, that she forgot all the foul weather and was very merry at supper.'[4]

By New Year's Eve, Anne had passed through Sittingbourne and reached Rochester, where she stayed at the old Bishop's Palace. The following day, she was watching a bull-baiting when a party of nine disguised men in hoods and cloaks entered the room. Completely reliant upon her translators and still uncertain of courtly protocol, let alone Henry's penchant for disguise, she was taken by surprise when one of the men approached her, took her in his arms and attempted to kiss her. In fact, considering the protocol of her sheltered childhood, and the strict way in which she had been covered up for the viewing of the ambassadors, such behaviour probably appeared scandalous to her. She had no way of knowing it was Henry, so she did not respond, but turned coldly away.

Abashed at the failure of his romantic gesture, Henry retired and changed into regal purple, before returning and declaring his true identity. Recognising her mistake, Anne bowed low and, according to Wriothesley, the pair 'talked lovingly together', although Lord Russell reported that he 'never saw His Highness so marvellously astonished ... as on that occasion.' Hall related how 'she with most gracious and loving countenance and behaviour, him received and welcomed on her knees, whom he gently took up and kissed,' after which, they dined together.[5] Anne's reaction had disappointed the King, but her appearance had been an even greater surprise. In his opinion, she was not as attractive or as young-looking as he had been led to believe and although he afforded her the respect her position demanded, his growing anger seethed behind his diplomatic mask. Riding back to Greenwich, he informed Cromwell in no uncertain terms that he did not like his new wife. However, now that she had arrived, pulling out of the wedding without causing a scandal seemed impossible.

On Saturday 3 January 1540, Anne travelled to Shooter's Hill, in London. Dignitaries, clergymen and servants lined the lane in their ranks, from the park gates to the cross of Blackheath, and Henry's retinue alone numbered between 5,000 and 6,000. Anne arrived at about midday, drawn in a chariot, flanked by a hundred horsemen. Margaret Douglas, Frances Brandon, Mary, Duchess of Richmond and other 'ladies and gentlewomen to the number of sixty-five' welcomed her and led her into a gorgeous tent or pavilion of rich cloth, where they helped her dress in a Dutch gown of raised cloth of gold, a round bonnet or cap, set with orient pearls 'of a very proper fashion', a black velvet cornet and, about her neck, a partelet, set full of rich, glistening stones.[6] Despite his initial dislike, Henry played his part, meeting her 'with most lovely countenance and princely behaviour ... saluted, welcomed and embraced her, to the great rejoicing of the beholders.'[7] She, in turn, received him with 'most amiable aspect and womanly behaviour (with) many sweet words and great thanks and praisings given to him.' Placing her on his right, he accompanied her to Greenwich Palace, where he embraced and kissed her, bidding her 'welcome to her own.'[8] While Anne settled into her privy chamber with her ladies, Henry then hurried back to Cromwell to seek a way that he could avoid having to make her his wife. There was one glimmer of hope: Anne's pre-contract with Francis of Lorraine.

Anne's former betrothal had been investigated the previous autumn. Then, the English ambassadors at Cleves had been entirely satisfied with the explanation that the parties had both been below the age of consent, making Anne now free to marry. Henry instructed Cromwell to investigate again, but Anne's Dutch secretary could only repeat the former verdict, promising to summon the relevant legal paperwork from Cleves at once. Anne willingly swore an oath to the effect that she was not obligated to Lorraine, so there was nothing Henry could do, unless he wanted to create a diplomatic incident with the Duke of Cleves. Seething with rage, backed into a corner, he decided that he was 'not well handled'. However, the wedding took place as planned, on 6 January 1540, in the Queen's closet at Greenwich. Cranmer officiated and the Dutch Earl of Overstein gave Anne away. Henry placed a ring on her finger that bore the legend 'God send me well to keep' and they walked hand in hand back into the King's chamber to hear Mass and take wine and spices. According to Henry's later accounts, the wedding night was not a success.

*

At some point early in 1540, Henry's path crossed that of a newly arrived young woman at court. The teenaged Catherine Howard may have been coached by her relatives, particularly her grandfather the Duke of Norfolk and her step-grandmother, Duchess Agnes Tilney, to attract the attention of the dissatisfied King. As long-standing enemies of Cromwell, recognising that the royal marriage was unlikely to last, they might have encouraged Catherine once it was clear that Henry was interested. Or it may simply be that his head was turned by a pretty face. The Duchess believed that the King's attraction was stirred almost as soon as the girl arrived at court, perhaps even by autumn 1539, saying that 'the King's Highness did cast a fantasy to Catherine Howard the first time that ever his Grace saw her.' By late April, the King was smitten, making the first grant of land to his new love, indicating a possible time when the affair was consummated. From that point, the chance of Catherine becoming pregnant meant that Anne's days were numbered. When she took her seat to watch the May Day jousts at Westminster, followed by a week of tournaments and feasting at Durham House, Anne could not have anticipated it would be her last public engagement as Queen.

On 24 June, 'the kyng caused the queen to Richmond,' purportedly for 'her health, open air and pleasure'[9] and to escape the illnesses that often broke out at court during the summer months. It was a beautiful palace, and Henry promised that he would be joining Anne there shortly. The days passed and she waited patiently. Instead, her husband established a commission to investigate the legality of his marriage, with the aim of securing a divorce and easing the path of Catherine Howard into his bed. On 6 July, Henry sent a written message to Anne at Richmond, informing her that the inquiry had found their marriage invalid. According to the Earl of Rutland, who understood her with the help of an interpreter, she took the news 'heavily' and did not respond to his encouragement to 'discharge her conscience' and 'rejoice and not … be sorry.'[10] That afternoon, Henry sent a delegation of gentlemen to Richmond to explain the matter further and urge her to co-operate. More composed, Anne replied that she was 'content always with your majesty' but she was forbidden to send any messages to Henry.[11] The case was heard at Westminster the following day. On July 8, Anne summoned her advisor Carl Harst twice, to explain the situation further to her, and when he saw her the second time, late that night, she was 'sobbing so loudly and crying so violently it almost broke his heart.'[12]

On 9 July, Parliament agreed that Henry and Anne had never been legally wed and that both were free to remarry.

Anne was now in a difficult situation. In a foreign country, far from home, she was no longer Henry's wife and Queen, and her status and future were uncertain. To return home as an unwanted bride, only six months after the lengthy journey and elaborate ceremony of her arrival, would be a terrible disgrace. She sent Harst to Henry to lodge her complaints, but his lone voice could accomplish little against the King's decision, backed by his Council, and her ambassador knew it. Returning to his mistress, he advised Anne to capitulate. On 11 July, she wrote to the King, accepting the verdict regarding their 'pretended matrimony', stating her 'worldly affection' for him and signing herself his 'sister and servant'. A relieved Henry responded with a generous settlement.

Anne became the King's sister by adoption, second only in status to his children and future wife, with extensive properties, a considerable annual income of £4,000, hangings, plate, furniture, jewels, pearls and the occasional invitation to court.[13] Henry wrote that 'when Parliament ends, we shall, in passing, see and speak with you, and you shall more largely see what a friend you and your friends have of us.' In the meantime, he required her to be 'quiet and merry'.[14] Faced with this solution instead of an ignominious return to Cleves, or worse, Anne returned her wedding ring with the message that 'it might be broken in pieces as a thing which she knew of no force or value.'[15] She confessed to the 'integrity of her body' and wrote to her brother, Duke William, on 21 July to reassure him that she had given her consent to the matter, 'wherein I had more respect (as beseemed me) to truth than to any worldly affection that might move me to the contrary, and did the rather condescend thereunto for that my body remaineth in the integrity which I brought into this realm.' She was 'well satisfied' that the Anglo-Cleves alliance would 'not be impaired for this matter', declared her intention to live in England and signed herself as 'Anna, Duchess born of Cleves'.[16] Writing to Francis I, Ambassador Marillac reported on Anne's popularity: 'She is no longer to be called queen, but Lady Anne of Cleves, to the great regret of this people, who loved and esteemed her much as the sweetest, most gracious and kindest queen they ever had or would desire.' Anne would make her home in England for the remainder of her life, living predominantly at Richmond, whilst being a regular attendant at court. She died in 1557.

*

Henry's frequent visits across the Thames to Catherine Howard at Lambeth had been noted. As Marillac wrote, 'It is commonly said that this King will marry a lady of great beauty, daughter of Norfolk's deceased brother. If permitted to write what he hears, he would say this marriage has already taken place and is consummated; but as this is kept secret he dare not yet certify it as true.'[17] Henry and Catherine were married on 28 July 1540 by Edmund Bonner, Bishop of London, at Oatlands Palace, when he was 49 and she was around 16 or 17. The news was made public on 8 August, when prayers were said for the new Queen in the chapel at Hampton Court. Marillac reported that he was 'so amorous of her that he cannot treat her well enough and caresses her more than he did the others.' The King's secretary, Ralph Morice, wrote that 'the King's affection was so marvellously set upon that gentlewoman as it was never known that he had the like to any woman.'[18] As the King's wife, Catherine's role was simply to please Henry in bed, to be cheerful and merry, to divert him from his illness and increasing old age, and as Queen, to appear on ceremonial occasions in the new clothes and jewels he showered her with. Henry's health was no longer what it had been, but any pregnancy that resulted would have been welcomed.

Like Anne Boleyn and Jane Seymour, Catherine Howard had been intended as an aristocratic wife. She was one of at least six children of Edmund Howard and Joyce Culpepper, born between 1524 and 1527. Her aunt was Elizabeth Howard, mother of Anne and Mary Boleyn, making her their first cousin, and Edmund's own cousin, Margery, was the mother of Jane Seymour. Her first years were spent at Norfolk House in Lambeth, the London home of the Howard clan, but in 1531, she was entrusted to the care of her step-grandmother, Agnes Tilney, Dowager Duchess of Norfolk, at Chesworth House, Horsham, in Sussex. The large property provided shelter for a number of young people, who were supposed to learn and make themselves useful until such time as they could find their way in the world of their own accord. For Catherine, it proved to be a period of sexual awakening: her years at Chesworth would come back to haunt her and underpin her downfall as Queen.

Of two surviving portraits claimed to depict Catherine, one is far more likely to show the new Queen. Recently, historian David Starkey has identified a Holbein miniature of an unknown woman as Catherine, by matching the jewels she is wearing to records of those in her possession. The sitter wears gold and brown against a blue background, her auburn hair pulled back under a gold French hood lined with pearls, more pearls and golden embroidery line her bodice and a further string and pendant sit around her neck. The sitter's face is pale and serene, with heavy-lidded eyes, delicate lips and rounded chin. She wears a gold wedding ring, indicating that the portrait was probably painted between mid-1540 and late 1541. It is less certain that the full-length Holbein 'Portrait of a Lady' in a black dress depicts Catherine, as although the features are similar, the sitter appears to be older than Catherine is thought to have been.

In September, Marillac visited the court at Grafton, where Henry was staying 'with a small company' for hunting and 'banquets being given to the new Queen'.[19] There, he saw Catherine for the first time, describing her as 'rather graceful than beautiful' and of short stature, dressed in the French style, along with her ladies.[20] Henry lavished wedding gifts on his new bride, including jewels from the royal coffer that had previously adorned his other wives: a pendant of gold set with a diamond, ruby and pearl, a square necklace of clustered rubies and pearls, the gold trimming for a French hood, adorned with diamonds and more. Through the second half of 1540, Catherine continued to entice and captivate her husband. Always taking a keen interest in medicine and cures for various bodily ailments, Henry approached his fiftieth birthday with a new-found enthusiasm for life, no doubt continuing to ask the advice of Dr Butts when it came to his ability to perform in the bedroom. In total, the surviving records of Henry's doctors show over two hundred different prescriptions for his various afflictions, to which total Henry also contributed his own remedies as plasters and ointments. That December, under the guidance of Dr Boorde, he began a new regime designed to assist in weight-loss, which involved rising at dawn and riding for two hours. However, this regime proved more dangerous than transformative, as Henry's leg ulcer closed over, making him very unwell, even to the point that his life was despaired of. Catherine was left alone for long periods, as Henry did not wish her to see him in that condition, only seeing her again once he had started to recover.

Margaret Douglas, Henry's niece, had been forgiven her scandalous betrothal to Thomas Howard and allowed to return to court in 1539, as part of the new household of Anne of Cleves, tasked with the responsibility of meeting her at Blackheath. Now aged twenty-four, and still unwed, she quickly made the transition to Catherine Howard's service, where she met the new Queen's brother, Charles. Just as before, a secret friendship developed, blossoming into a romance, but this time it did not take on the tragic dimension that her former affair had done. It is also likely that the events of autumn 1541 separated her from Charles before things went too far.

In the summer of 1541, Catherine took a more public role as Queen, appearing beside Henry as he travelled north in the hope of meeting James V of Scotland at York. On 1 July, they were at Enfield, moving on three days later to St Albans, then Dunstable on 8 July and Ampthill on the ninth. The party had moved on to Grafton Regis by 15 July, then Collyweston House, former home of Henry's grandmother, Margaret Beaufort, and Grimsthorpe on 7 August, where they were hosted by Charles Brandon, Duke of Suffolk, and his third wife, Catherine Willoughby. It was an important projection of majesty, and her responsibility, as Catherine was dressed in her finery, was to be seen by her subjects along the roads and in the cities and towns they visited, to inspire loyalty and devotion in a region that had rebelled five years before; a task both onerous and potentially dangerous.

On 10 August, the royal party arrived at Temple Brewer, seven miles outside the city of Lincoln, where tents had been erected for Henry and Catherine to replace their crimson and green velvet clothing with cloth of silver and gold. An account of their arrival lists the order of precedence as they rode into the city:

> The heralds put on their coats, the gentlemen pensioners and train rode according to the ancient order, then came lord Hastings bearing the sword, then the King, then his horse led by the Master of the Horse, then the children of honour, each after other on great coursers, then the earl of Rutland, Queen's chamberlain, then the Queen, then her horse of estate, then all the ladies, then the Captain of the Guard and the Guard, then the commoners.[21]

They were welcomed by the Mayor and other city dignitaries to the ringing of church bells before processing to the cathedral, where stools, carpet and cushions of gold had been set out for them. Wreathed in incense, they heard Mass before retiring to their lodgings.

From there, the progress moved to Gainsborough on 12 August and Hatfield Chase, where they rested in a village of splendid tents and enjoyed hunting and feasting, before moving on to Pontefract Castle on 23 August. Three weeks late, they arrived in York, awaiting King James of Scotland in vain, while in the meantime, a thousand men worked night and day to complete the conversion of the dissolved Abbey of St Mary's into a royal palace, sparking rumours that Catherine was to be crowned there. No coronation took place. By the beginning of October, they had arrived in Hull, and after a sojourn there, began the long journey south. It was at Ampthill, in Bedfordshire, that the King suffered an attack of malaria which exacerbated the ulcers in his legs, forcing him to stay in bed. Once he had recovered, as was often his pattern, Henry showered his wife with gifts, presenting her with a gold brooch set with diamonds and rubies. On 29 October, they arrived back at Hampton Court, where Henry gave 'most humble and hearty thanks' for his good life with Catherine, which he 'trusted to lead' in the future.[22] The following week, the storm broke.

*

On 2 November 2, as Henry went to attend Mass in his private closet, he found a letter which had been left on his seat. In it, the Archbishop of Canterbury, Thomas Cranmer, exposed the secret relationship Catherine had been conducting with Thomas Culpeper, a gentleman of the Privy Chamber, and one of Henry's favourites. Knowing the affection in which the King held his young wife, it was a wise move on Cranmer's part to lay down all the evidence against the Queen in writing, to allow Henry to read it as his leisure and limiting the inevitable dramatic scene that would ensue. At first, the King refused to believe the report, but ordered an investigation into Catherine's behaviour prior to her marriage. It was this process, over the first two weeks of November, which led to the uncovering of liaisons with Culpeper, which had been ongoing throughout the summer progress. The investigation uncovered that during her youth at Chesworth, Catherine had sexual relationships with her music teacher, Henry Manox, courtier Francis Dereham and her cousin Culpeper, to whom she had promised her hand. In addition, she had recently promoted a number of her former Chesworth inmates to positions within her household, possibly as rewards for holding their tongues. Henry had been duped into believing in her virginity and deceived about her intimate friendships as Queen.

On the night of 6 November, Henry left Hampton Court for Whitehall. There, in a Council meeting that ran from midnight until the early hours, Henry broke down in tears, lamenting his 'ill-luck in meeting with such ill-conditioned wives' and calling for a sword so that he might kill her himself, so 'that wicked woman (would have) never such delight in her incontinency as she should have torture in her death.'[23] Left behind at Hampton Court, Catherine would never see him again. On the evening of the following day, a delegation of the Council confronted her with their findings, which she initially denied. At a meeting with Cranmer later than night, however, she admitted her guilt and made a full confession, tearful and distraught, 'in such lamentation and heaviness as I never saw no creature, so that it would have pitied any man's heart to have looked upon her.'[24] Catherine was despatched to Syon Abbey and her household was disbanded. Margaret Douglas and Mary Howard, former Duchess of Richmond, were sent to Kenninghall House in Norfolk, a residence of the Dukes of Norfolk. On 10 December, Dereham suffered the full traitor's death of hanging, quartering and disembowelling at Tyburn, while Culpeper was beheaded. Afterwards, their heads were placed on spikes on London Bridge, as a macabre and powerful deterrent.

The weeks passed. Catherine waited at Syon as Christmas was succeeded by New Year. All may have seemed quiet in the seclusion of the old Abbey, but the King's Council were working furiously to pass the legislation required to allow her downfall. In late January, an Act of Attainder made it treason for a woman to become the King's wife without 'plain declaration before of her unchaste life' and confirming that adultery, to facilitate adultery, or the failure to admit adultery, was treason.[25] Before this, Catherine had hoped she might still gain Henry's forgiveness: Chapuys described her 'making good cheer, fatter and more beautiful than ever, taking great care to be well apparelled and more imperious and troublesome to serve than even when she was with the King.'[26] Yet, the new Act made her death inevitable, delayed only in order for the legal process to take its due course. On 10 February, Catherine was conveyed from Syon House to the Tower, 'with some resistance', dressed in black velvet. Two days later, she was informed that she would die the following morning, and 'wept, cried and tormented herself miserably without ceasing,'[27] before requesting that the block be sent to her, in order to place her head on it 'by way of experiment'.[28] Catherine and her lady-in-waiting, Jane Rochford, the widow of George Boleyn, were executed one after the other, early in the morning on 13 February, on the same spot where Anne Boleyn had died. Their bodies joined hers in the Tower's Chapel of St Peter ad Vincula.

Catherine's eighteen months of queenship were characterised by her youth and high spirits, breathing life back into the court of an ageing King. She attempted to exercise queenly mercy, pleading for the lives of two of Henry's high-profile victims of 1541, securing the release of Thomas Wyatt, who had been imprisoned on grounds of treason and adultery, but unable to save Henry's aunt, Margaret Pole, Countess of Salisbury, who went to the block for treason and the alleged support of her son Reginald's claim to the throne. After the precedent had been set by Anne Boleyn's execution, Margaret suffered brutally at the hands of her incompetent executioner, in a way that had been unthinkable a decade before. Catherine also welcomed Anne of Cleves at court and tried to bring Mary and Elizabeth back into favour, with the sisters exchanging gifts. In 1542, the first Christmas after Catherine's fall, Henry's three children spent their first Christmas together at Enfield. As Queen, she also provided a high-profile figurehead during the northern progress, fulfilling her ceremonial duties and her role in civic welcomes. The period of her reign was not always easy, and Henry's illnesses contributed to long periods of isolation which highlighted their age-gap, but Catherine demonstrated the potential to succeed in the public aspects of queenship before the exposure of her private life made her position untenable.

Catherine's death prompted a resurgence of interest in the fate of Anne of Cleves, giving rise to speculation that she was to be reinstated as queen. *The Remonstrance of Anne of Cleves* was printed by John of Luxembourg, Abbot of Ivry. It depicted Anne as overwhelmed with sorrow, taking the form of a direct appeal from her to Henry, lamenting that 'wives are given to men to obey them ... if then the King chooses to leave you and take another, ought you to go contrary to his will?' All the clothes and jewels, properties and lands she had received at his hands had 'been contaminated and defiled by the bad treatment, the wrong and the injury, exhibited by him to her.' This fictional 'Anne' continued, 'If it be said that she is not so personally attractive in the King's eyes as he desired to find her, let it be replied that she did not seek the King, but he sought her' and by 'becoming entirely conformed to his desires ... she should be far more agreeable to him than any of those whose company he might (with scandal and sin) desire to use.'[3] The French Ambassador, William Paget, implored Francis I to suppress the tract, but without success. It was an embarrassment, but it did nothing to advance Anne's cause, even if she was aware of its existence, or had desired to become queen again. Henry continued to treat her as his sister and that March, when she lay ill at Richmond with 'tertian fever', he sent his doctors there to tend her. After Henry had been so adamant to escape her, and with so many other options at court, there would be no second shot at the throne for Anne of Cleves. Her queenship was over before it had begun.

21

Weathering the Storm
1543–46

Henry's final Queen, Catherine Parr, was born around 1512. She was the daughter of Sir Thomas Parr, a descendant of Edward III and Maud Green, a cousin of Edward IV's wife, Elizabeth Woodville. The family home in Blackfriars had been granted to the Parrs by Henry VIII for their services to the crown: Thomas had been Master of the Wards, Master of the Guards and Comptroller to the King, before his death in 1517. Maud was a lady-in-waiting to Catherine of Aragon, so it was convenient for the family to be raised close to the court, as well as in their other main property of Rye House, Hertfordshire. Catherine's education included the traditional regime of womanly accomplishments, but she was also able to speak French and Italian, and as her later writing and pursuits proved, she was clearly the possessor of a formidable curiosity and no little intelligence. At some point in her young life, she became a firm believer in reform, and the need to spread that message, but like all women of her station, she was destined to become a nobleman's wife and a mother. Although her queenship lasted less than four years, and she did not bear the King a child, Catherine was able to make significant contributions to Tudor family life, the intellectual and religious climate of the court, national security and international politics.

Catherine was first married at the age of seventeen. Her husband was Sir Edward Burgh, the son of Anne Boleyn's Chamberlain, who had carried her coronation train in May 1533, although this had not prevented him receiving a severe warning after he defaced Catherine of Aragon's coat of arms. What the young Catherine Parr thought of Anne is unrecorded. She would certainly have shared her reformist sympathies, although Catherine's childhood connection to Princess Mary and her mother might suggest her loyalties lay there. The young couple lived first at Gainsborough Old Hall in Lincolnshire, then at nearby Kirton-in-Lindsey. There were no recorded surviving children from the marriage on Edward's death three years later.

A year later, Catherine remarried, to John Neville, Lord Latimer, a Catholic widower with two children, who lived a quiet life away from court after having served in Henry's 1513 French campaign. The bride was then twenty-one, the groom forty-three. Their married life was mostly spent at Snape Castle in Yorkshire, a sprawling residence with solid square turrets built of yellow-grey stone. It was a good career move for Catherine, taking her up a social step and providing her with a good home and public standing, although her husband's unfortunate involvement with the Pilgrimage of Grace in 1536 made the future path of the Latimers less certain. It was unclear to Henry exactly what role Latimer had played in the uprising, whether as a supporter of the rebels, or someone drive of necessity to negotiate with them to ensure the safety of his family at Snape. With family assistance, Latimer was given the benefit of the doubt, although his reputation never fully recovered. The exact date of his death is unclear: it may have been as early as December 1542 or as late as March 1543, when his will was proved. It is likely to have been closer to the former, as in early February Catherine was already at court, to visit her siblings and, perhaps, to renew her friendship with Princess Mary. She may also have been hoping to make a new marriage, to the man who had already captured her heart, Prince Edward's handsome uncle, Thomas Seymour.

Catherine was left a wealthy woman. Having gone through two marriages of duty, and with both her parents dead, she was ready to follow the precedent set by Tudor princesses and choose a husband of her own. The marriage of Jane Seymour had catapulted her brothers into prominence as uncles of a future king. Thomas was a dashing, handsome figure, described by Nicholas Throckmorton as 'hardy, wise and liberal ... fierce in courage, courtly in fashion, in personage stately, in voice magnificent, but somewhat empty of matter.' He also had an air of danger about him and in September 1540, the Privy Council had bound him and an Edward Rogers to keep the peace towards each other, at a penalty of £1,000 each.[1] Like many of his noble contemporaries, Seymour had benefited from Henry's policy of dissolving the monasteries. In June 1541 he had been granted lands that belonged to the late monastery of Cirencester and the following month the manor attached to that at Amesbury, receiving further land in Berkshire and Westmorland before the end of the year.[2] Described as Henry's 'trusty and well-beloved servant ... knight, one of the gentlemen of his Grace's privy chamber',[3] Seymour had been ambassador to Vienna for eight months by the end of 1542. He wrote to Henry from Nuremberg on 29 December, where he was investigating the possibility of hiring mercenaries to fight for the King, although he 'hoped to return to England shortly.'[4] He was back at court in the early spring, at which point Catherine hoped he would make her his wife. However, the emergence of a more significant suitor would delay this love match for another four years.

Catherine was a good catch. At the age of thirty, she was experienced and wise, without being too old that her childbearing years could be considered to be over. According to John Foxe, she possessed 'rare gifts of nature, as singular beauty, favour and a comely personage; things wherein the King was delighted,' as well as the 'virtues of her mind'.[5] Her appearance was 'lively' and 'pleasing' and her 'cheerful countenance,' as painted by William Scrots, shows a round, open face with brown or auburn hair and the fashionable pale skin. A second image, a miniature by Lucas Horenbout, depicts her with a slimmer face and lighter hair.

In spite of the religious leanings of her second husband, the identification of her mother with the Aragon faction, and her friendship with Princess Mary, Catherine was passionately interested in religious reform, welcoming Hugh Latimer and Miles Coverdale at her house. The reformer Latimer had been preaching in favour of an English translation of the Bible since the late 1520s and had recently been imprisoned for opposing Henry's six articles of faith: later he would suffer a martyr's death by burning at the stake. Coverdale was responsible for translating and publishing a 1535 version of the Bible, building on the work of the martyred William Tyndale, although Henry had welcomed this, ordering a copy of Coverdale's work to be placed in every church. He would become Catherine's chaplain and almoner in the years ahead. Catherine was well aware of the dangers of her faith: that July, just after her wedding, four men were burned at Windsor for preaching and holding heretical beliefs.

By January 1543, according to Chapuys, rumours circulated at court that Henry was considering remarriage. He staged a great feast and summoned Princess Mary and her ladies in order to act as host: 'This came very *a propos* for the Princess, who, in default of a Queen, was called to Court triumphantly, accompanied by many ladies... Many think that before the end of these feasts the King might think of marrying again, but hitherto there is no appearance of it.'[6] Henry's interest in Catherine may have pre-dated her Lord Latimer's death and he had probably known her all her life, as the daughter of courtiers. In February, Catherine had joined the household of Princess Mary, when the King paid her tailor's bill for 'numerous items' of cotton, linen, buckram, hoods and sleeves, Italian, Venetian, French and Dutch gowns, costing over £8.[7] As with his other wives, one of the first signs was the advancement of her relatives. That March, Catherine's brother William became a member of the Privy Council and was elected to Knight of the Garter in April. He also granted William a divorce, on 17 April, after his wife, Anne Bourchier, was accused of adultery. By this point, Catherine cannot have failed to be aware of his interest and struggled to reconcile what she later came to consider to be God's will with the brief hope she had glimpsed of personal happiness. Henry needed to ensure his rival, Seymour, was out of the way. Nothing was more effective than putting a large distance between him and Catherine, so in April, Thomas received his instructions for a new embassy to Flanders. He left in May. By this point, Henry had probably already proposed to Catherine.

While the King awaited her reply, news arrived at court of the death of one of his previous loves. Following the scandal of 1536, Mary Boleyn had lived in quiet obscurity with her second husband, William Stafford, at Rochford Hall, Essex. She had lost both her parents, Elizabeth Howard dying in 1538 and Sir Thomas Boleyn the following year, from whom she inherited further property in the area. Mary was fortunate in her quiet life; she had married Stafford for love, stating in the 1530s that she would rather 'beg my bread' with him than be 'the greatest Queen in Christendom'. This in itself was a significant statement regarding the role of queenship, in the wake of her sister's experience. Mary's final years are as elusive as her first; she had briefly enjoyed the limelight of Henry's affection, then witnessed the meteoric rise and fall of her siblings before retreating into what appears to have been domestic harmony. When she died in June 1543, she was the King's last link with the glittering, dangerous world of a decade before.

Henry was keen to plunge into married life again. In reality, Catherine had little choice but to accept his offer and the necessary licence was issued by Cranmer on 10 July. Two days later, Catherine and Henry were married in the Queen's closet at Hampton Court by Bishop Gardiner, 'in the presence of noble and gentle persons' including Princess Mary, but 'privately and without ceremony'.[8] Catherine wrote to her brother describing the marriage as 'the greatest joy and comfort that could happen' to her. He replied that it 'revived my troubled spirit and turned all my care into solace and rejoicing.'[9]

*

One of Catherine's most important contributions to the Tudor dynasty was the warmth with which she brought together Henry's children. She had maintained good relationships with her Latimer stepdaughters and now invited Mary, Elizabeth and Edward to share each other's company on a number of occasions, beginning soon after her marriage. While she and Henry were away in August, she persuaded her husband to detour on their way to Ampthill to visit his children at Ashridge in Hertfordshire. From this time onwards, Mary also had a permanent base at court until her father's death, giving her greater stability and access to court resources at a time when she was experiencing the continuing ill-health that had dogged her since adolescence. In March 1535, she had been so ill that the physicians feared for her life, prompting Henry to travel to Greenwich, although when he arrived and learned she was out of danger, he did not see her in person but accused the doctor of plotting to reunite Mary with her mother. He later sent his daughter a message saying she was the cause of mischief throughout Christendom, that he had no greater enemy than her and her resistance was the cause of conspiracies against him. Mary was also repeatedly told by Lady Shelton that she would share the fate of Carthusian monks who had recently been hung, drawn and quartered for their refusal to swear the Act of Supremacy. That September, Mary was ill again, with a lingering cold, and she feared the return of her 'ordinary complaint, which she dreads, in the coming winter.'[9] Occasionally, such as on New Year's Day 1539, she was so faint that she had to stay in bed. In April 1542, she experienced heart palpitations and lay in bed 'as one dead'[10] so that Henry was afraid enough to send in his own physicians. In September 1543, she was 'very ill of a colic' and the following July, had 'been nothing well' for a number of days.[13] Her apothecary bills were large, and she was frequently bled in a bid to alleviate her symptoms.

At least one historian has dismissed Mary's illness dating from after the death of Anne Boleyn as 'clearly not stress related' and suggested that it 'may have been mere hypochondria'.[4] This is unwarranted. Mary's symptoms are consistent with the decade and a half of trauma that underpinned her adolescence and young adulthood. Mary had experienced being forcibly separated from her mother and was unable to see her before Catherine's death. She had been denied her status and degraded, bullied and manhandled, forced to submit in fear of her life and witnessed the dismantling of her faith and the rejection of her spiritual hero, the Pope. By 1543, she experienced the violent or premature deaths of three stepmothers. A number of men who had championed her cause, such as Thomas More and John Fisher, were executed for refusing the Act of Supremacy. This would have been ample cause for Mary to experience continuing anxiety, post-traumatic stress or depression, with all the ensuing physical symptoms those could manifest. This reductive approach to female suffering, and its long-term effects, has appeared in many pre-revisionist biographies and histories of Mary and her contemporaries. New narratives of Tudor women's lives must centralise the battle against such perpetuation of patriarchal attitudes and gender imbalance. To fail to understand the cumulative effects of ill-health, and to distance health from other aspects of individual identity, is to misapprehend individual character. While historians are eager to point out Henry's increasing infirmity as a significant element of his decision-making and changes in mood, the same truth must be fairly acknowledged for issues of mental and emotional health in women. What is heartening are the instances of kindness suffering women could experience from other members of their sex. While Lady Sheldon and Anne Boleyn contributed to Mary's trauma, the constant, kind presence of Catherine Parr was of beneficial effect to her in ways which can hardly be overestimated.

With the restoration of her position, Mary again became her father's instrument in the negotiation of a dynastic marriage. Husbands were considered for her from France and the Empire, during which she was sometimes presented as a legitimate daughter, and sometimes not. Yet the one suitor who did visit and attempt to woo the princess in person, did so unofficially, of his own volition, over a period of seven years. Duke Philip of Bavaria was the son of the Elector Palatine, of the house of Wittelsbach, based in Bavaria, and thirteen years Mary's senior. He first visited England in December 1539, asking for Mary's hand and offering an alliance with military support. His approach to Henry was courteous enough.

> Thanks him for having received him so honourably at his palace. Was particularly glad that an opportunity had offered of showing the desire he has always had to serve Henry; and, in deference to Henry's wish that he should come with the least possible company, set out, in the very month this was announced to him, with a very small train, notwithstanding the dangers of the journey and the inclemency of the weather. He accordingly now presents himself. The King knows why he has come... It remains for the King to say what he will do with his daughter.[15]

Henry allowed investigations to take place, but Mary was put off by Philip's Lutheranism, protesting that she would prefer not to 'enter into that kind of religion' but that she would be guided by her father's wishes. French ambassador Marillac anticipated the problem, recognising 'the probability that they will not give her to a powerful prince, lest he should afterwards raise some claim to this crown.'[16]

Mary met the Duke in the gardens at Westminster on Boxing Day, when they conversed with the help of a translator and he was so bold as to kiss her, and promised to make her his wife. As Marillac reported:

> The news is confirmed that he wrote on the 24th touching the marriage of Lady Mary with this duke of Bavaria; who three or four days ago, as secretly as he could, went to visit her in a house of the abbot of Westminster, in the gardens of the abbey, a mile from this town, whither she had been brought. After having kissed her, which is an argument either of marriage or of near relationship, seeing that since the death of the late Marquis no lord of this kingdom has dared to go so far, the said Duke had a long conversation with her, partly in German through an interpreter, and partly in Latin, of which she is not ignorant. Finally, they mutually declared, the said lord his resolution, taken with this King, to have her for wife 'pourveu que sa personne luy feust agréable,' and the said lady her willingness to obey her father. Cannot tell when the marriage will be consummated; but some say in 15 or 20 days.[17]

In spite of the groom's religion, a treaty was drafted in which Philip promised to accept that Mary would not inherit the English throne, and to marry her within a month of his return to England. Henry was to pay a dowry of 20,000 golden florins of the Rhine, followed by another 20,000 after a year of marriage. Within three months of the vows being exchanged, Philip was to convey Mary to his home and the King and Duke would support each other in a state of perpetual peace.[18] A number of revisions to this document survive, but in the end it was never implemented, and Philip left England a month later. Marillac reported with some suspicion on 2 February 1540 that 'this Duke Philip of Bavaria, feigning a wish to return home through the Emperor's countries, embarked at Dover and departed with three or four ships which had been secretly equipped, not towards Calais but towards the country of the Easterlings.'[19] It may have been Philip's close relation to Anne of Cleves, being her third cousin on the side of both parents, which deterred Henry from pursuing this match.

Philip returned to England unexpectedly in May 1543, as recorded by the Imperial ambassador, Chapuys: 'The King and Council are surprised at his coming, and especially at his having been here about eight days before the King was informed of it. He spoke to the King on Tuesday last after Mass, at some length, and was well received.'[20] However, on this occasion he did not even see Mary and departed on 4 June 'ill-satisfied'.[21] His third visit took place three years later. On 27 March 1546, Dutch merchants wrote to Charles V that 'Count Palatine Philip of Bavaria was expected, having come down the Rhine to Dordrecht and thence to England incognito. People have been sent to meet him and he arrives at Court this evening.'[22] On this occasion, Philip did obtain a second meeting with Mary, who was then aged thirty, but no details of the event survived. He left and returned again that September, for the final time, but the marriage did not proceed any further. As the Admiral of France's correspondent related, 'Duke Philip of Bavaria is here, as he was last spring, having come both times to get the daughter of England in marriage or else persuade the King to give him some present and pension; and the King has now given him a present of 5000 angelots and pension of about 3000 cr., but has no mind to give his daughter, and the Duke has little hope of obtaining her.'[23] Philip did not renew his efforts to marry Mary, even after the succession of her brother, and died in 1548.

*

Catherine's queenship also encompassed an active role in the defence of England. With the Scots in submission following the death of James V, Henry concluded a secret alliance with Emperor Charles and turned all £650,000 of his military force against his old friend and adversary, Francis I. In spite of the agony from his leg ulcer, and his frequent inability to walk, Henry was determined to lead the army in person, clad in his giant-sized newly made armour. In February 1544, when his ulcers had flared up again, leaving him bedridden in a fever, Catherine requested that her bed be moved into a closet leading off his bedchamber, ordered plaster and sponges, comfits and pastilles from her apothecary and was glimpsed sitting with his bad leg in her lap.[24] Henry's doctors urged him not to travel to France in person but to deputise the role, as he had done in Scotland. It seemed impossible to think of a man who could barely stand, leading an army across the Channel. Nothing would change the King's mind though.

On 7 July 1544, Henry appointed Catherine as Regent in his absence, that his process of government would pass to her and that 'a commission for this be delivered to her before his departure.'[25] She was to be assisted by Cranmer as Archbishop of Canterbury, Lord Chancellor Wriothesley, Edward Seymour, Earl of Hertford, Stephen Gardiner, Bishop of Westminster and secretary Sir William Petre, who were to report to her once a month on 'the state of the country'.[26] Catherine was also granted the manors of Chelsea, Hanworth and Mortlake. It marked the height of her influence. Henry's health had significantly improved by the time of the campaign, to the extent that Edward Seymour commented that he was in 'as good health as I have seen his Grace at any time this seven year.'[27]

Before his departure, Henry and Catherine attended the wedding of his niece Lady Margaret Douglas to Charles Stuart, Earl of Lennox, which took place in the chapel royal of St James's Palace followed by a feast of five courses. Mary, Elizabeth and Edward also attended, with Mary giving her friend the gift of a ruby and diamond, with three small pearls suspended from them. Lennox was a great grandson of James II through the maternal line, recently supported by Henry VIII in his bid to take the Isle of Bute from the Scottish Regent, the Earl of Arran. Forgiven for her infatuation with Charles Howard, Margaret was then twenty-nine, and considerably older than average for a first marriage. Her situation must have drawn attention to the status of her close friend, Princess Mary, who was only four months her junior and still unwed. With at least ten years of their most fertile years behind them, Margaret and Mary highlight a specific problem for their generation of Tudor women. Their proximity to the throne made their marriages both very valuable as bargaining tools but also potentially explosive. The problem of finding the 'right' husband was the first question, but also complicated by the shifting sands of international negotiation, meaning that what was considered the most beneficial alliance could rapidly change. Understandably, Henry did not want to bestow his only adult daughter upon just anyone, nor open the door to a foreign king, but Mary was not getting any younger. In 1542 she confided in one of her ladies that it was 'folly' to think that any marriage would be arranged for her during her father's lifetime, and that while he lived, she would only be Lady Mary, the most 'malheureuse' lady in England.[28]

Henry was in France from 14 July until 30 September, laying siege to Boulogne, which finally fell to him after almost two months. In his absence, Catherine played the role of the 'humble, obedient loving wife and servant', writing soon after his departure that 'the want of your presence, so much beloved and desired by me, makes me that I cannot quietly enjoy anything until I hear from your Majesty' and that 'love and affection compels me to desire your presence.'[29] Yet she combined this with the strength and steel required to oversee the running of the country, from dealing with Scottish prisoners to equipping the French campaign. Only 25 July, she was at Hampton Court, where she wrote to Henry to inform him that a further £40,000 was being advanced to him by the Council and that 4,000 men were ready to be sent as reinforcements at an hour's notice.[30] A week later, she wrote again from the Palace with news from the Lieutenant of the North and enclosing other letters of business, concluding with her usual reassurance that the children were all in good health. They had all spent a brief spell together at Enfield and Oakham Castle, to exchange the dangerously pestilent air of the capital for that of the countryside. On 6 August, Catherine was back at Greenwich and reported that stories were circulating that the French had landed on the English coast, knowing that 'such vain rumours fly fast, and this may have reached the King.'[31] On 9 September, she was at Westminster to issue proclamations to deal with deserters: 'for the examination of persons returning from the king's army in France and punishing of such as have insufficient passports to do so' and for the containment of a fresh outbreak of the plague.[32] Catherine proved herself an active and capable Regent, overseeing finances, organisation and provisions, signing royal proclamations and maintaining strong links with her agents in the north to monitor the Scottish situation.

By the 1540s, Catherine was part of a continuing European tradition of women engaging in warfare, either directly as aggressors and defenders, or indirectly through the role of Regent or facilitator. Her English precedents included Elizabeth Woodville, nominally left in charge in 1475 without any experience, and Catherine of Aragon, who had drawn from the experiences of her mother, Isabella of Castile. Across Europe, other women had been dramatically holding their own for decades: Christina of Saxony repelled the Swedes who were attacking Stockholm in 1501, Constanza, Duchess of Francavilia, defended Ischia against the French in 1503, while in 1505 Ingeborg Tott held her Finnish castle when it came under assault. Further examples can be found in Finland and Spain, and in 1520 Anna Eriksdotter Bielke successfully defended the Swedish city of Kalmar after the death of her husband. In the same year as Catherine Parr's regency, Catherine Segurane is reputed to have defended the city of Nice when it came under attack from the Ottoman Empire, and when England sent an army into Scotland in 1545, a number of women are reported to have fought against them in defence of their realm. English women had defended their property for centuries, most notably recorded in the Paston letters, but this increasing redefinition of the role of queens as martial figures was built upon by the contributions of Henry's first and final wives.

In 1544, Henry left Calais disappointed. He had succeeded in taking Boulogne, but knew his victory was a pyrrhic one, with the Emperor and Francis immediately reconciling. He crossed the Channel despondently, anticipating that the French would retaliate. Francis did not keep him waiting long. The attack came in the summer of 1545, when a fleet of French galleys sailed up the Channel and burned Brighton on the Sussex coast, then a small fishing village, before moving west towards the Isle of Wight, where they sank Henry's flagship, the *Mary Rose*.

While he was digesting this information, Henry received word that his oldest and closest friend, and one-time brother-in-law, Charles Brandon, Duke of Suffolk, had died. It was a shattering loss of a man who had been present in the King's life since his early childhood – and a reminder that his own days were numbered. The mood at court that autumn must have been a sombre one, especially as it had been a terrible year for Henry's health. It may be that this had an impact upon Henry and Catherine's marriage. Some outside observers perceived that all was not well. In February 1546, the new Imperial Ambassador, Francois Van der Delft, wrote to the Emperor that 'there are rumours of a new queen. Some attribute it to the sterility of the present Queen, while others say that there will be no change during the present war. Madame Suffolk is much talked about and is in great favour; but the King shows no alteration in his behaviour to the Queen, although she is said to be annoyed by the rumour.'[33] Catherine many have been annoyed by the rumours about her personal life, but far greater dangers were to be faced in the challenge mounted to her religious beliefs. As a devout reformist, a leader among the proto-Protestant sect, her formidable intelligence and faith were to pose a challenge to a King whose religious position had fluctuated like a weathervane. And her enemies knew it.

22

Such a Brief Happiness
1545–49

By the 1540s, England's religious landscape had been transformed. The Pope, once a national symbol of hope and salvation, was now the enemy. The saints, once kindly invisible allies who could intercede for one's benefit, had been destroyed in effigy and their shrines dismantled. The monasteries, countrywide centres of faith, learning and medicine, with their extensive libraries and infirmaries, had been gifted to the crown and nobility. Pensionless monks and nuns swelled the increasing numbers of the homeless, leading to the Elizabethan Vagabond Acts and Poor Laws. The rituals that had punctuated people's lives, hourly, daily, weekly, monthly, annually, were stripped away, leaving a cultural vacuum into which the reformed faith attempted to feed a greater sense of personal connection and accessibility to God. In 1541, John Calvin returned to Geneva after a period of exile during he would establish his own branch of Protestantism, while in 1542, Pope Paul III established the Holy Office, or Congregation for the Doctrine of the Faith, to defend Catholicism against heresy and false doctrines. Thinking outside the old systems also produced some incredible leaps in understanding during these years. In May 1543, Nicolas Copernicus published his mathematical arguments for a heliocentric universe. In June, Andreas Vesalius challenged previous Galenic understanding about human anatomy in his *On the Fabric of the Human Body*. It was a time of unparalleled and seismic revisions.

Catherine's queenship provided a figurehead for those interested in religious reforms. She established a circle of women at court who shared her evangelical leanings, including her sister Anne Parr, Anne, Countess of Sussex, Catherine, Duchess of Suffolk, Anne Stanhope,

Lady Hertford, and Lady Denny. Her passion for humanist teaching and the direct, personal interpretation of the Bible extended into her relationship with her stepchildren, as she encouraged Princesses Mary and Elizabeth to undertake English translations of Erasmus's *Paraphrase of the Gospel of St John* and Marguerite of Navarre's *The Mirror of the Sinful Soul* respectively.

Catherine was also an accomplished writer, publishing *Psalms and Prayers* in 1544 and *Prayers Stirring the Mind unto Heavenly Meditations* in 1545, which Elizabeth would translate into Latin, French and Italian, bound in crimson silk, for her stepmother's Christmas present that year. These were significant works in the narrative of female literacy, written in English to be accessed by a wide audience, in which the Queen took the role of editor and compiler of material. However, her next book, *Lamentations of a Sinner*, would push female authorship much further, with a narrative of her own invention, charting phases of her spiritual development with a self-deprecating tone and reference to herself as author. She was not merely collecting or translating a man's work, she was creating a work of her own.

Catherine held back some of her more extreme views from her husband, however, waiting until after his death to publish *Lamentations*. Although the book presented Henry as an English Moses, leading his people to the light, it also argued in favour of consubstantiation, instead of transubstantiation, that the bread and wine of Mass was only a metaphor for the body and blood of Christ, rather than becoming the real thing. She would also argue against Henry's 1543 Act for the Advancement of the True Religion, opposing the premise that the lower classes should be banned from reading the Bible in English. It was such views as this that aroused the animosity of conservatives Thomas Wriothesley and Bishop Gardiner, who wanted Henry to halt the process of reform. In the spring of 1546, the emergence of an unusual woman named Anne Askew provided them with an opportunity to pose a challenge to the Queen.

Anne was one of those dangerous Tudor women who challenged patriarchal conceptions of gender roles. She had left her husband to become a preacher of reformed ideals, breaking the sacred bond of matrimony, her promise of obedience and displaying herself in public for a controversial cause. Yet she was well-connected at court, with one brother as cup-bearer to the King, and a half-brother as a gentleman of the privy chamber; her father was also a gentleman of the court, having participated in the trial of Anne Boleyn. His daughter was provocative. Taking lodgings in the city, she met other religious radicals, preaching to large crowds and resuming her maiden name, as if her husband had never existed. Whatever her religious message, this alone was an affront to the perceived order of things. After having been arrested twice for her outspoken pronouncements, her engagement with Catherine's circle came under scrutiny and the usual rules about the treatment of female prisoners were broken when she was subjected to physical torture in the Tower.

Alarmed by reports of heresy at his court, Henry sanctioned a search at court for banned books, focusing particularly on the chambers of the Queen's ladies. This led to the hasty changing of locks and concealment of those texts that could be considered heretical, and on this occasion, the investigators went away empty-handed. However, they had not given up. As a result of Anne Askew's interrogation, something changed the King's attitude towards his sixth wife. In early July, after working on his master over recent months, Gardiner managed to persuade Henry to sign a warrant for Catherine's arrest. The crisis came after Catherine contradicted her husband in debate, which irritated the unwell King, and played upon the fears of a dominant or argumentative wife that harked back to his volatile union with Anne Boleyn and stereotypes of female dominance. Henry snapped to the Bishop that 'a good hearing it is when women become such clerks and a thing much to my comfort to come in my old days to be taught by a woman.'[1] Such words were ominous indeed, when the manhood of the King was called into question.

Yet the Queen did not lack for friends at court. By accident or design, a copy of the warrant was left in a place where Catherine could find it and, suddenly understanding the extent of the danger she was in, she hurried to explain herself to Henry, claiming she was only contradicting him in order to learn from him through debate and take his mind off his pain, and 'your majesty (has) very much mistaken me, for I have always held it preposterous for a woman to instruct her lord.' Luckily, she caught Henry in time, found the right words, and he was in a forgiving mood.

No doubt Catherine was terrified of suffering the same fate as Henry's previous wives, or even that of other heretics. Her clever and quick response showed just how adept she was at reading her husband.

She understood that Henry required her intellectual submission and so she used the traditionally weaker role of a wife as a shield, repackaging her faith as something she had used to help her husband. In this case, she turned the tables of gender expectations to her advantage. She had been lucky though, that the tip-off, possibly from Henry's doctor, had allowed her to pre-empt the strike before Henry refused to hear or see her, as he had done in the cases of Catherine of Aragon, Anne Boleyn, Catherine Howard and even briefly, Anne of Cleves, physically removing himself from their presence. Once Henry had made such a decision, he was implacable. Catherine understood that Henry's objection was less to her religious views than the fact that she had dared to publicly oppose him, and her deft capitulation brought an instant reconciliation. Foxe related that Henry took his wife on his knee and reassured her of his love, before ordering 'all manner of jewels, pearls and precious stones ... skins and sable furs ... for our dearest wife, the queen'.[3]

Catherine had talked her way out of her arrest, probably saving her own life. Henry, though, had forgotten to call off his henchmen. The following afternoon, while they sat in the privy gardens, Wriothesley appeared with a armed guard of forty men and Catherine had a glimpse of what her fate would have been. His mood rapidly changing, the King berated him and ordered him to leave. As Catherine attempted to comfort her husband, in the full knowledge of what she had witnessed, Henry told her 'You little know how evil he deserves this grace at your hands.'[4] On 16 July, Anne Askew was burned at the stake at Smithfield, having been carried there in a chair, as the extent of her torture made her incapable of walking. Her broken body must serve as a metaphor for the wrath of a patriarchy unprepared to tolerate independence of thought in a woman. Anne was not a Tudor queen, but she was the close friend of one, and the public disharmony her voice created helps explain why Catherine chose to keep her reformed views secret from such a husband as Henry.

*

The late summer and early autumn were a period of quiet happiness for Catherine and Henry. A peace treaty was signed with the French and on St Bartholomew's Day, 24 August 1546, the King appeared, 'richly appareled' with the Admiral of France, for which occasion many costly banquet houses were built, with great masques and hunts being held for their pleasure and the visitors being lodged in tents made of cloth of gold.[5] Catherine loved to dance, but the King, who had once relished this and appearing in disguise, could only sit and watch. That year, Henry found it increasingly difficult to walk on his swollen legs and spent more time shut away in his rooms. The eight-year-old Prince Edward had taken his place to formally welcome the French at Hounslow, before they had arrived at Hampton Court. That summer, a short progress had taken Henry and Catherine to Oatlands, where a ramp was installed to allow him to mount his horse, and he was able to hunt at Chobham that August, but the effort exhausted him, so the plan to visit Guildford was abandoned and the royal party returned to Windsor. Van der Delft related that Henry's physicians had been in despair, giving up all hope for his recovery and opining that he was in 'great danger'.[6] Two 'trams', or moveable chairs, were built, 'for the King's majesty to sit in, to be carried to and fro' and that October, Van der Delft described Henry as 'passing in his chair'. Hall related that Henry required 'an engine' to help him climb and descend staircases and the Duke of Norfolk confirmed that a device was installed for him on the stairs.[7] The bill for the King's medicines increased from £5 in August to £25 in December.[8] In November, Henry moved to Whitehall and undertook a series of medicinal baths, combining herbs, spices and salts believed to have a soothing effect. His rooms were freshly perfumed, to obscure the smell of his rotten leg and the evil vapours of disease and several pairs of velvet slippers were made for the comfort of his swollen feet.

Princess Mary was also unwell in the autumn of 1546, as Chapuys suggested she often was at that time of year. Her physician Thomas Alsopp's expenses from September included 20d for a box with powder for her breast, 5s for a pot of green ginger from Venice, enemas and perfumes for her person and her chamber. October necessitated more enemas and perfumes, with lozenges and pills. Throughout the rest of the season into spring, she required more of the same, with black cumin seeds, cumin bread, liquorice, cinnamon and comfits. Mary also had a new white-grey gelding costing £5 so she could ride for exercise.[9]

Likewise, Margaret Douglas, now Countess of Lennox, ran up considerable expenses in the same months, although some of hers may have been the result of childbirth and recovery. She had borne Henry Stuart in 1545 and, besides her one other surviving child who arrived in 1455, delivered six others who did not survive. Margaret's health needs required wormseed, or mustard, mastic gum, sperm whale oil, liquorice, quince, rose and prune conserves, breast powders, sugar candy, almond milk, apples and quinces; she also needed treacle for her pet monkey.[10]

On Christmas Eve 1546, Catherine, Princess Mary and Princess Elizabeth, were ordered to leave Whitehall and spend Christmas at Greenwich. It was a significant step by the King, designed to distance his wife and daughters from him because of his deteriorating health. Catherine sent a gift of a double portrait of Henry and Edward to her stepson, who was passing the season at Ashridge, while the women observed the season quietly. On the first day of 1547, fever stuck Henry again and Catherine may have heard the rumours that he was dead, although she would not have dared believe them until official confirmation arrived. Her husband rallied yet again, but his strength was completely gone and his body was 'wasted'. Van der Delft reported that 'the King is so unwell that considering his age and corpulence, fears are entertained that he will be unable to survive further attacks.'[11]

Catherine would not see her husband again. On 10 January 1547, she returned to Westminster but was not permitted to see the King, who was, by that point, prostrate in bed. The next two weeks were spent waiting. In his final days, Henry made provision for her future, giving her a generous annual allowance of £7,000 and stipulating that she should be afforded the treatment due to a Queen, although she was not to be appointed to act as Regent for the young king-to-be, the nine-year-old Edward. Henry died at two o'clock on the morning of 28 January. Catherine dressed herself in the now-familiar widow's weeds and headed for her manor house at Chelsea. She was joined there by the ten-year-old Jane Grey, daughter of her close friend Frances Brandon, and by her stepdaughter, Princess Elizabeth, then aged thirteen.

*

Having been a dutiful wife to three elderly husbands, Catherine was finally free. Her thoughts turned again to love. She wrote to Thomas Seymour that spring, 'I would not have you think that this mine honest goodwill towards you to proceed of any sudden motion of passion; for, as truly as God is God, my mind was fully bent, the other time I was at liberty, to marry you before any man I know.'[12] Seymour was as keen to have her as his wife, as he had been back in 1543. They probably reached some swift private arrangement but kept this secret on the understanding that the Council would not wish to see her married so soon. Yet Catherine and Thomas could not wait to be together. She was thirty-five, an advanced age for any potential childbearing and deeply in love: he was approaching forty and knew a good match when he saw one. They were wed in secret that May, just four months after Henry's death. When the secret was discovered later that year, the pair were censured by the court, especially by Edward Seymour, whose wife now sought to take precedence over Catherine and demanded the return of certain royal jewels for her own personal use.

Catherine considered her new-found happiness to be worth the censure. Behind their private façade though, the new bride may not have known that she had not been her husband's first choice. Back in February, in the days following the coronation of the young Edward VI, the ambitious Seymour investigated the possibility of marrying the thirteen-year-old Princess Elizabeth, writing to her in a way that made his intention plain:

> I have so much respect for you my Princess, that I dare not tell you of the fire which consumes me, and the impatience with which I yearn to show you my devotion. If it is my good fortune to inspire in you feelings of kindness, and you will consent to a marriage you may assure yourself of having made the happiness of a man who will adore you till death.13

Unaware of the extent of her husband's interest in her stepdaughter, Catherine could no longer remain in ignorance after she and Seymour lived together at Chelsea. The dowager queen had been denied the regency of Edward and had damaged her relations with Mary after remarrying so soon, but she still maintained a warm connection with Elizabeth, whom she invited to live with them permanently. Seymour's attentions to the young girl soon strayed into the inappropriate, when he would come into her bedchamber early in the morning before she had risen and 'strike her on the back or buttocks familiarly.' If she was still in bed, 'he would put open the curtains and make as though he would come at her and one morning he strove to have kissed her in bed.' On another occasion, they 'romped in the garden' and he cut Elizabeth's gown 'into a hundred pieces', even getting Catherine to hold the girl while he did it.[14] Her governess, Kat Ashley, described how Seymour loved Elizabeth 'but too well, and had done so a good while, and that the queen was jealous of her and him, in so much that one time the queen, suspecting the often access of the Admiral to the Lady Elizabeth's grace, came suddenly upon them, when they were all alone, he having her in his arms.'[15]

Technically, Elizabeth had reached the age of consent, but the family dynamic and her place in the succession makes this a very uncomfortable situation for the modern reader. As a child of fourteen, Elizabeth may have found Seymour's attentions flattering, and it appears she considered him attractive, even fancied herself in love, but the imbalance between their ages and her relation to Catherine made this a situation of deep inequality. The adult sexuality Elizabeth was unable to avoid, as a dependent, conflicted with the deep admiration she held for her stepmother. In addition, Catherine was now six months pregnant, unexpectedly for a woman in her mid-thirties, after not previously conceiving in her three former marriages. Whether or not Elizabeth been a willing participant in Seymour's affections, the status dynamics of the triangle made it potentially explosive.

Predictably, the idyll blew apart dramatically. Catherine discovered her stepdaughter in the arms of her husband and recognised the true nature of the relationship. In May 1548, she arranged for Elizabeth to leave Chelsea and go and live at Cheshunt. Elizabeth wrote to her, that she was 'replete with sorrow to depart from your highness, especially leaving you undoubtful of health.'[16] Catherine was also keen to leave the house associated with such memories and took her other ward, Jane Grey, to her manor at Hanworth, whilst Seymour was busy at court. Seymour appears to have suffered no repercussions, writing to Catherine fondly about their child's quickening; 'I hear my lettell man doth shake hys belly, trusting, if God shall give him life to live as long as his father' and asking Catherine to 'keep the lettell knave so lean and gaunt with your good diet and walking that he may be so small that he may crepe out of a mouse hole.'[17] By mid-June, Catherine departed for Sudeley Castle in Gloucestershire, where she prepared a suite of rooms on the south side of the inner quadrangle, in which she would deliver her child.

Elizabeth had clearly been deeply affected by her encounter with Seymour, but she was aware of the need to balance her affection against the consequences of their actions. She wrote to Seymour, excusing or exonerating him from some promise and assuring him of her continuing friendship:

> *My Lord,*
> *You need not to send an excuse to me, for I could not mistrust the not fulfilling of your promise to proceed for the want of good will, but only the opportunity serveth no; wherefore I shall desire you to think that a greater matter than this could not make me impute any unkindness in you. For I am a friend not won with trifles, nor lost with the like. This I commit you and all your affairs in God's hands, who keep you from all evil. I pray you make my humble commendations to the queen's highness.*
> *Your assured friend to my power, Elizabeth.*[18]

Elizabeth also wrote to Catherine, thanking her for her letters, but grieved to learn 'what pain it is to you to write,' and prayed God to send her a 'lucky delivery'.[19] On 30 August, Catherine went into labour and bore a daughter, whom she named Mary. The birth had been a success but within a few days, Catherine descended into a fever, and reputedly, into a state of raving. Too weak to sign her own will, she died on 5 September 1548 and her daughter was given over to the care of Catherine, Duchess of Suffolk, although she appears not to have survived infancy. Catherine was buried two days later at St Mary's Chapel, Sudeley Castle, with Jane Grey as her chief mourner, in what is often cited as the first Protestant funeral in Britain.

*

The contributions made by Catherine Parr to the Tudor dynasty must been seen in the context of the 1540s. England was a considerably different place from when Henry had married Catherine of Aragon or Anne Boleyn. He was a changed man from the adoring bridegroom of Catherine Howard. He had become old, fractious, dominated by health problems, presiding over a country that was a strange new hybrid of old and new, with overt tensions between religious factions and the ever-present threat of the executioner. With the King's marital record, it seems surprising that any woman was brave enough to marry him, but it would have taken a strong woman to resist the desires of her ruler. Catherine Parr had stepped into this role with private reluctance, having already bestowed her heart after two marriages made out of duty. She was aware it would be a dangerous role to play, that she may be sacrificing the opportunity to bear children, as well as the potential clash over reformist views and the irascible nature of her husband. The fact that Catherine undertook the role of Queen in spite of everything was a significant dynastic contribution in itself.

Although the circumstances were not easy, Catherine's queenship was important in four main areas. Firstly, in national terms, she was an active and committed Regent during Henry's absence in France, organising supplies, liaising with key players and overseeing the Council. The international impact of this was to enable Henry's invasion of France and capture of Boulogne. At the same time, she monitored the volatile Scottish border. Secondly, Catherine was a crucial figure in facilitating the harmony of Henry's family, building on her existing friendship with Mary and drawing in Elizabeth and Edward, to bring them together under one roof where possible. There is also the undoubted influence she exerted over the three children in religious and intellectual ways. Although she held utterly different views to Mary's devout Catholicism, Catherine did not allow this to affect their relationship, which remained affectionate. When it came to Edward, and especially Elizabeth, the queen's evangelicalism and intellect shaped their developing faith and made her a role model for the young Elizabeth, who absorbed her approach to dignified, restrained academic pursuits. Thirdly, she was a figurehead for proto-Protestant thinkers at court, building a sympathetic circle at court and offering hope to her subjects who shared her reformist views. The potential risks she took during this were apparent in the Anne Askew case, which Catherine survived through her understanding of Henry and her skills of diplomacy. Finally, Henry's sixth wife was clearly able to soothe and placate a difficult man, from a position of compassion and understanding. Henry was a notoriously difficult patient, but when he allowed her Catherine was able to make his final, afflicted years a time of relative quiet in the royal household.

Catherine's queenship was one of maturity and emotional restraint, but also of progressiveness, in religion and female education. After Anne Boleyn, she was, at thirty, the second oldest of Henry's wives at the time of marriage. But where Anne had spent her years abroad, and in pursuing her own love affair at court, Catherine had been married to two much older men, cared for her stepchildren and watched her husbands ail and die. Instead of the vivacity and provocativeness Anne offered, Catherine brought a sensible compassion, which valued peace above conflict, and an understanding of the needs of a man of Henry's character and age. Her queenship was a success because she was the right woman at the right time, and her frequently overlooked contribution to the Tudor dynasty deserves greater recognition.

It did not take long for Catherine's widower to renew his efforts to marry Elizabeth. In tandem, he attempted to gain control over the young King, perhaps with the intention of replacing or equalling his brother's influence. In January 1549, he was arrested when breaking into the King's apartments at night, and his close associates were questioned, including Elizabeth and her household. Here, the young Elizabeth demonstrated the characteristic shrewdness and caution that would mark her reign. She confessed she had hesitated to send Seymour a letter of condolence upon Catherine's death, 'lest she be thought to woo him,'[20] and that she would only marry with the will and consent of her brother and the Council. On 21 January, her closest attendants, Kat Ashley and Thomas Parry, were arrested and sent to the Tower for questioning, while John Ashley was sent to the Fleet prison. But it was when Elizabeth heard that Seymour was to be put on trial that she could not conceal her distress, saying she 'could not hear him discommended, but she was ready to make answer therein'[21] and clearly mourned the loss of her friend. Seymour went to the block in March 1549, accused of treasonous activities including the wooing of Elizabeth and the attempt to abduct King Edward.

Elizabeth began the process of rebuilding trust with her brother and the Protector, Edward Seymour, to whom she wrote frequently that spring. In May, she sent a portrait of herself to court, as a gift for the King and reminder of her loyalty: 'in which if the inward good mind toward your grace might as well be declared as the outward face and countenance shall be seen,' she would not have hesitated to offer it. She was bashful about her appearance; 'for the face, I grant, I might well blush to offer, but the mind I shall never be ashamed to present' and assured him of her devotion, 'of this, although yet the proof could not be great because the occasions hath been but small, notwithstanding ... so may I perchance have time to declare it in deeds, where now I do write them but in words.'[22] While she privately mourned the loss of her friend, her public actions show her to be a survivor.

That December, when Elizabeth was invited to spend Christmas at court with her brother, the Princess presented herself modestly and plainly, in simple, unadorned clothes. She retreated to her country house at Hatfield and completed her education under the guidance of Roger Ascham. The twelve-year-old Jane Grey had left Catherine Parr's household in the autumn of 1549 and returned to Bradgate, where she continued studying under John Aylmer in theology and classics and learning Italian from Michelangelo Florio. Ascham famously commented that he had discovered her reading alone at Bradgate while the rest of the household were out hunting, but Guilio Raviglio suggested that her upbringing was less than harmonious, as she was 'urged by the mother and beat by the father.'[23] It was not uncommon for parents to use corporal punishment to correct children; indeed, it was recommended by contemporary manuals, but the ambition with which the Greys drove their eldest daughter would escalate in the coming years.

PART FIVE

A Woman on the Throne

1547–1558

23

Dangerous Women

1547–53

In 1547, Lucas Cranach the Elder, court painter to the Electors of Saxony, completed an ambitious and daring work. The altarpiece depicting the Last Supper at Wittenberg Church was unusual in taking a typical medieval subject and updating it for a reformist audience. Among the apostles are portraits of German theologians Martin Luther, Philip Melanchthon and Johannes Bugenhagen, as well as local figures from the reformist community. The former narrative of conservative Catholicism was replaced by the faces of those advocating the new faith, surrounding the figure of Christ. It was a daring grafting of an emerging tradition onto the old. Part of this redefinition extended to the changing role of women, in terms of the authority permitted them, and in their relation to men.

The defining events of secular women's lives were still marriage and motherhood. Even for queens, facing danger and responsibility, such events were shaped by their union with a king, and the outcomes were often determined by the children they bore, or did not bear. Queens were, however, exempt from the strictures placed upon other women through the law of coverture. Generally, a woman's legal rights and obligations were taken over by her husband, as the law considered man and wife to be one person, with the wife's state as one of dependence, as a *feme covert*. Queens, especially those with royal blood rather than those who became royal through marriage, had the ability to exercise greater independent power, but also had to face the consequences of their choices. Even queenship did not undo the cultural dynamic by which a husband was his wife's master, able to exercise corporal punishment, use her body as he wished, and any woman who committed mariticide was considered guilty of petty treason. More in keeping with the desired relationship between husband and wife was Tintoretto's 1547 work depicting Esther fainting before her husband Ahasuerus, because of his majesty and fierce expression.

Wives in Tudor England were defined by their husband's status, even if they were originally of higher birth, just as Jacquetta Woodville had been in the 1430s. He took ownership of her property and possessions, even money she may have earned, and continued to hold them in the event of her death. Because of this, a wife was not permitted to make a will disposing of such items if she was to predecease her husband, or at any time that he remained alive. She was only allowed to bequeath her 'paraphernalia', or small necessary, personal items, with his permission. Rights, claims and titles could be transmitted through a female line to a son, although a woman would not be able to enjoy these in her own right. Unmarried women or widows, known as *femes sole*, fared better with the law, being able to keep their earnings, own property and sign legal documents.

Worse than the legal fiction of the *feme covert*, popular culture depicted women as weak-willed, changeable, shrews, gossips and sexually licentious. As a gender, they were considered weak and susceptible due to the constitution of their bodies, the urge to reproduce and their menstrual cycles, which made them unpredictable and dangerous. Contemporaries believed that Nature had framed women as 'weak, frail, impatient, feeble and foolish', their behaviour was 'variable, cruel and lacking the spirit of counsel or regiment'. They were 'apt to lie, flatter and weep, all in extremes ... either loving dearly or hating deadly, desirous to rule than be ruled.'[1] The perceived physical and mental differences framed a narrative of conflict, in which it was the woman's part in law, religion and nature, to submit, although this was frequently the source of humour and challenge. Tudor literature, in pamphlets, songs, plays and poems, portrayed an ongoing battle of the sexes, and the victors were not always the men. From Chaucer's earlier lascivious Wife of Bath, cunning Alysoun, and adulterous May, through to Shakespeare's lewd nurse and Kate, the tamed shrew, women constantly sought ways to outsmart their men and gain the upper hand in the marriage and the bedroom. Sometimes they succeeded.

Outspoken and powerful women of the era were frequently challenged and found themselves in trouble with the law. In the late 1520s, the Catholic visionary Elizabeth Barton was reported as addressing a crowd of 3,000, and enjoyed personal interviews with Henry VIII, whose religious line she then accorded with. Later, as Henry became more radical and sought a divorce from Catherine of Aragon, Barton's ideas were redefined as heresy and she was hanged for treason. Anne Askew's unspeakable torture and burning was as much the result of her status as a controversial woman as they were of her heresy. She had left her husband and petitioned Henry for a divorce before she began preaching to London crowds in favour of religious reforms.

This period witnessed a number of high-profile divorce cases, with several at court including that of Edward Seymour, Jane's brother, William Parr, Catherine's brother and the poet Thomas Wyatt. Although scandal was accrued on both sides, men often weathered the storm better than women, who could be cast out and denied financial support, status and access to their children. Henry VIII set a new precedent with the execution of wayward women who deviated from male expectations of behaviour, morally, religiously or sexually, from Askew and Barton to Anne Boleyn and Catherine Howard. The question of independence for divorced or prominent women, and especially as potential rulers in their own right, challenged the status quo and raised doubts about the security of the realm in the event of a queen regnant's marriage. Through the mid-part of the sixteenth century, the contribution of women to the Tudor dynasty would become part of this emerging gender narrative.

Scotland had already been forced to confront the question of female inheritance. The death of James V in 1542 left his infant daughter Mary, six days old, to inherit the throne. Henry VIII had proposed a union between her and Prince Edward, ratified in the Treaty of Greenwich, by which Mary would come to live in England at the age of ten, under Henry's watchful eye. However, Anglo-Scots relations did not survive the terms of the Treaty, and by the time Mary was ten, Henry was dead, and his son nearly so. In 1548, at the age of five, Mary was betrothed to the French dauphin, Francis, son of Henry II, second son of Francis I, whom he had succeeded the previous year. With a small group of companions, Mary left Scotland for France that August, where she would remain for the next thirteen years, being raised as a future Catholic queen. Her infancy at the time of succession was problematic, allowing for power struggles among the nobility, but her right to inherit the throne as a woman set a precedent that England would soon be forced to embrace.

*

On the death of Henry VIII, the succession passed to the nine-year-old Edward, the next in line being Mary, Elizabeth, Frances Grey, and her daughters. Mary and Elizabeth were each left an annual personal allowance of £3,000, a generous sum for unmarried princesses, and when Mary's estate was valued at £3,819, it made her the third or fourth richest person in England.[2] In 1547, a London apprentice might receive 6d a day, a casual day labourer at court was paid 4d and weeders in the royal gardens 3d a day. A pair of Spanish gloves cost 6d, a gelding for a princess was £5 and a gilt and engraved saddle £10. Particularly well-favoured servants, such as governesses and wet nurses, could receive annuities of £20.[3]

Mary and Elizabeth were provided with money for dowries upon their marriage of £10,000 or more, as the Council saw fit, delivered in 'money, plate, jewels and household stuff'. It was not a huge sum for a dowry, though, as one witness commented, 'I have known many a nobleman's daughter left as great a legacy, nay, a larger dowry.'[4] In 1501, Catherine of Aragon's dowry of 200,000 crowns equated to approximately £120,000, paid in instalments, also made up of plate. A dowry was dependent upon the Council approving the marriage. One special clause was added for Elizabeth in 1547, stating that if she married without permission, she would be struck out of the succession, 'as though the said Lady Elizabeth were then dead.' This dowry for the Tudor princess may well have been deliberately set low in order to deter potential husbands who saw England as a meal-ticket.

Control of the Council passed to Edward, Duke of Somerset, Jane Seymour's brother, uncle of the new King. With a male on the throne, and another male in charge, Mary and Elizabeth fully accepted this passage of authority from father to son as the natural and proper order of gender relations, and anticipated life as the King's sisters, perhaps to be advantageously married and bear children. One of the Council's first acts immediately limited their power and autonomy by substituting their income for property, so Mary went to Framlingham Castle in Suffolk, while Elizabeth went to Chelsea with Catherine Parr, where the love triangle with Thomas Seymour played out. Elizabeth must have been conscious of the additional clause regarding approval for her marriage, as her resulting interactions with those questioning her repeated that she would never act without their approval. By Christmas 1549, she was back in favour, being invited to spend Christmas at court, where she was 'received with great pomp and triumph, and is continually with the king.'[5] The following spring, Elizabeth was granted lands to the value of £3,000 she was due, including Thomas Seymour's former Berkshire estate. That summer she also acquired Hatfield House in Hertfordshire, a favourite residence of hers, and engaged William Cecil as her surveyor.[6]

Mary's properties included former Howard estates in Essex, Suffolk and Norfolk, and the houses of Kenninghall, Newhall, and Hundson. This geographical concentration overlapped with the old pilgrimage route through East Anglia to the principal Marian shrine at Walsingham, dotted with Catholic symbolism along the way, which had been brutally destroyed within the last decade. One unexpected consequence of this allocation was that Mary's position as the new figurehead of the old faith guaranteed her considerable support in her new base. With Edward's ardent desire for reform driven by that of Somerset, it was probably a wise move for Mary to remove herself discreetly from the centre of emerging Protestantism. However, she observed these developments with concern, writing to Seymour to protest about the new religious direction. The Protector replied that Henry VIII had left the Reformation half-finished, and that his legacy must be protected by stamping out the last vestiges of popery and popish practice.

Whatever the intentions of the Protector, the Catholic Mary remained her brother's heir. She had stayed away from court through 1548, and was distressed to learn of the first major religious reform of 1549, by which the English Book of Common Prayer replaced the Mass in churches nationwide. When the exchange came into force at Whitsun, she ordered Mass to be celebrated as usual in the chapel at Kenninghall. The Council responded with a letter of admonishment, requesting that she be 'conformable and obedient to the observation of his Majesty's laws'. Mary replied by rejecting the law they were imposing, calling it 'a late law of your own making for the altering of matters of religion, which in my conscience is not worthy to have the name of law.'[7] When the Council summoned her chaplain, her controller and another of her servants, Mary wrote again at length, saying she had been treated with unnecessary urgency, ungently and without friendship.

For the time being, Seymour and the Council had more pressing concerns. Rebellion in Devon was threatening to get out of hand, the volatile Scottish border required troops to keep the peace, and a third uprising against enclosures broke out that summer in Norfolk, under local landowner, Robert Kett. Mary had no involvement in the enclosures debate and some of her own property was damaged by the rebels, so she was not suspected of involvement. However, by mid-July 1549, the rebels were calling for a change of regime and submitted a list of grievances to Somerset. The Imperial Ambassador reported that September that Mary was secretly approached to become regent for her brother once Somerset had been overthrown. In December, a coup at the heart of the Council replaced Somerset with John Dudley, Earl of Warwick, on the grounds of Somerset's ambition, vainglory and his acting in a warlike manner. Somerset was imprisoned in the Tower, then released, but rearrested on charges of treason and executed in January 1552.

The changes in religion posed no danger to Elizabeth, whose embrace of the reformed faith was welcomed by her brother. When she visited court early in 1551, she was 'most honourably received by the Council who acted thus to show how much glory belongs to her who has embraced the new religion.'[8] Thus, at the highest level, and in the popular imagination, Elizabeth and Mary were established as religious opposites, representing new and old, Protestant and Catholic, and drawing supporters from among those groups. This was to prove definitive when it came to their inheritance and their future queenship.

*

Having passed the age of thirty, Mary's marital future was causing concern among Edward's councillors. A potential Portuguese union was discussed in early 1550 but it came to nothing, so when in April that year Albert V, Marquis of Brandenburg, asked for her hand, the proposal was given serious consideration. Albert was in his late twenties, a member of the Hohenzollern family who had earned himself the nickname of 'the warlike' for his constant, fiery engagements in European warfare. Mary, though, was uncomfortable about the bridegroom's Lutheranism, as she had been with the candidacy of Philip of Bavaria, aware that preserving her religious independence would be difficult, if not impossible, after marriage.

Mary was also fearful for her own survival. The Imperial ambassador described her in April as being on the verge of hysteria about her relationship with the Council, and their curtailing of her freedom to worship. She continually feared arrest, or worse. This finally prompted her cousin, Emperor Charles and his sister, Mary of Hungary, to offer

Mary the opportunity to escape England. A plan was hatched at the end of June 1550 for Mary was to visit her residence of Woodham Walter in Essex, while Imperial ships docked at the nearby port of Maldon, the emperor's agents posing as merchants. Mary would join them under cover of darkness and sail to safety under her relatives' protection. Leaving the country was a dramatic move to say the least, and the fact that she even considered it was indicative of the danger that Mary felt Edward's regime posed. It was a potentially destabilising move to leave the country she was set to inherit. Instead of fleeing, she sent the Controller of her House, Robert Rochester, to intercept Charles's agent, Jehan Dubois. Rochester told him that Mary was not in any immediate danger, and that if she were out of the country in the event of King Edward's death, her succession to the throne would be compromised. Dubois would not abandon his commission so easily, arguing for the prioritisation of Mary's life, and following Rochester back to Woodham Walter. There, he found Mary in the process of packing but claiming she would not be ready for another two days. It was Rochester who ruled that the whole enterprise was too risky, but it would ultimately have been Mary's decision not to leave, and her lengthy packing is likely to have been designed as a delaying tactic.

Dubois' account presents Mary in a state of distress, torn between the duty of remaining as a Catholic queen-in-waiting, and the desire to escape. He reports her words as 'I am like a little ignorant girl, and I care neither for my goods nor for the world, but only for God's service and my conscience ... if there is peril in going and peril in staying, I must choose the lesser of the two evils.' She was also concerned about the influence of the new religion upon her servants: 'What gives me most pain is the thought of leaving my household, which, though small, is composed of good Christians, who may, in my absence, become lost sheep and even follow these new opinions'[9] Mary remained in England and found that the pressure on her briefly eased.

This was only the lull before the storm. Edward's Council wrote to Mary, indicting two of her chaplains for following Catholic rites, asserting that they were not covered by the private immunity extended to those under her roof. Until now, Mary had been able to argue that her brother was being misled by his advisors, but in January 1551, the thirteen-year-old King wrote to his sister, that it 'miscontent'[10] when she disobeyed his laws and clarifying that his laws were his wishes. Mary was summoned to court and made her entrance into the city amid a spectacle of Catholic symbolism and rosaries. Edward, though, chastised her for her behaviour, arrested some of her gentlemen and insisted that breaches of the law would not go unpunished. That August, the Council decided to rescind Mary's private licence to practise Mass, but she rejected their authority to do so. Her messengers were arrested again, and a deputation arrived at Copthall in Essex, where Mary was staying, with the news that Edward ordered her to follow the legally prescribed means of worship, and no other. Mary respected the letters sent by her brother, receiving them on her knees, but again rejected his councillors, shouting after their departing backs, 'I pray God to send you to do well in your souls and bodies, for some of you have but weak bodies.'[11] An uneasy stalemate followed, with the Council reluctant to take the step of imprisoning the King's sister.

Mary's contribution to the Tudor dynasty through these difficult years was complex. According to the terms of her father's will, she was next in line to the throne, and the poor health of her young brother was widely known. Aware that she might inherit sooner rather than later, she was torn between her duty to an increasingly reformist England and her duty to her Catholicism. Mary believed that England had been led astray by heretics, and her refusal to keep her faith private was as central to her vision to save the souls of her future subjects, as her dedication to the higher authority of her God. With the same martyrdom mindset displayed by her mother in the 1530s, Mary risked personal danger to remain true to her faith, for what she considered to be her calling. She was answerable to God above anything or anyone on earth, and this would definitively shape her approach to her queenship.

In autumn 1551, a storm in the Channel brought an unexpected visitor to English shores. Marie of Guise, widow of James V of Scotland, mother of the young Mary, Queen of Scots, had been returning north following a visit to her daughter in France, and was forced to land at Portsmouth on 22 October. Marie was then thirty-six, just a year older than Mary Tudor, and an imposing figure of the Catholic faith, familiar with dangers and loss, and an habituée of the French and Scots courts.

Marie stayed at Southwick Priory, then headed to London by way of Hampton Court and Fulham Palace, before meeting Edward and Elizabeth at Whitehall. Edward presented her with a diamond ring that had formerly belonged to Catherine Parr. A number of Tudor women also travelled to London to meet her, including Frances Brandon and her daughters Jane, Catherine and Mary, Margaret, Countess of Lennox and Mary Fitzroy, widow of the Duke of Richmond. Mary Tudor, however, with whom she perhaps had most in common, chose not to attend. Frances and Margaret were given seats of honour beside the guest at the banquet that evening, and all reconvened to bid Marie farewell at St James's Palace as she began her journey north. Briefly, a number of the disparate female members of the family were reunited.

*

In October 1551, King Edward celebrated his fourteenth birthday, achieving the majority that enabled him to rule alone. A new Council for the Estate was created for him, for which he chose the members himself. Power shifted to John Dudley, Earl of Warwick, who was created Duke of Northumberland, and acted swiftly to remove the obsolete Duke of Somerset and replace former officials with members of his own faction and family.

In 1551, Northumberland signed a peace treaty with France, and Edward was betrothed to Elizabeth, daughter of Henry II, King of France since 1547. The Duke proceeded apace, cutting back on military spending, handing over financial control to experts and enacting religious reforms that pushed Henry VIII's even further, removing iconography and introducing a new English prayer book. However, Edward's health was failing. Both he and Northumberland were desperate to prevent their changes being undone and the country being returned to Catholicism in the event of Mary's succession. Instead, they looked to the King's cousins, to the eldest daughter of Frances Brandon, Lady Jane Grey, and one of Warwick's own sons, Guildford Dudley, as the potential saviours of their work. Warwick's elevation to the dukedom of Northumberland may have been designed, as well as to secure his position, to make his son a more eligible match. By 1553, the Grey and Dudley parents came to hope that a marriage between their children could provide an alternative king and queen for a Protestant nation.

Jane was then around sixteen, 'a beautiful young woman, pretty and endowed with intelligence, educated and well-dressed'.[12] Chronicler Richard Grafton, who knew her, stated that she was a 'fair lady whom nature had so not only beautified, but God also had endowed with singular gifts.'[13] With Jane's Tudor blood, Guildford was not the first husband who had been suggested for her, and he was the most humble in rank. In 1541 the French Ambassador had proposed that she marry Charles, Duke of Orleans, the third son of Francis I, placing her in the line of succession to the French throne, but the young man had died in 1545 of the plague. Ten years later, Edward Seymour, Duke of Somerset, saw Jane as a potential bride for his eldest son Edward, Earl of Hertford, the King's cousin, but this was abandoned after Somerset's fall from power. Matches had been suggested for Guildford too. He had already been considered as a potential husband for Margaret Clifford, Jane's cousin, and the daughter of Eleanor Brandon, but Margaret was only thirteen in 1553 and her father opposed the match.

At first, Jane did not seem to like Guildford, as she responded by 'strongly deprecating such marriage'.[14] However, as dutiful children of high-profile parents, they understood that their personal preferences were outweighed by family interests. Jane does not appear to have been told about the intention to make her queen at this stage, simply believing she was being married for dynastic advantage. The match was the work of the two fathers, Protector Northumberland and Henry Grey, Duke of Suffolk. His wife's cherished hopes that Jane might marry Edward VI were clearly now impossible. On 28 April, Jane and Guildford's betrothal was announced at court, with the approval of King and Council.

On 25 May 1553, the Feast of the Holy Spirit, three weddings were held in the chapel of Durham Place, the former bishops' seat on the Strand, which Northumberland had recently acquired. Formerly the residence of Catherine of Aragon during her widowhood, the great hall abutted the river, being described as 'stately and high, supported with loftie marble pillers. It standeth upon the Thamise very pleasantly.' Just two years before, Durham Place had lodged the French ambassador, when it was well provisioned and 'richly hanged ... and had at his cominge ready sett in the court of the same, for a present from the Kinges Maiestie, certeine fatt oxen, calves, sheepe, lambes and all manner of wyld foule of every sorte, a certain [number] all alive, and also of all manner of freshe fyshe of the best that might be gotten, with wyne allso in his cellar.'[16]

The day was a triple celebration. As well as Guildford marrying Jane, both his sister, Catherine Dudley, and Jane's sister, Katherine Grey, were also wed. Catherine Dudley was the youngest of Northumberland's children and possibly still underage when she was united to Henry Hastings, Earl of Huntingdon. A clause in the will of Jane Dudley, who died in 1555, suggests that Catherine was less than twelve, allowing for the match to be dissolved later, 'if it so chance that my Lord Hastings do refuse her or she him.'[17] Hastings was then aged around seventeen and had been educated alongside Edward VI. The pair did not repudiate each other in the end, but lived together as man and wife from at least 1559, inheriting the Huntingdon title although they remained childless. The third couple to marry at Durham House on that summer day in 1553 were Jane's sister Katherine Grey and Henry, Lord Herbert, heir to the Earl of Pembroke. Katherine was definitely twelve, nearly thirteen, having been born in August 1540 and Henry was perhaps a year or two older. Their marriage did not become permanent, though, being dissolved the following year after the Dudley family had fallen from favour. In something of a marital coup, the third Grey daughter, Mary, was also betrothed on this occasion, to a distant relative, Arthur Grey, Lord Grey de Wilton.

King Edward was unable to attend the wedding because of his failing health, but he sent the couple wedding gifts including cloth of gold and tissue, in silver, purple, black, crimson and white, a collar of great pearls and enamelled flowers, thirteen table diamonds set in gold, enamelled black, a gold girdle and many other jewelled ornaments.[18] The King also gave permission for Northumberland's brother, Sir Andrew Dudley, his Master of the Wardrobe, to equip them with wedding clothes from the royal collection. Jane was issued a wedding dress of purple with gold and silver brocade, embroidered with pearls and diamonds, Frances had a 'loose gown of black velvet, embroidered', while Guildford's mother Jane was also given clothes and jewels.[19] Some of the clothing had a macabre heritage, having been forfeited to the King by Edward Seymour, Duke of Somerset, who had gone to his death in the Tower seventeen months before, but the guests either did not know they were wearing dead men's shoes, or else did not care.

There were jousts, games and two masques, one of men and one of women, accompanied by feasting in the great hall. It was a 'very splendid, and royal, wedding, with a large gathering of people, and of the principal (people) of the realm'. The Venetian and French ambassadors were among the guests. The only sour note was when Guildford and a few others experienced severe food poisoning after a cook made a mistake when preparing a salad, 'plucking one leaf for another'.[20] He appears to have still been ill into the middle of June. Even if Guildford had not been unwell, it may have been decided that the wedding was not to be consummated at once on account of the age of the pair.[21] Jane's biographer though, Nicola Tallis, believes that the pair did share a bed during this time, to ensure that the match was legally binding.[22]

Spiralling into decline, Edward drafted a new will on 21 June naming Jane as his heir. Her sudden promotion, above her cousins and aunts, 'caught me quite unaware' and 'very deeply upset me,'[23] as she later deposed. Jane wished to leave Durham Place and go to her mother, but she was forbidden from doing so. Soon afterwards she fell ill and was given permission to go to Old Manor, Chelsea, now owned by Northumberland, but where she had formerly spent happy months living with Catherine Parr. Her statement, this control of her movements, and her response to her marriage, make Jane's involvement in the process appear reluctant at best, and at worst, she was acting under duress.

Edward had another reason for taking the revolutionary step of nominating Jane to rule. It was not just about religion; it was about the patriarchal control of women. Edward was afraid that his sisters would make foreign marriages and that their husbands 'would rather adhere and practise to have the laws and customs of his own native country to be practised and put in use within this our realm ... which would then tend to the utter subversion of the commonwealth.'[24] This was indicative of the paradoxical attitudes about female subjection in marriage. Whilst it was desirable, on the one hand, for a man to control and influence his wife, it was not a condition that could be tolerated in the marriage of a potential queen regnant. If England was to be inherited by a woman, that woman must have an English husband, or else the kingdom would be lost. The problem played on the worst fears of Edward's councillors and subjects. They knew that with Jane as Queen, Northumberland would effectively remain in charge.

On 4 July, Princesses Mary and Elizabeth were both summoned to court by Edward's Council, supposedly to comfort their brother during his last illness. Both delayed, with Elizabeth remaining at Hunsdon apparently too ill to move, and Mary travelling very slowly, only covering the five miles to Hoddesdon over the next forty-eight hours. Edward died at Greenwich two days later, at the age of fifteen. His passing was initially kept secret, but Mary's loyal supporters had already crept away from Greenwich and brought her the news. She was expecting to become queen, but instead, on 9 July, an announcement was made in London that 'the Lady Mary was not fit to succeed because of the divorce that had separated her father, King Henry, from her mother, Queen Catherine... Lady Mary was unable to administer the kingdom, being a woman and of the old religion; and mutations and changes might take place that would cause the ruin of the country.'[25] Mary gave out that illness was rife in her household, and retreated north to Kenninghall.

Jane was summoned from Chelsea to Northumberland's house of Syon, formerly the Abbey where Catherine Howard had spent her final weeks. There she was greeted and banqueted, and found the Council awaiting her, probably Guildford too, joining forces to persuade her to accept the throne. The following afternoon, attended by a 'noble train of both sexes',[26] Jane travelled by boat to the Tower, and around four or five o'clock made her ceremonial entrance, 'with accustomed pomp'[27] being greeted by Northumberland, the Council, the Tower's Constables and prominent citizens. Jane's train was carried by her mother and all the guns were set off and there was a great fanfare of trumpets. Guildford walked alongside her, his cap in his hand.

A proclamation was issued on Jane's behalf, declaring her new queenship in accordance to the will of Edward VI. Bishop Ridley preached at St Paul's cross about the bastardy of Mary and Elizabeth, Mary's papist view and the fears that they would open the country to a foreign alliance. 'However,' added Schefvre, 'no one present showed any sign of rejoicing, and no one cried: 'Long live the Queen!' except the herald who made the proclamation and a few archers who followed him.'[28] An apprentice named Gilbert Potter had the bravery, or foolhardiness, to cry out in response that Mary was the rightful queen, for which he lost his ears.[29] On the same day, all the foreign ambassadors were formally briefed 'that the new King and Queen are to be proclaimed this very day in the Tower of London and at Westminster; and we have heard that the Council have quite decided not to allow the Lady Mary to succeed.'[30]

Mary, though, had other ideas. She wrote to the Council asserting her right to the throne and stating that she was 'astonished and troubled'. The stage was set for a dramatic showdown between the first two Tudor women to become queen by right of inheritance. But this unprecedented clash had been engineered entirely by men.

24

Queens in Conflict
1553–54

Neither Jane nor Mary wanted a fight in 1553. Through the wills of Henry VIII and Edward VI, the reformist agendas of Edward Seymour and Northumberland, and the lack of male heirs, the patriarchal Tudor inheritance became derailed. It was the ambitions of men that placed the queen-cousins in opposition, who were otherwise inclined to be merciful, even amicable, towards each other. Although that summer's immediate crisis was initiated by religious tensions, the potential succession of two female descendants of Henry VII created a swathe of new questions about the ability and status of women. It played into patriarchal fears of national identity, masculinity and the exercise of power.

Within days of Edward's death, the first contention arose, revealing Jane to be every inch a proud Tudor. The crown was conveyed to Jane's apartments from the jewel house for her to try on, upon which William Paulet said that she 'could take it without fear and that another also should be made, to crown (her) husband.'[1] Jane had not expected this, and immediately replied that Guildford was not automatically to become king. The royal blood line was hers, not his. Their marriage had been made to secure Northumberland's position, his faith, and to prevent the threat of a foreign king, but Jane had clear ideas about the power balance between her and her new husband. She informed Guildford that if he was to become king, it would only be by an act of Parliament; in the interim, she offered him the Duchy of Clarence. As the ambassadors related to the Emperor:

Guilford (sic) tried to induce his wife to cede her right to the Crown to him, so that he might not only be consort and administrator (*administrateur*), but king in person, intending to have himself confirmed as such by Parliament. But she refused to do so, and gave him the title of Duke of Clarence, which is reserved for the younger son of the king. He already had himself addressed as 'Your Grace' and 'Your Excellency,' sat at the head of the Council board, and was served alone.[2]

Guildford was caught in a difficult position between his wife and his parents, who urged him towards kingship. Determined to assert the majesty he felt was his due, he chose to dine in state, alone, and attempted to preside over council meetings, in the hope of wearing his wife down. The extent to which Jane's refusal angered Guildford's mother is clear from Lady Dudley's order that he should refrain from sleeping with her until she complied, and urged him to leave her in the Tower and return to Syon House.[3] Whether out of affection, pique, or level-headed loyalty to the path upon which they were now embarked, Jane intervened to prevent his departure. She understood they were stronger together than divided. She may not have been involved in the process of her own advancement, but her initial reluctance was conquered by religious appeals, and she understood her position to be that of a national saviour. Her devotion to the new faith convinced her of the need to oppose Mary's Catholicism, and once Jane was committed, her brief period of authority reveals an educated and strong mind.

*

On 12 July, a rallying cry was issued for London men to join the army heading to arrest the Lady Mary and bring her back to the city.[4] Jane's father, the Duke of Suffolk, was assigned to lead them, but she begged to have him remain by her side, so Northumberland went instead. Two days later, the Duke departed with 3,000 men, promising the Council he would bring Jane's rival back either captive or dead, 'like a rebel, as she was.'[5] However, he had not travelled very far before he discovered that many refused to support him or join his cause, and that the local nobility had flocked to Mary's side, along with increasing defections from his own ranks. Northumberland was also heavily reliant upon German and Spanish mercenaries, who, although they were paid for their work as individuals, were uneasy that they were being asked to support a Protestant candidate against a Catholic relative of their Emperor, Charles. Mary had retreated further east to the stronghold of Framlingham Castle, within reach of the coast, where she awaited the Duke's approach. But the Duke did not come. Messengers from London caught up with him and warned him that his London powerbase was crumbling.

In Northumberland's absence, his supporters began to fear reprisals. His prestigious talent had been the co-ordinating glue, driving and uniting the Council and, although Jane had been proclaimed Queen and oaths of loyalty sworn, this proved insufficient once he had left. Supremely able as he was, Northumberland's plot crumbled because he could not be in two places at once and lacked a second-in-command of equal calibre. As Cardinal Commendone noted, Jane's father, the Duke of Suffolk, was 'not held as a man of great valour and therefore lacked authority,'[6] and at the first signs of opposition he capitulated. In addition, popular support in London favoured Mary, with Bishop Ridley being shouted down when he preached about her illegitimacy. On 20 July, the Council met at Baynard's Castle and declared in Mary's favour. Her rule was then pronounced from St Paul's Cross. Their motivation appears to have been a straightforward belief in Mary's right of succession over that of Jane, but also the conviction that Northumberland had acted out of self-interest, 'which moved the Duke to seize the Crown of England in order to transfer it to his own house.'[7] As soon as Suffolk heard of the Council's defection, he left the Tower, broadcasting 'I am but one man,'[8] and declared in favour of Queen Mary. Then he returned to the Tower and entered his daughter's chamber while she was at dinner, sitting under a canopy of state, and dramatically tore the hangings down around her. Jane found her status changed in a second, now becoming a prisoner and removed from the royal apartments to the Gentlemen Gaoler's lodgings. It must have been difficult for her to avoid the angry conclusion that she had been betrayed by her father, that he had made her the instrument of his ambition only to turn on her with the tide. Her mother and ladies-in-waiting were permitted to return home, which they did at once, but Suffolk found himself confined under lock and key.

Halfway across East Anglia, Northumberland was forced to recognise that the mood had turned against him. He had no choice but to accept the Council's volte-face, although he was keen to stress that all his actions had been fulfilled with their express permission, and that he had documents as evidence. He 'declared to them loudly that all he had done up to that time had been enacted with the authority, consent and knowledge of the Council, in proof of which he had documents sealed with the Great Seal of England.'[9] The Duke presented himself as obedient to the Council's fluctuations, 'supposing that they had been moved by good reasons and considerations'[10] and proclaimed the rule of Mary. It would not be enough.

Waiting in trepidation at Framlingham, Mary's supporters flocked to her side. Finally, official confirmation arrived that at the age of thirty-seven, the Catholic, disinherited, bastardised daughter of divorce was to become England's first queen regnant. It was unprecedented in terms of the law, and a chance to revoke the religious reforms that had attacked the faith of her mother. Mary's first act was to order the erection of a crucifix in the chapel at Framlingham. She saw these events as nothing less than a clear mandate from God, as her mission to return England to its former Catholic state and reverse the estrangement with Rome. At Newhall in Essex, she received the dignitaries of London, who pledged allegiance to her as their queen and presented her with a crimson purse containing £500 in half sovereigns. Accompanied by her gentlemen in green and white, 700 supporters and 1,000 armed horsemen, Queen Mary I rode triumphantly towards London.

Wearing a gown of regal purple velvet, Mary entered the city at around seven on the evening of 3 August 1553. She received the sceptre from the Mayor at Aldgate, where streamers had been hung and the length of the street from Leadenhall to the Tower was laid with fresh gravel.[11] The city guilds displayed their banners in prominent support, trumpets sounded and the guns of the Tower were fired. She paused at the gateway of the Tower to be greeted by its officials and meet with the Council. Riding behind her, the twenty-year-old Elizabeth witnessed the welcome given to a woman who had succeeded in her own right, legitimised after being dismissed as a bastard, and must have taken heart from it when thinking of her own future. It was expected that Mary would marry, and her son would inherit her throne, but she was old in terms of first-time motherhood, and her health had been consistently poor. Until she succeeded, Elizabeth was next in line, and Mary's reign removed any gender barriers that might have previously stood in the way. However, Elizabeth also understood the danger she was in, and the double-edged nature of her relationship with Mary. As Mary's fortunes rose, bringing her the opportunity to restore her mother's marital status and return to Catholicism, so the status of the Protestant daughter of Anne Boleyn could not help but fall. It was a tragedy created by their parents and circumstances, that Mary and Elizabeth's fortunes would forever be pitted against each other, replicating the dynamic between their mothers.

Mary's supporters immediately began to celebrate the Mass again, and many religious artefacts, such as crosses, statues and icons came out of hiding in Catholic homes. The new Queen issued a proclamation forbidding accusations against her supporters of papacy and heresy, and she instructed Dr Bourn, a canon of St Paul's, to preach at the cross, denouncing Protestantism. An unruly crowd attempted to interrupt, which led to violence, and the leaders were arrested and imprisoned. The former bishops who had been deprived of their positions by Edward because of their adherence to the old religion, were restored in a judicial hearing and leading Protestants were arrested due to their 'seditious demeanour'. Mary tried to insist that Elizabeth attend Mass, which she did initially, before expressing her distaste and complying only on sufferance. With her reluctance widely known, Elizabeth soon became a symbol of hope for proponents of the new faith and established in the popular imagination as an alternative to her sister.

John Dudley, Duke of Northumberland, was executed on Tower Green on 22 August. In their quarters in the Tower, Jane and Guildford would have been aware of the Duke's execution, hearing the guns announce his death, perhaps even witnessing the fall of the axe from their windows. Their trials were fixed for 13 November, at the imposing fifteenth-century Guildhall where the fates of Catherine Howard and Anne Askew had been pronounced. They were forced to process publicly through the streets, headed by an officer carrying a great axe with the blade turned away from the accused, denoting their innocence until the verdict had been passed. But this was merely a ritual. Guildford went first under heavy guard, followed by Jane dressed in black, with a Bible in her hands, after which came the other Dudley brothers, John, Ambrose and Robert. All were pronounced guilty and the men were sentenced to be hung, drawn and quartered, while Jane was to be 'burned alive on Tower Hill or beheaded as the Queen should please.'[12]

And yet, it seemed that Mary was willing to shown leniency to Guildford and Jane, seeing them as the victims of a plot arranged by

Northumberland. Frances Grey, Duchess of Suffolk, had ridden into Essex to intercept Mary on her approach to the capital and plead for mercy for her daughter, drawing on her long relationship with her cousin, and their shared history. The pair were returned to the Tower, but no date was set for their execution and, as the weeks passed, Jane was permitted to walk within the gardens. Perhaps Guildford was even permitted to see her, as he was able to write a message to her father in Jane's prayer book: 'your loving and obedient son wishes unto your grace long life in this world with as much joy and comfort as I wish to myself, and in the world to come joy everlasting.'[13] As the new year of 1554 dawned, the pair must have entertained a degree of hope that they might be permitted to live. They had every right to hope, they may well have been pardoned and permitted to live in obscurity, or Guildford could have found a place at Elizabeth's court. Even the ambassadors were convinced that there was no need for Jane to die:

> As to Jane of Suffolk, if for the reasons she gave you, or for others, she does not wish to inflict the pain of death upon her, let her at least consider whether it would not be well to keep her in some safe place where she could be watched and guarded so that there should be no fear of her attempting to trouble the kingdom.[14]

*

Mary's coronation took place at the end of September 1553. The day before, she followed the custom of riding through the streets of the capital from the Tower to Westminster, buoyed on a wave of popular support. Dressed in purple velvet furred with powdered ermine, she had her head covered with a cloth of tinsel set with pearls and gems, topped with a gold circlet, and rode in a gold chariot under a canopy. Courtly and civic dignitaries rode before and after her, draped in colourful finery, with the Mayor of London, Sir Thomas White, freshly knighted by Mary, bearing the gold sceptre. After her, in another chariot made of white cloth of gold, rode Princess Elizabeth and Anne of Cleves, drawn by six horses, and then ladies and gentlemen of the court, in red velvet, with their horses decked out to match.[15]

Mary encountered the first pageant at Fenchurch, which had been made by Genoese merchants, the second at Gracechurch corner being staged by Easterlings, or traders from the Baltic. As she proceeded into Gracechurch Street, a third installation presented a triumphal arch in the Roman style, in line with the Renaissance architectural passion for the Antique style. With three arches, it was topped by four pictures and, above them, an angel dressed in green holding a trumpet to proclaim her approach. The fourth pageant was arranged by the city itself and situated at the Great Conduit at Chepe, which ran with wine. Mary and her procession passed along Cheapside, the main axis in the north of the city running from east to west, and containing the most expensive shops in the city, owned by merchants and goldsmiths. The Standard in Cheapside had been painted for the occasion and the cross, one of the original twelve Eleanor Crosses, was washed and burnished. At the end of Cheapside, on the approach to St Paul's Cathedral, stood the Aldermen of London, who welcomed Mary with a short speech. Her chamberlain, Sir John Gage, presented her with a purse of cloth of gold containing a thousand marks.[16]

Mary paused in the churchyard St Paul's, close to the school founded by John Colet, Dean of St Paul's and chaplain to Henry VIII. There, the poet and playwright John Heywood, a devout Catholic, was sitting in a pageant under a vine, reciting verses in English and Latin. A Dutchman called Peter climbed up on top of the cathedral steeple and waved a streamer that was five yards long, scaffolds around him were set with more streamers and torches, although these would not burn due to the wind. After the event, Peter was paid over £16 by the city for his efforts.[17] Another pageant awaited Mary at the Dean's gate, featuring choristers singing and playing on the viol. From there it was a short distance to Ludgate, the westernmost gate in the city walls, which had been repaired, painted and hung with cloth and tapestries as a backdrop to a troop of minstrels.[18] Mary passed out of the walls, over the Fleet River and into Fleet Street, the main road that ran down through Whitehall and on to Westminster. Another pageant was set up at the conduit there, and Temple Bar had also been painted and adorned with hangings. The procession ended at Whitehall, where the Queen thanked the Mayor and Aldermen and took her rest. The coronation ceremony took place at Westminster Abbey on 1 October, where Mary became the first queen regnant to be anointed and make her vows.

It was Mary's marital plans which put an end to Jane's hopes of survival. Until 1553, marriage had not seemed a realistic proposition for the ageing princess whose status underwent constant change.

She confided in the Imperial ambassador Simon Renard that, in spite of her half-hearted suitors, she had 'never known that thing which was called love ... nor harboured thoughts of voluptuousness.' She had never even 'thought of marriage until now, when God had been pleased to raise her to the throne.'[19] Now she was Queen, though, she was mistress of her own destiny and she was determined to select a spouse of her own choosing. Bishop Stephen Gardiner and Mary's former allies on the Council advised that she should marry Edward Courtney, Earl of Devon, a great-grandson of Edward IV, who was not only English, but also Catholic and personable; he was a younger than her by about a decade, and theoretically able to father sons. Courtney had been imprisoned by Henry VIII in 1538 under suspicion of conspiring to support the exiled Yorkist Reginald Pole, whilst only a boy of around eleven, and had remained in the Tower until Mary freed him in 1553. But Mary was keen on the Spanish heir Philip Hapsburg, son of her cousin, Emperor Charles V. Also her junior, he was widowed with one son and a reminder of Mary's mother's family and faith. The Council advised against marriage to Philip, whose commitments meant he would hardly be able to visit England much, and such an alliance fuelled national fears of the country becoming a Spanish colony. Imperial ambassadors nevertheless met with Mary through the summer and promoted Philip's virtues. Mary agreed to marry Philip in August 1553 and public notice was given in November, after the Queen told Parliament that her choice of husband was her business and they were not to interfere.

On 15 January 1554, the official announcement was made that the Queen would be married to Prince Philip II, son and heir of the Emperor. It was exactly what many of her subjects had feared and what Edward had attempted to avoid in the terms of his final will: the dismantling of religious reforms and a return to Catholicism, followed by marriage to a foreign prince whose influence would reduce England to being the mere annex of another country. As early as the previous August, the Emperor had foreseen the dangers of this and advised that the matter be delayed a little:

As to the Queen's marriage, as we know by your letters that her inclinations are for a foreign alliance, it would perhaps be better to forego this point for the present, as they (the English) are resenting her actions with regard to religion. If we were to pursue the matter now, evil-minded people might take advantage of it to maintain that the Duke of Northumberland's objections were well-founded.[20]

Yet Mary was keen to wed. During the negotiations, the first signs came of a worrying deference that England's Queen was expected to show to her foreign husband. The Council informed the Imperial Ambassador that they did not advise her to sign the nuptial agreement 'before His Highness had done so, for custom prescribes that the husband shall speak first, not the wife.'[21] Simon Renaud saw Mary's naivety making her vulnerable, as 'the Queen, being a woman, cannot penetrate their knavish tricks nor weigh matters of state.'[22] Discussions about this kind of protocol sparked concern among Mary's subjects, which soon spread to rebellion. On 18 January, Renaud wrote to the Emperor concerning a case in the west of England, where a Peter Carew had assembled a group of gentlemen in Exeter to sign a letter to the Queen. It stated that they did not wish Philip to disembark in the West Country because they believed that the 'Spaniards would wish to do as they pleased and violate their daughters.' Instead of enduring this, they preferred to 'choose death'. Carew excused himself by saying he 'had been induced to believe that the Spaniards were coming in arms to England to oppress the people'.[23] But he was not the only one. And so, said Renaud, 'the revolt and commotion (had) begun.'[24]

The most dangerous and organised rebellion took place in Kent. Thomas Wyatt, the son of the poet, published a proclamation at Maidstone, near his home of Allington Castle, to the effect that 'liberty and commonwealth' were being threatened by the Queen's 'determinate pleasure to marry with a stranger'.[25] The ambassadors reported that 'Wyatt is fortifying himself to the best of his ability in a house of his in Kent, laying in stores, munitions and arquebuses.' They failed to be convinced by his professed motives: 'Although the rebels are taking the foreign match as a pretext, their real objects are religion and to favour Elizabeth ... and it is said that the rising is spreading.'[26] The rebels championed Courtenay, Earl of Devon, as a replacement monarch, planning to marry him to Princess Elizabeth to continue an English, Protestant rule. Mary summoned her sister to court and despatched the old Duke of Norfolk, Henry Fitzroy's father-in-law, now aged around eighty, to put down the uprising. Norfolk found himself outnumbered and, embarrassingly, many of his men defected to Wyatt. Another strategy was required. Instead, the royal troops sat back and waited, allowing the rebels to reach London before encircling them and capturing their leader.

It is likely that Elizabeth was aware that the rebels favoured her cause, but she remained wisely aloof. After Mary's succession, she spent autumn with her at court, but left in December for her house at Ashbridge. Her reformed faith, coupled with the rebels' demands, fostered mistrust between the sisters, whose personal circumstances had always set them at odds. Mary had urged Elizabeth attend Mass with her, but the Princess always went reluctantly, complaining of feeling ill, and excusing herself because she had not been raised in the old faith. On her knees, Elizabeth had begged Mary to send her instructors, so she might learn the tenets of Catholicism, and thus 'might know if her conscience would allow her to be persuaded.'[27] Mary had rewarded her with jewels when she did attend, but Elizabeth refused to wear them, adopting plain clothing, and her absence from court over the winter of 1553-4 had made it difficult for her activities to be monitored. Now, her distance and her reluctance lent support to the suspicions that she had been involved in the uprisings, or was at least sympathetic to them. Mary was also influenced by Renard, whose identification of Elizabeth as a dangerous and cunning creature, prone to follow some 'dangerous design' out of ambition or persuasion, Mary was finding convincing. After hearing his thoughts, she replied that 'the same considerations had occurred to her.'[28]

Wyatt's uprising left Mary distressed, not just by the threat to her own person, but because it necessitated a suspension of her marriage plans. She began to see enemies everywhere, perhaps not without cause. By February, Courtney was back in the Tower and Elizabeth was confined to her quarters at Whitehall. It emerged that Suffolk had given his support to the anti-Spanish faction, and he was found hiding on his estates, while his brother Thomas was apprehended in a hollow tree, his presence sniffed out by a dog.[29] This effectively signed death warrants for Jane and Guildford, sitting passively in the Tower, waiting and praying as events unfolded outside but powerless to influence them. The decision to order their executions, taken by the Queen at the start of the month, may have the feel of a knee-jerk reaction, but Mary clearly considered it essential for the security of her realm and marriage.

*

The executions of Jane and Guildford were scheduled to take place on the same day, 9 February 1554, but they were granted a brief respite, during which Mary intended that Jane should convert to the Catholic faith. To encourage Jane to her way of thinking, Mary sent her chaplain John Feckenham to visit her in her apartments, with whom she spent many of her final hours. Feckenham was then almost forty, a staunch Catholic, who had been a monk at Evesham Abbey until its dissolution in 1540. He had been sent to the Tower by Archbishop Cranmer for resistance to reform in around 1549, where he had undertaken reflection and study, so that he was frequently required to take part in theological disputes. *The Literary Remains of Lady Jane Grey*,[30] published in 1825, contains an account of a dialogue between Jane and Feckenham, showing the process of questioning he employed in a final effort to save her soul. He asked her what was required of a Christian; whether faith alone was justification for salvation; what was the purpose of good works; what was the nature of communion and how many sacraments were there? His methods of persuasion failed to move Jane, but something of a brief friendship flourished, so that she asked him to accompany her to the scaffold.

The day before her execution, Jane wrote to her sister Katherine, giving an insight into her faith and her preparations for death. Sending her sister her own copy of the New Testament in Greek, Jane described it as 'not outwardly trimmed with gold or the curious embroidery of the artfulest needles, yet inwardly it is more worth than all the precious mines which the vast world can boast of.' It was the Lord's 'last will,' Jane explained, 'which he bequeathed unto us wretches and wretched sinners, which shall lead you to the path of eternal joy.'[31] If Katherine read the book, it would 'bring (her) to an immortal and everlasting life,' it would teach her to live 'and learn you to die.' In a comment upon their dynastic failure, she added that the book would bring her sister 'greater felicity than you should have gained possession of our woeful father's lands, for as if God had prospered him, you should have inherited his honours and manors.' Jane urged Katherine to 'live to die, that you by death may purchase eternal life and trust not that the tenderness of your age shall lengthen your life.'[32] At sixteen, Jane's faith helped her come to terms with the executioner's act, considering it to be the will of her God. Katherine was to 'defy the world, defy the devil, and despise the flesh and delight yourself only with the Lord ... desire with St Paul to be dissolved and be with Christ, with whom, even in death there is life.'[33]

To her father, Jane wrote more bitterly, with the opening that 'it had pleased God to hasten my death by you, by whom my life should rather have been lengthened,' yet she gave thanks for it and accounted herself blessed. '(I) washed my hands with the innocence of my fact, my guiltless blood may cry before the Lord, Mercy to the Lord!' Although her father may be sorrowful at her death, she assured him that there was 'nothing that can be more welcome than from this vale of misery to aspire to that heavenly throne of all joy and pleasure.'[34] Guildford requested to see Jane one last time on 11 February, but she refused the meeting, saying that it 'would only ... increase their misery and pain, it was better to put it off ... as they would meet shortly elsewhere, and live bound by indissoluble ties.'[35] It is impossible to deduce whether there was any affection between the young married couple. They had been united so briefly, and the few indicators of an emotional connection may equally point to convention. When Jane wrote a letter to Mary in August 1553, explaining how she had ended up claiming the crown, she described herself as merely acting as 'a wife who loves her husband.'[36] It may have all happened too dramatically for any sense of romance: far more likely is the sense of destinies irrevocably united, of two inexperienced young people who had joined forces in a venture that had failed.

Guildford was the first of the two to die. He was taken to Tower Hill at around ten o'clock in the morning where a crowd had assembled and shook hands with many well-wishers, including John Throckmorton, who had links to the Grey family by marriage, and whose brother was involved in the Wyatt rebellion, and Sir Anthony Browne, who had stayed out of the succession crisis. After this, Guildford was handed over to Thomas Offley, the Sheriff in charge of his execution. Reputedly, Jane watched the process from a window.[37] Guildford had no 'ghostly father' with him, but made a short speech, which does not survive, before kneeling and asking the people to pray for him, 'holding up his eyes and hands to God many times.'[38] He was killed by a single blow of the axe. Richard Grafton related that 'even those that never before the time of his execution saw him, did with lamentable tears bewail his death.'[39] His body was placed in a wooden box on a cart which, according to the Grafton Chronicle, was seen by Jane on her way outside, the 'dead carcas, lying in a car in straw was again brought into the Tower, which miserable sight was to her a double sorrow and grief.'[40] Guildford was interred in the chapel of St Peter ad Vincula.

Jane was then led out to the green beside the White Tower. The anonymous *Chronicle of Queen Jane and of Two Years of Queen Mary* includes the speech she delivered moments before her death:

> Good people, I am come hither to die, and by a law I am condemned to the same. The fact, indeed, against the Queen's highness was unlawful, and the consenting thereunto by me: but touching the procurement and desire thereof by me or on my behalf, I do wash my hands thereof in innocency, before God, and the face of you, good Christian people, this day. I pray you all, good Christian people, to bear me witness that I die a true Christian woman, and that I look to be saved by none other means but only by the mercy of God in the merits of the blood of his only son Jesus Christ: and I confess, when I did know the word of God I neglected the same, I loved myself and the world, and therefore this plague or punishment is happily and worthily happened unto me for my sins. And I thank God of his goodness that he has given me a time and respite to repent. And now, good people, I pray you to assist me with your prayers.[41]

Jane concluded by reciting Psalm 51 and asking forgiveness of her executioner. Feckenham was on hand to guide her, as she was blindfolded and fumbled for the block. Eleven days later her father shared her fate.

At the age of sixteen, Jane's contribution to the Tudor dynasty was of course cut short before it had the opportunity to flourish. Undoubtedly, she was an intelligent, devout and astute girl for her years, proud and conscious of her duty, but until the spring of 1553 she had been quietly engaged in the business of being a member of the royal family. Her life had been significantly more private than that of her cousins, Mary and Elizabeth, who were placed before her in the succession, and it had been devoted to her education, in anticipation of a successful marriage and motherhood. In many ways, so far as she had developed by 1553, Jane would have made a model Tudor queen. She might have continued to steer the country through the processes of reform, created a family with Guildford, including sons who would have reigned after her. The Tudor dynasty might even have lasted longer than its remaining fifty years.

It would be wrong to dismiss Jane Grey as merely the pawn of ambitious men. Although her value for them lay primarily in her birth, personal ambition was not the only motivation of those members of Edward's Council who sought to preserve his legacy. Jane was selected because of her Protestant sympathies, a cause which she felt deeply, and considered a question not just of life and death, but of the afterlife, and the salvation of souls. As such, she overcame her initial scruples about the succession, in the belief that it was necessary for the good of her country. She placed duty and faith above personal inclination, troubled by the expectation that Edward's reforms would be undone and committed reformers would suffer, a fear Mary's later reign proved to be justified. Briefly, Jane was a figurehead of hope, a Tudor queen in the making, driven by an ideology that ultimately was not strong enough to counter the laws of succession. Her contribution was that she responded to the call, when it summoned her, and sacrificed her person, her freedom and her life, for the sake of her beliefs. Her inclusion in John Foxe's polemic, *The Book of Martyrs*, reflects her position in the history of the reformed faith. Her nominal reign, of nine days, also exposes the nature of Tudor society, inheritance and government.

The events of July 1553 expose the volatility of the Tudor realpolitik, which was shaped by a handful of strong individuals and could easily collapse in the face of challenge. Tudor notions of duty were strong, both in the rebels who proclaimed for Jane and those who reverted to Mary's seniority in the 1544 succession plan. Both sides believed that this was the right thing to do for the country. The concept of God's plan was ingrained, even when this denied methods of worship of that same God. The mid-Tudor crisis arose from the tension between religious fears and dynastic obedience.

It is also impossible to divorce these events from the question of gender. The struggle was established between two women, by men, and out of necessity, it was the men upon whom they depended. Men provided the power and numbers to achieve victory or failure. Neither Jane nor Mary could have acted without them. Had there been a male reformist claimant in July 1533, things might have turned out very differently, with gender proving a stronger cultural force in determining the outcome. Had Frances Grey's first child been a boy, had it been James Grey, not Jane being proclaimed as heir, Mary herself might even have capitulated in the face of patriarchal beliefs.

25

The Half-Spanish Queen
1554–55

England in the 1550s was a nation with a strong identity. Centuries of war with France and Scotland, and insurrections in Wales and Ireland, had bred stereotypical cultural representations of foreigners, to the extent that foreign ambassadors expressed surprise at the level of 'extreme hostility' they experienced when visiting. Although Catherine of Aragon had been welcomed in 1501, her personal charms and royal status allowed her to be accepted by her subjects, in spite of the undercurrents of xenophobia that criticised her ladies' looks and the Spaniards' clothing. Immigrants who made a success of themselves in London, such as merchants and bankers, came under attack in the May Day riots of 1517 and foreign ships in the Channel were considered fair game for privateers, especially after the French had sunk Henry VIII's flagship the *Mary Rose*. In 1530, Henry had banned gypsies from the country on the pretext that they 'many times, by craft and subtlety, have deceived the people for their money, and also have committed many heinous felonies and robberies.'[1] The possibility of England being ruled by a foreign king by virtue of marriage to a queen regnant, was unacceptable to many of Mary's subjects. This feeling did not dissipate simply because Wyatt's rebellion had failed.

The volatile national mood made Elizabeth's situation even more tenuous. Although Wyatt and his other conspirators repeatedly denied that the Princess had any involvement in their plot, it was difficult for Mary to shake the suspicion from her mind. Renard wrote 'the queen is advised to have her thrown into the Tower, as she has been ... mentioned by name in the French ambassador's letters ... and it is certain that the enterprise was undertaken for her sake.'[2] Elizabeth could not be allowed to succeed for the sake of the true religion, as Mary was convinced that she 'only went to mass out of hypocrisy, she had not a single servant or maid of honour who was not a heretic, she talked every day with heretics and lent an ear to all their evil designs.' Moreover, it would 'burden her conscience too heavily' to allow Elizabeth to succeed ... it would be a disgrace to the kingdom to allow a bastard' onto the throne.[3] Thus, either Mary must marry and bear an heir, or Elizabeth must be isolated or die. Mary summoned her sister to London from Hatfield, under pretence of being concerned for her safety, but secretly convinced that Elizabeth would 'bring about some great evil unless she is dealt with.'[4]

Elizabeth pleaded that illness made her unfit to travel, a line she frequently employed when placed in difficult circumstances, but often rooted in fact. Unwilling to believe her excuse, Mary dispatched Dr George Owen and Dr Thomas Wendy, experienced physicians, who discovered that she was indeed suffering from nephritis, an inflammation of the kidneys, but certified that Elizabeth was well enough to attend her sister's summons. Elizabeth travelled slowly to London, arriving at Whitehall on 22 February, being carried for at least the final stretch in a litter, pale, swollen-faced and dressed in white. Expecting to meet Mary, she was surprised when her sister refused to see her, and pleaded for an audience, but was instead interrogated about her activities by a number of Mary's officials. It was only ten days since Jane Grey's beheading, and Elizabeth must have feared the worst. Mary was convinced of her guilt, but in spite of the admissions of conspirators that they had written to her and sent messages, no evidence survived. Even though she told Renard that Elizabeth's character was 'just what she had always believed it to be,' [5] she could not convict her of treason without proof.

On 17 March, Henry Radcliffe, Earl of Sussex, and Sir William Paulet, Lord High Treasurer, arrived at Whitehall to escort Elizabeth to the Tower. The associations of this, connected with her mother's fate eighteen years before, proved too much for the Princess. Terrified that her execution was imminent, she begged for time to write to her sister, composing a letter to remind Mary of a promise she made last December, that Elizabeth would 'be not condemned without answer and due proof' and asked her 'to let me answer afore yourself.' She signed it from 'your highness' most faithful subject that hath been from the beginning and will be to my end,' and scored lines across the unused paper beneath, in order to ensure no false information was added once it was out of her hands.[6] In pleading for an audience, she could not refrain from mentioning the fate of Thomas Seymour, still raw, from five years earlier:

> If any ever did try this old saying – that a king's word was more than another man's oath – I most humbly beseech your majesty to verify it in me, and to remember your last promise and my last demand: that I be not condemned without answer and due proof. Which it seems that now I am, for that, without cause proved, I am by your Council commanded from you to go unto the Tower, a place more wonted for a false traitor than a true subject. Which though I know I deserve it not, yet in the face of all this realm, appears that it is proved. Which I pray God I may die the shamefullest death that ever any died afore I may mean any such thing. And to this present hour I attest afore God (who shall judge my truth whatsoever malice shall devise) that I never practised, counselled nor consented to anything that might be prejudicial to your person any way or dangerous to the state by any mean. And therefore I humbly beseech your majesty to let me answer afore yourself and not suffer me to trust your councillors ... afore I be further condemned.
>
> ...in late days I heard my Lord of Somerset say that if his brother had been suffered to speak with him, he had never suffered.[7]

Elizabeth's letter only bought her a few hours. As she wrote it, the tide turned, and the barge was unable to embark from Whitehall until the next day. So it was on Palm Sunday, in the pouring rain, that Elizabeth was conducted downriver to the Tower, under arrest. Collapsing on the Privy Stairs, she addressed her guard, insisting that they bear her 'witness that I come in no traitor but as a true woman to the Queen's majesty as any now is living, and thereon will I take my death' but that she 'knew her truth to be such that no man would have cause to weep for her.'[8] Some sources state that Elizabeth was placed in the same rooms where Cardinal Fisher had awaited his execution in 1535, and above those of Sir Thomas More, in the Bell Tower, while others place her in those rooms where her mother had awaited her fate. Elizabeth was catered for according to her state, but the constant fear of accusations and imminent condemnation made it a time of tension and terror that she would never forget. Elizabeth's protestations went in vain, her removal urged upon Mary by Emperor Charles V as a necessary step to secure peace in the kingdom ahead of the arrival of the Spanish bridegroom. She was repeatedly questioned about her involvement in the uprising and her intentions, but her interrogators were mindful that they faced their potential future queen, and some were influenced by her great uncle William Howard, and treated her with less harshness than Mary may have wished.

In April, Wyatt made his final speech upon the scaffold, exonerating Elizabeth, after which the pressure eased off her a little. Following his execution, she was granted permission to walk in the Tower Garden, although the windows of other cells opening onto it were closed and the prisoners within were ordered not to look at her. During this time, as legend suggests, Elizabeth may have been aware of Robert Dudley, elder brother of Guildford, who was still imprisoned in the Beauchamp Tower, situated, like the Bell Tower, in the south-west corner of the complex, overlooking Tower Green. Born in June 1532, Robert was known to her as Northumberland's son, and it is likely the pair would have met at court on many occasions. Dudley later stated that he had known her since she was at least eight years old, probably dating from the time he was a boy at the court of Prince Edward.

While arrangements for the wedding of Mary and Philip were being discussed that spring, Charles V continued to urge Mary to organise the trial and execution of Elizabeth and Courtney for treason. But Mary could not bring herself to do it. Although there were alleged ciphers carved into violins and coded letters, these had somehow disappeared, so there was not sufficient evidence to condemn either. If she had been involved, Elizabeth was very careful not to leave a paper trail, or to reply to any suggestions, plans or gestures of support. Mary explained to Charles that 'the law as laid down by the English Parliament did not inflict the capital penalty on those who had consented to treason if they had committed no overt act.'[9] It was a nicety her father would probably not have heeded.

There was also the question of succession. The Royal Council believed that Elizabeth was far too important as the heir to be put to death, and so persuaded the Queen that Elizabeth should be released from the Tower but remain under house arrest. On 19 May 1554, the eighteenth anniversary of her mother's execution, Elizabeth was conducted by 100 royal guards led by Sir Henry Bedingfield to Woodstock in Oxfordshire. Her popularity with Londoners was exhibited when a large crowd of well-wishers turned out to cheer her progress, and many others appeared along the route for the same purpose.

If Elizabeth was not to be executed, the Council planned that she should be married instead. Mary's trusted advisor, Sir William Paget, stated that 'if insufficient evidence to put her to death were not discovered, he saw no better means of keeping her quiet than to marry her to a foreigner.'[10] This was a considerable turnaround from the xenophobic attitudes expressed towards Mary's marriage, and indicates Paget's conviction, or at least the conviction he professed to Mary, that Elizabeth was unlikely to inherit the throne. Or perhaps he reasoned that such a marriage would undermine her popularity. Similar marriages had been suggested for the Princess in recent years. In 1551, the Duke of Guise had offered his brother, and Elizabeth had her portrait painted for Guise to take back to France. The Duke of Ferrara's son was also suggested by a Florentine merchant, who described him as 'one of the goodliest young men of all Italy', and that match had been pursued until March 1553. The Duke of Florence's son was also raised, although he was then a boy of eleven, along with the son and heir of the King of Denmark. But as of her arrival at Woodstock, no serious candidate as a husband had been considered for Elizabeth. She wrote to Mary, pleading her cause and asserting her innocence, but the letter's informal address only served to annoy her sister, and so Elizabeth was banned from contacting her.

*

In April 1554, Mary's second Parliament passed the Act for the Marriage of Queen Mary to Philip of Spain, to ensure that England would not become a colony of Spain. Philip was to enjoy his wife's titles for the duration of their marriage and his name was to appear first on legal documents, in accordance with beliefs about the precedence due to a husband. The act of ruling was designated to Mary, and while there was an understanding that Philip would co-reign, he would not be able to appoint foreigners to positions of power. Parliament was to be called in their joint names, coins issued bearing both their heads and all matters of state conducted in Latin or Spanish, as the new King could not read English. Philip was barred from claiming the throne in event of Mary's death, nor could he remove his wife and any children born to them, from the realm. Should Philip's son from his first marriage, Don Carlos, die without issue, any son borne by Mary would inherit his father's lands as well as England and Ireland. It was on these terms that Philip agreed to become Mary's husband, willing to undergo a degree of humiliation bordering on emasculation in order to become King of England. However, this was not without precedent for him, as his more powerful grandmother, Isabella of Castile, had dictated the terms of her marriage to Ferdinand of Aragon.

The Spanish fleet was spotted off the Isle of Wight on 19 July 1554, and Lord William Howard set off to guide them into Southampton Water. Philip landed a day later, disembarking on the quay where the queen's minstrels and dignitaries were waiting to welcome him. He made his way to Winchester in Hampshire, where he gave thanks in the cathedral and changed into a coat embroidered with gold and matching hat with feathers. The future King of England was a twenty-seven-year-old Hapsburg, 'well-favoured with a broad forehead and grey eyes, straight nose and manly countenance', with a princely pace, gait straight and upright, of which 'nature cannot work a more perfect pattern.'[11] He rested in his lodgings for a few days, showing himself eager to adapt to English customs, and then, on 23 July, set out to meet his bride. Considered well-dressed, courteous and gracious, he came face to face with Queen Mary, thirty-eight, thin, slight, pale and plain, upon whom decades of ill-health had taken their toll. The pair met in the deanery, where Mary's grandmother, Elizabeth of York, had given birth to Prince Arthur over half a century before. Philip was conveyed there by a secret route, through the driving rain, to meet his bride, to whom he could speak no English. The couple conversed in a mixture of Latin, French and Spanish and parted after half an hour. The following day, they dined together and Philip surprised her with the announcement that his father had granted him the kingship of Naples, so that she might be married to a king, not a prince, which delighted her so that she caused it to be read aloud by the heralds.

Hans Eworth's portrait of Mary in 1554 was painted from life in order to impress her future husband. Standing before a panel of fringed green velvet, Mary rests her hands upon a surface of the same material and looks directly into the eye of the viewer with something of her father's boldness. Detailed analysis of the artist's technique, done in recent years, indicate that Eworth went to some lengths to make Mary appear attractive. Her nose has been lowered, her left eyebrow lifted a little and the outlines of jaw and chin adjusted. She wears a brown bodice with elaborately decorated sleeves in white and gold, holding her gloves in her left jewelled hand and a red rose in her right. Inside her high starched white collar sits a pearl collar, from which hangs a black and gold crucifix. A large rectangular jewel sits on her breast, under which is hooked a teardrop pearl, probably part of the royal collection inherited from Catherine Parr. Her features are small and pretty, if determined, with a brightness and intelligence in her eyes, and her reddish hair is visible, centrally parted, under her headdress.

The wedding took place at Winchester Cathedral on 25 July, with visual manifestations of Philip's subsidiary position to Mary, not least the insistence that he abandon his Spanish dress and appear in the French outfit designed for him, so that the bride and groom would match. Mary wore purple satin lined with taffeta and embroidered with rich tissue set with pearls, and white kirtle with silver and a long train, while Philip was provided with a gown of gold set with rich stones and other details to echo hers. They walked side by side through a cathedral hung with arras and cloth of gold, up a scaffold covered in red carpet. Before the altar, the usual positions of husband and wife were swapped, so that Mary stood on the right, as an indicator of her superior status. This was a first for an English royal marriage and designed to establish the tone of their relations. Her marriage ring was a 'rownde hoop of gold without anye stone, which was her desire, for she said she would be married as maidens were in the old time.'[12] A similar nostalgia for her youth would characterise Mary's reign.

After the ceremony, the Queen and her new King consort proceeded to kneel under a rich canopy where they heard Mass. They then proceeded the short distance on foot to Wolvesey Castle, former residence of the Bishop of Winchester since the twelfth century. There, in the great hall, they sat beneath a canopy held by English Lords and ate from gold plates. Mary and Philip danced to a German tune before retiring to a bed which had been blessed by the Bishop. Mary wrote afterwards to Charles, now her father-in-law, that the marriage 'renders me happier than I can say, as I daily discover in the king my husband, so many virtues and perfections that I constantly pray God to grant me grace to please him, and behave in all things as befits one who is deeply bounden to him.'[13] Mary fell deeply in love, very quickly, but Philip did not. His companion Ruy Gomez commented that she was 'older than we have been told' and suggested that 'if she dressed in our fashions she would not look so old and flabby.' He added to a friend that 'it would take God himself to drink this cup, and the best one can say is that the king realises fully that the marriage was made for no fleshly consideration, but in order to cure the disorders of this country and preserve the Low Countries.'[14] Philip was said to have cursed Hans Eworth for having exaggerated Mary's charms.

In early August, the royal pair moved from Winchester to Basing, and then to Windsor, where they hunted and Philip was installed as a Knight of the Garter. On 11 August, they reached Richmond, and after passing six days there, took a barge down river to Southwark and stayed at the Bishop's Palace at Lambeth. The following day, 18 August, they passed over London Bridge, where more guns and cannons were fired than in living memory. A pageant of the giants Corineus and Gogmagog had been set up. Following the same route as Mary's coronation, they encountered the freshly painted conduit at Gracechurch Street, where a display of the nine worthies included the figure of Henry VIII, depicted in armour, holding a sword in one hand and a book in the other.[15] This book, entitled *Verbum Dei*, The Word of God, was being passed by Henry to a figure representing his son Edward, in a clear reference to the transference of religious reforms from father to son. This was far too controversial for Mary. The painter was summoned by Chancellor Gardiner and berated as a traitor and villain, whereupon the image was wiped away, although it is not clear whether this took place before England's new King had seen it. A more congenial pageant depicted five famous Philips from history, including Philip of Macedon and Philip the Bold. He was also presented as Orpheus, playing his harp to charm the savage and brutish population of England. At St Paul's a Latin oration was delivered, but in an ill-omen, an acrobat performing on the cathedral roof fell to his death.[16]

*

In spite of the pre-eminence Mary's status insisted upon before and during her wedding, she proved willing to let Philip take over the majority of dealings with the Council. Since before her succession, Mary had admitted her lack of understanding of politics and the world, insisting that her focus was on her faith and God's purpose for her. Philip stepped into this role with relish, and it did not take long before he had undermined the condition that England would not be drawn into wars on Spain's behalf. His plan was for a joint English-Spanish force in the Netherlands, and he hoped that his own coronation would give him greater credibility and authority in English eyes. The Council also discussed the impact of Mary's return to the Catholic rites, including how to deal with the pockets of resistance where the Mass was refused, the heretical books being smuggled in and out of the country, and discontent against the Spanish influence. While Philip met with varying degrees of resistance, Mary was preparing herself for a different kind of role, that of pregnancy and childbirth. Desperate for a child, she happily embraced a far more traditional division of labour and typical gender roles.

In September 1554, Mary's menstruation ceased and she started putting on weight. In Tudor terms, at thirty-eight, she was old for a first-time mother, having reached an age when her contemporaries were grandmothers and had even begun the menopause. As the weeks passed, though, she became increasingly convinced that she was pregnant and delighted at the prospect of bearing an heir. In November, she and Philip opened Parliament together and, on the first Sunday in Advent, they attended High Mass at St Paul's, as administered by the newly returned exile Cardinal Pole. The future seemed to be rosy for Mary, with her beloved husband at her side, and his child growing in her womb.

In January, Parliament passed an act making Philip regent in the event of Mary's death in childbirth, and for the provision of education for any children. However, for some reason, Philip was not entirely convinced that his wife had conceived, according to letters he wrote to his brother, but he still signed the circulars that had been produced in advance to spread the news. At the end of April 1555, Mary retired to Hampton Court to prepare for her lying-in. Perhaps it was a mark of Mary's belief in her imminent motherhood that Elizabeth was released from house arrest at Woodstock and summoned to support her sister. At the end of the month, a false report reached London that she had delivered a prince, so bonfires were lit and bells rung in celebration. But then the bells went quiet. Weeks later, Mary was observed in the garden, 'stepping' so well that her delivery date was rapidly revised. May and June passed and then her swollen abdomen began to go down. She had probably suffered an infection or pseudocyesis, a phantom pregnancy. There was no baby. Elizabeth was at Greenwich to witness Philip depart for the Netherlands, leaving Mary inconsolable. On 3 August, she admitted defeat and departed for Oatlands. Alone, ailing and old, with her domestic happiness cruelly snatched from her, she became convinced that God was punishing her for her failure to ensure the nation's return to Catholicism. Just as her father had interpreted his inability to father a son as divine disapproval for an invalid marriage, Mary viewed her phantom pregnancy as judgement upon her religious policy; and she responded with equal vigour.

26

Saving the Nation's Souls
1555–58

In 1550, the monumental first text of Giorgio Vasari's *Lives of the Artists* was published in Florence. By recording artists' lives in gossipy detail, preserving their biographies and works for posterity, Vasari enshrined the concept of the artist as a creative genius, an individual master rather than an anonymous worker. The art world was still patriarchal. In the whole of Vasari's six books, only four women are mentioned; the sculptress Properzia de Rossi, and artists Sofonisba Anguissola, who would become court painter to Philip in Spain, Sister Plautilla, and Madonna Lucrezia, although even these are only afforded a few sentences each. While the artist was permitted to become a master, that master was still male.

Vasari's *Lives* was dedicated to Cosimo I de Medici, Grand Duke of Tuscany, whose wife, Eleanor of Toledo, had been born in 1519, making her three years younger than Mary. She had been married at seventeen in 1539 and enjoyed an unusual marriage of affection and influence with Cosimo, being his partner and true consort, bearing him eleven children. Eleanor was appointed regent in her husband's absence on several occasions and pursued a devout Catholic agenda, founding churches and encouraging the Jesuits to settle in Florence. It was the kind of marriage and achievement that Mary would have wished to replicate. Mary's other contemporary, Catherine de Medici, Queen of France, was unhappily married and often overlooked in favour of her husband's mistress Diane de Poitiers. However, after initial difficulties, she had borne eight children and in 1555 was pregnant for the last time, at the age of thirty-six. Later, Catherine would also pursue an aggressive anti-Protestant agenda in France, which would far outstrip the effects of Mary's policy between 1555 and 1558.

By the mid-sixteenth century, opposition to religious reforms and the emerging Protestant faith found full voice in a Catholic Counter Reformation. The Council of Trent, initiated by Pope Paul III, had first sat in 1545 and would continue to do so when conditions were favourable, until 1563. Most recently, the second session had met from 1551-2, under Julius III, although little had been achieved due to his reconciliation with France and the scandals that dogged his personal life. Across Europe, significant steps had already been taken to fight back against the rising tide of Protestantism, challenge heresy and reassert the old practices of pilgrimage, saints, icons, imagery, relics, indulgences and the cult of the Virgin Mary, transubstantiation and the seven sacraments, as well as making the church the only interpreter of the Scriptures. It was to this movement that Mary enthusiastically signed up in 1555, after a more tolerant start to her reign, in the belief that she was enacting God's will. Mary's contribution to the Tudor dynasty from 1555 onwards must firstly be evaluated in terms of what she intended it to be.

Upon her succession, Mary had insisted that she did not intend to impose religious conformity, but instead restored former leading Catholic bishops to their positions and attended public celebrations of the Mass at influential venues like St Paul's Cathedral. She interpreted popular support for her succession and the failure of the Protestant coup in favour of Jane Grey as approval for her religious agenda to go ahead. In October 1553, Mary's first Parliament passed the First Statute of Repeal, undoing the Edwardian reforms, banning the new Prayer Book and outlawing clerical marriage. This took England back to the religion of the Six Articles in 1547. In November, the Archbishop of Canterbury, Thomas Cranmer, who had married Henry VIII to Anne Boleyn, was arrested for heresy along with Bishops Latimer and Ridley and others, and despite being tried and condemned to death, experienced a brief reprieve in their transference to prison in Oxford.

By December, the Mass was reinstated by law, but after heated debate, Parliament refused to vote to penalise those who would not accept it. On 26 December, the Second Statute of Repeal was instituted, reforming Henry VIII's religious legislations and implementing a return to Rome. Mary was also keen to undo the closures of many of England's religious houses, re-founding seven between 1555 and

1558, with round £60,000 from her own coffers. This was a small percentage of the total her father had confiscated and his scheme of selling monastic land to the nobility, many of whom now sat in Mary's Council, meant that she was unable to reverse the dissolution further. In March 1554, English bishops were instructed to only follow legislation passed in 1547 and all Protestants were removed from their positions and replaced. A brief lull followed, as Mary was occupied with the arrangements for her marriage and the excitement over what she believed to be her first pregnancy.

November 1554 saw the revival of the medieval heresy laws by which capital punishment was available for those convicted. This was designed to avoid 'errors and heresies, which of late have risen, grown and much increased within this realm,' and drew on the statues made by Richard II and confirmed by Henry IV, at a time when Lollardy was rife. At the end of the fifteenth century, a proto-Protestant focus on the vernacular scriptures, consubstantiation and a rejection of Catholic practices, had led to a handful of burnings. The term had lingered into the sixteenth century, with prosecutions for Lollardy being held into the 1530s. The revival of these measures came into effect on 20 January 1555, and within weeks the first heretics had been burned according to its terms. John Rogers was one of the self-made men who rose from lowly ranks under Henry VIII to a Cambridge education. He translated the Bible into English, contributing to the new edition of 1539, studied in Wittenberg, became friends with Melanchthon, English exiles William Tyndale and Miles Coverdale, and ran a Lutheran church in Germany before returning to England. Promoted by Edward VI for his reformist vision, Rogers was appointed lecturer and prebendary of St Paul's, but royal favour was withdrawn upon Mary's succession. He was arrested in 1554, imprisoned for a year, and became the first victim of the new heresy laws, being burned alive at Smithfield on 4 February.

Until this point, Mary's reign had been one of comparative tolerance and forgiveness. Ironically, it was largely a Protestant powerbase which had supported her challenge to the succession of Jane Grey, showing that the climate of 1553 allowed loyalties and obedience to the correct order to override religious conviction. Leading Protestants had been instrumental in her campaign, such as Sir Nicholas Throckmorton, who rode out to Hoddesdon to warn her of a plot to arrest her, and John Hooper, who called on his flock to fight for Mary as their rightful queen, even if she was a Papist. Through the rebellions against her in 1553 and 1554, only those actively bearing arms against her, or intending to supplant her, had lost their lives. In a show of clemency, around 400 of the Wyatt rebels were brought into the courtyard of Whitehall Palace, where Mary appeared on a balcony to pardon them in true theatrical Tudor style. The influence of Philip also seemed to have been beneficial to Mary's opponents, as he had pleaded with his wife in January 1555 for the release of the final prisoners involved in the Wyatt uprising. Those arrested under suspicion of heresy at this point might have been condemned to death, but still languished in prison or house arrest, often for up to twelve months, with the possibility of forgiveness if they recanted. Married priests, discovered in 1554 to be almost 10 per cent of the clergy, were also ordered to set aside their wives and families or else lose their living with no recompense, but none were burned. Foreign Protestants in London were expelled rather than persecuted, including Peter Martyr, and English ones like Throckmorton and John Foxe and the Scottish John Knox, fled abroad for their own safety, often illegally, without the valid passport.

In 1555, Mary's religious policy changed, but her inspiration appears to have been personal. The move towards greater savagery followed her phantom pregnancy and her grief at the absence of Philip, both of which she interpreted as punishments from God for her failure to punish heretics with sufficient severity. Incredible and barbaric as it might seem to the modern mind, Mary's actions must be viewed in terms of contemporary ideas of salvation. As Queen of England, she believed she had a genuine calling, a religious mission, to return the country to the true path. Temporal, or earthly, life was considered merely a brief space before the soul's passage to eternal salvation or damnation. What really mattered was the afterlife. It was part of Mary's Catholic doctrine that heretical souls could only be saved through the process of cleansing fire. Thus, Mary truly believed that the burning of unrepentant Protestants was not simply a punishment meted out to these individuals but their salvation from their sin. By burning them, she was saving them. By saving them, she genuinely believed she was implementing a national imperative. She was the religious leader who would deliver her errant countrymen from the devil's influence, back to God's grace. By these standards, as powerful and dedicated as her mother's refusal to accept Henry's changing faith, and her grandmother Isabella's expulsion of Jews and Moors from Spain, her vision was that of a crusader. It was echoed in the Netherlands and in France, where Philip and Henry II were aggressively persecuting Protestants, who were tortured before burning, many of whom would seek refuge in England after the accession of Elizabeth.

Mary's vision was in some ways was already archaic. Her grandmother's policy of the 1480s and 1490s, and her mother's resistance in the 1530s, belonged to a world of simplistic, medieval and dichotomic reactions that had passed. The religious dialogue of the 1550s was complex, in both England and Europe, and although Catholicism might be the largest religion, Protestantism had gained a cultural foothold that permeated areas beyond the pulpit. When Cranmer, Ridley and Latimer were summoned to Oxford in April 1554 to take part in a debate about the Real Presence, they found the respectful and academic tone of the establishment debased by constant interruption and unchecked personal insults directed towards them. Intellectual rigour had been replaced by religious fanaticism, rudeness and intolerance, and the three of them faced a hostile crowd of almost a thousand, making the event more like a trial, at the end of which they were condemned as heretics.

In many ways, Mary's succession to the English throne had been due to the impact of Reformation thinking about the abilities of women. Fifty years earlier, it had seemed unthinkable that a woman might rule alone. While Mary tried to turn the clock back on religious practices, she could not undo the cultural and intellectual aspects of the new learning, with its emphasis upon the autonomy of the individual. It was these which had helped put her where she was. The Protestants who had supported her in 1553 had done so in the belief that the authority of the law, the Act of Succession, was sacrosanct and that it surpassed questions of faith. They had hoped, or expected, that Mary would respect the move towards greater freedom of expression. Many were to be disappointed, and some found their new-found rights stripped away, their autonomy lost along with their liberty and sometimes their lives. Whilst Mary's motivation was the salvation of their souls, the martyrs she created in 1555-8 contributed to a wider dialogue about the tension between the individual and state, in the crucible which formed the early modern world. Even Charles V and the Imperial ambassador Renard urged her to be cautious when reintroducing Catholicism and when it came to the punishment of Protestants.

In November 1554, Cardinal Pole accepted the submission of Mary, Philip and England to the supremacy of Rome. Pole had written the opening address of the Council of Trent in 1545 and was to be instrumental in persuading Mary to take more severe action. Bishop Stephen Gardiner, a devout Catholic and Lord Chancellor, had urged Mary to restraint when it came to the persecutions, but his death in November 1555 and replacement by Pole removed a voice of caution and stepped up the rate of burnings. Through the winter and spring of 1555, the burnings continued. Later in February, three preachers suffered martyrdom in Gloucester, Suffolk and Warwickshire, while among the ten who went to their deaths in March were 'ordinary' individuals such as a fisherman, a weaver, barber, butcher and apprentice. With two burned in April, two in May and seven in June, the burnings slowly gathered pace, until the first mass event at Canterbury in July 1555, and the death of the first female martyr, Margaret Polley, at Tunbridge Wells. The only person burned in August was another woman, Elizabeth Warne, at Stratford-at-Bowe, in London, who, like Margaret, was also a widow. That October, Hugh Latimer, former chaplain to Edward IV, and Nicholas Ridley, a former Bishop of London, met their deaths outside Balliol College, Oxford. In total, in 1555, seventy-six individuals were burned. There were eight-seven in 1556, seventy-seven in 1557 and forty-one in 1558, making a total of 281, of which 62 were women. Thomas Cranmer, former Archbishop of Canterbury, was martyred in March 1556. In addition, a further thirty-four died in prison, including three women and a child. The professions of the men indicate that, alongside the clergymen, most held relatively humble positions in society: carpenters, shoemakers, labourers, glovers, hosiers, teachers and similar. The women are invariably listed as either maids, widows, wives or servants, with one blind woman and another who was pregnant.[1] When it comes to evaluating the contribution of women to the Tudor dynasty, the sacrifices made by those ordinary individuals who gave their lives for the new faith must stand in contrast to the actions of their queen.

The Protestant reaction to Mary's program of burnings was to question her queenship. From the first arrests, reformist pamphleteers were responding that 'none but papists or traitors can justly accuse them of treason or disobedience.' Protestants continued to meet in secret and hope that God would intervene to turn Mary 'from idolatry' or else 'shorten her days'.[2] To imagine the death of a monarch was treason indeed, let alone to actively wish for it. Scandalous verses were circulated that not only attacked Mary's Spanish husband, and her inability to bear a child, but also the tenets of her faith. The preacher John Knox had fled into exile in January 1554 and settled in Calvin's Geneva, where he composed a pamphlet attacking Mary, claiming that either she was not the rightful queen, or else that she was wicked, and everyone had a duty to disobey and displace her. Calling her a 'wicked woman, a traitress and a bastard', he reopened the gender debate, adding that it was 'more than a monster in nature that a woman should reign and have empire over men.' He hoped God would inspire her supporters with a new, deadly hatred of that 'horrible monster Jezebel of England' and that they would carry out his judgement against her.[3] Mary even lost the papal support she had long dreamed of retaining when, in March 1557, Paul IV revoked the legation of Cardinal Pole.

There is little doubt that Mary was the driving force behind the burnings, as is evident from letters she wrote berating her bishops for their delay in enacting the given sentences. Her subjects could see this; both the persecuted Protestants and those Catholics who believed more in tolerance and education than capital punishment. In fact, by 1558 her policy was alienating even devoted Catholics, when it was reported that less than a third of the expected numbers were turning up for Mass. Instead of the hoped-for national, unified Catholicism, her policy only succeeded in sowing division and pitting her subjects against each other. It is possible to understand Mary's motivation in the context of contemporary beliefs, but difficult to justify such a radical and relentless campaign against a group of formerly royal-approved clergymen and 'normal' people. The humble victims of the burnings, including widows, apprentices, the young, the blind and the lame, posed no threat to Mary or her regime, but had offered the incorrect answers when asked certain questions of faith, or had their private conversations or practices reported. They were easy targets, sacrificed with the intention of placating Mary's God. Her contribution to the Tudor dynasty in this aspect, was one of division and detriment, inflicting a national wound that set back the development of reform, rights and tolerance.

*

Mary's program of burnings intensified the succession debate. Just as in 1553, many Englishmen still felt that the correct line of inheritance should be followed regardless of religious persuasions, but increasingly Mary's subjects began to fear for their future. Her Catholic followers, with their faith and relationship with Rome so newly established, did not wish to see Elizabeth inherit. Equally, the Protestants were afraid that Mary would nominate a Catholic successor such as her cousin Margaret Clifford, and that their persecution would continue. In the 1530s and 1540s, the debate had centred upon the gender of England's heir, but by the 1550s, because the main concern became the heir's religious beliefs, the inheritance of a woman became almost a given.

A number of female members of the Tudor family were present at court during Mary's reign, navigating their way through the difficult religious climate and seen at different times as potential successors to the throne. Lady Jane Grey's younger sisters made a relatively swift transition back to favour with the help of their mother. After the executions in 1554 of Jane and their father, the Duke of Suffolk, Katherine, then aged thirteen, was forcibly divorced from Henry, Lord Herbert, even though the pair pleaded that they had consummated the match and wanted to remain together. Young Mary's betrothal to the much older Lord Grey of Wilton was also dissolved. Both girls were sent back to live with their mother at Bradgate where they wisely played the game of religious conformity, despite having been raised in the reformed faith. In July 1554, Frances was invited to join Mary's Privy Chamber, so she and her daughters re-joined the Tudor court, taking part in the Queen's daily routine, attending her in private, at her table and in public ceremony, which probably included attendance at Mary's wedding. It was suggested that Frances Grey be married to Edward Courtenay, who was released from the Tower in April 1555, but instead, Frances took matters into her own hands and married her Master of the Horse, Adrian Stokes, a former soldier and Protestant, after which she spent more time in retirement. Frances and her daughters were probably still at court to witness the marriage of Katherine and Mary's cousin, the seventeen-year-old Margaret Clifford, daughter of Eleanor Brandon, to Lord Strange, on 7 February 1555. It would become a stormy marriage, and Margaret would bear four children before it descended into scandal in the reign of Elizabeth.

Frances may have been inspired to marry for love after the precedent set by her parents and the more recent example of her young stepmother. Catherine Willoughby, the widow of Charles Brandon, had remarried in 1553 to her Master of the Horse and Gentleman Usher, Richard Bertie, who supported her devout reformed faith. Catherine was also active in the support of the printer John Day, who brought out a number of reformist books bearing her coat of arms in the late 1540s. She offered support to foreign Protestants in England and employed Hugh Latimer as her chaplain. In 1555, the Berties were among the reformers who fled England to safety in Europe, as was later recounted in *Foxe's Book of Martyrs*, to return when Elizabeth's succession made it safe to do so. Other Tudor women of the reformist persuasion wisely kept a low profile during Mary's reign. Like Elizabeth, Mary Fitzroy, Duchess of Richmond, lived quietly in the countryside, dying in her late thirties in 1557.

Elizabeth stayed at court until October 1555, and then departed for Hatfield, where she would spend much of the next three years. The following year, she received a warm invitation to attend court for Christmas, but her welcome was brief and by early December she was heading back to Hatfield, probably because she had rejected the proposal of Philip's cousin, Emmanuel Philibert, Duke of Savoy. Mary threatened that her sister would be returned to an official status of illegitimacy if she refused to comply, and would lose her place in the succession. Elizabeth considered escaping across the Channel, much as Mary had in 1553, but instead she retired to the country to weather the storm. It was also suggested that she might wed Don Carlos, Philip's son, even though he was now showing signs of mental instability. Again, Elizabeth refused, confessing to the Venetian ambassador that 'the afflictions suffered by her were such that they had ... ridded her of any wish for a husband.'[4] She continued to resist Mary's instructions to attend Mass, only doing so under duress, prevaricating and avoiding the question, making just enough concessions to placate her sister.

Mary's religious policy may have alienated her sister, but it won the support of her cousin, Margaret Douglas, Countess of Lennox. The daughter of the former Queen of Scots was also a devout Catholic, part of the same generation as Mary, born in 1515 and educated and raised in Catholicism before Henry's split with Rome. Although she made nominal, public concessions to the new faith, by the early 1550s, she was practising Catholicism in the privacy of her home, with rosaries, statues, icons and the regular visits of priests to perform the Mass. Her young son Henry, born in 1545, and his brother Charles, who would arrive in 1557, were both brought up in the Catholic faith. Upon Mary's succession, Margaret had hurried to her side in London and was rewarded with gifts of dresses and jewels amounting to £500. Already, Mary was thinking about her Catholic legacy and informed ambassador Renard that autumn that, 'if God were to call her without giving her heirs of the body, the Lady Margaret Douglas ... would be the person best suited to succeed.'[5] Margaret and her husband were given permanent positions at court, with expensive tapestries hanging in their chambers. They were promoted and allocated sources of revenue, taking their food from the Queen's kitchens, and receiving generous gifts at New Year. Margaret and Frances Brandon were also given precedence over Elizabeth when she visited court, finding herself required to walk behind her older cousins and occupy inferior rooms below theirs. When Margaret later stated, in 1558, that she always believed her claim to the throne to be stronger than that of Elizabeth, it is clear to see that the foundations of this belief were laid by Mary.

In March 1556 a new plot was discovered to invade England from France, to replace Mary with Elizabeth. It coincided with the appearance of a comet in the sky, visible for a string of nights, during which rumours were rife that the day of judgement was nigh. The details are obscure, but it was led by John Throckmorton and Henry Dudley, brother of Guildford and Robert, and better organised and financed than Wyatt's attempt, with a simultaneous uprising in the west led by Sir Anthony Kingston. Reputedly, they had the support of Henry II of France, who was reported to have listened with relish to plans to have Mary poisoned.[6] Elizabeth may have known of it, but she was careful not to be drawn in or implicated, and when her house was searched and her staff were questioned in May, nothing was found, and Mary sent her sister a ring accompanying a reassuring letter. Courtenay, whose name had again been coupled with hers, went into voluntary exile in Brussels at Easter, to remove himself from the burden of suspicion. The conspirators were questioned, racked and condemned, with ten ringleaders suffering a traitor's death.

The experience left Mary drained, according to the Venetian ambassador, and lonely. She hardly appeared in public, her guard was doubled, and it was rumoured that she scarcely slept and often wore protective armour. Another uprising in July 1556 was swiftly suppressed but took a further toll on the queen. Mary was also missing her husband, and obviously, there was no opportunity for her to conceive when he was not even in the country. She sent William Paget to the Imperial court to persuade him to return and wrote pitifully to Charles, begging for Philip's presence, as her 'chief joy and comfort', whose absence left England in 'miserable blight'.[7]

Finally, in March 1557, Philip returned to England, although it was primarily to organise his campaign against the French. The pair were reunited after almost eighteen months at Greenwich, to Mary's great happiness. Almost at once, another uprising broke out, when around forty Protestant exiles landed at Scarborough from a French ship named the *Fleur de Lys* under the leadership of Thomas Stafford. Twenty-seven rebels including Stafford were executed, and again Elizabeth survived unscathed. The involvement of Henry II, again, was a step too far, prompting Mary to agree to Philip's request and declare war upon France. However, in other matters, including Elizabeth's future, she refused to listen to his wishes, or to follow his proposal that her sister wed his cousin, the Duke of Savoy. Mary accompanied Philip down to the docks at Dover, when he sailed away at the head of an army in July. She would never see him again.

Once more, Mary was convinced that she had conceived, this time at the age of forty-one. Hearing her news, Philip wrote to Cardinal Pole that it is 'the one thing in the world I have most desired and which is of the greatest importance for the cause of religion and the welfare of our realm.'[8] He did not, however, believe it. In January 1558, the French retook Calais, and Mary was left heartbroken at the loss of the last English possession across the Channel.

By March 1558, eight months had elapsed since Philip's departure, but no practical plans had been made for her lying-in. Mary made her will 'thinking myself to be with child ... foreseeing the great danger which by God's ordinance remain to all women in their travail of children.'[9] She appointed Philip as Regent during the child's minority and summoned Elizabeth to London to be with her. At this point, even Renard acknowledged that Mary was unpopular, and that Elizabeth was now 'honoured and recognised' as heir to the throne by the 'leading men of the realm'.[10] By 1 May, it was clear that there was to be no child. Increasingly, Mary was unwell, she could not sleep and suffered from an excess of black bile. Pitifully, she begged Philip to return, but they continued to disagree over Elizabeth's marriage and their letters become bitter. In August, Mary fell ill with a fever whilst travelling from Hampton Court to St James's and did not improve, By

October, she had worsened, adding a codicil to her will recognising that she would not bear 'fruit nor heir' and asking her sister to honour her religious reforms. Philip despatched one of his own physicians to England and Elizabeth was informed in early November that her succession was imminent. Mary heard Mass early on the morning of 17 November 1558 and died before the dawn. The cause of her death is unknown. A deadly outbreak of influenza would claim the life of Cardinal Pole on the same day, but Mary's gynaecological history suggests the possibility of uterine or ovarian cancer. She was forty-two.

*

Assessing Mary's contribution to the Tudor regime is complex and full of pitfalls. Hers was not simply the clearly defined role of previous generations, fighting for the rights of an heir as her great-grandmothers did, modelling queenship like her grandmother and mother, or asserting her right to personal happiness like her aunts. As the first queen regnant with a particular religious vision, she was the most powerful of them all thus far, and her decisions had an impact that was experienced in different ways by her subjects than those of former queens consort and queen mothers. She exercised power in a more public, independent and direct way, which conflicted with contemporary gender expectations. As with all these women, Mary's character and reign were shaped by her specific moment in time, and that moment encapsulated a unique set of problems. Mary was born and educated under Catholicism, as the influence of the Renaissance and Reformation was beginning to be felt in England. Her adolescence witnessed the complete destruction of all her foundations, religious, personal and secular, which she spent her maturity attempting to recover.

Mary's birth in 1516 located her early years within the 'golden age' of her parents' marriage and her father's reign. The old medieval Catholic certainties about her life, family, position and faith, defined her character as a child. She had experienced elements of a humanist education, designed to expand her mind with information, but it was not intended to encourage her to challenge the mores of her day. Despite her position, the purpose of her education was to equip her to be a better wife, and for most of her life, that was her own intention, to be the consort of a powerful European prince or king. Until the age of eleven, her childhood was secure and happy, as the treasured only child of loving parents, and she participated in political and cultural engagements, feasts and festivities, patronage and rituals, events of the religious year, the reception of ambassadors, royal progresses and moved freely through her parents' glittering world.

When Mary reached the age of eleven, her childhood security crumbled. Over the course of the next decade, she was sent away from her mother, bullied by her attendants, deprived of her titles and status, treated like a servant, abandoned by her father, experienced continual ill-health and even feared for her life. Perhaps the worst of all was being forbidden to see her mother from 1531 when she was only fifteen, and later they were not permitted even to write to each other. Worse still, during this period of distance, Catherine sickened and died without being able to see her daughter, knowing the degree of her suffering and the dangers that lay ahead. In the turbulent last years of her father's reign, Mary experienced some reconciliation with Henry but this was only after she had made humiliating concessions, abasing herself, accepting her loss of status and that her parents' marriage had been invalid. She had mixed relationships with the four stepmothers who followed in quick succession and increasingly turned to God for comfort. She witnessed her father systematically dismantling and disrespecting the religion that had been central to her survival and represented her Spanish heritage from her grandparents, the Christian crusaders of Spain.

It is difficult to underestimate the devastation of the Reformation and growth of Protestantism upon English Catholics of Mary's generation. Whilst many could agree with the need for reform, they witnessed the national religion of past centuries, whose rituals defined their lives from beginning to end, abused, dismantled and criminalised. The structure of English cultural life was changed, as well as its faith, with the loss of monasteries as infirmaries and benevolent landlords, as repositories of learning, libraries, medical knowledge, social care, and charity. Their buildings and lands were given or sold to the nobility, their wealth and symbolic artefacts destroyed, and their followers denied the comfort of shrines, saints, rituals, ceremony and the figures of priests as conduits and interpreters of the Bible.

More religious heartbreak followed for Mary during Edward's reign, in which she must have feared the complete obliteration of practices that had defined and sustained her life. Throughout her brother's reign, Mary feared her faith would lead to her displacement in the succession, even to punishment as she clashed with Edward and his Council about her right to practise in private. The tension of those years made her ill, with friends like the Emperor not as supportive as they might have been, even when she thought of fleeing abroad. When she survived the Jane Grey scandal, largely through the swell of popular English support, it is little wonder that she sought to restore the old certainties of her childhood.

Mary's short reign was dogged by a range of problems beyond that of religion. Her marriage was unpopular on a national level, provoking a significant anti-Spanish discourse and Wyatt's rebellion. One aim of the malcontents was to replace Mary with Elizabeth, which strained the relationship between the sisters to breaking point and led to calls for the Princess to be put to death. The fear of leaving her legacy in the hands of a Protestant was ever-present for Mary, increasing as the years passed and she did not produce a child. Although she was deeply in love with Philip, she was forced to recognise the inequality between their feelings and suffered much personal unhappiness from his long periods of absence. She had to endure the shame of two phantom pregnancies, the awareness of her failure in the eyes of her contemporaries and the increasing ill-health that led to her death.

Mary's most important contribution to the Tudor dynasty was to be its first queen regnant. She succeeded because she had popular sympathy and people believed she was the rightful heir. To have achieved that in spite of the machinations of a powerful Council, to have endured the years of waiting and ridden triumphantly into the capital to take control, showed great courage. Once she was in place, though, how much autonomy did Mary exercise as Queen? Her gender and the nature of her power can be explored by considering the delicate balance between her ruling as an individual, or as a wife, led by her husband, advisors and councillors. Monarchs have often been suggestible or susceptible to favourites, but until 1553, they were men, without the additional complication of perceived female subservience. Mary certainly asserted her will at the start over her marriage, even though it was unpopular and caused rebellion. Her Council wanted her to marry an Englishman, but she rejected their candidate. Just how much, though, was marital choice a true representation of her independence? It was still a female preserve to have a say in choosing one's own husband, as shown by Mary's earlier rejection of Lutheran candidates and Elizabeth's refusal to marry a Catholic. The Queen's marriage was a national decision for her to make, but also a personal one, in which considerable freedom had already been exercised by her female relations.

In 1554, Mary faced the balancing act of maintaining her authority as a female sovereign whilst not being seen to emasculate her husband. Philip's last-minute title of King of Naples brought greater equality, embedded by his succession to the Spanish throne in 1556, but the events of summer 1553 and Wyatt's rebellion made it essential for Mary alone to be England's monarch. She elevated her authority over Philip in small but symbolic ways, such as in the wording of titles, her precedence during the marriage service, by teaching him English ways and controlling his appearance. In a society that gave men precedence in the home, extending to corporal punishment, marital rape and absolute compliance, these could have been difficult concessions for Philip to swallow. For a man of his standing in the 1550s, Philip was remarkably accommodating to these challenges to his masculinity, and the implied subservience, trading this against the benefits he received from being England's King. It helped that Mary was keen for him to play the active, 'masculine' role in government, encouraging him to take over business in the council chamber and listening to his advice. Ultimately, because of this, Mary's queenship cannot be seen in any way as progressive. She may have been the first anointed Queen, but she was happy to relinquish the more active role and embrace motherhood and, later, religious questions, following her councillor's advice.

Mary was a Catholic figurehead for many years, especially before she succeeded to the throne. During the suppression of the monasteries, the growth of the new faith in the final years of Henry's reign and the accelerated reforms under Edward VI, many English subjects looked to Mary as their hope for the future. Her succession was a marked relief for them, allowing for the open exercise of practices that had been banned or discouraged. The stigma of illegality, fear and prosecution was removed for Catholics. However, it did not take long before the religious pendulum swung too far the other way. Whilst advisors such as Pole led Mary to a harsher, uncompromising position, it was ultimately her decision to burn Protestants, and the numbers were greater than any other religious persecution by Tudor monarchs. This makes Mary's regime of heretical burnings appear extreme, fanatical and casts a long shadow over the rest of her legacy.

Mary's complex legacy resulted from the overlap of her positions as the first queen regnant and as a religious zealot. It was unfortunate that her gender gave her critics an easy explanation for her extreme behaviour, citing a lack of male governance and sexual frustration, which all played into contemporary stereotypes of a hysterical woman's lack of control over body and mind. The health of the Queen's body was metonymic for the health of the nation, and this extended to Mary's appearance and fertility. It was a culture which celebrated feminine youthfulness but feared female sexuality, channelling their physical impulses and reproduction through the narrow conduit of marriage. Women were considered naturally libidinous and those who were denied the opportunity for release through sex were thought to suffer from internal vapours rising from the womb to suffocate them, resulting in irrational behaviour. Mary's failure to inspire love in her husband and her physical unattractiveness for him, as well as her advancing age and failure to conceive, evoked the contemporary caricature of the ageing woman of literature and popular culture; a woman who had lived beyond her patriarchal 'usefulness' but clung to power.

It was unfortunate for Mary that some of her choices undermined perceptions of the ability of women to rule wisely. She represented positive change for Catholics at the start of her reign, but many of them considered it unnecessary to persecute Protestants to the degree she did. In fact, her actions served to undermine the new intellectual freedom and individual autonomy achieved by the Renaissance and Reformation. Mary's interpretation that her failure to bear a child was a sign of God's disapproval, which prompted the need to burn heretics, was no more extreme or crazy than her father's actions of 1527-36, yet, as a woman, it seemed to confirm deeply entrenched national gender stereotypes. As monarch, Mary's gender was an inescapable factor in both her succession and her ability to rule. While she achieved the seemingly impossible for womankind by being the first queen regnant, aspects of her rule undermined this victory and reopened the vituperative debate about the comparative abilities of the genders.

It was the reign of Mary, as well as that of Mary of Guise, regent in Scotland, which prompted John Knox to compose his misogynistic polemic *The First Blast of the Trumpet Against the Monstrous Regiment of Women*. A Protestant Reformer exiled in Geneva, he completed it anonymously in 1558, railing against the inversion of the natural order in having a woman ruler. 'God, by the order of his creation, has [deprived] woman of authority and dominion.' It was repugnant to nature, he was certain, 'that the blind shall be appointed to lead and conduct such as do see.' Women, in his eyes, were weak, sick and impotent, foolish, mad and frenetic, and should not therefore be permitted to govern the whole, strong and discreet. All women were so, 'compared unto man in bearing of authority.' Women's sight was blindness, their strength was weakness, their advice was foolishness and their judgement was frenzy.[11]

Knox's timing ensured his thesis would be soon seen as spectacularly wrong. In 1558, the English throne was inherited by a woman who was a humanist, an intellectual, Protestant and moderate, wise, strong and authoritative. On the morning of 17 November, Elizabeth was formally proclaimed Queen outside Westminster Palace.

PART SIX

Gloriana

1558–1603

27

Autonomy

1558–62

Elizabeth stares back from the canvas, with her mother's black eyes. She is dressed in her coronation robes, cut from shimmering cloth of gold embroidered in silver thread with the dynastic symbols of the Tudor rose and the fleur-de-lys. Her bodice is narrow, trimmed in pearls and gems, skirts wide and full, while her thick cloak is trimmed with ermine. Her left hand holds the black orb of ceremony, and the sceptre sits upright in her left. Her golden hair ripples down over her shoulders, long, loose and virginal, against a background of dark blue, which almost makes her seem like a painted icon. The original of Elizabeth's coronation portrait has been lost, but copies made at the end of her reign survive to capture the moment of her triumph. After two decades of waiting, often through danger, despair and privation, the daughter of Anne Boleyn was to set a new precedent in queenship. Her reign would prove that women could stand alone, pursue their personal and religious paths of choice, inspire and lead a nation through alternative methods to the patriarchal norms, reinvent their identities and retain their autonomy.

For women, one of the major changes in recent years was in education and literacy. However, this varied depending upon class and the materials to which women had access. Literacy statistics are almost impossible to estimate, and even David Cressy's method of assessment by the number able to sign official documents is fraught with difficulties. Literacy levels were higher among men, with 100% of male gentry being able to read and write, and fewer of the women of their class, although the majority could at least sign their name. On average, though, Cressy estimated that 30 per cent of all men and 10 per cent of women could read and write by 1600.[1] Yet how we define literacy complicates this, as does the explosion in disposable printed materials, like pamphlets, and the publication of the Bible in English. Women like Mary, Elizabeth and the Grey sisters received fuller, more 'academic' educations than princesses of previous generations, in response to cultural reforms and Renaissance influences, but they were not typical. The education and literacy of wealthy women improved hugely between 1450 and 1550, and influenced intellectual families like that of Thomas More, but middle- and lower-class females were lucky if they attended one of the few newly founded girls' schools, and were more likely to access broadsheets and religious texts. It is likely that a larger proportion of women were able to read to some degree, rather than form their own letters. The overall population of England had risen from around 2,000,000 in 1450 to a little over 2,800,000 by 1540, and would pass 3,000,000 at the time of Elizabeth's succession.[2]

1558-9 saw sweeping political change across Europe. Shortly before Elizabeth' succession, the death of Emperor Charles V ended the domination of huge swathes of Europe by one man, and although the Hapsburgs remained pre-eminent, their control was fragmented among a range of different individuals. Many of these were women in the 1550s, following in the footsteps of Charles's aunt, Margaret of Savoy; his daughters Maria and Joanna were Regents of Spain during the absence of Philip, and even his illegitimate daughter, Margaret of Parma, became Regent of the Netherlands for her brother. In 1558, Charles's sisters, Eleanor and Mary, died. Eleanor, former Queen of Portugal and France, and Mary, Queen consort of Hungary and Bohemia, had both spent a year being educated with Anne Boleyn at Mechelen in their youth. April 1559 marked the end of the Hapsburg-Valois war that had been running since the 1490s, with the signing of the Peace of Cateau-Cambresis. By the treaty's terms, Mary's widower, Philip of Spain, was remarried to Elizabeth, daughter of Henry II of France, while his cousin, the Duke of Savoy, married Henry's sister Margaret. Thus, Spanish foreign policy shifted its focus from England and two potential suitors for Elizabeth's hand were removed from the game. On 30 June, Henry II was fatally injured in a joust and his fifteen-year-old son, Francis II, and his wife, Mary Queen of Scots, become King and Queen of France. The end of 1559 also saw the arrival of a new Pope, when the anti-Spanish Paul IV died and was replaced by the Medici, Pius IV.

The twelve months following Elizabeth's succession have been identified by some historians as marking the end of the Renaissance, or at least its first phase. An eighty-two-year-old Michelangelo completed his final architectural commission, the Sforza Chapel in Rome's Basilica di Santa Maria Maggiori. Benvenuto Cellini began writing his autobiography, a punchy and colourful account of his life and work as a goldsmith, which is now considered the most important of the century in its genre. Tintoretto painted his symbolic struggle between *St George and the Dragon*, which could be taken as a fitting metaphor for the emergence of the English nation from the identity crisis of the mid-sixteenth century. In Madrid, Philip II invited Italian artist Sofonisba Anguissola to be lady-in-waiting and court painter to his new wife, Elizabeth, where she would remain for fourteen years, depicting the Spanish royal family in delicate portraits with a dark palette. Her parallel at Elizabeth's court was Levinia Teerlinc, the Flanders-born miniaturist who had arrived in England in 1546 and was granted an annual pension by Henry VIII, which she retained until her death thirty years later. In Antwerp, Pieter Bruegel the Elder completed his *Landscape with the Fall of Icarus*, a work typical of northern Mannerist art, in which a large genre picture foregrounded 'low' subject matter, whilst the 'high' subject took place on a smaller scale in the background. This motif, and the theme of high and low, public and private, would be central to the evolution of the early modern world and appear in the many portraits of Elizabeth that would help define her public identity.

The year 1558 was an important one for women's literature, with the posthumous publication of Margaret of Navarre's *Heptameron*, a collection of stories about love and adventure, based on the structure of Boccaccio's *Decameron*. It also saw the birth of Robert Greene and Thomas Kyd, future leading lights of the Elizabeth dramatists, the formulation of Gresham's monetary law by Thomas Gresham, merchant and financial advisor, and the arrival of tobacco at the French court. But while this period saw the close of one phase of the Renaissance, it was to witness the rebirth of personal freedoms that would allow for the greatest flourishing of English art and culture yet seen under the Tudors.

*

Tradition has Elizabeth sitting under a great oak in the park at Hatfield when she was brought news of her succession. She remained for the next week at the house so associated with her childhood, as loyal servants flocked to her side making preparations and plans, in what must have been a surreal, invigorating time. On 23 November, the new Queen made her entry to London, staying first at the residence of Edward North, first Lord North, at Charterhouse, before heading to the Tower, to the accompaniment of cheering crowds and celebratory gunfire. Her subjects travelled great distances to see her and, as one chronicler reported, 'all her faculties were in motion ... her eye was set upon one, her ear listened to another ... distributing her smiles, looks and graces so that thereupon the people again redoubled the testimonies of their joys.'[3] She spent a week at the Tower, where there was 'such shooting of guns as was never heard before,'[4] then moved to Somerset House before heading to Westminster for the Christmas season. During this time, she appointed her staff, her privy councillors and made plans for her coronation. The funeral of Mary took place during this lull, the old Queen's body laid to rest in Westminster Abbey with appropriate ceremony, her coffin topped with the usual jewelled, life-sized effigy. On 12 January, Elizabeth returned to the Tower, sailing from Whitehall in a barge covered with tapestries, to the sound of drums and fifes. Entering by a private bridge, she commented on the ironic comparison with her last arrival in 1554, that she had been saved like Daniel, by God, from a den of raging lions.

In his collection of royal pageantry through the ages, the nineteenth-century antiquarian publisher, John Gough Nichols, identifies Elizabeth's coronation as a turning point. To his eyes, it marked 'an Augustan age of pageantry, where the Monarch herself was willing to take her part in their exhibition, and mixed in the dialogue of the fictitious characters that addressed her.'[5] When previous queens had been celebrated through the city streets, their responses had been gracious but distant. The coronation processions of Elizabeth of York, Catherine of Aragon, Anne Boleyn and Mary Tudor had been magnificent and costly, but they were set pieces on the journey of a queen who bestowed her approval from a distance, listening, observing and accepting gifts. Mary had been the most distant, being cited as not acknowledging singers along her route, a complete contrast to her sister, whose journey from the Tower to Westminster was an interaction between monarch and people. Like her Yorkist great-grandfather,

Edward IV, Elizabeth possessed the ability to connect with her subjects, the 'common touch' of making all feel included and valued, according to accounts from her foreign ambassadors. She drew on the existing popularity she had among her subjects, but her accessibility increased this popularity and marked a redefinition of the Queen's role as a populist heroine.

No expense was spared on the day, estimated at around £20,000, or 10 per cent of the entire royal revenue[6] and work had been progressing, day and night, weekdays and holidays, for weeks. Dressed in twenty-three yards of gold and silver tissue, embroidered with sparkling 'powderings'[7] Elizabeth left the Tower in a chariot at around two in the afternoon of 14 January 1559. It was snowing lightly, settling on the sloping roofs and freshly gravelled streets, but this did not keep the people away. Civitas Londinium, a wood-block map dating from 1561, attributed to the surveyor Ralph Agas, captures the feel of her sprawling capital, with its crowded streets, houses, shops, churches and marketplaces. It shows the Tower, with its thick walls, and the city's postern gate in the east, Tower Hill where tiny gallows are drawn, and the church on the corner at Barking, before the procession headed north to Fenchurch Street, along which the King's Head Tavern was located, where Elizabeth reputedly ate her first meal as a free woman when she was released from the Tower in May 1554. At Fenchurch, a band of players stood upon a richly decorated scaffold, where a child welcomed the queen in a 'poetical address', then she passed St Gabriel's Church to the point where the street met Gracechurch, running north-south, at the church of St Benet.[8]

At the top end of Gracechurch, before the sign of the Eagle, a huge arch had been built spanning the entire street, with three portals and battlements topped by three platforms. Here, a boy and girl sat enthroned, representing Henry VII and Elizabeth of York, the boy holding a red rose, the girl with a white one. Out of these roses sprung two branches reaching up to the level above, where Henry VIII and Anne Boleyn were depicted, from which another branch spread up to Elizabeth herself on the top level. The personal significance of this was immense, as it was the first time since 1536 that Anne was acknowledged as Henry's legitimate wife and queen. Bearing the legend 'The Uniting of the Two Houses of Lancaster and York', the new Queen's family tree was explained in verse by another child, followed by music. Elizabeth requested that her chariot be moved back so she might better view it, and 'personally desired to have the matter opened to her' before she thanked the city profusely for its efforts and promised she would endeavour to keep peace in the realm. Turning left into Cornhill, Elizabeth was met by a similar gateway labelled 'The Seat of Worthy Governance', where the personifications of Justice, Wisdom, True Religion and Love of Subjects trampled beneath their feet the vices of Rebellion, Bribery, Superstition, Ignorance, Folly, Vainglory and others. More pageants emphasising her virtues sat on the Great Conduit along Chepe Street and at the junction with Soper Lane. Further along Chepe, the Standard and Cross had been decorated and the City Waits (municipal minstrels responsible for providing the music for state and civil processions) played in the porch of St Peter's Church.[9]

Elizabeth's attention was particularly caught by the next display, at the Little Conduit, and she paused to enquire about its meaning. When informed that it symbolised Time, she replied that 'Time hath brought me hither' and listened to the detailed explanation offered by the pageant's keeper. She was presented with a copy of the Bible in English, delivered down to her on a silken lace, and a crimson purse containing a thousand gold marks. Then she addressed the crowd, making the promise that 'whereas your request is that I should continue your good Lady and Queen, be ye assured that I will be as good unto you as ever Queen was to her people,' and that if need be, she would not spare 'to spend my blood', at which the crowd cheered.[10] She then passed on to the pageant depicting the Bible, where two contrasting hills represented a decayed and a flourishing commonwealth, the former withered and decayed, the second fresh and flowering. Underneath was a cave, out of which came the figure of Time, holding a scythe, and his white-clad daughter, representing the word of truth, who delivered another copy of the Bible to the Queen. She kissed it and clasped it to her breast, promising to read it often. She heard children sing at St Paul's and heard musicians perform at Ludgate before she came to the final pageant at the Fleet Street Conduit, just at the Western edge of the city walls.[11]

This was the last and most impressive of all Elizabeth's coronation pageants. Mounted on a stage with four towers, it was painted and decorated, with a throne set beneath a large tree hung with green leaves and fruit, identified as a palm tree. Upon it sat the Biblical queen Debora, dressed in parliamentary robes, the judge and restorer of the house of Israel, indicative of the active political role Elizabeth was to take and her symbolism as the saviour of her dynasty and people. Debora was flanked by two commoners, two clergy and two noblemen, and a child gave an oration about their significance. Again, Elizabeth asked for her chariot to be brought closer and called for silence that she might better hear.[12] Another child spoke outside Christ's Hospital, as she witnessed the creations of two giants, Gogmagog the Albion and Corineus the Briton, who wrestled, figures that had also graced the city during Philip's arrival four and a half years previously. In Latin and English, the pair gave a summary of the pageants and a farewell to the Queen, who then exited the city over the Fleet bridge, down to Whitehall and Westminster.

The following day, 15 January, had been chosen as an auspicious coronation date by Elizabeth's astrologer John Dee. She processed the short distance from the palace to the Abbey, where she took her oath and was anointed by Owen Oglethorpe, Bishop of Carlisle, before being crowned with St Edward's Crown and then the Imperial Crown of England. The Lords and Bishops paid her homage, Mass was celebrated and the Bible was read in English and Latin, an important indication of her religious intentions. Afterwards, she processed in her robes, carrying orb and sceptre, back to Westminster Hall, where the banquet lasted from three in the afternoon until after midnight.

*

It did not take Elizabeth long to clarify a religious settlement for the country, a pragmatic and tolerant approach, based on the Protestant settlement of Edward's reign, but retaining Catholic elements, and with the monarch as the head of the church. Her personal view of religion, shaped by the influences of figures like Catherine Parr, was that 'she had rather talk with God devoutly by prayer than hear others speak eloquently of God,' and as Francis Bacon put it, 'Her Majesty did not like to make windows into men's hearts and secret thoughts.' Thus she sought a moderate approach, flexible and tolerant, to move on from the years of division and persecution, in the belief that 'there was only one Jesus Christ, and one faith, and all the rest they disputed about but trifles.'[13]

Elizabeth's first parliament debated the proposed settlement hotly that January, with the House of Commons in full agreement, although the

Lords required more persuasion. One of the main areas of dispute was the question of gender, as it was considered inappropriate to nominate a woman as Head of the Church of England, even if that woman was its queen, but Elizabeth diplomatically accepted the substitution of 'Supreme Governor' instead of Head, while relinquishing none of her powers. All clergymen, lawmakers and royal servants were required to swear an oath to serve Elizabeth under this title, but the penalty for not doing so was loss of office, instead of loss of life. The harsh heresy laws reintroduced under Mary were repealed. In March 1559, the Act of Uniformity and Act of Supremacy were passed, confirming England's separate status from Rome, re-introducing Edward's Common Prayer Book of 1552, with moderations for Lutherans and Catholics, and allowing for variation in beliefs about consubstantiation and transubstantiation, or the presence of Christ during the Mass. The death of Cardinal Pole, on the same day as Mary, left the Archbishopric of Canterbury vacant and Elizabeth appointed the moderate Matthew Parker, her mother's former chaplain, who accepted the position reluctantly in August 1559. Elizabeth's religious settlement was generous and pragmatic, a much-needed balm to the deep divisions and harsh penalties of her sister's reign.

While English wounds began to heal, divisions opened across the Channel. In 1559, persecution of Protestants marked the first signs of the French Wars of Religion that would last for decades and see the flight of thousands of Huguenots to the more tolerant atmosphere of England. The fifteen-year-old Francis II had been crowned eight months after Elizabeth, and his young wife, Mary Queen of Scots, becoming Queen of France. Francis's poor health meant that governance was handed over to his Guise relatives, who pursued a hard Catholic line comparable to, if not worse than, that of Mary I. The regime of burnings and maimings, usually the cutting out of heretics' tongues, led to the Amboise Uprising of March 1560, which aimed to kidnap the King and liberate him from the Guise's influence. The rebels were initially pardoned but after further insurrection, over a thousand conspirators and their associates were killed. It was the Queen Mother, Catherine de Medici, who influenced the Council towards greater tolerance, and the Edict of Romorontin, signed that May, took France a step closer towards freedom of conscience.

Annoyed by Francis and Mary's continuing use of the English coat of arms, Elizabeth had lent support to Scottish rebels in January

1560, blockading the French-held port of Leith, the main access by water to Edinburgh. Marie of Guise found herself a virtual prisoner in the capital and the French were unable to bring in more or troops. That July, the Treaty of Edinburgh was signed between the rebels, the English and the French delegates, by which Francis was to withdraw his troops and stop using the English arms. However, when the treaty was presented to the French King and Queen, they refused to acknowledge or sign it and rejected the Scottish Parliament's requests. The Scots Parliament then moved to establish Protestantism as the national religion, a move which was acceptable to the English Queen but not to Mary.

By the middle of November 1560, Francis was seriously ill. He lost consciousness perhaps due to otitis, an ear condition that could lead to dangerous abscesses, or possibly as the result of mastoiditis, meningitis or some other unknown condition, and rapidly declined. He died in Orléans on 5 December and was succeeded by his ten-year-old brother, Charles IX, whose regency was overseen by his mother, Catherine de Medici. Francis's marriage to Mary had probably not been consummated, and now, having been raised in France since the age of five, she was grief-stricken. Nine months later, she returned to the country of her birth, a teenaged widow, a Catholic and almost a foreigner to her subjects. Her choice of a husband would shape her reign.

*

For years, the question of Elizabeth's marriage had caused concern in the Council, even more so after Mary's union with Philip demonstrated how dramatically the personal could eclipse the national interest. Four days after her succession, Ambassador Feria wrote that 'the more I think about this business, the more certain I am that everything depends upon the husband this woman may take,' and that Elizabeth had a 'certain air of authority about her' and 'gives her orders and has her way absolutely as her father did.'[14] As with Mary, the question of her marriage was bound up with contemporary concepts of her gender's abilities to reason and rule dispassionately. Yet, early on, Elizabeth demonstrated herself to be more capable and diplomatic than her sister, and more willing to enter the 'masculine' arena of the Council debate chamber. She was just as certain of her own wishes as

Mary had been, but her understanding, priorities and her conclusions were vastly different, as her tolerant religious settlement displayed. Equally, Elizabeth did not shy away from the 'masculine' skills of giving orders, rebuking servants who had shown disrespect with words they would 'carry to their graves' or from debating with her Council.[15] Like her father, as Feria had observed, she had her own mind and knew what was due to her. In January 1559, she told her first Parliament that it was 'unfitting and altogether unmeet for you to require them that may command ... or to draw my love to your liking, or to frame my will to your fantasies.'[16] She was aware of the stereotypes of female behaviour and addressed them directly with the men of her Council, commenting that her gender could have made her show 'some fear to speak, and bashful besides,'[17] while this was clearly belied by her authoritative voice and articulacy.

It was anticipated that in spite of her talents, Elizabeth's own desire would be to conform to expectations and relieve herself of the burden of authority by placing herself in the capable hands of a husband. In fact, to purloin Austen's pithy opening to *Pride and Prejudice*, it was a truth universally acknowledged that a single woman in possession of a good kingdom must be in want of a husband. The German ambassador summed up the mood that any 'wish to remain a maid and never marry is inconceivable.'[18] Since the 1480s, the Tudor dynasty had been defined by its need to create sons to promulgate a line which had replaced a family blessed by an abundance of male heirs. After the initial triumph of Arthur's birth in 1486, it had been a source of anxiety to Henry VII after that premature death left only one remaining son, towards whom he became overprotective. Then it had driven Henry VIII to break with Catherine of Aragon and Rome, and caused a crisis in the succession and the pitting of one cousin against another. Fertility and infant mortality had been critical issues for the Tudor women, as had the survival of sons. Of the thirty-six births resulting from the marriage of Henry and Elizabeth in 1486, only nineteen had lived beyond childhood, of which seven had been males and twelve were females. Of those seven males, two had inherited the English throne, one was illegitimate, two died prematurely, one was a Scottish king and three were descendants of the house of Stewart. Ruling out the Scots and Henry Fitzroy as illegitimate, as undesirable heirs, and with Arthur and Edward VI dying at the age of fifteen, Henry VIII was the only male Tudor heir who reached maturity.

However, Elizabeth did not feel the need to conform to such universally acknowledged truths, when their disadvantages were painfully apparent to her. She had rejected previous suitors on the grounds of religion, but when she had received a proposal from the Prince of Sweden before her succession, she replied that 'I like so well of this estate (spinsterhood) as I persuade unto myself there is not any kind comparable to it.'[19] Soon after, she added that she would rather enter a nunnery or suffer death than renounce her spinster state against her will. Yet, throughout her long reign and even into her forties, when the chance of childbearing was slim, Elizabeth flirted with the idea of marriage. She may well have wanted to be married on a personal level, she may even have fallen in love, but she knew that it involved a compromise that would forever alter, undermine, or actively destroy, the autonomy that was essential to her queenship. It may have been deliberate policy to send out mixed messages, to keep the pleas of her councillors at bay. By remaining single, she made no unfortunate foreign alliance, alienated none of her subjects, maintained the integrity of her kingdom and self, and did not have to bow to any man. She remained married to her subjects and was the only governor of her destiny.

In 1527, Anne Boleyn had sent Henry VIII a gift of a silver carving, of a maiden on a ship, tossed upon stormy seas. It was an apt metaphor for the emotional turmoil of the commitment she was about to make to him, as her lover and her King. Elizabeth was certain that she, and only she, would remain at the helm. Elizabeth's decision, either by accident or design, was revolutionary for the Tudor dynasty. It transformed the nature of queenship, established a new standard for female intelligence and capabilities but, as she well knew, it was also responsible for the demise of her family line.

The process of negotiations and suitors, favourites and marital settlements proved a delicate dance throughout the next two decades. It began almost at once, on 6 February 1559, when Elizabeth's first Parliament presented her with a petition to marry as soon as possible. While she replied that she did not rule it out, she asserted that she had felt no inclination for it so far and it may 'please Almighty God to continue me still in the mind to live out of the state of marriage,' and she would have little regrets if she 'lived and died a virgin,' also that children may not be such a blessing, as they might 'grow out of kind and perhaps become ungracious.'[20] In 1561, she told the

Scots ambassador that 'Princes cannot like their children, those that should succeed unto them,' because they were 'likeunto their winding shroud.'[21]

One of the first suitors to emerge had been Elizabeth's brother-in-law Philip, who offered to marry her for the sake of continuity of the Anglo-Spanish alliance. Elizabeth was not convinced and Philip had made a hasty withdrawal into the arms of France. She also rejected the son of Ferdinand I, Holy Roman Emperor, with the news that her spinsterhood was 'no new or suddenly formed resolution' but one she had long held.[22] Also appearing as candidates were the King of Denmark's brother, Prince Eric of Sweden, and the Dukes of Holstein and Savoy, none of whom appealed to the Queen. Her councillors rejected her reservations and continued to speculate about her husband, becoming divided over whether or not she should marry a foreigner or an Englishman. Both considerations had serious disadvantages, either opening the door to the influence of another country's regime, or promoting a man of inferior position, inciting the jealousy of others. The main rivals were the 'very handsome' Sir William Pickering, the old Duke of Norfolk, and the Earls of Arundel and Westmorland, but not Edward Courtney, who had died in 1557. However, for the first two years of Elizabeth's reign, there was an added complication, as the man she may have desired as her husband was off limits.

Elizabeth's relationship with Robert Dudley was rooted in their childhoods and their shared experience of danger. Handsome and accomplished, he was described by William Camden as 'a man of tall personage, a manly countenance, somewhat brown of visage, strongly featured, and thereunto comely proportioned in all lineaments of body,' while his face had a 'sweet aspect, but high-foreheaded, which was of no discommendation.'[23] Robert had navigated the dangerous waters of the 1540s and 1550s, enjoying power and influence under Edward when he was Master of the Buckhounds and Keeper of Somerset Place, then losing his father and brother to the executioner, his mother to illness, and almost his own life. In 1558, he was present to witness Elizabeth receiving the royal seal at Hatfield, was soon appointed her Master of the Horse, oversaw her coronation and spent Christmas with her, in lavishly decorated new apartments. There is no doubting the genuine attraction between them, evident from the amount of time they chose to spend together, to the scandal of the court. Philip was informed that 'Lord Robert has come so much into favour that he does whatever he likes with affairs and it is even said that her majesty visits him in his chamber day and night.'[24] Such rumours so disturbed the envoy for the Archduke's suit that he employed secret agents to reassure him that Elizabeth had never behaved inappropriately with Dudley. The problem was, no matter what the Queen's powers might afford her, Robert was out of bounds. He already had a wife.

Born on 24 June 1532, Robert Dudley's long association with Elizabeth was unparalleled. As the fifth son, he had never been intended for greatness, but illness and warfare had removed three of his elder brothers, so that he was next in line after Ambrose Dudley inherited the title. Well educated, excelling in languages and mathematics, Robert's youth overlapped with that of Edward VI, and it was likely that he was placed in the Prince's household at some point, as one of the 'young lords attendant'.[25] It was during Kett's rebellion of 1549 that a seventeen-year-old Robert accompanied his father into Norfolk to suppress the rebels, staying at Stanfield Hall, the Norfolk home of Sir John Robsart. The following summer, at Richmond on 4 June 1550, Robert was married to Robsart's daughter and heir, the eighteen-year-old Amy. It was not a particularly prestigious match for him, although it promised to bring significant lands and estates, and was overshadowed by the far more splendid celebrations that took place the day before, to celebrate the nuptials of Robert's elder brother John to Anne, daughter of Edward Seymour, Lord Somerset. These circumstances have led historians to deduce that Robert and Amy's marriage was one of affection, as seems to have been later confirmed by William Cecil's comment that 'carnal' marriages begin in joy and end in weeping.[26]

Once Elizabeth had become Queen, her inclination, and Robert's job, kept him at court whilst Amy remained in the countryside. In March 1559, he treated Elizabeth to a lavish banquet, games and dancing in St James's Park. The following month he was promoted to Knight of the Garter and attended Elizabeth at a feast held at Baynard's Castle on St Mark's Day, 25 April, at which he presented her with a gift of perfumed gloves and set tongues wagging about their constant intimacy. Ambassador Feria reported that people openly declared 'that his wife has a malady in one of her breasts and the Queen is only waiting for her to die to marry Lord Robert ... they say she is in love with Lord Robert and never lets him leave her.'[27] This was echoed by the Venetian ambassador, who wrote that 'if his wife, who has been ailing for some time, were perchance to die, the Queen might easily take him for her husband.'[28] Robert visited Amy at Easter 1559 while she was staying with friends at Throcking but was back at court on 8 April, where he remained at Elizabeth's side. That June, Amy travelled to London, according to the Spanish Ambassador, having overcome her recent malady,[29] and Robert spent a few weeks with her in early June before departing with Elizabeth on progress. Amy returned to the countryside, first staying at Compton Verney, then at Cumnor Place in Oxfordshire. She would never see her husband again. On 8 September 1560, her body was discovered at the bottom of a flight of stairs at Cumnor, with a broken neck. Worse, Ambassador de la Quadra reported that shortly before this happened, Elizabeth remarked to him that 'the wife of Milord Robert was dead or almost so and asked me not to say anything.'[30] Amid the ensuing scandal, Elizabeth exiled Dudley at Kew while the death was investigated. The suspicious circumstances suggested she could never risk making Robert her husband.

*

Another sexual scandal erupted at court in 1560, making Elizabeth wary of the dangers of marrying for love. This time it involved a member of her family, close in succession and tainted by the upheavals of 1553, whose secret romantic activity gave the Queen pause for thought. Jane Grey's sisters Katherine and Mary had been Ladies of the Bedchamber to Mary I, but Elizabeth disliked them, perhaps because of their close blood relation, and demoted them to be maids of honour, so they were out of her bedroom and confined to a more formal role. Katherine was then aged around twenty. Her first marriage to Henry, Lord Herbert, had been annulled as unconsummated by Archbishop Cranmer, even though the couple swore that they had slept together. The match was no longer politically expedient after the failure of the Jane Grey coup, so Katherine had returned to her mother at Bradgate until Frances was forgiven and restored to her position at court.

Technically, Katherine was Elizabeth's Protestant heir, next in line to inherit, and preferable to the Catholic Mary, Queen of Scots, who had returned to Scotland in 1561 and was claiming to be England's rightful queen. Katherine was being considered as a bride for the Earl of Arran, and thus a means of uniting the two thrones and maintaining the Protestant settlement. But once again, as with so many Tudor daughters, love intervened. In 1559, Katherine began a relationship with Edward Seymour, Lord Hertford, son of the former Lord Protector and in the late autumn the pair were married in secret, with only Edward's sister Jane as witness. The following spring, Jane died at the age of nineteen and Hertford was sent to Europe, leaving behind a pregnant Katherine who could no longer conceal her condition.

Feeling deserted, with her letters to Hertford going unanswered, Katherine wrote to her first husband, Henry Herbert, who responded warmly and sent her tokens of his affection. Approaching her eighth month of pregnancy, she panicked and attempted to contact Hertford again, at which point her news was leaked. Herbert withdrew his offers to reunite and requested the return of his gifts, and Katherine embarked with Elizabeth upon her summer progress on 14 July. By 10 August, heavy with her impending child and fearful of discovery, Katherine appealed to Robert Dudley for help, asking him to ease her path to the Queen. However, when Dudley broke the news to Elizabeth the following day, she was furious, and ordered Katherine to be sent to the Tower. Guards were sent into France to arrest Hertford and bring him back. On 17 August, the Queen wrote to the Lieutenant of the Tower, Sir Edward Warner, to 'examine the Lady Katherine (sic) very straightly how many hath been privy to the love betwixt the Earl of Hertford and her from the beginning, and let her certainly understand that she shall have no manner of favour except she will show the truth … for it doth now appear that sundry personages have dealt therein.'[31] Elizabeth's health was apparently so affected by the discovery that she swelled up with dropsy. A month later, a visitor to Hertford Castle where Elizabeth was staying described her as looking depressed and ill: 'To all appearances she is falling away, and is extremely thin and the colour of a corpse.'[32]

On the afternoon of 24 September, while Katherine was still incarcerated in the Tower, she delivered a son, who was not just the product of an illicit connection, but a pointer to Elizabeth's marital failings and a potential heir to the Tudor throne. The Queen feared that Katherine's son might provide a figurehead for malcontents to contest her throne, a concern deepened by the appearance of a tract by John Hales, *A Declaration of the Succession of the Crown Imperiall of England*, arguing in favour of Mary Tudor's descendants. Katherine named the child Edward and, despite all odds, he survived and would grow to adulthood. Hertford had joined her in the Tower upon his return from the continent and was permitted to visit his wife in her rooms. Elizabeth was furious to discover this arrangement, but not before Katherine had conceived for a second time and, to her cousin's horror, bore a second healthy son, Thomas, in 1562 or 1563. No longer able to tolerate this threat to her position, Elizabeth ensured that the couple's marriage was declared void, they were denounced as fornicators and their sons ruled as illegitimate and barred from the succession. It was a drastic and dramatic response to her cousin's love story, which the Queen undoubtedly saw as a threat to her own security. Katherine was released into the custody of various relatives, moving from house to house in the country, before her death from tuberculosis in 1568 at the age of twenty-eight. Her short, tragic life reveals that the dangers of marriage for love had increased dramatically among the Tudor women, since the dowager Queens Margaret and Mary chose their own second husbands in the 1510s and 1520s.

28

Gender Politics
1563–69

On 10 October 1562, Elizabeth was at Hampton Court, the red-brick fantasy palace on the Thames which her father had commandeered from Thomas Wolsey and transformed into a dynastic icon. Inside an archway under the clock tower, the entwined initials H and A remained as a reminder of her parents' marriage, having escaped obliteration by the stonemason. That summer, Elizabeth's wan appearance and thinness had been remarked upon by observers. With the arrival of autumn and the change in season, the Queen had started to feel unwell, believing herself to be coming down with a cold. She took a bath and had a brisk walk around the gardens, but was still capable of conducting business, writing letters to her ambassadors and giving orders over the next few days. On 15 October, she wrote to Mary, Queen of Scots, regarding the cruelties of Henry, King of France, concluding by telling her 'the hot fever' which was upon her prevented her writing more.[1] The same day, she was taken seriously ill, shivering and sweating.

The first to treat Elizabeth was Dr Burchard Kranich, referred to as 'Dr Burcot', a German who first appears in English documents in June 1553, in relation to mining in Derbyshire. He had come to Elizabeth's attention by the summer of 1461, when she granted him denization and he settled in London to practise medicine, swiftly establishing a reputation by curing ladies of the court. When he was summoned to Hampton Court on 15 October, his initial diagnosis was smallpox, even though the Queen was not displaying the full range of symptoms, which could encompass headache, sore throat, palpitations, dry mouth and the notorious itching. Elizabeth dismissed him as a 'knave' and demanded that he be removed from her sight. However, the following day, her worsening condition confirmed Burcot's fears. She lost the power of speech, developed a rash and weakened so completely that her life was despaired of. Burcot was re-summoned by Elizabeth's cousin, Henry Carey, and prescribed a lotion to apply to her skin, that she be wrapped in red flannel and sat close to the fire. Within two hours she regained consciousness and Burcot's swift diagnosis meant that her complexion was not terribly scarred from the pockmarks that affected her devoted servant Mary Sidney, who nursed her throughout. By 25 October, she was sufficiently well to carry out a limited amount of official business, but it was not until early November that the scabs cleared from her face and she was prepared to reappear in public.

For a brief time, though, Elizabeth's life had been despaired of. She also believed in her imminent demise, later writing that 'death possessed every joint of me.' A mid-century chronicler reported that there was 'great lamentacon made' and 'no man knoweth the certenty for the succession; every man asketh what parte shall we take.'[2] Her illness prompted panic at her bedside, and disagreement among the councillors about whether to back Katherine Grey, Margaret Lennox or Henry Hastings, Earl of Huntingdon, as her heir, with 'nearly as many different opinions about the succession to the crown' as there were people present.[3] None dared speak up for the Queen of Scots, but no doubt she was the elephant in the room for those of a Catholic persuasion. Elizabeth's behaviour when she believed herself to be dying was also indicative of the true nature of her relationship with Robert Dudley. As soon as she could speak, her first thought was of him, and she swore that she loved him but that nothing improper had ever passed between them, and named him as Protector in the event of her death.

Upon Elizabeth's recovery, the question of her marriage was raised again, as a matter of urgency, to avoid what Parliament feared could lead to a future outbreak of civil war. In fact, her illness had prompted a plot headed by Arthur Pole, great-grandson of George, Duke of Clarence, and thus a distant cousin of the Queen, with a claim to the throne. Pole's intention was to invade with troops supplied by France and Spain and place Mary, Queen of Scots, on the throne, to restore the Catholic faith. Under interrogation in the Tower, he admitted his guilt, but insisted that the intention was to act only in the event of Elizabeth's death, but the alchemist they consulted had predicted Elizabeth's imminent demise, so Pole, his brother and their conspirators were convicted of treason and sentenced to death. For the time being, Elizabeth commuted their sentences, and they were held in the Beauchamp Tower.

When Parliament reconvened in January, Elizabeth's spinster status came under attack from the very opening ceremony, when the Dean of St Paul's asked her 'If your parents had been of your mind, where had you been then?' She was also compared to her sister, in terms of creating a different but parallel form of chaos; Mary's marriage had been a 'terrible plague to all England ... so now for want of your marriage and issue is like to prove as great a plague.'[4] The playwright Thomas Norton warned Elizabeth to marry whomever she chose to prevent

> ...the great dangers, the unspeakable miseries of civil wars, the perilous intermedlings of foreign princes with seditious, ambitious and factious subjects at home, the waste of noble houses, the slaughter of people, subversion of towns, intermission of all things pertaining to the maintenance of the realm, unsurety of all men's possessions, lives and estates, daily interchanging of attainders and treasons.[5]

It was not until the closing ceremony that the Queen gave her response to Parliament. Elizabeth framed her speech as if her illness had been a mere interruption to business, nothing more. She told her councillors that it saddened her to be pressed to name a successor when she was still of an age to marry and produce an heir, adding that although she felt little personal inclination for matrimony, she recognised that her duty as Queen may require it. She would have nominated a successor, she explained, but the question was so fraught with difficulties that she needed more time to recover, asked for their understanding on the matter and assured them she was seeking ways to deal with the problem. Even Pole's conviction on 26 February did nothing to force her hand. However, after this, she prorogued Parliament until 1566, and came no closer to marriage or naming whoever might be next in line.

Through the next three years, the possibility of Elizabeth's marriage to Robert Dudley loomed large over the court. Their relationship was volatile, passing through phases of closeness, complicated by the legacy of Amy Dudley and Elizabeth's reluctance to submit. Sometimes it was overtly flaunted before her household, when she danced with him, kissed him, or entertained him in her rooms. It was understood that she preferred him, even during his absence from court or when she favoured another courtier like Sir Christopher Hatton or Sir Thomas Heneage, both of whom she promoted and flirted with, causing Dudley jealousy. The long-standing nature of their relationship was unlikely to be shaken by passing fancies, though. When the Spanish Bishop de Quadra travelled in the royal barge with the pair in 1561, Dudley jested that the Bishop should marry them then and there, but Elizabeth joked that the bishop's English was probably insufficient for the task. In 1562 she told the Duke of Saxony's ambassador that she was 'more attached' to Dudley, 'than any of the others because when she was deserted by everybody in the reign of her sister, not only did he never lessen in any degree his kindness and humble attention to her, but he even sold his possessions that he might assist her with money.' She felt, therefore, that 'she should make some return for his good faith and constancy.'[6] Dudley was elevated to Privy Councillor upon her recovery from smallpox and, the following June, she granted him Kenilworth Castle, the traditional seat of the Earls of Warwick, a title she returned to Dudley's elder brother Ambrose, and in 1564, she made Robert Earl of Leicester.

The nature of Elizabeth and Dudley's relationship inverted the usual gender power balance. With Elizabeth holding all the cards and Dudley's dependent upon her for advancement, it most closely resembled the intricate dance of medieval courtly love. Elizabeth understood this well, playing the game with all her male courtiers, making their material rewards and political advancement depend upon the favouritism they found in her eyes. Through nicknames, gifts, flirtation and personal charms, they vied for her attention in a way that has prompted historians to draw an apiarist analogy, of the Queen and her hive.[7] This also created a clear division between the Queen's all-female privy chamber, her all-male Council and the erotic charge of her court. It was a change of culture, method and tone at the English court, which was the direct consequence of Elizabeth's gender and character. To introduce a consort would change the dynamic entirely and result in her loss of the control by which she managed her closest advisors, maintained her court, and sustained her reign.

Throughout the dance of gendered politics in the mid-1560s, the subject of Elizabeth's marriage continued to cause her concern, although she was always clear about the personal dangers involved. Sir Nicholas Bacon told her in 1563, that 'if your Highness could conceive or imagine the comfort, surety and delight that should happen to yourself by beholding an imp of your own ... it would, I am assured, sufficiently satisfy to amove (sic) all manner of lets, impediments and scruples.' But the Queen could not contemplate the loss of her unique position.[8] The Scots ambassador, Sir James Melville, accurately deduced her situation when she told him in 1564 that she wished to remain single, to which he replied, 'I know the truth of that, Madam ... your Majesty thinks if you were married, you would be but Queen of England, and now you are both king and queen.'[9] The following year, Elizabeth told the French ambassador that the only thing a husband could give her was an heir, as she had no intention of relinquishing control over the traditional 'masculine' preserves of the army and her finances. She was also aware that the man she married would be in a good position 'to carry out some evil wish, if he had one.'[10]

None of this deterred foreign suitors from seeking the hand of the Queen of England. The Protestant Eric XIV of Sweden was the same age as Elizabeth, an intelligent and cultivated King, although he was reputed to show signs of mental instability, especially from 1563. A portrait commissioned from Steven van der Meulen to send to Elizabeth shows a typical man of fashion, although perhaps somewhat sombre despite his red hose and gold embroidered doublet, in comparison with some of the English portraits. His appearance is pleasant enough, with long forked red beard, even features and mannered pose, but the expression in his eyes is wary, even suspicious rather than commanding, as the depictions of Henry, Mary, Elizabeth and even Edward Tudor are. Nor can he compare with contemporary images of Dudley, which convey something of the magnetism and charisma that held Elizabeth's affections. Elizabeth rejected two proposals conveyed to her by Eric's brother, Duke John of Finland, who reluctantly returned home bearing the bad news. The more significant candidate, Philip II's cousin, Archduke Charles of Austria, represented an Anglo-Hapsburg alliance that certainly had its attractions. Younger than Elizabeth by seven years, Charles' Catholicism and promotion of Jesuits proved an obstacle, but nevertheless, negotiations were strung out from 1564 for about five years, whilst Charles also made a play for the widowed Queen of Scots. His ambassadors to England found Elizabeth's prevarications and affection for Dudley frustrating, as Count Feria reported: 'Sometimes she appears to want to marry him (Charles) and speaks like a woman who will only accept a great prince, and then they say she is in love with Lord Robert, and never lets him leave her.'[11]

With Elizabeth so reluctant to commit elsewhere, even Dudley's critics began to view his marriage to her as a lesser evil than her prolonged virginity. Thomas Radcliffe concluded that as 'no riches, friendship, foreign alliance or any other present commodity that might come by a husband, can serve our turn, without the issue of her body, if the Queen will love anybody, let her love where and whom she lists, so much thirst I to see her love. And whomever she shall love and choose, him will I love, honour and serve to the utmost.'[12] Yet despite her great love for Robert, Elizabeth was prepared to make an offer of his hand to her greatest rival.

*

When it came to taking a husband, Mary, Queen of Scots, was facing the same dilemma as Elizabeth. Nine years younger than the English Queen, she had the advantage of time and, having been married once already, had fewer scruples about taking a second husband. The pressing question was, exactly who would be a suitable match for a Catholic queen in a Protestant nation, who might match her royal blood and guide her without impinging upon her inherited power? Mary's religious approach had been wisely tolerant upon her return to Scotland, retaining her half-brother, the Earl of Moray, as her royal advisor and only insisting that a quarter of her Council were Catholic, reappointing existing Protestants with a proven record of service. It was Mary's Guise relatives who pushed the suit of Charles, Duke of Austria, while she was more interested in Don Carlos, the unstable son of Philip II, until Philip himself rejected her overtures. It was to counter such a possible union that Elizabeth made the unusual move of offering Mary the man she trusted most as a husband, to 'best remove out of her mind all fear and suspicion, to be offended by usurpation before her death,' as she trusted him so much, knowing he 'would never give his consent nor suffer such a thing to be attempted during her time.'[13]

Her suggestion that Mary wed Dudley, even that they lived in England under her supervision, shocked her court. It also shocked Robert himself, and was perhaps made in the knowledge that it would never transpire, as William Cecil related that Elizabeth was 'very desirous to have my Lord of Leicester placed in this high degree to be the Scottish Queen's husband, but when it cometh to the conditions, which are demanded, I see her then remiss of her earnestness.'14 Dudley was not keen either, telling the Scottish ambassador that it was a scheme dreamed up by his enemies, prompting Lord Melville to write, 'I cannot get the man to take her.'15

Unsurprisingly, like Elizabeth, Mary had her own ideas about choosing a husband for herself. She had already developed a liking for her cousin, Henry Lennox, Lord Darnley, the eldest son of Margaret Douglas and a grandson of Margaret Tudor, Queen of Scots, who thus had a claim to both thrones. Darnley had been raised a Catholic and with a suitably royal education, studying Latin, French and Gaelic, excelling in hunting, horsemanship and hawking, as well as the courtly pursuits of dancing and lute playing. Elizabeth was aware, though, of the questionable loyalty of his mother, who had been a close friend of Mary I, and considered by her as her heir at one point. Margaret had been described as loving 'neither God nor the Queen's majesty' and regarding her Catholic beliefs, was 'beyond measure hostile to religion, more violent indeed than even Mary Tudor herself.'16 She also denied Elizabeth's legitimacy, saying 'either Queen Mary I, or the Queen's Majesty ... behoved to be a bastard. As for Queen Mary, all the world knew that she was lawful.'17 When Margaret left court in 1561, she was placed under surveillance, where her treasonous activities with the French were uncovered as she first considered a match between Mary and her son. From November that year until February 1563, she and her husband were placed in separate confinement in London.

Born in 1545 or 1546, Henry was nineteen at the time of his marriage, but his heritage and personal charms caught the attention of the Queen, who described him as the 'lustiest and best proportioned long man that she had seen.'18 From February 1565, he was Mary's constant companion at court and was elevated to Lord of Armanoch and Earl of Ross that May, and Duke of Albany in June. In Mary's eyes, Darnley's charms may have been enhanced by Elizabeth's disapproval of the match, and also by the effrontery of Dudley's offer, which may have propelled her more swiftly into a love match. When

Elizabeth recalled Darnley to England, he did not obey the summons. Her Parliament debated the dangers this potential marriage would propose to the English throne, as a dual Catholic claim, with the result that the censure of Katherine Grey for her illicit marriage was relaxed and she was considered a more desirable heir than Mary, or any child she might bear. On 24 July, Margaret Douglas was sent to the Tower for encouraging the relationship, but five days later Darnley and Mary were married in the Queen's private chapel at Holyrood. Although she refused to give him the crown matrimonial which would have made him her heir, it was announced that government would be equally in both their names, which gave Darnley precedence as Mary's husband. It was a decision she would swiftly come to regret.

Within months, Mary was disillusioned about Darnley's character. It was precisely the type of situation that Elizabeth feared, as the Queen realised she had gifted her autonomy to an unworthy mate. Darnley proved to be immature, vain, arrogant, petulant and impulsive, with his drunken behaviour angering Mary's court and driving away her councillors, even his own father, the Earl of Lennox. Sir Thomas Randolph reported that he was 'of an insolent, imperious nature, and thinks that he is never sufficiently honoured,' and another source called him 'wilful, haughty and, some say, vicious'.[19] Unsurprisingly, Mary's half-brother, James, Earl of Moray, rose in revolt that August against Darnley's influence and bad governance, in the name of the Scottish Reformation. With the rebels pursued back and forth across Scotland by the royal army, the revolt became known as the Chaseabout Raid, and was swiftly concluded without conflict, as Moray fled into England and headed towards London. He was intercepted by a message from Elizabeth proclaiming that he was a traitor for rising against his Queen and was not welcome. Withdrawing to the north, he remained in exile until the following March, when Mary summoned him north for trial.

By March 1566, Mary was already six months pregnant, conceiving soon after her marriage, but almost completely estranged from her husband. He was, wrote Cecil, 'in great misliking with the queen. She is very weary of him, and as some judge, will be more so ere long.'[20] The situation had been made worse when Mary passed over Darnley's father for the role of governing the borders and gave it to his rival, the Earl of Bothwell. In addition, Mary had acted without the consent of her husband to pardon a number of the rebels of the Chaseabout Raid who were members of the Hamilton family, enemies of the Lennoxes. Randolph communicated with Robert Dudley about the tense situation in Scotland, and the plans that were brewing: 'I know that there are practices in hand, contrived between the father and the son, (Darnley and Lennox) to come by the crown (matrimonial) against her will ... many things grievouser and worse than these are brought to my ears, yes, of things intended to her own person.'[21] Randolph continued:

> The matter is this, there have been jars between the Queen and her, husband, partly because she has refused him the crown matrimonial, and partly for that he has assured knowledge of such usage of herself as altogether is intolerable to be borne, which if it were not overwell known they would be very loath to think it could be true. To take away this occasion of slander he is himself determined to be at the apprehension and execution of him, whom he is able manifestly to charge with the crime and to have done him the most dishonour that can be to any man.[22]

There had also been rumours building about the nature of Mary's relationship with her private secretary and Italian musician, David Rizzio, who was reputed to be the father of her unborn child. Rizzio's closeness to the Queen and his status as a foreigner sparked Darnley's jealousy, and he instigated a plot against the controversial favourite, with the support of Lord Ruthven and other dissatisfied Lords. The bond they made to him included the oath that they would be 'true subjects to Henry, King of Scotland ... to grant him the crown matrimonial and to maintain his title to the crown failing of the succession of the queen.' Randolph commented to Leicester that 'if that take effect which is intended, David, with the consent of the king, shall have his throat cut within these ten days.'[23] The situation that Elizabeth had always feared, of promoting a husband to a position by which he was able to 'carry out some evil wish,' was coming to pass in Scotland.

On the evening of 9 March, while Mary was dining with Rizzio in a private chamber, Darnley and his men overpowered her guards and burst in, dragging Rizzio away, although the Queen attempted to shield him. She claimed that a gun was pointed at her belly, and another threatened to stab her, whilst Rizzio was murdered, receiving fifty-six stab wounds, his body thrown down the stairs. A terrified

Mary saw that her immediate safety lay in reaching a truce with Darnley. Convincing him they were both in danger, she fled with him at midnight through the basement, only returning to Edinburgh when it was safe to do so. Two weeks later she publicly cleared Darnley of any involvement, even though his 'dagger was left standing in Rizzio's body', but only after he had betrayed his accomplices. Reputedly, Mary and Henry were reconciled, but the die was cast. The Scottish Queen appealed to Elizabeth. From Dunbar Castle, Mary wrote, on 15 March:

> Marvels that she credits the false speaking of her unworthy subjects, whom she will hereafter know never deserved her favour or assistance to their mischievous enterprises. They have taken her house and slain her most special servant in her presence, and thereafter held her person captive treasonably, whereby she was constrained to escape at midnight out of her palace. Desires to understand if she minds to support them against her as she boasts, for she is not so disprovided but that other Princes will help her to defend her realm.[24]

Although Elizabeth's greatest fear was being played out by her rival, Mary was also on the verge of achieving what her cousin most envied. On 19 June 1566, she bore a son at Edinburgh Castle, whom she named James Charles Stuart, a legitimate male heir to the Scottish throne. Two days later, the English ambassador Sir Henry Killigrew was admitted to Mary's presence, where baby James was being breastfed by his nurse, and saw him 'as good as naked, his head, feet, hands, all to his judgement well proportioned.'[25] Before the delivery, Mary had made an inventory of her jewels and possessions, as was customary, in case she did not survive, leaving a number of items to Darnley, including her wedding ring. Through that summer she continued to bestow gifts upon him, a magnificent bed in August and gold cloth in September, while she tried to bring together her husband, Moray and the Earl of Bothwell at a hunting party. It was during this time that Mary may have become close to Bothwell, whose wedding she had attended in February 1566, but who divorced his wife the following May on the grounds of his adultery. Lennox later wrote that 'setting apart her honour and good name (she) became addicted and wholly assotted unto the said Bothwell. Not only for the lust of her body, but also to seek the blood of her dear husband in revenge for the death of her servant David.'[26] She reputedly refused to sleep with Darnley any more, even suggesting that he take a mistress, and turning more to her new friend. Her behaviour was described in typically patriarchal terms, with one chronicler describing her as 'flinging away like a mad woman,' in her desire to visit him when she heard he had been wounded that October. She was so unhappy in her marriage that in November, though she prayed that God would 'mend' Darnley,[27] she also wished that she was dead, prompting her advisors to suggest a divorce. It was Bothwell who wrote the next chapter of Mary's life, precipitating her into disaster.

*

Baby James Stuart was baptised at Stirling on 21 December and Elizabeth was one of his godparents, sending a gold font as a gift. Three days later, Mary pardoned all the conspirators in Rizzio's murder. Darnley was aware that their return to favour placed him in danger and immediately attempted to leave court and go to his father's house in Glasgow. On the way, he was taken ill with 'very great pain and dolour in every part of his body'[28] with blue blisters and his hair falling out, perhaps suggestive of an attempt to poison him, or of the syphilis he had contracted during his wild drinking nights in Edinburgh.

Within weeks, Darnley was back in Edinburgh, staying in the Old Provost's Lodgings at Kirk o' Field, a short distance from Holyrood Palace, where Mary was attending a wedding. On the night of 9-10 February 1567 an explosion destroyed the house, and although they had apparently escaped the blast the bodies of Darnley and his manservant were discovered in an orchard nearby, strangled or smothered. Sir James Melville later wrote in his memoirs of how Darnley was urged out of the house before the explosion and choked to death in the stable, with a cloth stuffed in his mouth. He was told by Bothwell that the house had been destroyed by a thunder bolt and that there was no mark visible upon Darnley's body, although he was prevented from seeing it. The Scottish Parliament promised a reward of £2,000 and a pardon to any who might reveal the names of the conspirators. It may be that Mary's Guise relatives were behind the killing, as was suggested by Sir William Drury to William Cecil on 14 February, because of the letters sent her by the Cardinal of

Lorraine, warning her to 'take heed whom she trusted with her secrets, and gave her warning that her husband would shortly be slain.'[29]

Suspicion immediately fell upon Mary and Bothwell. Just weeks after his acquittal in a trial staged that April, the pair were married, when Bothwell performed a semi-abduction of the Queen under the guise of protection. She agreed to accompany him to Dunbar for her safety, but he allegedly imprisoned and raped her, until she agreed to become his wife. Sir William Drury wrote that although the manner of things appeared to be forcible, it was known to be otherwise. Mary's feelings and consent in the matter are unclear. Forced marriages did take place, but her closeness to Bothwell had been growing, and her elevation of him to the Dukedom of Orkney and Marquisate of Fife, and the personal gift of a fur-lined gown, suggest affection. How far she was forced to act cannot be ascertained. Events moved swiftly afterwards, with talk of Mary being deposed and her infant son crowned in her place.

Elizabeth could not hold her tongue. Seeing her cousin make what she considered a disastrous error of judgement, she wrote to the Earl of Bedford in Scotland, having seen some of the letters containing gossip about Mary. Her position is one of investigation but also of concern for a fellow-queen, and for Mary's heir. She asked that Mary be delivered from bondage and said that Bothwell was maligned because he had rescued her from her enemies. She was concerned by reports that Prince James was to be smuggled out of Scotland and entrusted to the care of his grandmother, her cousin, Margaret Douglas. She most strongly advised against Mary's remarriage, and the complications that would bring. Their situation differed from that of Dudley in the aftermath of Amy's death in 1560, but Elizabeth understood better than many how the delicate balance of power could be upset by the pair's marriage:

> As to the third, which is the pursuit of the murderers of the King, she sees great difficulties if the Earl Bothwell marry the Queen. Thinks it very necessary to have further explication how they mean to prosecute these matters. If she cannot be trusted with the protection of the Prince she thinks intermeddling with the rest of the matters should prove more hurtful than profitable. Thinks it strange that the Lords mean to crown the Prince if the Queen marry Bothwell, which is a matter hard to be digested by her or any other monarch.[30]

Just a month later, Mary and Bothwell were forced to part, when the two sides clashed at Carberry Hill. He headed to Norway, where he was pursued and arrested, while she was taken by a rebel army to Edinburgh, jeered by crowds calling her an adulteress and a murderess, then imprisoned in the castle on Loch Leven Island. Towards the end of July, she miscarried twins. On 24 July, she was forced to abdicate in favour of the one-year-old James. Mary remained in captivity for a year, before escaping and heading for the English border where she hoped to be offered shelter by her cousin. However, the threat her presence posed to Elizabeth was too great for her to be received at court and she was conducted to captivity at Carlisle Castle. Mary wrote to her cousin, entreating her to 'Send to fetch me as soon as you possibly can, for I am in a pitiable condition, not only for a Queen, but for a gentlewoman.'[11] Elizabeth sent her clothes, but did not send to fetch her.

In January 1568, Katherine Grey died at the age of twenty-seven. She had remained in custody, forcibly separated from her husband, living a quiet, respectable life in the countryside under house arrest, according to Elizabeth's wishes. Her doctor wrote that she had given up hope of recovery and was resigned to her fate, telling her ladies that her time had come and it was not God's will that she live any longer. She asked for her regrets to be conveyed to Elizabeth, and asked forgiveness for marrying without her consent, as well as requesting that her cousin be good to her sons and not assign any blame to them. On her death bed, she called for her diamond engagement ring and asked that it be sent to Hertford, with the message that she had been 'a true and faithful wife' and hoping he would be 'a loving and natural father unto my children'. She also sent him a memento mori ring, with a miniature of her inside, and the message 'While I lived, yours.'[32] Her death removed the main Protestant heir to Elizabeth's throne, which could both be a problem and a security. Although it reopened the succession question, it brought Elizabeth relief. The Queen entered official mourning for the loss of her close relative, but it was merely for show, as the Spanish Ambassador commented, because 'she was afraid of her.'[33]

Katherine's death left one remaining Grey sister, Mary. The youngest of the three, she was destined to live as unhappy and turbulent a life as Jane and Katherine, following the latter's route of marrying in secret for love. Mary was extremely short, even perhaps with a degree of deformity, described by the Spanish ambassador as 'little, crook-backed and very ugly', so was not considered a realistic contender for the throne. Elizabeth appointed her as one of her maids of honour, with a small pension, but it was in this role that Mary attracted the attention of Elizabeth's serjeant-porter, Thomas Keyes. It was a strange match, with Keyes notoriously tall at six foot eight, and a widower with seven children, as well as being Mary's social inferior. The pair married secretly whilst Elizabeth was attending a wedding in July 1565, but their happiness had lasted only six week, when news of their marriage was leaked at court. Mary was sent to stay in the countryside at Chequers, in Buckinghamshire, where she was confined to a single room, while Keyes was sent to the Fleet prison. Two years later, Mary was sent to live with her step-grandmother, Katherine Brandon, who had remarried to Richard Bertie, and had two children, Susan and Peregrine, then aged thirteen and twelve. Mary's illicit marriage, as well as her physical afflictions, invalidated her claim to the throne. Her story, and that of her sister Katherine, is a sad one in comparison with that of their Tudor cousins, Mary and Margaret Tudor, whose closer relation to the throne meant that they could pursue the path of love without such devastating consequences. Fifty years earlier, the Tudor sisters might choose their own husbands, but only after they had first fulfilled their duty to the crown; the tragic Grey girls were not so fortunate for having been once removed but too close to be able to enjoy love and freedom.

The death of Katherine Grey and disgrace of her sister Mary reopened the succession question, and its connection with Elizabeth's faith. With Mary, Queen of Scots now on English soil, the Catholics had a focus for their discontent, fuelled by the Pope's increasing condemnation of Elizabeth's policy of religious tolerance. It was a time of rising religious persecution in Europe, a turmoil that England would not fully escape in the coming decades. In France, the wars of religion had created a pendulum of conflict that seemed to be perpetual. At the Battle of Jarnac in March, the Huguenots suffered a terrible defeat, but that June and July the Protestants won a victories at La Roche l'Abeille and Orthez, slaughtering vast numbers of their enemies, before the Catholics took ascendancy back in October at Montcour. It was the intervention of the Queen of Navarre, Jeanne d'Albret, that brought about a peace to end this phase of bloodshed with a treaty signed at St Germain-en-Laye, by which Jeanne agreed to the marriage of her son, Henry, with Marguerite, the daughter of Catherine de Medici. This window of opportunity allowed for the possibility of two French marriages for Elizabeth in the 1570s, either of which which her councillors were keen to bring about, despite the differences in faith.

Having finally recalled Parliament two years earlier, Elizabeth had undergone another barrage of demands to marry or name her heir, but had finally rejected the Hapsburg Archduke Charles of Austria, saying that her conscience could not permit him to practise his religion. By 1568, when the Queen turned thirty-five, a late age for contemporary childbirth, the situation was becoming critical. Her closeness with Dudley, which was seen by many as underpinning her reluctance to wed, was under strain during these years, when he grew close to the widowed Douglas Sheffield, Baroness Sheffield, frustrated by the dance Elizabeth was leading him. Dudley also made an enemy of the Catholic Duke of Norfolk through his overfamiliarity with the Queen. The disaffected Duke began to consider himself as a possible suitor for Mary's hand, and Mary as a potential replacement for Elizabeth. In public, he denied his intention to marry the Scottish Queen, even telling Elizabeth directly that he liked to 'sleep upon a safe pillow' and calling Mary a 'wicked woman ... a notorious adulteress and murderer'.[34] However, his supporters secretly conveyed his intentions to Mary, who welcomed the idea, and informed Philip II that with his aid, she might be 'Queen of England in three months, and Mass shall be said all over the country.' The Council, including Cecil and Dudley, were in favour of the marriage, hoping that it would enable them to control Mary, but were unaware of the extent of Norfolk's ambition. Elizabeth was the last to learn of the proposal. Her fury prompted the Duke to flee and consider open revolt, before he was arrested on 3 October and committed to the Tower. That November, a large uprising among Catholic Earls in the north attempted to liberate Mary with the intention of bringing about the Norfolk marriage and Elizabeth's deposition. The Scottish Queen was moved to Coventry Castle to remove her from the rebels' reach. They were subdued by the presence of a large English army, perhaps as many as 10,000, which resulted in the execution of what has been cited at around 750 participants. On this occasion,

Norfolk received a pardon and was released the following August. Mary was removed to Tutbury Castle, under the custody of the Earl of Shrewsbury and his wife, Bess of Hardwick.

Elizabeth, though, was upset by the rebellion, angered by the disloyalty of subjects she thought ungrateful for the 'exemplary treatment' they had always received from her. She believed, though, that ultimately they would not choose a foreign queen over her, saying that 'the English hate the very name of foreigner,' and that their xenophobia would triumph over religious concerns. It was a shift in position to that taken by Mary, who had hoped her and Philip's shared Catholicism would overcome doubts about their countries' union. Elizabeth considered her subjects to be English men and women first and foremost, whose religious convictions took second place to their loyalty to the crown, a position which would, in itself, help to mould a sense of nationhood over the coming decades.

29

The Queen's Person
1570–88

By 1570, the late Renaissance had well and truly metamorphosed into Mannerism, with its exaggeration, asymmetry and disproportion, shown in the elongated, sculpted figures and chiaroscuro effects of artists such as El Greco, Tintoretto and Caravaggio. The second edition of Vasari's *Lives of the Artists*, published in 1568, described Mannerism as the modern style, copying and improving what had been created in works that were simulacra of reality, more elegant, more sensuous, than the simply representational. While the technique was developed in Italy in the 1520s and 1530s, it travelled slowly to England in printed books. Soon, artists at Elizabeth's court such as Marcus Gheerats and Nicholas Hilliard were adopting a Mannerist approach in their depictions of the Queen. Using art in its fine and applied forms, Elizabeth was to create a lasting cult around her person that created powerful projections of the dynasty, and of national identity.

It was the 1575 Darnley Portrait, named after a former owner rather than the unknown artist, which epitomised the Queen's emerging iconography. Painted from life, Elizabeth's face as depicted in this image, with its white mask and red cheeks, set the pattern for all the faces in her subsequent portraits. The colours of the work are faded now, so that the vivid reds daubed by the artist are more orange and brown. The Queen stands in a white and gold embroidered dress, with the huge, puffed sleeves and wide shoulders indicative of status, and the masculine doublet that equates her with the other European ruling men of her generation. As a concession to her femininity, Elizabeth holds a colourful fan and a string of pearls are looped over to one side on her doublet. Her large pendant jewel depicts the figures of Minerva, Jupiter, Venus, Cupid and Mars, an allegorical mix of wisdom, warfare and love. She stares back at the viewer with confrontational, steely black eyes from above a stiff ruff, creating an impression of authority and strength, which is reinforced by the crown and sceptre visible on the table behind.

Another depiction of the Queen made in the same year, known as the Phoenix portrait, after a jewel the queen is wearing, is symbolic of chastity and purity. Attributed to Nicholas Hilliard, in a departure from his usual scale as a miniaturist, the work depicts tight curls framing the queen's face under her headdress, with the similar white painted mask and dark eyes, above an intricate ruff and black lace collar. Elizabeth wears her favourite colours of black and white, representing constancy, with her complicated dress featuring many symbolic devices, pearls and slashed sleeves. The top of a white feather fan is visible, being held in the Queen's left hand, while her right is drawn up to her breast, where she holds a red rose in her famously long fingers. The fan might be one mentioned in Elizabeth's new year gifts of 1574 from Robert Dudley, which is listed as 'a fan of white feathers set in a handle of gold, the one side thereof garnished with two very fair emeralds...fully garnished with diamonds and rubies, and the backside and handle of like gold, garnished...and on each side a white bear and two pearls hanging, a lion rampant with a white muzzle bear at his foot.'[1] The submissive symbolism of the muzzled bear representing the Warwick line, at the foot of the rampant lion of England, would not have been lost on Elizabeth.

The unusual Serpent Portrait, painted at some point in the 1580s, shows Elizabeth wearing the Lesser George, the sash medal of the Order of the Garter. A black mantle studded with pearls hangs from her gold headdress and her gold and white dress is slashed and features the masculine doublet again. The deterioration of the work makes it difficult to properly assess, but recent conservation has revealed the original intention of the artist in depicting the queen with a serpent in her hand, before it was painted over with a rose. It is likely that the artist reconsidered when he balanced the serpent's symbolism of wisdom and judgement against the usual Christian context of the creature, with its connotations of temptation and sexuality. With all the Queen's images carefully crafted to send coded messages about her standing, artists had to choose their symbols with care.

Through the portraits of the 1570s, Elizabeth deliberately crafted a persona that exuded aspects of both feminine and masculine authority, portraying a Queen who had found a balance between the expectations and the reality of her gender and her unique position. Typically, she projected the plain white mask, the impartial face of governance, with the dark eyes and small mouth, the high doublet in the male style, the instruments of authority, and the feminine touches of the flower or fan. Apart from the doublet, her clothing is inescapably gendered, but her structured ruffs, intricate lace, puffed and slashed sleeves, headdresses and accoutrements are a female architecture of power, achieved through the extremes of angles, width, height, certain colours, lengths of fabric and the display of jewels. Several historians have considered Elizabeth's iconography, with Susan Doran[2] arguing that the gender-virginity question has been overplayed, and Susan Bassnett[3] and Carole Levin[4] arguing for a more feminist reading of Elizabeth's choices. In her portraits, the Queen's choices of clothing alone created the first visual library of what a Queen might be. This was an obviously gendered contribution towards defining the dynasty, but was something which Elizabeth exploited and accentuated to send a clear message about the equality of her abilities and influence to that of any man. Elizabeth used her gender to define a new kind of regal image, but Elizabeth was always far more than simply her gender. As the works show, her sum was greater than her constituent parts.

Elizabeth was initially playing to a limited audience in paint. The expensive and intensive production of royal portraits meant that only a small number were commissioned by the Queen, or those close to her, and were displayed within royal palaces, whilst copies were made based on sketches of these originals and might end up hanging in the homes of courtiers. This was, however, Elizabeth's target audience, the elite market upon whom she needed to impress her majesty; to impress foreign dignitaries and ambassadors, and to subdue malcontents like the Duke of Norfolk and Margaret Douglas. The majority of her subjects would have been more used to seeing her image on the coinage issued during her reign, familiar with the profile with the aquiline nose, long flowing hair, prominent crown and Tudor rose.

Numbers of English men and women also saw Elizabeth in person, if they happened to be in a location that she visited on one of her summer progresses or on her frequent moves between palaces.

Elizabeth travelled widely, as far west as Bristol, talking with local people and appreciating the displays and pageants they created to welcome her. Walter Raleigh's comment that she was 'a queen of the poor as well as the rich' helps explain her considerable popularity. In 1572, on a typical progress, she travelled through Essex and Buckinghamshire to Woburn Abbey, and on to Dudley's seat at Kenilworth Castle, in Warwickshire. She then proceeded to Berkley Castle, Woodstock, Reading and ended at Windsor, passing through villages and along main roads, attracting attention with her heralds riding ahead. Told of her approach, her subjects turned out to cheer her and give her gifts. Courtiers often spent huge sums of money building, rebuilding or improving their properties in order to host the Queen for a few days. In 1573, she visited the home of Sir Percival Hart at Orpington in Kent, who had prepared a pageant representing a sea battle for Elizabeth's three-day sojourn. As she passed through Kent and Sussex, towns and cities staged lavish welcomes, such as that in Sandwich on 31 Augus, when she was met by a hundred guards dressed in black and white, and every house was painted black and white, the doorways strewn with branches and flowering vines hung across the streets. Two days later, she was feasted on an eighteen-foot table set up in the schoolhouse, at which were served 160 dishes, and she was presented with a gold and silver cup. Two days she spent in Faversham shortly afterwards cost the town a considerable £44 19s 4d, two-thirds of which was taken up by a presentation cup.[5]

Gift-giving was central to Elizabeth's travelling, from the humble flowers, fruit and eggs from poor people along the route, to the gold cups and ewers, crystal bowls, tankards, jugs and precious jewels listed in her accounts. On progress in 1574 alone, her hosts feeling obliged to give her the best gifts they could afford, she received a gold, diamond, ruby and pearl pendant from Sir Edward Umpton, a crystal falcon adorned with gold, rubies and emeralds on a gold chain from old Lady Shandowes, a phoenix and salamander set in agate with rubies and diamonds from Sir John Young, an emerald and pearl falcon preying on a bird with diamonds and rubies from Sir John Thynne, a dolphin of mother of pearl with a golden man riding on its back draped with gold chains, pearls and more from Sir Henry Charington, a gold enamelled eagle with precious stones from the Earl of Pembroke and a gold mermaid set with diamonds and pearls from the Countess of Pembroke.[6]

This adulation of the Queen was an essential part of her cult, expressed in the hope of gaining her favour. In many ways, this equates Elizabeth's position to that of the pre-Reformation cult of the Virgin, and the process of pilgrimage and offerings made for the intercession of the saints. But while Catholics would travel to shrines, this new shrine, embodied in the person of the Virgin queen, would instead travel to them. Thus, Elizabeth's cult of worship was a more active, imposed means of rule and of gaining her subjects obedience, an earthly, temporal cult, for all that she was considered God's divine instrument upon the earth. Elizabeth's public performances and the rewards she reaped in terms of monetary value and loyalty, were a conscious facet of her queenship, which she developed from her father's example and crafted into an art form, and the expression of a flourishing national culture. Her courtiers and subjects were obliged to celebrate her identity through performance and applied art forms, outdoing previous pageantry, using the Queen's own motifs and colours, transposing her personal iconography into their cities, towns and the English countryside. These were the years that made 'Gloriana' and gilded the Queen as an English icon, almost divine, almost mythical. This was a specifically gendered phenomenon, built upon the courtly adulation of Elizabeth's femininity and virgin status.

This gift-giving was also a way for Elizabeth's favourites to vie with each other for her favours, in keeping with the eroticisation of her court. In 1574, when Dudley gave her a white fan, his rivals tried to outdo him with jewels. Christopher Hatton gave her a gold jewel, enamelled with various colours, set with diamonds, rubies, emeralds and opals, with a small pendant of opal and a shell opal carved like a rose, featuring two figures receiving a garland from above. Thomas Heneage's gift was a ram made of agate with a stone pendant hanging on a gold chain, while John Harington presented her with a gold salamander painted black, with flowers and small pearls. By playing on the emotions of her courtiers as they competed for her favours, she kept them in subjection. To lose patience, or break faith with the Queen, would have been an ungentlemanly act to which no favourite would stoop until the next generation.

The most famous of Elizabeth's summer progresses, marking the epitome of the mid 1570s flowering in entertainments and pageantry, was her visit to Kenilworth in the summer of 1575. It marked the height of Dudley's success and refuelled the rumours that they might marry, despite the Queen's advancing years. It was around eight in the evening of 9 July when Elizabeth rode through the castle gates, saluted by musicians and an actress dressed as the Lady of the Lake who had guarded the lake since King Arthur's day, and now presented it to the Queen. Dudley had created a huge new bridge from the castle's base court, which Elizabeth was to cross, with gifts from the Gods upon each of its seven posts. There were caged birds from Sylvanus, bowls of fruit from Pomona, grains from Ceres, grapes from Bacchus, seafood from Neptune, arms from Mars and instruments from Phoebus. With banquets, fireworks, masques and dancing, Dudley wooed Elizabeth for three weeks, at a cost of around £60,000 to himself, including an unveiling of a pair of portraits, of himself and the Queen, in which Elizabeth wears the white doublet he gave her at New Year. His final assault upon her unmarried state came in verses before she left, imploring her to live with him and command him as her knight.[7] Yet, by this point, other serious suitors had emerged for both of them.

*

In 1570, in the belief that Norfolk's rebellion had been a success, Pope Pius V issued a bull of excommunication against 'Elizabeth, the pretended queen of England and the servant of crime.' The bill absolved her subjects of their allegiance to her, actively encouraged any who wished to rise against or even assassinate her, and threatened Catholics who followed her with excommunication. In response, a programme commenced of foreign priests, often Jesuits, travelling to England incognito, with the intention of spying upon the Queen, or even assassination. Elizabeth called upon William Cecil and Francis Walsingham to establish an espionage network in her defence, to work on a range of projects, from championing Huguenots in France to identifying plots against her.

In 1571, Walsingham's spies discovered that a Florentine banker and papal agent, Roberto Ridolfi, was intending to use foreign aid to depose the Queen and replace her with Mary Stuart. The assassination of the Earl of Moray by a supporter of Mary the previous year had removed a sympathetic figure with whom Elizabeth had been happy to negotiate, and replaced him with the Earl of Lennox, husband of Margaret Douglas, with whom Elizabeth had little sympathy. Ridolfi's messenger was intercepted at Dover, carrying incriminating letters that exposed a planned invasion from the Netherlands, to join with the Northern rebels and marry Mary to Norfolk, and with the intention to gain the support of Philip II of Spain with the Pope's blessing. Payments in gold and letters in cipher were discovered between Norfolk and Mary, resulting in Norfolk's execution for treason, and the English Parliament passed a bill barring Mary from the succession. Customarily cautious, however, Elizabeth refused to sign it.

In late August 1572, news arrived in England about a terrible massacre of Huguenots by Catholics in France on St Bartholomew's Day. Prompted by the marriage of Henry of Navarre to Marguerite of Valois, which had been intended to heal religious division, the slaughter in Paris ran to thousands, with many more in the provinces, and was welcomed by the Pope and Philip of Spain as divine intervention. Francis Walsingham, who had been in the French capital at the time, barely escaped with his life. Protestants across Europe were horrified, including Elizabeth, who wore mourning, especially in the light of marriage negotiations that had been taking place between herself and Henry III of France, who sanctioned the massacre along with his mother. It exacerbated existing religious tensions in England and encouraged Elizabeth to welcome Huguenots fleeing from France, to whom she had previously lent financial support, as well as those being persecuted in the Spanish Netherlands. An estimated 6-7,000 had arrived in the 1560s, but in the decade following the massacre, more continued to find shelter and freedom of worship in England.

In the 1570s, Elizabeth contemplated marriage with two of Catherine de Medici's sons, although she was only serious about one of them. Henry, Duke of Anjou, was eighteen years her junior when a match was proposed between them in 1570. As a fourth son, he was promoted to be Kingdom of Poland, as it was not anticipated he would inherit the French throne, but he appears to have objected to the English Queen personally, calling her an old creature with a sore leg, and a public whore. The arrangements were half-hearted and over by 1573, when he succeeded to the Polish throne, and shortly afterwards also became King of France, as the Catholic Henry III. His policy towards Protestants, undeniable after St Bartholomew's Day, meant that no English match could ever take place.

It was his younger brother, Francis, Duke d'Alençon, later Duke of Anjou, with whom Elizabeth made a serious, and apparently genuine, connection. At twenty-two years her junior, Elizabeth's 'frog' was young enough to have been her son, but romantic feeling developed between them when he visited England in person. This took place after considerable wooing by his ambassador, Jean de Simier, whose name led Elizabeth to designate him her 'monkey'. Elizabeth greatly enjoyed Francis's company, making him her favourite, carrying with her the book he had given her, so that de Simier had faith in her marrying Francis, confiding to a friend that he had 'every good hope' but would wait until 'the curtain is drawn, the candle is out, and Monsieur in bed.'[8]

Alençon himself arrived in August 1579, when Elizabeth was pleased to see the reports of his unattractive appearance had been exaggerated. Calling him her 'frog,' she described him as 'not so deformed' as portraits painted during his youth suggested and devoted two weeks to an unofficial courtship, which had all the tongues at court wagging, even though the unofficial nature of the visit meant he could not appear with her in public. The Queen gave all appearances of being in love, and when the visit drew to a close, 'the parting was very tender on both sides.'[9] In April, French negotiators returned, and were feasted under a huge temporary banqueting pavilion at Whitehall, but despite all the splendour on display, Elizabeth made a stumbling block of the discrepancy between her and Francis's ages, and expressed a fear that the marriage might be seen as encouragement to English Catholics. Refusing to be discouraged, the Duke appeared again in person on 31 October, and found himself much flattered by Elizabeth's obvious partiality, although she evaded the essential matter of her marital intentions. The Queen was exploiting the gap between public and private discourse between them, as she had on his previous unofficial visit, by 'pledging herself to him, to his heart's content ... as much as any woman could to a man,'[10] when they were alone together, but not acknowledging her promises in public. She finally broke this stalemate on 22 November, when she announced to the court that 'the Duke of Alençon shall be my husband,' and kissed him on the mouth, asking that the same be written to Henry III. However, the conditions she placed upon this, that she would not assist France in the Netherlands but would expect his support against Spain, were prohibitive. On the one hand she agreed to the match while on the other, she made it impossible.

Personal questions aside, Elizabeth may have been influenced by the strong anti-French, anti-Catholic feeling that arose against her marriage. Almost as strong as that which had opposed Mary's match with Philip, it found a voice in pulpits across the country, fuelled by Elizabeth's Protestant subjects who feared a return to the draconian measures of the previous reign, and prompted such sermons as that stating 'marriages with foreigners would only result in ruin to the country.' Ballads mocking Alençon were circulated, satires were posted on the door of the Mayor of London and a pamphlet was published entitled 'The Discovery of a Gaping Gulf whereinto England is like to be swallowed by another French marriage if the Lord forbid not the banns by letting her Majesty see the sin and punishment thereof.' The author, printer and distributor were arrested and punished by the loss of their right hands, under a law passed under Mary, even though it was technically obsolete. People also feared governance by the Valois, who were responsible for the massacre in Paris. The event had so captured the national psyche that it was later turned into a play, *The Massacre of Paris*, by Christopher Marlowe, who at the time of the event had been a boy in Canterbury, Kent, a city which Elizabeth visited the year after, and which welcomed Huguenot refugees. Elizabeth issued a proclamation that foreign princes were not to be abused in her realm, but when her Parliament met soon afterwards, it became clear that the majority were opposed to the match.

From urging the Queen to wed earlier in her reign, Elizabeth's fourth Parliament now advised the opposite. Their main concern was the Queen's age and the dangers of her bearing a child. By the end of the 1570s, when Elizabeth was in her late forties, the prospect of birth and the potential loss of both mother and child, posed a far greater danger to the nation than the chance of the Queen never delivering a live heir. Thus, the kingdom might be left with an infant on the throne, as Scotland had in 1542, or under a French regent, or a joint Franco-Scottish alliance, if Mary Stuart inherited. Again, the question of gender was central. Kings were at risk of illness and accident, like any mortal, but they could not die in childbirth. Elizabeth's body was perhaps more metonymic for the state than any king's, representing the dangers inherent in the transfer of power from one monarch to another, and the painful gestation and arrival of a new regime. Even more so as she advanced beyond the plausible age of conception, the well-being of the Queen was symbolic of national welfare, her health was reflective of its health, and any potential illness or disruption suggested a weakness in her kingdom. This extended to her sexual health, the sanctuary of her intact body and her outward appearance, all of which she carefully controlled to avoid giving any cause for criticism or fear, an effort that underpins all her gender-influenced decision-making. Although Elizabeth might later state that she had the body of a weak and feeble woman, overriding her gender's perceived fallibility with her strength of heart, she could not escape her gender. She might decide against marriage, refuse to bear a child, and dress in masculine doublets, but she used her female status when it suited her, being wooed by Francis, controlling her court with an erotic charge, using elements of dance and display, playing upon women's perceived frailties to buy herself time, employing the elaborate range of symbolism in art and in ceremony, so that her femininity was never in doubt.

The question of her spinsterhood was nevertheless in doubt, and it may have been as the result of other developments in her private life. Elizabeth may have felt more inclined to marry since she had discovered Dudley's secret relationship with Douglas Sheffield, one of her maids of honour, who bore him an illegitimate son in 1574. Then, finally despairing of ever making Elizabeth his wife, Dudley had entered into a secret marriage with her cousin, the red-haired Lettice Knollys, in 1578. She bore him a son, Robert Dudley, Lord of Denbigh, three years later, but the boy died at the age of three. Elizabeth's flirtation with France provoked great jealousy in Dudley, which may have ultimately been its purpose, but it was not a dance Elizabeth could maintain forever. In 1581, when she said goodbye to Francis for the last time, it was on the understanding that they could not marry. Her poem, reputed to have been composed upon his departure, suggests there was an emotional connection, even perhaps some regret, but not sufficient to overcome the religious and diplomatic barriers. It has also been considered as expressive of her love for Dudley, but the use of the French title suggests Francis:

> I grieve and dare not show my discontent;
> I love, and yet am forced to seem to hate;
> I do, yet dare not say I ever meant;
> I seem stark mute, but inwardly do prate.
> I am, and not; I freeze and yet am burned,
> Since from myself another self I turned.

My care is like my shadow in the sun --
Follows me flying, flies when I pursue it,
Stands, and lies by me, doth what I have done;
His too familiar care doth make me rue it.
No means I find to rid him from my breast,
Till by the end of things it be suppressed.

Some gentler passion slide into my mind,
For I am soft and made of melting snow;
Or be more cruel, Love, and so be kind.
Let me or float or sink, be high or low;
Or let me live with some more sweet content,
Or die, and so forget what love e'er meant.

*

The mid-sixteenth century had seen a variety of literature addressing gender differences and attempting to weigh the comparative qualities of men and women. From Thomas Elyot's 1540 *The Defence of Good Women*, to John Knox's 1558 *First Blast of the Trumpet Against the Monstrous Regiment of Women*, the question of female rule had moved from the hypothetical to the real, finding its way into popular pamphlets, songs and stories. In 1579, Londoner John Alday translated into English a French book entitled *Praise and Dispraise of Women*, which again raised the topic of gender stereotypes that remained central to Elizabeth's reign. Whilst the Queen remained comparatively young, the debate had focused on the workings of her physical body and potential childbearing, but after around 1581, when she finally refused the Duke of Alençon, the debate shifted to Elizabeth's identity as a childless woman, previously a role considered burdensome and obsolete in late sixteenth century England. Combating this cultural trope would be hard work, even for a woman of Elizabeth's extraordinary abilities and resources.

The majority of gender literature written during Elizabeth's reign was conservative in tone and did not challenge the stereotypes of behaviour, but punished female resistance, judgeed women by their virtue and reinforced their need to be ruled by men. One of the only voices to speak in their defence was Robert Burdet's in his 1541 *A Dialogue Defensive for Women, Against Malicious Detractors,* which challenged the double standards of behaviour, but he was in the minority, even among women. It may be a frustrating concept for the twenty-first century, post-feminist mind to embrace, but the extent of the Elizabethan patriarchy was enabled by women, who accepted their inferior position as the norm and colluded in masculine denigration of other women who defied convention. Yet nor can they be blamed, for being products of their time, centuries before concepts of female equality entered the popular imagination. Such notions ran contrary to what was considered feminine, desirable and worthy of social affirmation. Thus, plays like Shakespeare's *Taming of the Shrew,* written between 1590 and 1592, drew approval from both genders, for its tale of the spirited Kate, who needed to be tamed, or broken, by her husband, in order to become an obedient wife. It played upon what literary critic Jan Harold Brunvand describes as an existing oral tradition of the shrew-taming complex, which initially seems to sit at odds with the country's rule by a woman. Yet Elizabeth, along with those watching, would have recognised that whatever comedy, slanders or lessons were being presented by the shrew's taming, they were not applicable to Elizabeth. Her queenship made her exempt from such gender stereotypes; her status always superseded any questions of femininity. In a way, she was another gender entirely, a woman who was a monarch, neither male, nor typically female. Elizabeth understood that she was almost in a gender class of her own, and defined herself by drawing upon characteristics of each, whilst attempting to avoid the traps of both. She was not a wife or mother to a man, but she was both wife and mother to all her subjects, making her the universal figure of deference and authority, much as her Catholic and pre-Reformation subjects had related to the benign and caring protection of the Virgin Mary, a patriarchal love that wore a female face.

In 1589, a pamphlet appeared entitled *Jane Anger: Protection of Women*, which was ground-breaking in many ways. It was reputed to be written by a woman, although nothing is known about the author, and it does present a different, female perspective in response to the traditional male narrative and method of evaluating and subjugating women through their sexuality. For the first time, a genuine voice expressed the barriers that prevented women from speaking up, and the problems inherent in patriarchal interpretations of female behaviour and character. It explored just how difficult it was for women to express traditional 'masculine' qualities or emotions, without this being perceived to threaten their femininity, moving towards a new definition of gender that was probably shaped, at least in part, by the influence of two queens regnant. Its female authorship (whether actual of believed) also represented a significant shift as, hitherto, women had only been authors of previously male-controlled material, usually collections of prayers, poems or translations of men's works. Julian of Norwich's late fourteenth-century book, the first by an English female author, was a collection of divine visions. Even the early fifteenth-century Book of Margery Kempe, possibly the first English biography, had been dictated by the illiterate Margery to two male scribes, meaning she was unable to read exactly what they had written. Jane Anger's book was the first female creative work of this nature, the first female polemic, the first voice to fully delineate the female experience from a female perspective in England.

The female experience though, as experienced by those women close to the throne, was atypical. Throughout her reign, perhaps in recollection of her relationship with her sister and the coup that elevated Jane Grey, Elizabeth was concerned to keep her closest remaining female relatives under observation. Those women sharing the queen's descent from Henry VII, were too close in blood to be allowed to enjoy the usual pursuits of love and motherhood free of interdiction. It may have been Elizabeth's own childlessness that led her to treat her Tudor cousins so harshly, jealousy when they bore children, or fear of them as her successors. Katherine Grey had died lonely and forcibly divorced from the man she loved. Mary Grey had never been reunited with her husband, Thomas Keyes, who died in 1571. She was denied the right to care for her stepchildren and never remarried but had been invited back to court by Elizabeth at the very end, becoming a maid of honour shortly before her death in 1578. It was only by punishment, denial and abnegation of any personal aspirations that Mary was able to find her way back into royal favour, and probably the fact that her physical condition ruled her out of the succession. With the queen's appearance so central to the health of the state, her contemporaries would have viewed with horror the prospect of rule by a woman with disproportion and dwarfism. An able-bodied woman was barely tolerable, and the rumours and speculation about Elizabeth's menstrual cycle, potential female afflictions and ability to experience intercourse or childbirth, highlight the patriarchal obsession with the 'correct' workings of the female body.

On Elizabeth's mother's side, her female relations fared better, as they lacked the blood proximity to the throne which made them dangerous. Her Carey cousins, children of Mary Boleyn, had married and produced children, of whom many were present at Elizabeth's court. Catherine Carey's son, Sir Henry Knollys, was an Esquire of the Body, his brothers Francis, Robert, Richard and William were MPs, his sisters Lettice and Anne were Ladies of the Bedchamber. It was Lettice Knollys of course who caused Elizabeth the greatest personal pain through her secret marriage to Robert Dudley. The Queen was among the last to know it had occurred, discovering the truth about nine months later and banishing her cousin, never to forgive her.

Following the deaths of Katherine and Mary Grey, and Katherine's sons by Hertford being considered illegitimate, the next English great-grandchild of Henry VII and Elizabeth of York was Margaret Clifford, daughter and only surviving child of Eleanor Brandon. Margaret had married Henry Stanley, Earl of Derby, in 1555, and bore four sons, two of whom survived, in a tempestuous relationship that ended when Derby deserted her, leaving her with debts. In 1579, Margaret was overheard discussing the Queen's proposed marriage to the Duke of Alençon, in which she expressed fears that their marriage would displace her in the succession. Her physician, William Randall, whom she claimed was staying with her because he could 'cure sickness and weakness in my body' was arrested for sorcery and subsequently put to death. Margaret was accused of attempting to predict the Queen's death using magic, and of planning to poison her, and was placed under house arrest. Banished from court, she was never permitted to return, remaining 'overwhelmed with heaviness through the loss of your majesty's favour and gracious countenance,'[12] until her death in 1596. Whether there was any justification for Elizabeth's fear of her cousin, whether Margaret posed any real danger, her words had been injudicious and her sentence came in the context of the many real threats to the Queen's life and throne that escalated following her excommunication.

The experience of Margaret Clifford reflected a wider concern about witchcraft that developed at the end of the sixteenth century, especially fuelled by the paranoia of James VI of Scotland. Cases of witchcraft had been pursued before, notably against Eleanor

Cobham in 1441 and Jacquetta Woodville in 1469, but these had been politically motivated attacks against high-status women and bore little resemblance to what took place late in Elizabeth's reign. With Margaret's case as an exception, the focus shifted from the elite to women of the lower classes, the marginals who were often unprotected spinsters or widows, sometimes socially isolated, young or very old, as the women burned as heretics by Mary had been. This represented a new manifestation of misogyny and fear of the supernatural which manifested in a number of trials and hangings in England, or burnings in Scotland, that gathered momentum and peaked with the career of Matthew Hopkins, Witchfinder General in the 1640s. It is unlikely that Elizabeth considered these to be gendered acts, rather as acts of treason, murder and criminal damage, but it is undeniable that only a very small number of men were accused.

In 1563, an act was passed against conjurations, enchantments and witchcrafts, which was probably more lenient than previous acts, in that it only insisted upon punishment where actual harm had been done. In 1566, three women were condemned at Chelmsford for the possession of a familiar and confessions of murder, causing illness and damaging livestock. Agnes Waterhouse and her sister Elizabeth Francis were condemned in a high-profile hearing attended by the Queen's Attorney, the Justice of her Bench and her future Lord Chancellor, and hanged for their reputed crimes. In 1576, Bessie Dunlop was accused in Edinburgh of theft, communing with spirits and fairies, and of treating individuals with her potions and, according to the Scottish version of the Witchcraft Act, was strangled then burned. St Osyth, in Essex, saw the first mass trial in 1582, when fourteen women were put on trial, but only two were hanged: Ursula Kemp for her ability to 'undo' curses, and Elizabeth Bennet for the murder of four people, and for keeping two familiars. It was shocking, and potentially treasonous, when accusations of witchcraft were made in the royal family.

*

The biggest family challenge that Elizabeth faced, though, was her Scottish cousin. Still in captivity in the properties of the Earl of Shrewsbury since the Ridolfi Plot, Mary Stuart's presence had been causing Elizabeth anxiety for years. The potential threat of foreign invasion, papal hostility and Catholic-Protestant tensions made for a mixture of suspicion and intrigue that Walsingham and Cecil continued to monitor by ever more sophisticated means. In 1583, a plot was unearthed led by Sir Francis Throckmorton, cousin of Bess, one of the Queen's ladies-in-waiting. United by their Catholicism, Spain was to back an invasion led by Henry, Duke of Guise, head of the Catholic League, who would liberate and marry Mary, who would replace Elizabeth as queen. Francis was arrested carrying incriminating letters and executed the following year, the Spanish Ambassador was expelled and Mary was kept in close confinement. As a result, Cecil and Walsingham drafted the Bond of Association, by which all signatories were obliged to execute anyone attempting, or succeeding, to take the English throne, or threatening, or taking, Elizabeth's life. In a masterstroke of irony, Mary herself was made to sign it.

By 1586, Mary had been imprisoned in England for nineteen years, and had engaged in several plots designed to murder her cousin and place her upon the throne. The final straw was the Babington Plot, which aimed at a similar Franco-Spanish invasion and assassination of Elizabeth, but which was infiltrated by Walsingham's double agents, who then collected letters sent to Mary in the stopper of a beer barrel. Walsingham was determined that this scheme would mark the end for Mary, writing to Robert Dudley that 'so long as that Devilish woman lives, neither her Majesty must make an account to continue in quiet possession of her crown, nor her faithful servants assure themselves of the safety of their lives.'[13] Mary committed herself to the plot, in the knowledge that her son James supported Elizabeth, and agreed to the need to assassinate her cousin and support a foreign invasion. She saw it as the only means of restoring the Catholic faith, writing that 'the Catholics here remaining, exposed to all persecutions and cruelty, do daily diminish in number, forces, means and power ... if remedy be not thereunto speedily provided I fear not a little that they shall become altogether unable for ever to rise again.' She signed her final letter, 'Let the great plot commence.'[14] It was all the evidence Walsingham needed.

The conspirators were rounded up, tortured and executed in August and September 1586. That October, Mary went on trial at Fotheringhay Castle, before forty-six English lords and bishops, being denied the opportunity to review the evidence, call witnesses or mount her own legal defence. She was found guilty save for one vote and sentenced to death. Elizabeth deliberated for months over the warrant for her execution. Mary had pushed her to the limits of her tolerance, and would always represent a threat, but to kill a fellow queen was a heinous act, and would open the European floodgates, with a potential Franco-Scottish alliance. The number of assassination plots against her would no doubt increase as a result. Parliament urged her to sign but still she resisted. Elizabeth finally signed the warrant on 1 February 1587, but entrusted it to a privy councillor, rather than officially submitting it. However, Cecil arranged the meeting of an impromptu group without the Queen's knowledge two days later, who ruled that the sentence be carried out as soon as possible. Mary Stuart learned of her fate on 7 February, and spent the last night of her life writing letters and praying. The following morning she was beheaded upon a scaffold erected in Fotheringhay's Great Hall, draped with black cloth. She would be buried at Peterborough Cathedral that July, after Elizabeth denied her request for her remains to lie in France.

Despite having signed the warrant, Elizabeth reacted with indignation to the news of Mary's death. She had been deliberately vague with her instructions, probably hoping that the decision would be taken out of her hands, as Cecil had intuited. Now the deed was done, she blamed William Davison, the privy councillor with whom she had entrusted the paper, claiming her instructions had been disobeyed, and that her Council had acted without her authority. Davison was imprisoned for over a year until Cecil and Walsingham interceded, but if Elizabeth hoped her reaction distanced her from the event in the eyes of Europe, she was sorely mistaken. The result was the same: Mary, Queen of Scots, was dead. In France, Henry III was dealing with a crisis of his own, and would shortly have to flee Paris when the Catholics rose against his religious policies. Spain, however, had been on a collision course with England in recent years, and Philip was not prepared to let Mary's death pass unmarked.

After Spain's record of backing plots against Elizabeth, she sent a Protestant army to support Dutch rebels against Philip in the Netherlands in 1585. Relations between the two countries quickly deteriorated, exacerbated by the activities of English privateers in the Channel who regularly plundered whatever Spanish ships ventured there. Open hostilities were no longer avoidable following the execution of the Catholic Mary. In May 1588, Philip launched an armada heading for Flanders, where they were to collect an army to invade England. The fleet was spotted in the Channel off Plymouth, and swiftly assailed by Sir Francis Drake's ships, which were smaller and could move more easily between them. While the enemy anchored off Calais, awaiting re-enforcements from the Duke of Parma, the English employed fire ships, which the prevailing wind and tide carried down to the Spaniards, causing them to flee in panic and break their formation. A day of fighting followed, as the Spanish attempted to board the English ships for hand-to-hand combat, but the English kept their distance and turned their guns upon them. The weather then carried the Spanish north, where they were pursued until the border with Scottish waters, leaving them to sail around the top of Scotland and back home past Ireland, where many were wrecked.

Elizabeth had hurried to the port of Tilbury, in Essex, in anticipation of an invasion from Flanders which did not come. Amid a small group of loyal servants, and with Dudley at her side, Elizabeth left her bodyguard to mingle with the waiting soldiers and it was there, on 9 August 1588, that she delivered her most famous speech about defying her gender, or confirming that it was irrelevant compared to what lay within:

My loving people.

We have been persuaded by some that are careful of our safety, to take heed how we commit our selves to armed multitudes, for fear of treachery; but I assure you I do not desire to live to distrust my faithful and loving people. Let tyrants fear. I have always so behaved myself that, under God, I have placed my chiefest strength and safeguard in the loyal hearts and good-will of my subjects; and therefore I am come amongst you, as you see, at this time, not for my recreation and disport, but being resolved, in the midst and heat of the battle, to live and die amongst you all; to lay down for my God, and for my kingdom, and my people, my honour and my blood, even in the dust.

I know I have the body of a weak, feeble woman; but I have the heart and stomach of a king, and of a king of England too, and think foul scorn that Parma or Spain, or any prince of Europe, should dare to invade the borders of my realm; to which rather than any dishonour shall grow by me, I myself will take up arms, I myself will be your general, judge, and rewarder of every one of your virtues in the field.

I know already, for your forwardness you have deserved rewards and crowns; and We do assure you on a word of a prince, they shall be duly paid. In the mean time, my lieutenant general shall be in my stead, than whom never prince commanded a more noble or worthy subject; not doubting but by your obedience to my general, by your concord in the camp, and your valour in the field, we shall shortly have a famous victory over these enemies of my God, of my kingdom, and of my people.

The Armada Portrait of Elizabeth, painted in, or soon after, 1588, represents a new style in depictions of the Queen. It is usually attributed to George Gower, a Yorkshireman who bore the unusual title of sergeant painter at court from 1581, and had previously produced the Sieve Portrait, in which Elizabeth carries a symbol of her virginity. The style of Gower's new work rejected Renaissance classical unities of time and space in favour of Mannerist elements of perspective and allegory. The Queen stands in the centre of a tableau, wearing fashions that have taken the ruff, puffed sleeves, farthingale and ornament to the maximum, occupying greater space in a display of majesty. She has a full circular ruff, but it is intricate and lighter, with filigree lace, her golden hair is dressed in a crescent on top of her head and studded with pearls, topped with hat and feathers. Again, the Queen opts for her trademark black and white, with a doublet draped in pearls and immense leg-of-mutton sleeves with lace cuffs. Her skirt continues the black velvet of the doublet but is spilt at the front to reveal the same fabric as her sleeves. A matching black cape, lined with brown fur, hangs from her shoulders. Her left hand holds her white feather fan, while her right lightly rests on top of a globe, as its mistress, claiming control of her country, and preventing it from rolling off the table. To her right, a carved wooden mermaid is reminiscent of a ship's figurehead and suggests her mastery over the seas. But it is behind her, through two windows, that the scenes of the Armada are played out. Tied together by a green velvet curtain, the two images contrast control and chaos. The first uses a light palette to show ships sailing upon calm seas, while the second is dark and stormy, with vessels driven onto black rocks. The second image is smaller, encroached upon by the more dishevelled folds of the curtain, and the unparallel line of the chair below gives it a disordered feel. Elizabeth turns her back upon the chaos and her pale, mask-like face looks towards the scene of ordered calm. It epitomises female majesty and imperial power, showing the Queen's mastery over the worlds of men, diplomacy and, even the weather.

Elizabeth's joy in the defeat of the Armada was short-lived. In late July, as Commander of her army, Robert Dudley had invited the Queen to inspect his troops at Tilbury, and stood beside her as she delivered her famous speech on 8 August. He told her afterwards that her words had 'so inflamed the hearts of her good subjects' that he thought 'the weakest among them is able to match the proudest Spaniard that dares land in England.' The pair had dined together afterwards in Elizabeth's tent before she had returned to London. At the age of fifty-six, Dudley was in poor health and set out instead, with the intention of taking the healing waters at Buxton, Derbyshire. He stopped on the way at Rycote House in Oxfordshire, where he wrote to Elizabeth, wanting 'to know how my gracious lady doth, and what ease of her late pains she finds, being the chiefest thing in the world I do pray for.'[15] He told her he was taking the medicine she had given him and that it made him feel better than anything else he had been prescribed. Dudley them moved on to Combury Park, near Woodstock, where he was troubled with an 'ague', or fever. His condition worsened and he died on 4 September 1588. Receiving the words he wrote at Rycote, Elizabeth wrote upon the paper 'his last letter' and shut herself away in her chamber, until her councillors had the doors broken down. It was to mark a change in the queen, her court, and her reign, as Elizabeth entered her twilight years.

30

Finale

1589–1603

The question of Elizabeth's gender resurfaced towards the end of her reign. For thirty years she had successfully fought off demands that she marry and bear children, as well as doubts about her virginity. At Tilbury in 1588, she had stated that she had a heart as strong as a man's, but through her final decade, Elizabeth's femininity was increasingly challenged by a new generation who saw her as old, despotic and anachronistic. This was a consequence of her ageing, a process which was heavily influenced by gender issues and contemporary concepts of female 'usefulness' post-menopause.

But this was also a curse Elizabeth had brought upon herself. For most of her reign, she had nurtured an erotic tone at her court, flirting with her eyes and words, playing her favourites off against each other and demanding they submit to her with the loyalty of lovers. She was their Queen Bee, the life-giving sun, the Virgin Queen, and her male courtiers accepted the rules of the game as essential to their personal advancement. This extended to their intimate relationships to the extent that they feared her discovering their marriages and downplayed relations with their wives. By the advent of her fourth decade on the throne, though, most of Elizabeth's contemporaries were old men. Dudley had died in 1588, Walsingham followed in 1590 and Hatton in 1591, while Heneage would last until 1595 and Cecil until 1598. They were replaced with a younger generation of men who were not willing to play the same erotic game with an old woman, their eyes were turned to the future and the approaching seventeenth century. Some still played the game, in the belief that they had the upper hand. But even at the end of her life, Elizabeth was a force to be reckoned with; those who failed to distinguish between her as a woman and as a queen, suffered the consequences.

Into the void left by the old statesmen stepped Dudley's stepson, Robert Devereux, Earl of Essex. Thirty years her junior, with bright red hair, Essex was lively, ambitious and reckless, related to the Queen through his mother, Lettice Knollys. Born in 1565, he was depicted as a young man in a miniature by Nicholas Hilliard, posing as a 'melancholy youth' or 'young man among roses', in black and white doublet, white hose and black cloak that echo the Queen's colours. The image has subsequently become associated with the voice of Shakespeare's sonnets, but was inspired by frescoes and plasterwork Hilliard had seen at Fontainebleau when working at the court of Henry III. Hilliard had taken the place of miniaturist at Elizabeth's court after the death of Levinia Teerlinc in 1576, who specialised more in the portraits of prominent women. He was possibly even trained by her.[1] Similar to the poetic form of the sonnet in its exquisite precision, the miniature captured an ideal, and could be worn like a jewel, or exchanged as a lovers' gift. When Hilliard painted Essex in around 1588, perhaps as a gift the Earl was to give the Queen, he echoed tones of the tiny portrait he created of Elizabeth a year or two before, with the angle of their heads, the frothy ruff and blue sky behind. The portrait of Essex contains clues as to its intention. Bearing the motto 'my praised faith procures my pain,' his figure is wreathed in white eglantine roses, symbolic of the crown and of purity, whilst leaning against a tree representing steadfastness. The entirety seems to be declaring his forbidden love for Elizabeth.

For Essex, this love was a game to be played at court, a device to win favour. He was not pursuing a potential wife, as Dudley had been, and although he had taken over the title of Master of the Horse, he was no Dudley. Essex was courting a queen old enough to be his mother, and in his childish impetuosity, often ignored or rejected her commands. Volatility characterised their relationship from the late 1580s, when he absconded from court against Elizabeth's wishes to join the Drake-Norris voyage to Portugal. Elizabeth berated him that 'our great favour bestowed unto you without deserts has drawn you this to neglect and forget your duty.' She demanded his return, 'whereof see you fail not, as you will be loath to incur our indignation and will answer for the contrary at your uttermost peril.'[2] Essex ignored her request. When he did return, he did not prostrate himself at Elizabeth's feet so much as seek his pleasure among her ladies, making a secret marriage to Frances Sidney, daughter of the recently deceased Walsingham, whom he quickly made pregnant. Through the summer and autumn of 1590, he attempted to keep Frances away from court to conceal her condition, and she bore her son the following January at the Walsingham home in Seething Lane, London. Elizabeth forgave Essex fairly quickly, perhaps as a mark of how much less personal affection she felt for him than she had for Dudley. It was Frances who bore the brunt of her anger though, being forbidden from returning to court.

Frances' absence did not halt Essex's pursuit of pleasure, and around the same time that she bore her second son, early in 1592, another of Elizabeth's maids of honour, Elizabeth Southwell, delivered his illegitimate son, Walter. The birth was hushed up and the mother's absence explained by 'illness', while the child was raised by Essex's mother, Lettice. When the Queen became aware of Walter's existence, his mother blamed his paternity upon another court gentleman, who was imprisoned, but Elizabeth Southwell was banished. Nor was she the only one of the Queen's ladies to incur her wrath for pursing their heart during these years. In July 1591, her gentlewoman of the privy chamber, Bess Throckmorton, discovered she was pregnant by Walter Raleigh and begged him to marry her. They were wed that November and Bess remained at court as long as she dared, before leaving for her brother's house at the end of February. Having hoped for a quick delivery and return to court, she did not give birth until the end of March, and her absence was noted. Raleigh denied everything, asking Robert Cecil to 'suppress what you can any such malicious report. For I protest before God, there is none on the face of the earth that I would be fastened to,' and promising that he loved only the queen.[3] The truth was uncovered, though, and both Walter and Bess were sent to the Tower, Walter until September, Bess until December. She retreated to the country and bore a second son the following year, but Walter was not forgiven until 1597. Lady Bridget Manners also incurred the Queen's wrath with her secret marriage to Robert Tyrwhitt in 1594, the bridegroom imprisoned and only released after a considerable sum of money was paid to the Queen by Bridget's father. These were not marriages made by those close to her in blood, who might plot against her, but simply her servants falling in love in secret, which the Queen could not tolerate. The older Elizabeth got, the more out of touch she seemed with the younger generation, whom she expected to maintain a courtly façade at odds with their youth and needs. Whether due to jealousy, the desire for control, or her anger at the concealment of secrets, it paints the image of an increasingly unreasonable old woman.

Elizabeth's advancing age, and increasing physical ailments, prompted the predictable parallels with the state of the nation. Her short-sightedness led to frequent headaches, her sweet tooth created pain in the few remaining teeth she had, and she restricted herself to a very frugal diet, taking purges and remedies to appear youthful. She appeared less in public, but when she did, she was 'always magnificent in apparel' in the hope that by blinding her subjects with her ornaments, they 'would not so easily discern the marks of age and decay of natural beauty.'[4] Having lost her hair, she wore wigs, her false teeth were wooden. Layers of white lead mixed with vinegar were painted onto her face; the rouge on her cheeks and lips contained other heavy metals. The Queen attempted to hold back the inevitable change by exercising greater control over her public image. She understood that any evidence of female decrepitude would be taken for signs of immorality, unravelling court and country more so than the ageing process of a king, in which advanced years were equated more with wisdom. The presentation of older women in contemporary drama placed them either in the home, often as dependents, or as malcontents or outcasts, like Shakespeare's Elizabeth Woodville[5] or the Weird Sisters.[6] Older women who were still sexually active, or minded, were either figures of fun, like Juliet's nurse,[7] or disgust, like Gertrude.[8] Two portraits from 1592 show the dichotomy between the image and the reality, with the Queen portrayed as a shining icon in one, youthful, powerful and strong, while she appears old and tired in another, with the full light shining on her aged face.

The Ditchley Portrait was commissioned by Sir Henry Lee, Elizabeth's champion, to celebrate an entertainment he staged for her at Ditchley, his Oxfordshire home, in September 1592. Lee had fallen from favour when he retired to live with his mistress Anne Vavasour, to whom Elizabeth referred as a 'strange lady', and this event, and the work, marked his thankfulness for having been forgiven. The artist was Marcus Gheeraerts the younger, who was born in Bruges but appears to have been raised in England, painting from the late 1580s when he was in his late twenties. His style was more continental than the symbolism of Gower's Armada portrait, rejecting the bright, jewel-like colours of Hilliard's miniatures and depicting his sitters in a personal way, with closely observed features and expressions. Their faces were tonally observed though a grey and pale palette, moving away from the tiny scale of the miniaturists to vast, imposing canvases. Yet in spite of his more naturalistic style, Gheeraerts' work captures the 'icon' Elizabeth, rather than the declining figure she was. The Queen stands, doll-like, with her tiny feet peeping out the bottom of a wedding-cake of a dress, wide and solid, with curtain folds hanging from the prominent shelf of her farthingale. The bodice, sleeves, skirt and cloak are all in a heavy ivory fabric, decorated with gold roses, while the ruff has become a horseshoe, open to reveal her clear, white bosom, wrinkle-free and firm, draped with pearls and offset by a hanging jewel and pair of pink roses pinned to the lace. Her hands are clear, white and unblemished, her face a pale smooth mask and her waist impossibly small. Her golden wig is dressed high with pearls and, from behind her rise two gauzy wings, framing her in a heart shape, like the embodiment of Edmund Spenser's *Faerie Queene*. At almost eighty feet high, Gheeraerts' portrait perhaps might drown out another image, of which Elizabeth had disapproved.

The same year, Elizabeth had invited a French artist to portray her from life. Isaac Oliver had come to England as a small child with his Huguenot parents, fleeing from the wars of religion, and studying the art of miniature painting under Hilliard. Oliver had previously portrayed a plump and smiling Queen in a smaller work, representing her meeting the three goddesses associated with the Judgement of Paris that sparked the Trojan War. It was an interpretation of a familiar theme, already immortalised in paint by Hans Eworth in 1569. The allegory represents the pacific nature of Elizabeth's reign, with a smiling Queen in gold and black, against a landscape depicting a Tudor palace and what looks more like a European country scene. When planning his new work in 1592, Oliver chose to place the queen facing a window, contrary to her preference, so that the natural light fell on her face, with its drawn lips and sunken cheeks. Elizabeth was not pleased with the result, and make her dislike clear. Her privy council issued a statement that 'all likenesses of the queen that depicted her as being in any way old and hence 'subject to mortality' were to her a 'great offence' and would be destroyed.[9]

A recently discovered work of around 1595 is unusual in that it depicts Elizabeth with the verisimilitude of the Oliver portrait she had rejected. Shown in half-length, she wears a white silk gown, high ruff and faerie wings and is draped in pearls. But the mask has slipped: her face is gaunt, lined and wrinkled. This work has been attributed to Gheeraerts, and if he was the artist, it stands in contrast to the other images he produced preserving the Queen's youthful looks, so it is difficult to imagine who would have commissioned this depiction from him, and that he accepted and risked Elizabeth's censure. Perhaps this image, if it truly dates to the final years of her reign, is a herald of the 'truth' portraits that appeared posthumously, most famously the allegorical image of her sitting wearily in a chair, head in hand, with a grinning skeleton behind her.

More typical is the Rainbow Portrait of the Queen, also potentially by Gheeraerts in 1600, showing her with the plump, full face and red lips of youth, inscribed with the legend 'no rainbow without the sun.' This regina-centric vision ascribes the flourishing of her colourful court, the cultural rainbow of artists, dramatists and explorers, to the warmth of the Queen's influence. The painting has Elizabeth defying mortality, and the trope of her purity and as the mother of her people co-opts the Catholic cult of the Virgin Mary for national purposes. The palette is orange-brown, with the Queen dressed in a low-cut cream bodice, embroidered with flowers and puffed sleeves, along one of which is embroidered a twisting serpent, about to bite a small red apple. She is wrapped in a pale brown cloak with rich orange lining, upon which are embroidered eyes, ears and lips, signifying the Queen to be all-seeing, all-hearing and speech as the conduit of her knowledge and power. Her ruff has become even more slight, and the gauzy wings and cape are almost bridal. Her headdress, hair, bosom and wrists feature her trademark pearls and four tumbling red curls lie across a full, youthful bosom. It is the portrait of a woman half Elizabeth's age, or less, in the prime of life, exactly the image the Queen wished to perpetuate.

In 1600, Hilliard produced a miniature coronation portrait of Elizabeth, all white and gold against royal blue, reminiscent of the colours of the Virgin Mary, her loose hair flowing, her face open, youthful and looking straight at the viewer with a benign gentleness. The work has the feel of an icon about it, deifying a Queen who was approaching death.

The Queen's physicality increasingly featured in contemporary poetry. In 1590, Edmund Spenser, the son of a clothmaker who had attended Cambridge and served under Walter Raleigh, published the first three books of *The Faerie Queene*, which was reissued, with the final three books, in 1596. As an Arthurian allegory designed to honour the Queen's ancestry, it follows a number of knights who are the embodiments of certain virtues: holiness, temperance, chastity, justice and courtesy. Elizabeth appears in the work in a number of identities, as Gloriana and the virgin Belphoebe, and controversially as 'Lucifera', a maiden queen whose bright court masks a dungeon. The power of Belphoebe, a married woman, is depicted as located in her vagina, and as she exhibits a sexual ambiguity about her availability, she sends out confusing signals to men, one of whom attempts to rape her. Thus Spenser addresses the conundrum at the heart of Elizabeth's strategy to maintain power; the contemporary paradox of a virgin with authority, both sexually alluring, erotic and playful, whilst being unavailable. A similar theme had appeared in George Puttenham's The *Arte of English Poesie* the year before, in which Elizabeth's authority was situated in her breasts and access to her person equated to sexual intimacy. The *Faerie Queen* was dedicated to Elizabeth, who clearly approved, granting Spenser an annual pension of £50, but when he visited court, the poet found the reality of the 1590s did not live up to his vision. He was 'shattered by what he saw there'[10] recognising that the cult of Gloriana was flawed and unravelling, with a climate of volatility ruled over by Essex, whom the Queen could barely keep in check.

Early in Elizabeth's reign, playwrights had used allegory to address the question of the Queen's successor. The 1561 *Gorbudoc*, by Thomas Norton and Thomas Sackville, depicted a king who divided his realm between his sons during his lifetime, only for them to fall out. Both died as a result, and the kingdom was left in chaos. Raphael Holinshed carried a similar story in 1587 and Shakespeare developed this theme of ungrateful royal heirs in *King Lear*, which is estimated to have been composed between 1603 and 1606. It was Shakespeare's debut, *Venus and Adonis*, a poem published in 1593, which exaggerated the dynamic between Elizabeth and Essex, of an older, voracious queen pursuing a young, beautiful man in sexually explicit terms. If the relative status of the Queen and her favourite had reversed the usual order of gender relations, Venus and Adonis restored the patriarchal balance so the queen had to beg her young lover for attention. It was not a flattering message for Elizabeth, but the allegory kept it at one remove, and it proved an immediate popular hit.

The final decade of the sixteenth century witnessed a flowering of English literature with poems like Sidney's posthumous *Arcadia* and *Astrophil and Stella*, Harington's *Orlando Furioso*, Daniel's *Delia* sonnets, Barnfield's *Cynthia*, Constable's *Diana* and Marlowe's *Hero and Leander*, and dramatic works from Chapman, Dekker, Drayton, Greene, Johnson, Kyd, Lyly, Marlowe, Marston, Middleton, Nashe, Shakespeare and others, drawing people from all walks of life into the newly built theatres. After the influences of the Reformation and European Renaissance and a period of peace and stability, England experienced a literary renaissance of its own, unparalleled in its quantity and quality of creative works. Although this created some of the most memorable female characters, they were written and acted by men, so it was still a masculine phenomenon.

Women were writing creatively in the second half of the sixteenth century, but they were rare. The first play had been Jane FitzAlan's translation of *Iphigenia*, but it was very much an isolated case. Perhaps the first English poet, Isabella Whitney, who was writing in the 1560s and 1570s, was all the more remarkable in coming from a lower-class background. After losing a job in service, she made a living selling her poems to a London printer, many of which were semi-autobiographical and full of classical allusions, expressing disappointed love, perhaps for the first time from a female perspective. Whitney also wrote a number of poems directed at her 'sisters' and 'sister-mistress' containing advice for a happy domestic life, such as prayer, hard work, industry, honesty and virtue, in an atypical act of female solidarity for the times. The poet herself, though, intended to eschew such duties and employ her pen, although her second stanza suggests she felt excluded from the patriarchal supporting role:

Good Sister so I you commend,
to him that made us all:
I know you housewifery intend,
though I to writing fall:
Wherefore no longer shall you stay,
From business, that profit may.

Had I a Husband, or a house,
and all that 'longs thereto
Myself could frame about to rouse,
as other women do:
But till some household cares me tie,
My books and Pen I will apply.[11]

Surviving examples of female literature of the Elizabethan period are scarce. Women were still characters and muses, thought incapable of creativity and technical skill comparable with that of men. Literacy was still an issue, although the case of Isabella Whitney provides astonishing evidence of a lower-class woman's writing that is not only technically accomplished but rich in classical and cultural allusions. It is also amazing how well-informed and bold women's writing could be. Anne Dowriche, a member of the Cornish gentry, published an epic poem in 1589 retelling events of the French Wars of Religion and calling upon Elizabeth as a defender of Protestantism. Better known to the Queen in the 1590s was Emilia Lanier, who had been raised in the household of Susan Bertie, daughter of Catherine, fourth wife of Charles Brandon. Lanier went on to become the mistress of Elizabeth's cousin, Henry Carey, but it was not until after the Queen's death that she began to publish her poetry. The first female-authored play, created from scratch, is likely to have been Elizabeth Cary's *The Tragedy of Mariam, the Fair Queen of Jewry*, composed between 1602 and 1604, and thus classified as Jacobean rather than Elizabethan.

It was not until the arrival of Mary Sidney, niece of Robert Dudley, daughter of his sister who had been scarred nursing Elizabeth through her 1562 case of smallpox, that a woman played an active role as patron. Mary created a salon for writers at Wilton House, hosting Daniel, Drayton, Jonson and Spenser, and where her brother composed much of his *Arcadia*. The biographer described her home as 'like a college, there were so many learned and ingenious persons. She was the greatest patroness of wit and learning of any lady in her time.' Mary completed her brother's translations of the Psalms and presented them to Elizabeth in 1599, as well as translating Petrarch and contemporary French plays, Garnier's *Marc-Antoine* and de Mornay's *A Discourse of Life and Death*. Although the Elizabethan literary world was still dominated by men, through all its stages of production, from its inception, creation, production, performance and publication, women's voices were starting to be heard. And they were voices of knowledge, skill and authority. Still, though, male voices, even those closest to Elizabeth, continued to question those qualities in the Queen.

*

After a tempestuous career, Robert Devereux, Earl of Essex, persuaded Elizabeth to give him the role of Lieutenant of Ireland. In the 1590s, he had commanded a military force assisting Henry IV of France in the continuing Catholic-Huguenot conflict and had won glory for his capture of Cadiz in 1596, when he had metaphorically 'singed the king of Spain's beard'. Irish rebels had risen against English rule in 1595, with support from Spain, and had won two significant early battles. Essex set out from London in March 1599 at the head of 16,000 men, with the intention of bringing the conflict to an immediate halt. However, he found himself frustrated by lack of funding and Elizabeth's disagreement over appointments he made. Instead of confronting the rebels at Ulster, as had been planned, Essex went south and wasted money and time on inconsequential skirmishes, giving superfluous knighthoods and making grand ceremonial entries into towns, before entering into a truce with the rebels.

Once again, as reports to Elizabeth suggested, Essex appeared to be in it for the adventure, rather than to achieve results. By September, he wished to return to London, but Elizabeth forbade him, insisting that he remain in post. She was surprised, therefore, when early one morning at the end of the month, he burst into her bedchamber at Nonsuch, before she was dressed, and without her wig in place. Horrified, Elizabeth initially feared a plot against her life, and spoke to him civilly before it was established that he had come alone. Then, she confined him to his rooms, likening him to a beast that needed to be tamed, in a reversal of Shakespeare's motif. Essex's return was not only rash, it breached critical protocol about access to the Queen's person, for safety and hierarchy; but also it impinged upon the privacy of a proud woman, shattered her carefully groomed image and exposed her at her most vulnerable.

The following day, Essex was interrogated before the Council for five hours. They pronounced that his truce with the rebels was an indefensible departure from the aims of his mission, and that in leaving

Ireland against the Queen's express orders, he had deserted his post. He was confined within his own home, York House, from 1 October, until a formal trial in the summer of 1600, and deprived of his sources of income. During his confinement, he had rejected his friends' plans to help him escape to France, but he did correspond with James VI of Scotland, the last remaining of Elizabeth's likely heirs, professing his loyalty and asking for assistance. Essex's sister had previously been indiscreet enough to write to James that her brother was 'exceedingly weary, accounting it a thrall he now lives in, and wishes the change.'[12] This criticism, and anticipation of the Queen's death, was tantamount to treason. James had replied to Essex that 'He desires the continuance of his affection and promises to reward it in proper time and place.' In December 1600, Essex went further. He wrote to James that it was time to 'stop the wickedness and madness of these men, and to relieve my poor country which groans under her burden' and that Elizabeth 'must needs be led blindfold into her own extreme danger.'[13]

In February 1601, when his allies met to plan their next move, Essex was summoned to attend the Council but used the Queen's old ploy and pleaded illness. When councillors visited his home to investigate, they found the Earl far from ill and the place thronged with lively conspirators, whom Essex explained were his bodyguards, as he was in fear of being murdered. Luring the councillors into his house, the Earl then detained them as his prisoners and headed off into the street with his unruly followers, who were firing their guns, while he cried 'For the Queen! A plot is laid against my life!'[14] By the end of the day he had been arrested. At Whitehall, Elizabeth remained calm throughout, following her usual routine, even though one of Essex's friends made it to the door outside her privy chamber, planning to force her to sign a warrant for the Earl's release.[15] This time, Essex had pushed the Queen too far. He was tried on 19 February, accused of conspiring to 'deprive and depose the Queen's Majesty from her royal state and dignity, and to procure her death and destruction'.[16] The next day, Elizabeth signed her former favourite's death warrant, recognising that he was 'unworthy' of her mercy, and he went to the scaffold on 25 February 1601.

Despite his connection with Essex, James VI of Scotland still had the strongest claim to the English throne, as Elizabeth's first cousin twice removed. He also had the advantages of being male and Protestant. An English alternative existed in the elder son of Katherine Grey,

Edmund Seymour, who was forty in 1601 and favoured by the will of Henry VIII, which overlooked the offspring of Margaret Tudor in favour of those of Mary. The steps Elizabeth had taken in the 1560s to pronounce Edmund and his brother illegitimate, however, meant his claim was never taken seriously. There was also Arabella Stewart, daughter of Charles, the brother of Henry, Lord Darnley, grandson of Margaret Douglas, who was twenty-six in 1601, unmarried, and had attended Elizabeth's court. Yet Arabella was never a serious contender. Parliament favoured her cousin James as older, wiser, male, a father, and having been a king since he was a year old. Almost until the end of her life, Elizabeth continued to reject any talk of her succession or to nominate an heir. Her secretary, Robert Cecil, who had taken over from his father William, conducted the necessary negotiations with James in secret.

Elizabeth's health began to fail in the autumn of 1602. Depressed following the deaths of close friends including her cousin Catherine Carey, and perhaps mourning Essex, she installed herself on a cushion at Richmond Palace, refusing all entreaties to move or to go to bed. She ordered her coronation ring to be filed off her finger as it had become too tight, and was troubled by 'heat in her breasts and dryness in mouth', which kept her from sleeping. Her doctor reported that she was 'resisting physic' and was 'suspicious' of those around her, and that she exhibited a 'notable decay of judgement and memory'.[17] William Camden noted in January that she had always enjoyed 'health without impairment', or at least that was the impression she created, but that she was now aware of a 'weakness' or 'impairment' in her health.[18] By early March, she appeared to rally, sleeping better, and lifting the mood at court. However, soon afterwards, a Dr Beaumont described her as 'given up' and reported that she had said she 'wished not to live any longer, but desire to die.' She had her wish early in the morning of 24 March 1603, with her chaplain reporting that she 'departed this life mildly, like a lamb, easily like a ripe apple from a tree.' She was sixty-nine. She had reigned for over forty-four years, 'a far greater part of a man's age'.

The body of the Queen was placed in a lead coffin and transported down the Thames to Whitehall Palace. She lay there in state for a month, before her grand state funeral on 28 April, as witnessed and recorded by dramatist and pamphleteer, Henry Chettle.[19] A procession from Whitehall to Westminster preceded the coffin, comprising 260 poor women and 40 poor men, knights, sergeants, servants according to rank, trumpeters, city officials, delegates from Ireland and Wales, heralds, clerics and ambassadors. Elizabeth's coffin followed in a black chariot, draped in purple velvet and topped with a life-sized wax effigy, dressed in parliamentary robes and holding the orb and sceptre. On either side walked noblemen carrying banner rolls of the Queen's lineage, so that the arms of Anne Boleyn, Elizabeth of York and Elizabeth Woodville fluttered around the body of the final Tudor queen. It was reported that there was 'such a general sighing, groaning and weeping as the like hath not been seen or known in the memory of man.'[20] Her body was initially buried in the same vault as that of her grandparents, Henry VII and Elizabeth of York, but in 1607, it was relocated to that of her sister Mary. Her successor, James VI of Scotland, erected a white marble statue in her honour in the north aisle of Henry VII's Lady Chapel, which was painted in full colour at the time, at a cost of £1,485.

Elizabeth was succeeded by the son of her cousin, Mary, Queen of Scots. James Stewart, or Stuart, as he now became. He was thirty-six, the father of a family that included two surviving sons and an experienced Protestant ruler. He left Edinburgh on 5 April, arriving in London on 7 May, where he was welcomed by the crowds and made a smooth transition to power, being anointed as the first joint ruler of England and Scotland on July 25. The Tudor dynasty was no more, but the new King had the blood of Margaret Beaufort, Henry VII and Elizabeth Woodville in his veins.

*

Elizabeth's contribution to the Tudor dynasty is unparalleled. In many ways she was the epitome of the family's achievement, the embodiment of success, a national icon, the ultimate Tudor. Certainly, in terms of the female narrative, the cumulative efforts of her immediate forebears – Margaret Beaufort, Elizabeth Woodville, Elizabeth of York and Anne Boleyn – were building toward Elizabeth, as the individual to celebrate and benefit from their sacrifices. Unconscious as this was, as none of these women lived to see her reign, they had an abstract concept of a dynastic future, as queens or mothers, which found its fruition in the magnificent Tudor finale of Elizabeth's making. Her reign was the longest of all the Tudor monarchs, lasting for over a third of their tenure on the throne, but it was also the reign that ended the dynasty, as the result of Elizabeth's personal choices. The direct English blood line may have flowered under her, but then it died with her in 1603.

The first critical hurdle that Elizabeth's reign overcame was that she succeeded without opposition. Whereas Mary had faced a coup to prevent her inheritance along religious and political lines, Elizabeth was welcomed and feted by a population whose affection for her lasted almost all of her life. As a young, unmarried woman, and a Protestant, her succession went unopposed, and she continued to reign despite considerable challenges being mounted against her from foreign and Catholic forces, even after the Pope's bull of excommunication. This was the result of the loyalty she inspired, her more moderate religious approach and the work of her intelligence network. Elizabeth's commitment to religious and intellectual privacy, not seeking to meddle with men's souls, came as a relief after the period of Marian burnings, to Protestants and Catholics alike. By asking for her subjects' loyalty first as Englishmen and women, she move the country towards definition by nationality rather than religion, in contrast to her sister's attempts to unify the country within a wider Catholic international community, which had resulted in xenophobia and rebellion.

Elizabeth used her gender to form a new type of queenship. Where Mary had been keen to marry and adopt the role of mother while Philip was more active in the Council, Elizabeth rejected the thought of sharing her power with a man. She played the courtship game skilfully, allowing her suitors hope and permitting herself the pleasures of courtship but refusing to yield the autonomy she understood was the key to holding onto power. The flirtatious virgin was a difficult role to maintain as she aged, but by this point her reign was well established and the benefits of having a live, reigning queen outweighed the dangers of losing her in childbirth. How this decision sat with Elizabeth's personal feelings is a question biographers have been trying to untangle for centuries. She may have loved Robert Dudley, but she was not prepared to risk her crown for him, and as queen, she could insist that he remain by her side, and it was a trade-off she was prepared to live with.

Elizabeth's femininity dictated the nature of her court, with her privy chamber dominated by women and her presence and council chambers by men. It also shaped the nature of her interactions with her courtiers.

The Queen played a different courtly game of her own invention, actively deploying the tactics of female stereotypes to interact with her favourites and establish behaviours that felt more like courtship, or courtly love, in order for them to please her on a personal level. It was essentially an ego-driven court, as that of her father had been, but the manifestation of each was different, and Elizabeth never brought her male favourites as close as Henry VIII had, through marriage. While this style narrowed the gap between Elizabeth's dual identities as a woman and a monarch, her men quickly grasped that the way to the Queen's favour was to please the woman, but those who failed to recognise that the monarch might unexpectedly rear her head, and bite, suffered the consequences.

She also deployed the idea of women's physical frailty to her advantage, pleading illness or indisposition when required to travel, or make difficult decisions, and cited expected gender standards in her speeches to Council, only to defy them and carve her own path. The erotic edge to her interactions, her deliberate exploitation of perceived female weaknesses, allowed Elizabeth to use the patriarchal tropes to her own advantage. As the only Queen Bee at the centre of her buzzing hive, Elizabeth could give the impression of needing her men's service and devotion whilst, paradoxically, remaining stronger than them all.

The combination of Elizabeth's virginity and queenship gave her a distance which allowed her to establish herself as an icon or muse, a distant deity, an object of veneration in the courtly love tradition. There was essentially a chivalric cordon around the Queen which she never broached, unlike her father. As her reign progressed, she employed a combination of feminine and masculine elements in her clothing to communicate the image of the Virgin mother with patriarchal authority. Portraiture styles developed to promote the ever-youthful, untouched image of powerful purity, the like of which had only ever before been seen in divine contexts, such as in the cults of the Virgin Mary and female saints, or in martyrs such as Joan of Arc. Her public face, meaning that which she presented outside her bedchamber, was midway between Spenser's Faerie Queen and the Catholic Marian cult. This was entirely a construct of her gender, a new way of exercising and retaining power through feminine channels, which proved successful for forty-five years.

Elizabeth's effect on the Tudor dynasty and in international politics, religion and culture contributed to a golden age in England, which created a new sense of national identity and intellectual freedom. These owed much to the force of her personality, such as her stoicism through years of danger and her stirring address to the troops at Tilbury, but personality cannot be divorced from gender, and it was there that she made her famous speech about having the heart and stomach of a king. It was as a result of her gendered choices that Elizabeth made her greatest contribution to the Tudor dynasty. As a woman, she redefined a new way of being a monarch and slipped in and out of gender conventions as they suited her, exactly as her formidable paternal great-grandmother, Margaret Beaufort, had done. Elizabeth showed exactly what a queen regnant could do when she had sole authority, making the longest and most memorable contribution to her dynasty.

While Elizabeth's game-changing gender choices make her the most significant woman in the Tudor dynasty, it is impossible to deny that it was also her choices that led to the end of her family line. Elizabeth ended the Tudor dynasty. Had she lost her throne by being overthrown or assassinated, or had the Spanish successfully invaded or the smallpox done its worst, the end of her line would have been the result of factors that needed careful analysis, such as the depositions of Henry VI in 1460 and 1471, the defeat of Richard III in battle and the disappearance of young Edward V in 1483. But it was nothing more or less than Elizabeth's childlessness that ended her line. After four generations' struggles to secure and further their line, to produce and educate heirs, Elizabeth fulfilled many dynastic ideals save for, perhaps, the most important one. In this, and in her choice to remain single, it appears that Elizabeth promoted her own survival over that of her dynasty. As she stated on numerous occasions, a husband would threaten her autonomy and children would jeopardise her position. Ultimately, her decisions were made out of self-preservation, but if her self was synonymous with the state, then she chose in the best interests of her country. She handed over a peaceful, prosperous nation to her cousin's son by default, and without challenge, but in the knowledge that the name of Tudor would no longer be first in the land.

In around 1604-6, Caravaggio painted his controversial *Death of the Virgin*. Rejecting Mannerism for a chiaroscuro baroque style, the artists depicts a lifelike body sprawled on a bed, skirts rumpled, arm thrown out and feet bare, intense in its humanity and lack of dignity. The woman, dressed in red, lies before a gathering of largely older men, with bald heads and beards, draped in robes and also barefooted; one openly weeps over her body, but with his hands balled in his eyes, so the raw emotion is masked. The depiction of the Virgin was rejected in Rome as too irreverent, too confronting, as opposed to the usual idealised images of similar scenes, which showed Mary's assumption into Heaven, rather than the fact of her death. It would be the last Catholic image of the Virgin as dead, marking the end of an era, and providing a reminder that, at the end of her life, England's virgin, for all her wealth, status and palaces, could not defy mortality, and was stripped of her royalty. In death, she was reduced to her mere physicality by that great leveller so familiar to her medieval forebears. At Richmond, and at Rome, the brutal fact remained; the virgin, and the dynasty, lay dead.

31

How the Tudor Dynasty Was Built by Women

1437–1603

In her *Book of the City of Ladies*, finished in around 1405, Christine de Pizan wrote: 'If it were customary to send maidens to school, and teach them the same subjects as are taught to boys, they would learn just as fully and understand all the subtleties of arts and sciences.' Shortly before this, Geoffrey Chaucer had written in his *Canterbury Tales*, 'What is better than wisdom? Woman. And what is better than a good woman? Nothing.' At the start of the Tudor dynasty, the abilities of women were understood, in places, in theory. In practice though, levels of female literacy were very low, their legal rights were minimal, and there was little consideration given to their education, all of which came secondary to a woman's ability to bear children. Yet, through the patriarchal morass of suppression, the bright lights of individual women began to shine when the opportunity arose.

In literature produced during the years following Elizabeth's death, respect for women and their abilities had not only increased but was based upon the reality of female role models. In 1606, George Chapman wrote in his play *The Gentleman Usher*, 'Let no man value at a little a virtuous woman's counsel; her wing'd spirit is feather'd oftentimes with heavenly words.' Beaumont and Fletcher's *The Maid's Tragedy* contained the lines, 'Then, my good girls, be more than women, wise: at least be more than I was; and be sure you credit anything the light gives life to before a man.' In 1613, Miguel de Cervantes wrote: 'The woman who is resolved to be respected can make herself so even amidst an army of soldiers.' In 1621, Robert

Burton's *Anatomy of Melancholy* used the now famous adage, 'women wear the breeches.' In answer to the question posed by Joan Kelly-Gadol in 1977, of whether women had a renaissance, it seems that yes, women did experience change between 1437 and 1603, but it was only some women, as part of a cumulative narrative, and those changes trickled down slowly, from royalty to the nobility.

That timespan of the female Tudor narrative overlapped with immense cultural transformation, with the introduction of the printing press, the Renaissance, the Reformation, and the blending of the medieval into the early modern. As a result, religious, cultural and social life in England underwent irrevocable change, forging a new sense of national and personal identity, commensurate with the foregrounding of royal women. The two Tudor queens regnant developed the national dialogue about gender, but it is with hindsight that the behind-the-scenes work of their mothers and grandmothers becomes apparent, in laying the crucial foundations that enabled Mary and Elizabeth to inherit in their own rights. Directly and indirectly, women influenced the Tudor dynasty in four main ways. Firstly, as a result of circumstances; events, accidents or other people's successes or failures, which impacted upon their lives. Secondly, through exclusively female experiences, whether biological like childbirth, or cultural, such as living within the patriarchal tropes about gendered behaviour. Thirdly, and most significantly, they influenced their dynasty through decision-making, planning, behaviour and direct action. Finally, they left their mark through sheer ability, a number of truly exceptional women were born, or drawn into, the Tudor family. By these means, they established an alternative narrative of influence that gained momentum in the wings until the time came for it to take centre stage.

The lives of the dynasty's women were often shaped by circumstances beyond their control. Perhaps the most important of these was the low number of male heirs they bore, and the failure of boy children to survive to adulthood. Elizabeth Woodville's sons by Edward IV went missing in the Tower, presumed murdered, making their eldest sister, Elizabeth of York, heir to the Yorkist line. It was the lack of a son that ended Catherine of Aragon's marriage and brought Anne Boleyn into the Tudor family, as well as precipitating the wider religious and cultural implications of breaking with Rome. Between them, Catherine and Anne, Eleanor and Frances Brandon, only produced surviving daughters, the two sons of Mary, Duchess of Suffolk, died young, and even the illegitimate Henry Fitzroy predeceased his father, so that the line of succession according to the 1544 act became exclusively female save for the fragile life of Prince Edward. Only the death of their brother allowed for the crown to pass to Mary and Elizabeth, after which the only plausible alternatives were the sons of Katherine Grey, swiftly declared illegitimate, and the Scottish James. The greater number of live female births in the family, and surviving girl children, dictated that, by necessity, even by default, the crown was passed to women.

The circumstance of battle was another factor beyond women's control. As gender codes dictated, women did not bear arms on the battlefield and were powerless to directly affect the outcomes of the military clashes in which the Tudor dynasty was forged and defended. Sometimes, though, even defeat created circumstances in which a woman might find herself presented with a new, life-changing opportunity. Elizabeth Woodville could never have become Queen had her first husband not been killed in battle, and the outcome of Bosworth defined the path of Elizabeth, England's first Tudor queen. In Scotland, the Battle of Flodden ended Margaret Tudor's decade on the throne and thirty years later the death of her son at Solway Moss led to the succession of a six-day-old girl. Sudden death off the battlefield also shaped the journey the dynasty's women took. Catherine of Aragon's marriage to Henry VIII was possible only after the death of Prince Arthur at the age of fifteen. Mary, Queen of Scots' future was changed irrevocably as a result of the loss of Francis II, forcing her to trade her queenship of Catholic France for her Protestant homeland. Surviving a reigning king could be liberating, if it allowed a widow to make her own choice, as discovered by Mary Tudor, Queen of France in 1515, and Catherine Parr in 1547. Male-driven political change was another circumstantial factor in women's lives, such as the deposition of Edward IV in 1470, the coup of 1553 which attempted to replace Mary I with Jane Grey, and the events of 1566-7, which led to the abdication of Mary, Queen of Scots, although those might be argued to have been influenced by her choices. Battle, male deaths and politics were contributing factors to the ways in which women shaped the Tudor dynasty, but not necessarily ones they could control. What they could determine, were their responses.

Many women of the Tudor dynasty made their contributions through exclusively female experiences. At the risk of stating the biologically obvious, only a woman could bear an heir, although the success of that process was often not down to her, being influenced by paternal health, illness and environmental factors. Some bore a large number of children, such as Elizabeth Woodville, Elizabeth of York, Catherine of Aragon and Margaret Tudor, while others, like Mary I, failed to conceive despite trying. Elizabeth I chose not to have children, but Margaret Beaufort may have limited her conception, and circumstances stole the opportunity from Anne of Cleves, Mary Grey and later, Mary, Queen of Scots. Yet when the dynasty was desperate for boy children, the claims of those who did arrive against the odds were swiftly neutralised. Katherine Grey conceived for the second time despite her cousin's best efforts to prevent her, and her two healthy sons were barred as potential heirs. The experience could also prove deadly, costing the lives of Elizabeth of York, Jane Seymour and Catherine Parr. Childbirth configured the life of a late medieval or Tudor woman, especially a royal one, whether they were a mother, or hoped to become one, or decided not to be. Their gender meant that the subject of childbirth was something they had no choice but to negotiate.

Another exclusively female contribution to the dynasty, which provides a unifying thread between many of these women, was the way they acted as mothers. Often, the aim of their decision-making was to protect, or promote, sons or daughters who later played a significant role in the dynasty. Sometimes this necessitated painful choices, even negotiations with the enemy, as with Elizabeth Woodville's agreement to leave sanctuary in 1484 so long as Richard III provided for her daughters, and Margaret Beaufort's meetings with Henry, Duke of Buckingham and Richard III, in an attempt to secure her son's inheritance. Mothers also experienced a loss of control over their children, either from factors beyond their control, or due to their status. Yorkist and Tudor heirs were raised at Ludlow, including Princess Mary from 1525, and other royal children were established in their own households away from their parents. Political events might intervene between mother and child, such as the infighting which forcibly separated Margaret Tudor from James V during his childhood, and Mary, Queen of Scots from James VI for almost all his life. Margaret Beaufort lost control of Henry as a result of the regime change in 1461, when he was entrusted to the Yorkist Earl of Pembroke, then again after the Battle of Tewkesbury in 1471, when he fled to France.

Motherhood was the one area in which women's contemporaries permitted them to demonstrate a quasi-masculine strength and commitment, because they were acting in the interests of their dynasty. The 'she-wolf' trope applied to Margaret of Anjou's actions in the 1460s showed how this permission could easily edge into misogyny, and was a reminder that women could only wear borrowed robes in the gender battle, and must know when to remove them in order to reveal their femininity. Maternal activity might, from necessity, be covert, but it was definitely pragmatic, as with the return of Frances Brandon to court in 1554, with her surviving daughters. The drive and fire of mothers fighting for their children had a power that enabled them to transcend the limitations of their gender, and initially gave the dynasty an impetus which outlived the battlefield or the council chamber. The dedication and endurance of mothers, especially those prior to 1509, enabled the Tudor regime to establish itself against almost prohibitive odds. Equally, it was the dynasty's lack of a corresponding maternal force after 1547 tat led directly to its demise.

*

Between the reigns of Elizabeth of York and her granddaughter and namesake, the scope of royal women's queenship evolved, in stages, from a quiet, personal influence, to more formalised, public contributions and ultimately, independent rule. From helping to ease a husband's burden of power, they went to shouldering it entirely. Paradoxically, this assumption of the reins both confirmed and blew apart the Tudor stereotype of female dependency. Key dates on this timeline are 1485, when Henry VII's victory afforded Margaret Beaufort the authority of King's Mother, 1486 when Elizabeth became the first Queen to bear the name of Tudor, 1533 when the outsider Anne Boleyn officially married Henry VIII, 1553, which marked the succession of the first queen regnant and finally, the decision made by Elizabeth to rule alone, clarified by her final rejection of the Duke of Anjou in 1581.

Elizabeth Woodville's influence as Queen was established by her personal relationship with Edward IV, but after his death, her wishes as the mother of Edward V were overturned. She had no intrinsic power. Margaret Beaufort lacked royal backing initially but was motivated to act behind the scenes, through the media of letters, meetings and alliances, until her son's victory formalised her organisational capabilities. Before 1485, her wealth and bloodline gave her the security net to act, and the protection of husbands loyal to the throne shielded her from permanent repercussion. Yet, it was always Margaret's force of character in which her true power was rooted. In comparison, Elizabeth of York's queenship was of a gentle, domestic nature, through personal channels, and as a figurehead of national, almost religious, admiration.

Like Margaret had been, Catherine of Aragon was active in political affairs, advising, letter-writing, acting as an unofficial ambassador and organising, particularly visibly in the 1513 campaigns in France and Scotland, as well as being the presiding muse at court. In her attempts to balance this with the creation of a family, Catherine might have come to represent a combination of the best elements of Margaret and Elizabeth of York, but her heart-breaking personal losses undermined her best efforts. For the first sixteen years of her marriage, she and Henry were committed equals in work and play, as Catherine sought to replicate the example set by her parents, the united crusader monarchs of Spain. After their separation, Catherine saw her continuing duty as a wife and queen as opposing Henry's sins and upholding Catholicism; her sacrifice to the dynasty. As Catherine's replacement, Anne Boleyn's queenship was similar in that it was the extension of a companionate marriage. While Anne was equally active and involved in Henry's business, particularly his pursuit of a divorce, she also represented religious change, engaging in debate, patronising reformers, and creating an intellectual atmosphere as a cultured, equal player. The brutality that marred the end of her life brought an unprecedented danger to the role of queen, which cast a long shadow over the dynasty. Following her, Jane Seymour defined her queenship in diametric opposition to Anne, being quiet where Anne was vocal, submissive where her predecessor had been confrontational, parochial to Anne's European polish, and conservative instead of forward-looking. She also provided Henry with the long-desired son, for the lack of which his first two wives had lost their status, and one, her life.

The succession of Margaret Tudor's granddaughter in 1542 marked the appearance of the first queen regnant. It was a monumental step in terms of gender and royal inheritance, paving the way for later events in England, but in real terms it had little political impact, as Mary Stewart was only six days old, and the country continued to be run by a series of regents. Mary's inheritance made it easier to promote the candidacy of women to the English throne a decade later. While Mary Tudor was named on her father's act of succession, her brother overturned this in favour of the Protestant Jane Grey, proving that by this point, gender mattered less than religious conviction. Unfortunately, Mary's marriage and her harsh penalties for heretics encouraged the surfacing of patriarchal and misogynistic attacks upon her gender and dismissal of her abilities, culminating in John Knox's fiery anti-female tract of 1558. It may be that the two Marys made the mistakes, in marriage and religious policy, from which Elizabeth learned and used to inform her own decisions. By choosing to remain unmarried, Elizabeth had to craft her own method of rule, based on her personality and gender. She proved that a woman could reign alone, as a *feme sole*, and with great success and authority, remodelling her court and the nature of her interactions with her councillors and favourites. Although her decision was a success on a personal level, which correlated with national prosperity during her lifetime, it ultimately perforce meant the end of the Tudor dynasty.

*

A crucial aspect of the transformation of Tudor women's contributions was the Renaissance focus upon the individual. While royal men were already able to assert their personal desires, as in Edward IV's choice of Elizabeth Woodville, it was not until the second decade of the sixteenth century that royal women felt able to reject patriarchal pressure in pursuit of their own happiness. The brief emergence of the companionate union was driven largely by women. Mary and Margaret's choices of a second husband were a product of the culture in Henry VIII's early court, but also stemmed from the belief that they had fulfilled their dynastic duty. Henry chose a number of his wives for love. Of the three Tudor siblings, it was only Margaret whose status suffered as a result, and her relationship with her son was affected by her second marriage.

The motives of Jane Seymour, Anne of Cleves, Catherine Howard, Catherine Parr and even Anne Boleyn, were complicated by questions of duty and the ambition of their male relatives. Genuine affection may, or may not, have developed in their marriages, but 'love' was a multi-faceted emotion when it involved a man who was also a monarch. Catherine Parr certainly set aside her romantic desires in order to wed the King, only to pursue her chosen man again with rapidity, before her period of mourning had elapsed. The second generation of romantics, though, found themselves more harshly treated by Elizabeth I than their predecessors had been by her father. The efforts of the Grey sisters, Margaret Douglas and Mary, Queen of Scots, to find love, only ended in disaster. While Elizabeth rejected the preferences of her cousins for the threat they posed to her throne, it was national disapproval that made the marriages of Mary I and Mary Stuart so problematic.

A number of women who contributed to the Tudor dynasty were capable of powerful acts of Renaissance self-fashioning. Some had a well-defined sense of purpose and destiny from a young age, like Margaret Beaufort's narrative of divine inspiration, elective chastity, and her literal rewriting of Tudor protocol through her numerous Ordinances. Others were fixed upon their own path to the extent of martyrdom, with a lonely, rejected Catherine of Aragon refusing to relinquish the queenship she had been signed up for at the age of three. Perhaps the most surprising career arc of all was that of Anne Boleyn, whose meteoric rise to power raised questions of mobility and gender that eroded her security at the top. It was her daughter, Elizabeth, though, whose process of personal and artistic self-reinvention would leave the greatest mark upon national culture and identity. Each of these four women was possessed of extraordinary talents, and made commensurately larger contributions to the dynasty through the exercise of those abilities. Margaret, Catherine, Anne and Elizabeth were the milestones by which the female Tudor narrative progressed.

Many of the women on the family tree endured uncertainty, danger, grief and pain as a result of their dynastic connection. Between the 1460s and 1490s, Elizabeth Woodville, Margaret Beaufort and Elizabeth of York showed diplomacy, patience and resilience through years of waiting, and pragmatism when dealing with their enemies, regardless of the personal losses they had experienced. Catherine of Aragon underwent years of penury and ill health as a young widow after the death of her first husband, only to fall back into a worse condition in her final years. However, she would never give up and accept an easier compromise, remaining true to her vision. Both Mary and Elizabeth were shaped by the uncertainty they experienced as princesses, believing their lives were in danger and cautious about whom they might call their friends. Patience certainly had its rewards for those who survived. Anne of Cleves and Catherine Parr played the waiting game through Henry's final years of life, with Anne achieving peace as the King's sister and Catherine marrying for love. Yet queenship brought no contemporary certainties or guarantees. The forcible annulment of Catherine's marriage, the frequency of infant mortality, the deaths in childbirth of Elizabeth of York, Jane Seymour and Catherine Parr, the executions of Anne Boleyn, Catherine Howard and Mary Stuart, as well as the Marian burnings, remind us in the twenty-first century, of the extraordinary nature of these times, during which women's achievements shone despite the rigid definitions of the patriarchy.

These women form an alternative narrative of the Tudor dynasty to that of the powerful men on the battlefield, the throne and in the council chamber. When a family has been dominated by a figure so all-encompassing as Henry VIII, within a hierarchy designed to perpetuate existing male privilege, women are often relegated to secondary figures, particularly in male-authored biographies and histories. They continue to be wives, mothers and daughters in print, even Mary and Elizabeth, who have still been defined in terms of their relations with men. Some historians actually view them as aberrations in the patriarchal story. The reasons for this are partly practical, as the nature of female contributions has, of necessity, been of the informal kind, or gone unrecorded, or was recorded by male scribes. One advantage of the sixteenth-century cultural revolution was the greater amount of surviving written material from figures such as Catherine Parr, Mary I and Elizabeth I. Fortunately, in recent years, the rise of gender studies as a separate discipline, coupled with excellent biographies of these women, increasingly by female historians, has allowed for new perspectives and interpretations. The way women contributed to the Tudor dynasty was specific and different from that of men. Their cumulative narrative is one of change and gradual empowerment, reaching its fulfilment in the forty-five year reign of a *feme sole*, a woman who refused to share her throne, and redefined the nature and exercise of queenship, *all by herself.*

Notes

1 Elizabeth Woodville and Margaret Beaufort, 1437-60

1. Figure of 2,000,000 cited as the average of several academic estimates.
2. Cressy, David *Literacy and the Social Order: Reading and Writing in Tudor and Stuart England* Cambridge University Press, 2006
3. Baldwin, David *Elizabeth Woodville: Mother of the Princes in the Tower* Sutton, 2002
4. Ibid
5. Ibid
6. Ibid
7. Underwood, Malcolm, G and Jones, Michael *The King's Mother: Lady Margaret Beaufort, Countess of Richmond and Derby* Cambridge University Press 1992
8. Dictionary of National Biography
9. Underwood

2 Women as Witnesses, 1460-63

1. Baldwin
2. Various authors, *The Chronicles of the White Rose of York* F, B and C Limited, 2015
3. Ibid
4. Ibid

3 A Queen Is Made, 1464-69

1. Various authors, *The Chronicles of the White Rose of York* F, B and C Limited, 2015
2. Mancini, Dominic *The Usurpation of Richard III*, Sutton 1984
3. Baldwin
4. *Chronicles of the White Rose*
5. Ibid
6. Ibid
7. Ibid
8. Fabyan, Robert *The New Chronicles of England and France* Longman, 1811
9. Ibid
10. Unknown, *Ingulf's Chronicle of the Abbey of Croyland* AMS 1968
11. Waurin, Jean de *A Collection of the Chronicles and Ancient Histories of Great Britain, now Called England* Longman, 1864

12. *Chronicles of the White Rose*
13. CPR Edward IV 1464-6
14. Underwood

4 A Queen Is Unmade, 1469-72

1. Underwood
2. Baldwin
3. Griffiths, R A *The Reign of Henry VI: The Exercise of Power 1421-61* University of California Press, 1981
4. Baldwin
5. Ibid
6. Underwood

5 Elizabeth of York, 1472-85

1. Underwood
2. Ibid
3. *Chronicles of the White Rose*
4. More, Thomas *The History of King Richard III* Hesperus 2005
5. Underwood
6. Ibid
7. Stowe, John *Annales, or a General Chronicle of England* Richard Meighen, London 1631
8. Underwood
9. Ibid
10. Cooper, Charles Henry *Memoir of Margaret Beaufort, Countess of Richmond and Derby* Cambridge University Press 1874
11. Underwood
12. Ibid
13. Baldwin
14. *Croyland Chronicle*
15. Ibid
16. Underwood

6 The First Tudor Queen, 1485-86

1. Andre, Bernard *The Life of Henry VII* Longman, 1858
2. Brereton, Humphrey *The Most Pleasant Song Of Lady Bessy* Percy Society, 1847
3. Underwood
4. Croyland
5. Rotuli Parliamentorum
6. Ibid
7. Ibid
8. Calendar of Papal Registers Relating to Great Britain and Ireland, Volume 14 ed Twemlow, J.A HMSO
9. Andre
10. SLP Henry VII April 1486

11. SLP Henry VII July 1486
12. SLP Henry VII various, February-May 1486
13. Underwood.

7 Dynasty in Danger, 1487-92

1. Underwood
2. Weightmann, Christine B. *Margaret of York, Duchess of Burgundy 1446-1503* St Martin's Press, 1989
3. Calendar of Papal Registers 1486
4. SLP Henry VII May 1487
5. SLP Henry VII 1488
6. Underwood
7. CSP Spain 1488
8. Ibid

8 Tudor Princesses, 1489-01

1. Kelly-Gadol, Joan *Did Women Have a Renaissance?* Houghton-Mifflin 1977
2. Mattingly, Garrett *Catherine of Aragon* Little, Brown 1941
3. Ibid
4. Ibid
5. SLP Henry VII 1496
6. SLP Henry VII 1499
7. SLP Henry VIII November 1495, 1496
8. SLP Henry VII 1497
9. Hall, Edward *Hall's Chronicle of England* (ed. Grafton, Richard) J. Johnson et al, London 1809
10. CSP Spain 1498

9 The Spanish Bride, 1501-03

1. Nicolas, Sir Nicholas Harris *Privy Purse Expenses of Elizabeth of York: Wardrobe Accounts of Edward IV with a Memoir of Elizabeth of York, and Notes.* W. Pickering 1830
2. Ibid
3. Wardrobe Accounts Henry VII SLP 1501
4. Kipling, Gordon (ed) *The Receyt of the Ladie Kateryne* Oxford University Press 1990
5. Ibid
6. See Licence, Amy, *Catherine of Aragon* Amberley 2016 for discussion / SLP Henry VIII Volume 4 1529
7. Ibid
8. Ibid
9. Hall
10. SLP Henry VII January 1502
11. Ibid
12. Ibid

13. Underwood
14. *Privy Purse*
15. Ibid
16. Ibid
17. Ibid
18. Crawford, Anne *Letters of the Queens of England 1100-1547* Sutton 1997

10 The Two Margarets, 1503-09

1. Average taken from a range of population estimates.
2. Sneyd, Charlotte Augusta *A Relation, or Rather a True Account, of the Island of England: With Sundry Particulars of the Customs of these People and of the Royal Revenue under King Henry VII, Around the year 1500.* Camden Society 1884
3. CSP Spain 1503
4. Ibid
5. Bryson, Sarah *La Reine Blanche: Mary Tudor, A Life in Letters* Amberley, 2018
6. SLP Henry VII 1502
7. Underwood
8. Strickland, Agnes *Lives of the Queens of Scotland and English Princesses Connected with the Regal Succession of Great Britain* Blackwood, Edinburgh, 1850
9. Ibid
10. Ibid
11. Ibid
12. Ibid
13. Ibid
14. Ibid
15. Ibid
16. Ibid
17. SLP Henry VII 1504
18. Ibid
19. SLP Henry VII November 1504
20. CSP Spain October 1504
21. SLP Henry VII June 1505
22. SLP Henry VII March 1505
23. SLP Henry VII September 1505
24. SLP Henry VII September 1505
25. Brown, Mary Croom *Mary Tudor, Queen of France* Methuen 1911
26. Ibid
27. Ibid
28. Ibid
29. Ibid
30. Ibid
31. Ibid
32. SLP Henry VII August 1508

33. SLP Henry VII March 1509
34. Underwood
35. Ibid
36. Ibid
37. Ibid
38. Cooper, Charles Henry *Memoir of Margaret Beaufort, Countess of Richmond and Derby* Cambridge University Press, 1874
39. Halsted, Caroline Amelia *Life of Margaret Beaufort, Countess of Richmond and Derby* Smith, Elder and Co. 1845
40. Starkey, David *Six Wives of Henry VIII* Random House 2004
41. Jewell, Helen M *Women in Late Medieval and Reformation Europe 1200-1550* Palgrave Macmillan 2007

11 New Wives, 1509-13

1. SLP Venice June 1509
2. Ibid
3. SLP Henry VIII June 1509
4. Nichols, John Gough *London Pageants* J.B.Nichols and Son, London 1831
5. Ibid
6. Ibid
7. Hall
8. SLP Henry VIII November 1509
9. Kramer, Kyra *Blood Will Tell: A Medical Explanation for the Tyranny of Henry VIII* Createspace 2012
10. Strickland
11. Ibid
12. Ibid
13. Lesley, John *The History of Scotland*, Edinburgh 1830
14. Ibid
15. Ibid
16. SLP Henry VIII April 1512
17. Ibid
18. SLP Henry VIII June 1513
19. Ibid
20. Hall
21. SLP Henry VIII August 1513
22. Ibid
23. SLP Henry VIII September 13
24. Ibid
25. CSPS Spain 1513
26. SLP Henry VIII September 13
27. Ibid
28. SLP Henry VIII October 1513
29. Ibid
30. Ibid
31. SLP Henry VIII September 1513
32. SLP Henry VIII November 1513

12 Widows, 1513-15

1. Hall
2. SLP Henry VIII June 1514
3. CSP Spain June 1514
4. SLP Henry VIII June 1514
5. SLP Henry VIII July 1514
6. SLP Henry VIII August 1514
7. Hall
8. SLP Henry VIII 1515
9. Hall
10. SLP Henry VIII October 1514
11. SLP Henry VIII October 1514
12. Ibid
13. Ibid
14. SLP Henry VIII December 1514
15. SLP Henry VIII March 1515
16. Ibid
17. Hall
18. SLP Henry VIII October 1515

13 Legacies of Love, 1516-20

1. SLP Henry VIII July 1517
2. Ibid
3. Hall
4. Ibid
5. Ibid
6. Ibid
7. SLP Henry VIII December 1516
8. SLP Henry VIII January 1517
9. Erasmus, Desiderius *The Handbook of a Christian Knight* 1501 Methven 1964
10. Erasmus, Desiderius *Colloquies* (1522) University of Toronto, 1992
11. Ibid
12. SLP Henry VIII May 1517
13. Hall
14. SLP Henry VIII June 1517
15. SLP Henry VIII July 1518
16. SLP Henry VIII 1517
17. Hall
18. Ibid
19. CSP Venice October 1518
20. Ibid
21. Hall
22. SLP Henry VIII April 1519
23. SLP Henry VIII July 1519
24. Ibid
25. SLP Henry VIII August 1519

14 Gold, 1520-25

1. Hall
2. Ibid
3. Ibid
4. Ibid
5. Holinshed, Raphael *Chronicles of England, Ireland and Scotland in Six Volumes* J.Johnson et al, London 1808
6. Hall
7. Ibid
8. Ibid
9. Ibid
10. Ibid
11. SLP Henry VIII June 1520
12. Ibid
13. SLP Henry VIII June 1520
14. Ibid
15. SLP Henry VIII February 1521
16. Ibid
17. Hall
18. Ibid
19. SLP Henry VIII October 1518
20. SLP Henry VIII 1518-19
21. SLP Henry VIII October 1519
22. SLP Henry VIII 1524
23. Cressy, David *Birth, Marriage and Death: Ritual, Religion and the Life-Cycle in Tudor and Stuart England* Oxford University Press 1997
24. Kramer

15 Breaking the Queenship Model, 1525-33

1. Hall
2. Ibid
3. Ibid
4. Cavendish, George *The Life of Cardinal Wolsey* Samuel Weller Singer 1825
5. Ibid
6. Lydgate, John *The Dietary* George Shuffleton, (ed) from 'A Compilation of Popular Middle English Verse' 2008
7. CSP Venice August 1525
8. SLP Henry VIII Various, August-December 1525
9. Ibid
10. CSP Venice October 1532 824
11. De Carles, Lancelot *A Letter Containing the Criminal Charges Laid Against Queen Anne Boleyn of England* June 1536
12. Brantôme, Pierre de Bourdeilles *Oeuvres Complètes* Foucault Library, Paris 1822
13. Hall
14. Ibid
15. Ibid
16. SLP Henry VIII May 1525

17. SLP Henry VIII March 1527
18. SLP Henry VIII December 1528
19. SLP Henry VII May 1529
20. Ibid
21. Ibid
22. Ibid
23. Ibid
24. SLP Henry VIII 1532
25. Ibid
26. Ibid
27. Ibid
28. SLP Henry VIII September 1532
29. Hall
30. Ibid
31. Ibid

16 Wives and Daughters, 1533-34

1. Hall
2. SLP Henry VIII June 1533
3. Nichols
4. Ibid
5. Ibid
6. Ibid
7. Ibid
8. Ibid
9. Ibid
10. SLP Henry VIII July 1533
11. Ibid
12. SLP Henry VIII July 1533
13. SLP Henry VIII 1532
14. SLP Henry VIII June 1533
15. SLP Henry VIII July 1533
16. SLP Henry VIII 1532
17. SLP Henry VIII September 1533
18. SLP Henry VIII November 1533
19. SLP Henry VIII December 1533
20. Ibid
21. Ibid
22. SLP Henry VIII Jan/Feb 1534
23. Ibid
24. Ibid
25. Ibid
26. Ibid
27. Ibid
28. SLP Henry VIII March 1534
29. Ibid
30. SLP Henry VIII March 1534
31. Ibid

17 Queen, Interrupted, 1534-36

1. SLP Henry VIII April 1534
2. SLP Henry VIII June 1534
3. SLP Henry VIII July 1534
4. SLP Henry VIII, various, 1534
5. SLP Henry VIII 1535
6. SLP Henry VIII January 1536
7. Ibid
8. Ibid
9. Ibid
10. Ibid
11. Ibid
12. SLP Henry VIII March 1536
13. SLP Henry VIII April 1536
14. SLP Henry VIII May 1536

18 The Search for Love, 1533-37

1. SLP Henry VIII July 1536
2. Ibid
3. Ibid
4. SLP Henry VIII June 1536
5. SLP Henry VIII May 1536
6. Ibid
7. SLP Henry VIII June 1536
8. SLP Henry VIII May 1536
9. Ibid
10. Ibid
11. SLP Henry VIII June 1536
12. Ibid
13. Ibid
14. Ibid
15. Ibid
16. Ibid
17. SLP Henry VIII September 1536
18. SLP Henry VIII October 1536
19. SLP Henry VIII October 1537
20. Ibid
21. Ibid
22. Ibid
23. Ibid
24. SLP Henry VIII November 1537
25. SLP Henry VIII November 1537
26. SLP Henry VIII October 1537

19 Changing Times, 1537-40

1. SLP Henry VIII 1534
2. Ibid
3. Ibid

4. SLP Henry VIII June 1537
5. SLP Henry VIII October 1541
6. Lisle, Leanda de *The Sisters Who Would be Queen* Harper Press 2008
7. Ibid
8. Somerset
9. SLP Henry VIII August 1536
10. Ibid
11. Ibid
12. Somerset
13. SLP Edward VI September 1547

20 Women in Danger, 1540-42
1. SLP Henry VIII June 1539
2. SLP Henry VIII September 1539
3. SLP Henry VIII December 1539
4. Hall
5. Ibid
6. Ibid
7. Ibid
8. Ibid
9. SLP Henry VIII June 1540
10. SLP Henry VIII July 1540
11. Ibid
12. Ibid
13. Ibid
14. Ibid
15. Ibid
16. Ibid
17. Ibid
18. Ibid
19. SLP Henry VIII September 1540
20. Ibid
21. SLP Henry VIII August 1541
22. SLP Henry VIII October 1541
23. SLP Henry VIII November 1541
24. Ibid
25. SLP Henry VIII January 1542
26. Ibid
27. SLP Henry VIII February 1542
28. Ibid
29. SLP Henry VIII 1542

21 Weathering the Storm, 1543-5
1. SLP Henry VIII September 1540
2. SLP Henry VIII June, July, December 1541
3. SLP Henry VIII December 1542
4. Ibid

5. Foxe, John *Book of Martyrs* John Day 1563
6. SLP Henry VIII January 1543
7. SLP Henry VIII February 1543
8. SLP Henry VIII July 1543
9. SLP Henry VIII September 1535
10. SLP Henry VIII April 1542
11. SLP Henry VIII September 1543
12. Ibid
13. Ibid
14. Loades, David *Mary Tudor: The Tragical History of the First Queen of England* National Archives 2006
15. SLP Henry VIII December 1539
16. Ibid
17. Ibid
18. Ibid
19. SLP Henry VIII February 1540
20. SLP Henry VIII May 1520
21. Ibid
22. SLP Henry VIII March 1546
23. Ibid
24. SLP Henry VIII February 1544
25. SLP Henry VIII July 1544
26. Ibid
27. Ibid
28. SLP Henry VIII 1542
29. SLP Henry VIII July 1544
30. Ibid
31. SLP Henry VIII August 1544
32. SLP Henry VIII September 1544
33. SLP Henry VIII February 1546

22 Such a Brief Happiness, 1545-49

1. SLP Henry VIII 1546
2. Somerset
3. Foxe
4. Somerset
5. Hall
6. SLP Henry VIII August 1546
7. Hall
8. SLP Henry VIII August, December 1546
9. Ibid
10. Ibid
11. SLP Henry VIII January 1547
12. Somerset
13. SLP Henry VIII February 1547
14. Marcus, Leah S, Mueller, Janel and Rose, Mary Beth (eds) *Elizabeth I: Collected Works* University of Chicago Press 2002

15. Ibid
16. Ibid
17. SLP Henry VIII June 1548
18. Marcus et al
19. Ibid
20. Somerset
21. Ibid
22. Marcus et al
23. Lisle

23 Dangerous Women, 1547-53

1. Somerset
2. Loades
3. SLP Edward VI
4. Loades
5. SLP Edward VI December 1549
6. SLP Edward VI 1550
7. SLP Edward VI 1549
8. SLP Edward VI 1551
9. Loades
10. SLP Edward VI January 1551
11. Somerset
12. Tallis, Nicola *Crown of Blood: The Deadly Inheritance of Lady Jane Grey* Michael O'Mara 2016
13. Grafton, Richard *Chronicle* (1569) Middle English Texts Series, University of Rochester
14. Tallis
15. Loades
16. SLP Edward VI 1551
17. Lisle
18. Ibid
19. Ibid
20. Ibid
21. Ibid
22. Tallis
23. Tallis
24. Somerset
25. Ibid
26. Tallis
27. Ibid
28. Somerset
29. Ibid
30. Ibid

24 Queens in Conflict, 1553-54

1. SLP Edward VI 6 July 1553
2. Ibid

3. Lisle
4. Somerset
5. Ibid
6. Ibid
7. Ibid
8. Ibid
9. Ibid
10. Ibid
11. Somerset
12. Lisle
13. Tallis
14. SLP Mary November 1553
15. Nichols
16. Ibid
17. Ibid
18. Ibid
19. Somerset
20. SLP Mary August 1553
21. Ibid
22. Ibid
23. SLP Mary January 1554
24. Ibid
25. Somerset
26. Ibid
27. Ibid
28. Ibid
29. Lisle
30. Ibid
31. Ibid
32. Ibid
33. Ibid
34. Ibid
35. Ibid
36. Ibid
37. Lisle
38. Ibid
39. Grafton
40. Ibid
41. Nichols, John Gough *The Chronicle of Queen Jane and Two Years of Queen Mary* Camden Society 1850

25 The Half-Spanish Queen, 1554-55

1. SLP Henry VIII 1530
2. Somerset
3. Ibid
4. Ibid
5. Ibid

6. Marcus, Leah S, Mueller, Janel and Rose, Mary Beth (eds) *Elizabeth I: Collected Works* University of Chicago Press 2002
7. Ibid
8. Somerset
9. Ibid
10. Ibid
11. Prescott
12. Somerset
13. SLP Mary July 1554
14. Ibid
15. Nichols, *Pageantry*
16. Ibid

26 Saving the Nation's Souls, 1555-58
1. Foxe, John *Book of Martyrs* Partridge and Carey, Paternoster Row 1848
2. Somerset
3. Ibid
4. Ibid
5. Ring, Morgan *So High a Blood: The Life of Margaret, Countess of Lennox* Bloomsbury, 2017
6. Prescott
7. Ibid
8. Ibid
9. SLP Mary March 1558
10. Ibid
11. Knox, John *The First Blast of the Trumpet Against the Monstrous Regiment of Women* (1558) Edward Arber (ed) Echo Books 2006

27 Autonomy, 1558-62
1. Cressy, David *Literacy and the Social Order: Reading and Writing in Tudor and Stuart England* Cambridge University Press, 2006
2. Estimates of average population from a range of sources.
3. Skidmore
4. Machyn, Henry *The Diary of Henry Machyn, Merchant Taylor of London* Camden 1848
5. Nichols *Pageantry*
6. Skidmore
7. Nichols
8. Ibid
9. Ibid
10. Ibid
11. Ibid
12. Ibid
13. Skidmore
14. *Calendar of State Papers Domestic, Edward, Mary and Elizabeth 1547-80* Robert Lemon, London HMSO 1850

15. Marcus et al
16. Ibid
17. Ibid
18. CSP Domestic 1559
19. Marcus et al
20. Ibid
21. Whitelock
22. Somerset
23. Camden, William *Annals of the Affairs of England and Ireland During the Reign of Elizabeth* 1615
24. CSP Spain 1559
25. Skidmore
26. Ibid
27. CSP Domestic 1560
28. CSP Venice 1560
29. Ibid
30. Ibid
31. Whitelock
32. Ibid

28 Gender Politics, 1563-69

1. CSP Domestic 1562
2. Somerset
3. Ibid
4. Ibid
5. Ibid
6. Ibid
7. Sitwell, Edith *The Queens and the Hive* Macmillan 1962
8. Somerset
9. Whitelock
10. Somerset
11. Ibid
12. Whitelock
13. Somerset
14. Ibid
15. Skidmore
16. Somerset
17. Ibid
18. Fraser, Antonia *Mary, Queen of Scots* Weidenfeld and Nicolson 1969
19. Somerset
20. CSP Domestic March 1566
21. Lang
22. CSP Domestic 1566
23. Ibid
24. Ibid
25. Somerset
26. Ibid

27. Ibid
28. Ibid
29. Fraser
30. CSP Foreign 1567
31. Ibid
32. Lisle
33. Ibid
34. Somerset

29 The Queen's Person, 1570-88

1. CSP Foreign January 1574
2. Doran, Susan Monarchy and Matrimony: The Courtships of Elizabeth I Routledge 1995
3. Basnett, Susan Elizabeth I: A Feminist Perspective Berg Women's Series 1992
4. Levin, Carole The Heart and Stomach of a King: Elizabeth I and the Politics of Sex and Power University of Pennsylvania 2013
5. Nichols, *Pageantry*
6. Ibid
7. Marcus
8. Somerset
9. Ibid
10. Ibid
11. Ibid
12. Ibid
13. Fraser
14. Ibid
15. Hartweg, Christine *John Dudley: The Life of Lady Jane Grey's Father-in-law* Createspace 2016

30 Finale, 1589-1603

1. Strong, Roy *The English Renaissance Miniature* Michael Joseph 1975
2. Whitelock
3. Ibid
4. Ibid
5. Shakespeare, William *Richard III*
6. Ibid *Macbeth*
7. *Romeo and Juliet*
8. *Hamlet*
9. Whitelock
10. Green, Paul D 'Spenser and the Masses: Social Commentary in The Faerie Queen' Journal of the History of Ideas 35 (3): 389-406, 1974
11. Whitney, Isabella *A Sweet Nosegay, or Pleasant Posy: Containing 110 Philosophical Flowers*. Various eds. Montana State University-Bozeman 1995
12. Somerset
13. Ibid
14. Ibid

15. Ibid
16. Ibid
17. Whitelock
18. Camden, William *Annals of the Affairs of England and Ireland During the Reign of Elizabeth* 1615
19. Chettle, Henry *The Order and Proceeding at the Funerale of Elizabeth I* E. Short, London 1603
20. Camden

Bibliography

Andre, Bernard *The Life of Henry VII* Longman, 1858

Baldwin, David *Elizabeth Woodville: Mother of the Princes in the Tower* Sutton, 2002

Basnett, Susan *Elizabeth I: A Feminist Perspective* Berg Women's Series 1992

Benson, Pamela Joseph *Invention of the Renaissance Woman* Penn State Press 2010

Brantôme, Pierre de Bourdeilles *Oeuvres Complètes* Foucault Library, Paris 1822

Brown, Mary Croom *Mary Tudor, Queen of France* Methuen 1911

Bruce, John (ed) *A History of the Arrival of Edward IV in England and the final Recovery of his Kingdom from Henry VI* Camden Society 1838

Bryson, Sarah *La Reine Blanche: Mary Tudor, A Life in Letters* Amberley, 2018

Calendar of Fine Rolls Henry VI Volume 19 1452-61 HMSO 1911

Calendar of Patent Rolls Edward IV 1461-7 HMSO, London 1897

Calendar of Patent Rolls Edward IV, Edward V, Richard III 1476-85 HMSO, London 1901

Calendar of State Letters and Papers Henry VII 1485-1509 (ed G.A.Bergenroth) Longman, Green, Longman and Roberts, London 1862

Calendar of State Papers Domestic, Edward, Mary and Elizabeth 1547-80 Robert Lemon, London HMSO 1850

Calendar of State Papers Spain Volumes 1-5 Bergenroth, G.A, Mattingly, Garrett, Gayangos, Pascual de, 1865/1947

Calendar of State Papers Venice Volumes 1 and 2 Rawdon Brown, London 1864

Camden, William *Annals of the Affairs of England and Ireland During the Reign of Elizabeth* 1615

Cavendish, George *The Life of Cardinal Wolsey* Samuel Weller Singer 1825

Chettle, Henry *The Order and Proceeding at the Funerale of Elizabeth I* E. Short, London 1603

Cooper, Charles Henry *Memoir of Margaret Beaufort, Countess of Richmond and Derby* Cambridge University Press, 1874

Crawford, Anne *Letters of the Queens of England 1100-1547* Sutton 1997

Cressy, David *Birth, Marriage and Death: Ritual, Religion and the Life-Cycle in Tudor and Stuart England* Oxford University Press 1997

433

Cressy, David *Literacy and the Social Order: Reading and Writing in Tudor and Stuart England* Cambridge University Press, 2006

Cunningham, Sean *Prince Arthur: The Tudor King who Never Was* Amberley, 2016

Davey, Richard *The Nine Days' Queen: Jane Grey and her Times* Methuen 1909

Davey, Richard *The Sisters of Lady Jane Grey and their Wicked Grandfather...* 1911

De Carles, Lancelot *A Letter Containing the Criminal Charges Laid Against Queen Anne Boleyn of England* June 1536

Denny, Joanna *Anne Boleyn: A New Life of England's Tragic Queen* Piatkus 2004

Dixon, William Hepworth *History of Two Queens, Catherine of Aragon and Anne Boleyn*, Volume II. B Tauchnitz 1873

Doran, Susan *Monarchy and Matrimony: The Courtships of Elizabeth I* Routledge 2002

Erasmus, Desiderius *Colloquies* (1522) University of Toronto, 1992

Erasmus, Desiderius *The Handbook of a Christian Knight* 1501 Methven 1964

Fabyan, Robert *The New Chronicles of England and France* Longman, 1811

Fox, Julia *Sister Queens* Weidenfeld and Nicolson 2011

Foxe, John *Book of Martyrs* Partridge and Carey, Paternoster Row 1848

Fraser, Antonia *Mary, Queen of Scots* Weidenfeld and Nicolson 1969

Fraser, Antonia *The Six Wives of Henry VIII*, Weidenfeld and Nicolson 1992

Gairdner, James *Three Fifteenth Century Chronicles* Creative Media Partners 2019

Grafton, Richard *Chronicle* (1569) Middle English Texts Series, University of Rochester

Green, Paul D 'Spenser and the Masses: Social Commentary in The Faerie Queen' *Journal of the History of Ideas* 35 (3): 389-406, 1974

Griffiths, R A *The Reign of Henry VI: The Exercise of Power 1421-61* University of California Press, 1981

Gristwood, Sarah *Elizabeth and Leicester* Bantam, Transworld 2007

Hall, Edward *Hall's Chronicle of England* (ed. Grafton, Richard) J. Johnson et al, London 1809

Halsted, Caroline Amelia *Life of Margaret Beaufort, Countess of Richmond and Derby* Smith, Elder and Co. 1845

Harpsfield, Nicholas *A Treatise on the Pretended Divorce between Henry VIII and Catherine of Aragon* Camden 1878

Hartweg, Christine *John Dudley: The Life of Lady Jane Grey's Father-in-law* Createspace 2016

Henderson, Katherine U and McManus, Barbara F *Half Humankind: Contexts and Texts of the Controversy about Women in England 1540-1640* University of Illinois Press 1985

Holinshed, Raphael *Chronicles of England, Ireland and Scotland in Six Volumes* J.Johnson et al, London 1808

Howe, Professor Elizabeth Theresa *Education and Women in the Early Modern Hispanic World* Ashgate Publishing 2013

Hutchinson, Robert *Young Henry: The Rise of Henry VIII* Hachette 2011

Ives, Eric *The Life and Death of Anne Boleyn: The Most Happy* Blackwell 2005

Ives, Eric 'The Fall of Anne Boleyn Reconsidered' *The English Historical Review* Vol 107, No 427, July 1992 p651-664

Jewell, Helen M *Women in Late Medieval and Reformation Europe 1200-1550* Palgrave Macmillan 2007

Kelly, H A *The Matrimonial Trials of Henry VIII* Wipf and Stock 2004

Kipling, Gordon (ed) *The Receyt of the Ladie Kateryne* Oxford University Press 1990

Knox, John *The First Blast of the Trumpet Against the Monstrous Regiment of Women* (1558) Edward Arber (ed) Echo Books 2006

Kramer, Kyra *Blood Will Tell: A Medical Explanation for the Tyranny of Henry VIII* Createspace 2012

Lang, Andrew *The Mystery of Mary Stuart* Library of Alexandria 1901

Lesley, John *The History of Scotland* Edinburgh 1830

Levin, Carole *The Heart and Stomach of a King: Elizabeth I and the Politics of Sex and Power* University of Pennsylvania Press 2013

Lisle, Leanda de *The Sisters Who Would be Queen* Harper Press 2008

Loades, David *Mary Rose; Tudor Princess, Queen of France, the Extraordinary Life of Henry VIII's Sister* Amberley, 2012

Loades, David *Mary Tudor: The Tragical History of the First Queen of England* National Archives 2006

Loades, David *The Boleyns: The Rise and Fall of a Tudor Family* Amberley 2012

Luce, John (ed) *The Love Letters of Henry VIII and Anne Boleyn* John W Luce and Company 1906

Lydgate, John 'The Dietary' George Shuffleton, (ed) from *A Compilation of Popular Middle English Verse* 2008

Machyn, Henry *The Diary of Henry Machyn, Merchant Taylor of London* Camden 1848

Madden, Frederic *Privy Purse Expenses of the Princess Mary, daughter of King Henry VIII* W Pickering, 1831

Mancini, Dominic *The Usurpation of Richard III* Sutton 1984

Marcus, Leah S, Mueller, Janel and Rose, Mary Beth (eds) *Elizabeth I: Collected Works* University of Chicago Press 2002

Mattingly, Garrett *Catherine of Aragon* Little, Brown 1941

Neale, J E *Elizabeth I* (1934) Chicago Press 1992

Nichols, John Gough *The Chronicle of Queen Jane and Two Years of Queen Mary* Camden Society 1850

Nichols, John Gough *London Pageants* J G Nichols and Son, London 1831

Nichols, Nicolas Harris *The Literary Remains of Lady Jane Grey* Harding, Triphook and Lepard 1825

Nicolas, Nicholas Harries *Privy Purse Expenses of Elizabeth of York* William Pickering, London 1830

Norton, Elizabeth *Anne Boleyn: Henry VIII's Obsession* Amberley 2008

Norton, Elizabeth *Anne Boleyn: In her own Words and the Words of Those who Knew Her* Amberley 2011

Norton, Elizabeth *The Boleyn Women,* Amberley 2013

Oakley, Ann *Sex, Gender and Society* Routledge 2016

Penn, Thomas *Winter King: Henry VII and the Dawn of Tudor England* Simon and Schuster 2013

Pollard, A F *Henry VIII* London, 1913

Porter, Linda *Mary Tudor: The First Queen* Portrait 2007

Prescott, William H *History of the Reign of Ferdinand and Isabella, the Catholic, of Spain* Volumes 1, 2 and 3, Routledge, Warne and Routledge, London 1854, 1862

Ridley, Jasper *Bloody Mary's Martyrs* Robinson 2001

Ring, Morgan *So High a Blood: The Life of Margaret, Countess of Lennox* Bloomsbury, 2017

Rubin, Nancy *Isabella of Castile: The First Renaissance Queen* St Martin's Press, New York, 1991

Rummel, Erika *Erasmus on Women* University of Toronto Press, 1996

Skidmore, Chris *Death and the Virgin: Elizabeth, Dudley and the Mysterious Fate of Amy Robsart* Weidenfeld and Nicolson 2010

Sneyd, Charlotte Augusta *A Relation, or Rather a True Account, of the Island of England: With Sundry Particulars of the Customs of these People and of the Royal Revenue under King Henry VII, Around the Year 1500* Camden Society 1884

Somerset, Anne *Elizabeth I* Weidenfeld and Nicolson 1991

Starkey, David *Six Wives of Henry VIII* Vintage 2004

State Letters and Papers Henry VIII Volumes 1-10 J S Brewer, Gairdner, James London 1887/1920

Stewart, Alan *The Cradle King: A Life of James VI and I* St Martin's Press 2003

Stowe, John *Annales, or a General Chronicle of England* Richard Meighen, London 1631

Strickland, Agnes *Lives of the Queens of Scotland and English Princesses Connected with the Regal Succession of Great Britain* Blackwood, Edinburgh, 1850

Strong, Roy *The English Renaissance Miniature* Michael Joseph 1975

Tallis, Nicola *Crown of Blood: The Deadly Inheritance of Lady Jane Grey* Michael O'Mara 2016

Thurley, Simon *The Royal Palaces of Tudor England* Yale University Press 1993

Tremayne, Eleanor E *The First Governess of the Netherlands, Margaret of Austria*. Methuen 1908

Tremlett, Giles *Catherine of Aragon: Henry's Spanish Queen* Faber and Faber 2010

Tytler, Patrick Fraser *England Under the Reigns of Edward IV and Mary* Bentley, 1839

Underwood, Malcolm, G and Jones, Michael *The King's Mother: Lady Margaret Beaufort, Countess of Richmond and Derby* Cambridge University Press 1992

Unknown, *Ingulf's Chronicle of the Abbey of Croyland* AMS 1968

Various authors, *The Chronicles of the White Rose of York* F, B and C Limited, 2015

Vergil, Polydore *Anglia Historia* 1555

Walker, Greg 'Rethinking the Fall of Anne Boleyn' *The Historical Journal* Cambridge University Press Volume 45, No 1, March 2002 pp1-29

Bibliography

Ward, Allyna *Women and Tudor Tragedy: Feminizing Counsel and Representing Gender* Rowman and Littlefield 2013

Warnicke, Retha *The Rise and Fall of Anne Boleyn* Canto 1991

Waurin, Jean de *A Collection of the Chronicles and Ancient Histories of Great Britain, now Called England* Longman, 1864

Weightmann, Christine B. *Margaret of York, Duchess of Burgundy 1446-1503* St Martin's Press 1989

Weir, Alison *Henry VIII: King and Court* Jonathan Cape 2001

Weir, Alison *Mary Boleyn: The Great and Infamous Whore* Jonathan Cape 2011

Weir, Alison *The Lady in the Tower* Jonathan Cape 2009

Weir, Alison *The Six Wives of Henry VIII* Vintage 2007

Whitelock, Anna *The Queen's Bed: An Intimate History of Elizabeth's Court* Picador 2013

Whitney, Isabella *A Sweet Nosegay, or Pleasant Posy: Containing 110 Philosophical Flowers.* Various eds, Montana State University-Bozeman 1995

Wilkinson, Josephine *Mary Boleyn: The True Story of Henry VIII's Favourite Mistress*, Amberley 2009

Wilkinson, Josephine *The Early Loves of Anne Boleyn* Amberley 2009

Williams, Patrick *Katharine of Aragon* Amberley 2013

Wilson, Derek *The English Reformation* Robinson 2012

Acknowledgements

The creation of this book was significantly eased due to a generous award from the Society of Authors. I am deeply grateful for their support, and their faith in my project, which gave me a boost at a much-needed time. Thank you so very much to all those who have invested so generously in the Society.

A huge vote of thanks also goes to my editors at Amberley Publishing, Nicola Embery and Shaun Barrington, for their patience during the writing of this book and their diligence in bringing it to a conclusion.

I would like to thank my mother for her constant love and support, my two wonderful sons, Rufus and Robin, my kind godmother, Susan and dear friend Anne. I have been blessed with some great friends, comrades and supporters, whose encouragement has kept me going. They know who they are.

Index

Also available from Amberley Publishing

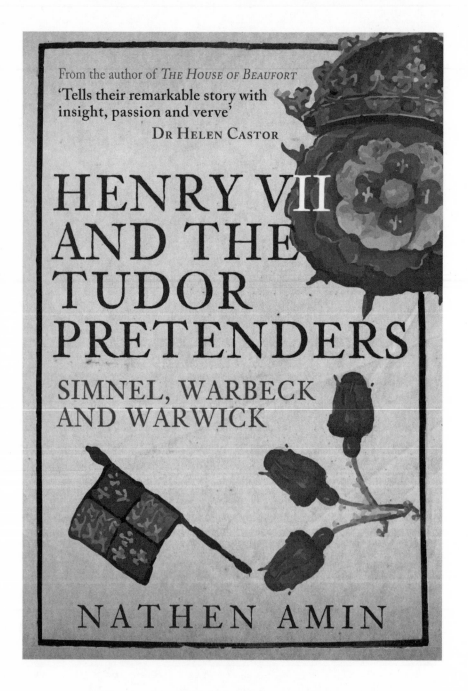

From the author of The House of Beaufort
'Tells their remarkable story with insight, passion and verve'
Dr Helen Castor

HENRY VII AND THE TUDOR PRETENDERS

SIMNEL, WARBECK AND WARWICK

NATHEN AMIN

Also available from Amberley Publishing

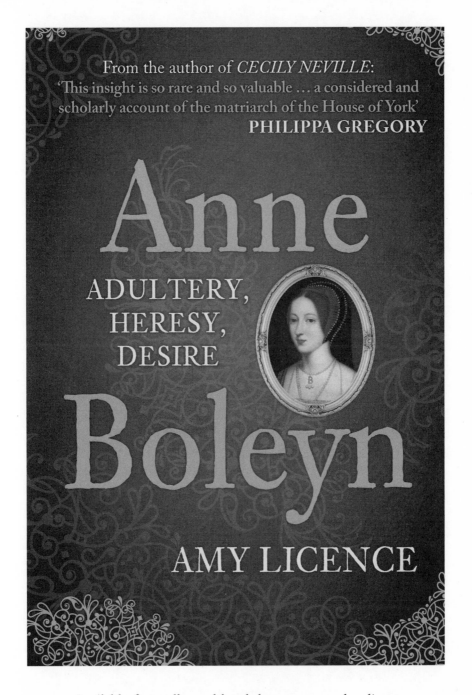